China Rising

China Rising

Capitalist Roads,
Socialist Destinations

The True Face of Asia's Enigmatic Colossus

Jeff J. Brown

CHINA RISING
Capitalist Roads, Socialist Destinations -
The True Face of Asia's Enigmatic Colossus
Incorporating Jeff J. Brown's geopolitical chronicles
Copyright © 2016 by Jeff J. Brown
All rights reserved.

New York   Punto Press **Publishing**   Rome

First electronic and paperback editions published in the United States by
Punto Press Publishing
P.O. Box 943, Brewster, NY 10509 USA
Address all inquiries to admin@puntopress.com

•

Summary: "An intimate social, cultural and political look into historical and modern China, while comparing these observations to the history and current trends of the United States and Europe."-Provided by publisher.

ISBN-13: **978-0-9964870-4-7**

China-United States-Europe-Anecdotes-History-Current Events.
I. Title.
Cover photo and section photos by www.redocn.com and Punto Press LLC.
Book design by Punto Press Publishing

•

First Print Edition

The eBook is available at Amazon worldwide and at Ganxy.com

•

Incorporating *Jeff J. Brown's geopolitical chronicles*

REVISED EDITION #1

A Lautarine Library Selection

Patrice Greanville • Editorial Director

Contents

FOREWORD

The Not So Quiet American

SOONER or later, certainly while you are deep into this book, say when you reach that part that explains what makes Xi Jinping run, you gotta ask yourself a question; why should I rely on a gaggle of pompous, redundant, ideologically impaired U.S. scholars self-billed as China "experts" when I can get my Sino-kicks with Jeff?

There's your answer. Leave those poor fools to die of thirst in the Gobi of ideas, and hop on the New Silk Roads with a Not So Quiet American. You're guaranteed not to be lost in translation.

Jeff and I met in my favorite Xinjiang restaurant in Beijing on a cold winter evening. We hit it off famously. We had already read each other's work, and we were – politically, even spiritually - in synch. So here we were: two *laowai* (old outsiders), originally from the Americas, him from the North, myself from the South, sitting on a tavern served by smiling Uyghur girls, discussing the Chinese century. If this was a western, the placid scene would have been disturbed by the spectacular entrance of a NSA-cleared deranged killer – but this was Beijing, and no one would dare mess with Chinese intel.

Let's cut to the chase; take this as your travel book of choice to navigate the 21st century Chinese dream. It's got historical background. It's got some of the best sights. It's got reams of symbolism. It radiates, all across the narrative, that elegant scent of Confucianism imbuing all levels of Chinese society and culture. And it's got the Chinese leadership planning, planning, more planning, and executing, executing, non-stop executing. Jeff makes it all so easy to digest, when he "affectionately" calls this powerful, mindful system *Baba* Beijing – as in "father".

You will read Jeff mocking all so predictable facets of *Exceptionalistan* – masters of stigmatizing "Red China", or the "communist dictatorship", or whatever. Nonsense. What matters is what you won't read on "indispensable" U.S. corporate rags; how *Xi Dada* is steering – and stirring – the Middle Kingdom with the Chinese Dream, the vision within, and the One Belt, One Road (OBOR), the vision beyond. Exceptionalists operate on the (flawed) assumption that China's expansion will fall dramatically. Jeff will give you elements to understand how it won't. What's declining here is not China, but U.S. influence, in parallel with U.S. deindustrialization. And if what Jeff says mirrors what the *People's Daily* says, so much the better; you're getting it straight from the dragon's mouth.

As Jeff put it; "just like the *Washington Post* and *New York Times* in the U.S., the *People's Daily* is a government mouthpiece, so whatever they say, you can take it to the bank that it is channeling Baba Beijing, just like a good Pentecostal speaking the word of God in tongues."

Turbo-capitalism has not yet depleted the development of its productive forces – especially in China, which may still absorb vast spaces that are non-capitalist, pre-capitalist or just plain agricultural. No wonder Baba Beijing predicts the beginning of socialization for…100 years from now. Talk about socialism as conceived by Marx and Engels: as a natural consequence of the historical development of capitalism. This is what Baba Beijing is really up to – and this is what you'll be offered a glimpse of by Jeff.

So get ready to be familiar with the *hexi* ("nucleus") of the leadership, and what makes *Xi Dada* run. Get ready to see the workings of what Russian Foreign Minister Sergei Lavrov loves to fully describe as Comprehensive Strategic Partnership of Cooperation (CSPC) – the Russia-China alliance. And last but not least, also get ready to grab a cab on a rainy day in Beijing (yes, it's epic).

Jeff spent 13 years living and working in China. He speaks fluent Mandarin. He's been to 30 of the 34 provinces. He met the full spectrum of Chinese society. He modestly frames it as "I am a changed person" since he first arrived in the Middle Kingdom in 1990 – when the spectacular post-modern version of the Long March was just beginning. In fact he metamorphosed into a priceless Western guide to the greatest story of the 21st century; China back to where it was during most of recorded history – on top.

Jeff, half in jest, says that the world is now officially in the Xi era. And he's only getting started; his next book will be a historical fiction – The Diaries of Xi Jinping. Rock on, *Jeff Dada*.

Pepe Escobar

Paris, April 2016

Prologue

ON a personal level, this book is a virtuous circle. My first book, *44 Days*, really gave me a deep understanding of China and its peoples. This book, *China Rising- Capitalist Roads, Socialist Destinations- The True Face of Asia's Enigmatic Colossus*, has enabled me to discover my own countries (the United States and France), past and present, as well as digging much deeper and wider into all things China, past, present and future.

This whole process has been a voyage to learn the truth and I slowly realized this means questioning a lifetime of conventional wisdom, the popular consensus and their accepted myths. Looking back, I was not really prepared to do this, until coming back to China in 2010. The alternating bookends of growing up in America and then living and working in Africa and the Middle East, 1980-1990; living in China, 1990-1997, France and the United States, 1997-2010 and then back to China, 2010-2016, were and are the doors of my newfound perception.

I now understand that getting de-brainwashed takes a lot of effort, humility and personal courage. I get inspired reading about others people's journeys to discover the truth. Please allow me to share mine.

I grew up in Oklahoma, USA, in the 1950s-1960s, a very unique period in modern American history. Every school day started with the Pledge of Allegiance, class prayer and singing the Broadway musical, state song, *Oklahoma*. Patriotism, God, country, the goodness of America's government and the nobility of its institutions. Beacon on the hill. America's selfless sacrifice to bring freedom, democracy and Adam Smith's invisible hand of righteous capitalism to the world's oppressed masses. Domino theory. Red scare. Commies. Nuclear bomb shelters. Teachers practicing with us, "When you see the flash of light, duck and cover". Sputnik. The space race. John F. Kennedy. RFK and MLK murdered. Vietnam. Nixon. Sex 'n drugs 'n rock 'n roll. Beatles, Rolling Stones, the Who, Led Zeppelin, Doors, Jimi Hendrix, Janis Joplin, Jefferson Airplane. Bob Dylan, Simon and Garfunkel, Motown, Stax. *Dr. Strangelove, Zorba the Greek, The Graduate, Manchurian Candidate, Fahrenheit 451, 2001:A Space*

Odyssey, Westerns and WWII movies on the big screen. Bertrand Russell, Friedrich Nietzsche, John Stuart Mill and Fyodor Dostoyevsky by the bedside. *The Honeymooners, Father Knows Best, Rowan & Martin's Laugh-In, Ed Sullivan, Twilight Zone, I Love Lucy, Leave It to Beaver, Gunsmoke, Bonanza, Andy Griffin* and Saturday morning cartoons on black and white, and then finally, color TV. Norman Rockwell. *Life Magazine. Reader's Digest.*

[IMG 0001]

My first indoctrination to government propaganda. Every week at elementary school, we had this drill, to "protect" ourselves from a Russian atomic blast. This massive disinformation campaign served two purposes: to make America's citizens think that atomic annihilation was feasible and that the Cold War nuclear arms race was a patriotic necessity. (#1 Image by Wikipedia)

https://www.youtube.com/watch?v=5gD_TLIBqFg

[VID 001]

This video link above of archival footage shows just how much duck and cover would have protected us. Yeah, sure, Uncle Sam. (#1 YouTube)

Spent half my time in the city and half on a family farm. Driving a tractor, harvesting crops, cleaning manure out of animal pens, helping ewes give birth to newborn lambs at 3am in the freezing cold, riding a horse, hunting and fishing – all this left an indelible mark on my psyche. Getting your hands dirty and living the science and art of agriculture will do that to you.

[IMG 0002]

Got a BS (Oklahoma State, 1976) and MS (Purdue, 1978) in Animal Sciences, thinking I was going to go back home and farm. But the Brazilian community at Purdue adopted me and I quickly learned Portuguese, discovering that I had a knack for languages (along with all the hard work to succeed). Went to Brazil to seek my fortune as a soybean and corn farmer. Couldn't get anybody to lend me the startup money. In retrospect, I am not disappointed. Had I done so, I would probably be impoverishing local natives, clearcutting rain forest and destroying the environment, while getting very rich, at the expense of the aforementioned. Looking back, it's not who I want to be during my time on Planet Earth.

But, Brazil whet my appetite to see the world. I became a volunteer for the Peace Corps, in Tunisia, as an agriculture extension agent (1980-1982), learning fluent Arabic, speaking, reading and writing. This background got me into international agricultural marketing in Africa and Middle East (1982-1990). During this time, I learned French, met my Parisian wife in Algeria in 1988, whereupon, we left for China in 1990.

We lived in China 1990-1997, during what I call the *Wild East Buckaroo Deng Days*. I learned Mandarin fluently and became a naturalized French citizen. I continued to work in agricultural marketing (which gave me the opportunity to travel over much of rural China) and then built and managed the first McDonald's bakery on the Mainland. Our two daughters were born while we were in China at this time. Needless to say, these seven years are a huge part of our lives.

Then, my wife and I owned and managed a retail business in Normandy, France (1997-2001). Since I had left the US in 1980, we moved back to Oklahoma, so we could spend time with my parents. I actually returned on the first flight (United from Paris to JFK) that was allowed back into US airspace, a few days after 9/11. After 21 years, what a symbolic way to return home, for what was to transpire.

The America I left and the one I came back to, were two different countries. I was shocked by how rundown everything was, all the poverty below the surface, how superficial and self-centered everyone was, and how reactionary and insular the people were. It was buy-buy-buy-me-me-me. Given our eclectic experiences, my wife and I were like exotic, Dr. Seuss creatures from an alien planet. We never fit in, but the time with all my extended family was wonderful. We built up a big real estate business and lost everything we owned in the 2008, thanks to the "Save the Big Banks" middle class implosion. Our plans of becoming teachers for our retirement years got moved up in a hurry. We started working in Oklahoma City's urban, minority schools that same year.

In 2010, we moved back to Beijing to teach in international schools, bringing our younger daughter with us. As depressing as it was returning to America in 2001, it was just as amazing and jaw dropping seeing China, after being absent for 14 years. Wow! This is the first time I began to sense that China was moving up and on, while the US was going down and out. The contrasts were that remarkable. I so much wanted to share what was happening, thus, I started a blog and doing extensive research in the process. Then I took a solo trip across China in the summer of 2012, to journal about

it. This morphed into my first book, *44 Days*, whose travels are really a metaphor about discovering China in history and current events, how it all relates to the West and what humanity can expect in the future. I then began writing my online column, *Reflections in Sinoland*, on my original www.44days.net. This book is an anthology of these articles. After reading this book, you can continue to follow my work at www.chinarising.puntopress.com, which now includes an audiovisual element, *Radio Sinoland*.

In the meantime and over the years, my classroom experiences inspired me to develop a method to teach English, which is published, *Doctor WriteRead's Treasure Trove to Great English*.

After Xi Jinping was elected president of China, I was and am still so impressed with him, that I am now writing an historical fiction, *Red Letters – The Diaries of Xi Jinping*, which will be out in print and ebook, late 2016. In the meantime, Badak Merah Press has commissioned me to write, *China Is Communist, Dammit! – Dawn of the Red Dynasty*. It will be out in print and ebook sometime in mid-2016. These two books involve a massive amount of research, learning and discovery. I'm having the literary time of my life.

My arc of personal enlightenment about how the world really works has been a long, slow hyperbolic curve that has skyrocketed upwards in the very recent past. In 1972, if my draft lottery number had been drawn, I would have patriotically gone to Vietnam. That year, I voted for Richard Nixon, not George McGovern. Working and living with peasant farmers for two years in the Peace Corps opened my eyes to how the other

85% of the world lives, as well as eight years traveling all over Africa and the Middle East. Since I was involved in agriculture, my work got me out of the big cities and into the hinterlands of each country where I traveled, so I got the see "the real" Africa and Middle East. It was very educational and humbling.

While sensing the inequities and injustices, I was still firmly rooted in the myths of America's moral superiority, divine righteousness and the perfections of capitalism. It was not until we returned to the US in 2001 and living in Bush World for nine years, that I began to see the rot of empire. Still though, I clung to the nobility of the "democratic" process, capitalism and the mainstream media's mind numbing consensus. I still believed at the time that the *New York Times* and the *Economist* were cutting edge (and dependable) journalism.

It was when we came back to China in 2010 that all the scales really started cascading off my eyes, traveling, researching and writing. Since then, I have spent thousands of hours studying genocide, empires, societal collapse, war, capitalism, colonialism, socialism, communism, fascism, false flags, the deep state, etc. I innately understood that I could never understand China and the Chinese, until I really knew the truth about the West. I was ready to question my 1950s-1960s upbringing, its conventional wisdom and official narrative. Like in the eponymous movie and its protagonist Neo, I was finally prepared to step out of the Matrix. There was no turning back.

After researching and writing *44 Days*, I had now given up on the US, but being a dual national French-American, I still clung to the illusion that Europe, with its vaunted socialism, UN Charter on Human Rights and the lessons learned from two world wars, was the world's last great hope for moral recovery. But then, like an amped up Hurricane Katrina, came the Western junta's genocide in the Ukraine. For months, I followed with morbid horror (and continue to do so), the ugly face of not only American, but *European fascism*. My utter disgust and disillusionment with my ancestral home, Europe, boiled over and I clearly saw that the American empire is nothing more than a continuation of European empire. I could now truthfully and coherently talk and write about a seamless historical spectrum: The West. And thanks to this epiphany, I could honestly and meaningfully write about China and its people, from their point of view.

Now it is all very clear to me. Western genocide, colonialism, false flags and color revolutions have never stopped since 1492, when Columbus "discovered" the "New World", as if it were devoid of humanity. The methods and instruments of destabilization, divide and conquer, exploitation and resource extraction have simply evolved and adapted. The West, with its foundation of racism and capitalism, perpetually spawns colonialism, imperialism, fascism and war; all underpinned by a steady stream of false flags. This bastard monster is a seven-headed Hydra and it is insatiable. Starting in 1922, with the US and Britain forcing the creation of Israel upon the Palestinians and world geopolitics, via their Orwellian "British Mandate", the Western Empire added a powerful, destabilizing death star to its arsenal: Anglozionism.

[IMG 0003]

China and Russia have their work cut out for them, fighting for their countries, peoples and ways of life. This, against the onslaught of Western racism and capitalism, and their evil spawn of colonialism, imperialism, fascism, war and false flags. (#2a Image by 1.bp.blogspot.com)

China has been struggling to rise up against this onslaught, since the first Europeans landed on China's shores in 1514. The Chinese, with the world's longest continuous civilization, were and are more than qualified to fight back. It is an irony of history that the West used four of China's great inventions, gunpowder, moveable type, the compass

and paper, to bring the Heavenly Mandate's long history to its lowest nadir, the century of humiliation, from 1839 to 1949.

There is a titanic struggle for the soul of humanity, our survival as a species into the 21st century, and it is China, Russia, BRICS, ALBA CELAC and NAM; it is Xi, Putin, Maduro, Castro, Correa, Zuma, Afwerki and all the hundreds of world leaders the West has assassinated or deposed, versus the Western empire, Obama, Cameron, Hollande, Merkel, Abe and their thousands of satraps in the hallowed hall of imperial power.

The world needs a million more voices like The Greanville Post, The Saker, Andre Vltchek, Pepe Escobar, Kevin Barrett, Rory Hall, Dave Kranzler, Moti Nissani, Gail Evans, Dan Yaseen, Mo Dawoud, Jason Bainbridge, Dean Henderson, Hrvoje Morić (all of with whom I've worked), and the many other journalists/authors involved in this worldwide struggle for humanity's very survival.

From the mouth of the Dragon and the belly of the New Century Beast, it is an honor to lend my voice from the viewpoint of China's people and their leaders, past, present and future.

Note about this book:

These chapters were written as columns on my website, www.44days.net, from November, 2013 to mid-2015. Earlier ones are referenced with footnotes and whereupon learning about embedded hyperlinks, the others are referenced as such. There is no chronological order, as the book has been divided into themes. In any case, there is enough research to follow up on, to keep you busy and entertained for months, while earning an honorary degree in Chinese and Geopolitical Studies.

Glossary

Here is a short glossary of key terms used throughout the book:

AIIB: Asian Infrastructure and Investment Bank. China' answer to the West's Asian Development Bank.

ALBA: Bolivarian Alliance for the Peoples of Our America, in Latin America.

Angloland: the world's major, historical and colonial English speaking countries: Canada, the United States, Britain, Australia and New Zealand.

Baba Beijing: my wry name for China's (communist) leadership. Depending on the context, Baba (Beijing) can either signify the singular "*it*" or the plural "*they*".

B&R: China's Maritime String of Pearls (Belts) and (Silk) Roads master plan, to integrate the infrastructure of all of Africa, Europe and Asia into an organized, coordinated whole.

BRICS: coordinating body comprised of Brazil, Russia, India, China and South Africa.

CELAC: Community of Latin American and Caribbean States. Every country in the Americas is a member, except the US and Canada.

CPC: Communist Party of China. Can also be *CCP*, the Chinese Communist Party.

CSTO: Collective Security Treaty Organization. Basically the former USSR, less Eastern Europe, organized like NATO.

Deep State: the people and groups governing a country behind the scenes – FIRE (finance, insurance and real estate), the military and intelligence communities.

Dreaded Other: from the viewpoint of the West, the 85% of humanity's peoples who are not Western.

EUAU (EEU): Eurasian Economic Union. Similar to CSTO, but for trade and cooperation.

Eurangloland: all the countries in Angloland, plus all the countries in the European Union.

Eurmerica: the United States and the European Union.

FOIA: Freedom of Information Act. Some countries have laws forcing secret documents to be made available to the public, usually 20-30-50 year after their creation. They can still be heavily redacted before release.

Great Western Firewall (GWF): The West's mainstream media propaganda bubble.

Heavenly Mandate: Going back for 5,000 years, across emperors and dynasties, this is China's unique interpretation of good governance, and it is still in force today. The leader(s) in power can continue to rule, keeping the Heavenly Mandate, as long as they protect the people, their livelihoods, wellbeing, keep society safe, and maintain the national borders of the country. If they fail in these criteria long enough, these leaders will lose the Heavenly Mandate and new leadership will be brought in.

KMT: the Kuomintang, Chiang Kai-Shek's political and military organ, which fled to Taiwan in 1949.

Moral Majority: The world's 85% non-Westerners, from their viewpoint.

MSM: mainstream media.

MWM: mainstream western media.

NAM: Non-Aligned Movement. Most of the world's countries outside of the G20.

NDB: BRICS' New Development Bank. Their answer to the IMF and World Bank.

NGO: non-governmental organizations, a number of Western ones which are front organizations of CIA, MI6, etc. to destabilize and overthrow foreign governments.

PLA: China's People's Liberation Army.

Princes of Power: the Western elite. The 1%. (Actually they are something like the 0.00002% of all humanity.)

RMB: China's currency, the *renminbi*. Also called the *yuan*. In some articles, the symbol "¥" is used.

SCO: Shanghai Security Organization. China, Russia and a number of Asian countries, organized for cooperation and trade.

Sheeple: a pejorative contraction of *sheep people*, an uninformed, obedient and apathetic citizenry.

Sinoland: My wry name for the People's Republic of China.

Dedicated to the peoples of China, without whom my personal voyage of discovery would have been impossible.

On China:

When one is in China, one is compelled to think about her, with compassion always, with despair sometimes, and with discrimination and understanding rarely. For one either loves or hates China. Perhaps even when one does not live in China, one sometimes thinks of her as an old, great, big country which remains aloof from the world and does not quite belong to it. That aloofness has a certain fascination. But if one comes to China, one feels engulfed and soon stops thinking. One merely feels she is there, a tremendous existence, somewhat too big for the human mind to encompass, a seemingly inconsequential chaos obeying its own laws of existence and enacting its own powerful life-drama, at times tragic, at times comical, but always intensely and boisterously real; then after a while, one begins to think again, with wonder and amazement.

From *My Country, My People*, by Lin Yulang

On the West:

The civilized have created the wretched, quite coldly and deliberately, and do not intend to change the status quo; are responsible for their slaughter and enslavement; rain down bombs on defenseless children whenever and wherever they decide that their "vital interests" are menaced, and think nothing of torturing a man to death: these people are not to be taken seriously when they speak of the "sanctity" of human life, or the "conscience" of the civilized world.

From *Collected Essays*, by James Baldwin

Note on Concordance

As a service to print book readers of *China Rising - Capitalist Roads, Socialist Destinations*, this print edition carries specific references to images, embedded hyperlinks and YouTube video links found in the ebook. Other than this, the ebook and print book are essentially identical. *China Rising* is divided into theme-based chapters and each one has a number of related articles. Obviously, each article's visuals compliment the subject at hand. There is a prologue and an epilogue.

Referenced images are denoted as they appear in the text—inline— as per following format:

[IMG 0000]. Thus, image #27 would be **[IMG 0027]**

All videos are denoted as **[VID 000].**

Full credit data for materials displayed is given on the online concordance file found on the author's website, China Rising

(http://chinarising.puntopress.com/2016/01/27/ china-rising-visuals-hyperlinks-for-print-edition-duplicate/)

Chapter 1

Deep State West (Wing)

This section of the book is put first for a very valid reason. It has taken me years and years, upon thousands of hours of reading and research, to understand that our Western governments have a long history of being and continue to be very evil and corrupt. Yes, the West invented penicillin and gave us Mozart, but since the 1400s, Eurmerica has been and continues to colonize the rest of the world's people's and resources, via war, overt and covert regime change, with their international financial institutions – and false flags. This global Western empire of exploitation and extraction continues unabated and it is a very hard and bitter pill to come to this realization. Like the vast majority of people, simply to avoid mental discomfort and to go along to get along, I was in complete denial until recently. It's just so much easier, to look the other way and survive the day.

What I have learned in writing this book, is that you cannot wrap your head around the popular notion of China's rise, without also recognizing Western colonialism's imperial past and ongoing decline, including the rampant use of false flags. They go together like soy sauce and steamed dumplings.

It takes great courage and overcoming an insurmountable mental hurdle to accepting the documented proof of just how common our Western governments commit false flags, in order to manipulate their citizens, get them to accept laws and norms against their own freedoms and safety and like all false flags throughout history, enabling our governments to victimize and attack perceived (fabricated) enemies at home and abroad.

No surprise then, that, Western false flags figure prominently in China's modern history.

Don't despair or be shocked. I know exactly how you feel. It took extensive research, while writing this and two other books, to have the scales of brainwashing and propaganda ripped from my eyes. The power of denial and conformity are oppressive. Ultimately, it is a very difficult and emotionally taxing journey to get there, but so liberating and cleansing when you finally reach the summit. While not a religious person, I think that when the clarity of the truth fulfills you, it is like an intellectual and spiritual baptism of sorts.

This section has many hyperlinks, which you can study at your leisure. In any case, Deep State West (Wing) is intended to be a solid primer to help you understand much of what I've discovered and presented here. You may not be ready to take the journey just yet, but you will understand my life's trajectory and this book's rationale much clearer, vis-à-vis China.

Behind the Great Western Firewall Is the Ugly Truth

*The Great Western Firewall vs. the Great Firewall of China:
different methodologies, identical results.*

A truth untold is a lie. A fact hidden is censorship. – Jeff J. Brown

This is a plea to everyone reading, that we Westerners had better wake up before it's too late. If we don't, we are going to continue to have many repetitions of Ukraine, Serbia, Georgia, Venezuela, Bolivia, Iraq, Iran, Syria, Afghanistan, Sudan, Libya, Mali, Yemen and the list goes on, non-stop, since at least the Bolshevik Revolution in 1917. That was when the West's elites perceived a genuine global threat to the status quo of capitalism and their dominion over Earth's resources: Communism. Now, with the world being more multipolar than ever, we come to China and Russia. As the Western Empire's decline continues, in desperation, America is trying to take down these two colossal civilizations. This, even as Russia and China work openly and secretly to interlock their cooperation and resistance. It is clear they are creating a unified front in the face of Western hegemony and bellicosity. The United States is delusional and megalomaniac in its attempts to maintain global dominion in the 21st century's rapidly changing world order. It is equally frightening to know that if carried to its logical conclusion, it could mean the end of humanity as we know it: global nuclear war.

A big part of this plea is for Westerners to quit using the mainstream media and to start seeking out alternative news sources, as frustratingly fractured as they are, and to invest a modicum of time to do some research and investigation along the way. A good place to start would be all the hyperlinks below and then take advantage of the list of resources in the chapter entitled, *What Jeff J. Brown reads and researches to write Reflections in Sinoland.* The other plea is to come to terms with just how evil and corrupt our Western governments and capital are, in spite of what we learned in school text books. All of our lives and future absolutely depend on it.

An author friend of mine, whom I'll call Miguel, sent me a hyperlink about Hillary Clinton and her possible political downfall. This is due to America's decision to destroy Libya, using France and the UK as proxies, starting in 2011. It was also a major slap in the face to China and Russia, who did not veto the US led, 2011 UN Security Council vote for a "no fly" zone over Libya. "No fly", as in bombs away, baby, much like Slim Pickens' Major Kong riding bronco on airborne bombs in the movie, *Dr. Strangelove*. Flagrant psyops propaganda about Viagra-crazed Libyan soldiers mass raping girls saturated the Western media. "The eminent genocide" of the people of Benghazi was another psyops agitprop, just as the supposed incubators being unplugged by Iraqi soldiers and WMD were used to justify invading that country. Lies and more lies swallowed as official truth.

We know how this flagrant disregard for international law is playing out across the planet. Under the guise of "humanitarian" wars, the West pushes its fatuous, well-worn R2P (so called "Responsibility to Protect"), to overthrow, or at least control, the governments of resource rich lands. In reality, R2P really means the West's "Right to Plunder".

According to this article series, Hillary apparently went over the heads of the Joint Chiefs of Staff and the CIA to push through the bloody regime change. I replied to my friend that given Americans' predilection to cheer on their government's slaughter and maiming of millions of dark skinned, mostly Muslims, across the planet (not to mention, by Kiev proxies, thousands of fair skinned Ukrainians as well), then surely this macho orchestration of Gaddafi's murder might actually help her win the White House. I then said that even if Queen Clinton is not the Democratic candidate, her replacement will just be another Wall Street-Angloziocon-Russophobe one percenter, so what difference does it make? Think Joe Biden or John Kerry. Miguel's closing comment was that I was probably right, but "he despises Bill and Hillary Clinton with a passion".

That got me to pondering how much my thinking has evolved and grown in the last five years of living in China. In 2010, I thought Bill and Hillary were good leaders and capable politicians. I voted for Clinton twice and Obama the first time. By 2012, I futilely wrote in the Green Party presidential candidate on my Oklahoma ballot, as my awareness of the truth was growing. But I still thought that Hillary would make a great president. Not anymore. Being a dual national, that same year, I also voted for François Hollande, thinking that he, as a so called socialist, would be different than Mini-Me Nicolas "W." Sarkozy. Wrong again and if I have to, I'll write in a name on my ballot for France's elections in 2017. Western leaders all unfailingly support global empire.

Working as a school teacher affords me a lot of personal time. We work about 190 days a year and I can usually leave my professional life on campus, so I have my evenings and weekends to myself. As a result, since 2010, I have spent thousands of hours writing books, columns and more importantly, doing the necessary research to generate my work as accurately and as truthfully as possible. It is this massive amount of investigation that has opened my eyes about how the world really works. Especially revealing has been the West and its 500 years of brutal colonialism, with its exploitation of our planet's human and natural resources. The myth is that the West has nobly done all this in the name of progress and the pursuit of knowledge. But the impetus has been and continues to be profit, empire and global domination. To legitimize it all in the eyes of its citizens, throw in God, Country and King. Voilà, the annals of history as told by the Princes of Power.

The second thing that happened was an exchange of emails with another writer friend of mine, whom I'll call Francis. This time, it was to congratulate them for having an article published in a heavyweight American newspaper. In their article, they forcefully condemned a communist country's use of censorship to control its version of history. To get published in this newspaper is a quite an achievement. It is one of those news sources which is so well respected, that if they print something, it's accepted as gospel truth. And if they don't write about an event happening in the world, it never occurred. So, my friend can now stake claim as a mainstream "made" (wo)man in the news establishment world, and I am truly happy for them and their success. It is a dream that many a writer and journalist fantasizes doing.

Yes, this communist country's censorship is more overt, compared to what I like to call the West's *Great Western Firewall* (GWF), but the aims and results are identical. Why do countries like Cuba, China, Vietnam, North Korea, Iran, Venezuela, Ecuador and countless others keep more proactive tabs on their media? Why can't they do what the West does? In the West, the state and capital know that merely controlling the mainstream media is enough to define what is true, not true, what happened and didn't happen. Western alternative media is too diffuse, too fractured and ultimately only constitutes feeble background noise, attenuated over time.

The difference is that for 85% of the world's people and their governments, the Dreaded Other, they have been the victim of five centuries of Western colonialism and exploitation. And these countries continue to be ceaselessly assailed by so called Western "civil society" and "democracy" NGOs, to effect psyops, destabilization and ultimately, regime change through assassinations, false flags, coups and armed uprisings (not to mention the economic and social predations of sanctions, the IMF and World Bank) – especially if they have valuable natural resources and/or strategic locations. With these examples of "superior" Western virtues and civilization trying to tear the 85% Moral Majority's countries apart, one can empathize with their belief that they need to be more controlling and heavy handed than maybe they would like to be.

Being the aggressor and not the victim, the West plays by a different, privileged set of rules. For 500 years, the West has had and continues to own the copyright to the human race's history books and current events. From the world's majority perspective, what I like to call the Moral Majority, their histories have been written for them, by the West, against their will. These countries must battle against this massive, distorting prism of perceived reality, which helps explain their sometimes obsessive nature about trying to fashion their own pasts and control the message surrounding current events.

A long time ago, I had a girlfriend who had been savagely raped at a young age. She kept a loaded pistol in her purse 24/7, even taking it to the bathroom, and slept with it under her pillow. She was paranoid and trusting of nobody, not even of me in our intimate relationship. Can't say that I blame her. And she reminds me of China, Vietnam, Cuba and all rest of the 85% of the people of the world, who have been and continue to be savagely raped during five centuries of Western colonialism. Like my old friend, I can empathize with their paranoia and lack of trust.

In any case, the West can be just as heavy handed at censorship as these more criticized countries. Westerners who lambaste Baba Beijing for setting up thousands of social media accounts to help control the official government narrative don't realize that <u>their governments spend billions doing exactly the same thing. If you think all those thousands of comment trolls who haunt mainstream and alternative websites across the planet work for free, think again</u>.

I have learned over the last five years that Francis' mainstream acceptance in a bigtime daily can sometimes come at a cost. They replied to another email I had sent. My original email contained a link for an article that explained the background history of this very same communist country which my friend wrote about. The revelations in this article that I sent were written by a non-establishment journalist who researches FOIA released documents, WikiLeaks, testimonies, court documents, interviews, etc., and has contacts in the dark, dank netherworld of spydom. I was very surprised to get back a reply from my writer friend, saying that this investigative journalist is, "a nut case conspiracy theorist". I wanted to reply to this riposte that I wasn't sure who was sending it, the friend I've known for 30 years, or the one who wrote the article for that high powered, establishment newspaper. I joked to myself saying maybe they wrote it, knowing that the NSA and America's 15 other spy agencies would store a copy for future reference. It would look good in his file, for when the time comes.

Alvin Toffler said,

The illiterate of the 21st century will not be those who cannot read and write, but those who cannot learn, unlearn, and relearn.

Being outside of the West for the last five years has afforded me the opportunity to leave the Matrix and its iron fisted control of the Washington-London-Paris consensus. As a born and trained scientist (I taught middle school multidisciplinary sciences for three years), I am in a never ending quest for the truth, as uncomfortable as it may be to discover. All my research has allowed me the luxury of unlearning and relearning humanity's ancient and modern history, up to our resulting current events. I am not sure that if I were still living in the West, I could have broken my brainwashed chains and set myself free from the bondage of its suffocating conventional narrative.

I worked in the corporate world for 25 years before becoming a teacher. Like almost all of us, I felt compelled to spout "the imperial party line" of the West's tightly scripted version of history and current events. In fact, until 2010, I still believed much of it was true. Conformity is society's most powerful control mechanism. Those who don't go along to get along can pay a very heavy price. Just ask Malcolm X, JFK, RFK, MLK, Oscar Romero, Gandhi, Ché Guevara, the four American nuns raped and killed in El Salvador, Jesus Christ and millions of other (less) well known martyrs, whose lives were and still are being cut short, or imprisoned, beaten, raped, tortured, bankrupted, ostracized, or made stateless or jobless. These fearless and principled martyrs are everywhere, such as the cases of <u>Sami Al-Arian</u>, <u>Barrett Brown</u> and <u>Mohamedou Ould Slahi's Guantánamo Diary, which brilliantly leaves in line after line of blacked out text – pages and pages of censored truth</u>. Makes you proud to be an American, doesn't it? There are many multitudes like them who are ignored by the mainstream media. And we know that if they are not reported on in the *New York Times, Washington Post* or on *CNN* and *Fox*, then they don't exist and they don't matter.

Gore Vidal said the same thing in his own inimitable way,

To keep information <u>from</u> the public is the function of the corporate media.

It takes courage to leave the Matrix and seek the truth. For the multitudes who escape martyr status, sacrifices still often have to be made, both professional and personal. Rejection and ridicule by the vast majority, who is still ensconced in the mainstream propaganda bubble, are commonplace. It means being labeled a conspiracy theorist. In reality though, it is those in the Matrix who are the real conspiracy nuts, for trying to rationalize and justify the world they are selectively presented, in the suffocating cocoon of the GWF. Baba Beijing has its just as ruthless and controlling Great Firewall of China and the outcomes are identical. Only the methodology is different [and the ultimate purposes can be defended, once one understands the broader issues and larger stakes]. The big difference is that most Chinese know their information is censored. Most Westerners obediently believe they have "freedom of the press" and that censorship is everybody else's problem. Sadly, Westerners are deluded, gullible and easily manipulated. But this has been true of all citizens of Empire, since the dawn of civilization.

It is hard to accept and very disillusioning to realize just how irredeemably corrupt and evil are the West's supposedly democratic systems and the political and business leaders who own the process. All my thousands of hours of extensive research confirm this and nothing surprises me anymore. Especially that false flag operations are not the exception, but the banal norm of imperial national governments. They most certainly have been the weapon of choice since the first civilizations in Mesopotamia, China, India and Africa, and they continue at a fast and furious pace in current events. This article lists many false flags that governments have admitted to, or were exposed by WikiLeaks and FOIA laws, while they last. False flags routinely change the course of human history: the USS Maine, Reichstag, Gulf of Tonkin and Iraq's WMD. Let's remember that Maidan in Ukraine was a classic false flag and since then, it seems weekly, the West is launching one after another there, which has brought our planet to the threshold of World War III.

False flags are ingrained in the DNA of Empire, to control and manipulate their subjects, as well as demonizing an internal or external group in the eyes of the masses. The Empire keeps on perpetrating false flags relentlessly, because they are so ruthlessly successful at achieving their aims. False flags brilliantly create mass fear and uncertainty among the people and justify the persecution of the group to be dehumanized for exploitation or destruction. The shock and awe of false flags allow governments and capital to herd the masses like sheeple (sheep people), to induce them to gleefully go to war, commit genocide, accept economic servitude and environmentally destructive resource extraction, while willfully renouncing their free will to the tyranny of fascism and oligarchy, for "security and safety". It's been working like a charm since 5,000 BC and will undoubtedly continue to work, because of all our embedded social memes for group survival and evolutionary genes for individual survival. At the end of the day, in spite of our "superior" intelligence, we as a species are not much better than a herd of gazelle or a colony of ants.

Unless we get smart and get involved, it brings me to a frightening conclusion: false flags will continue unabated, until they cause the demise of the human race. To put the challenge before us into perspective, following are a few recent cases, going back in time. Trust me, based on my life experiences, your gut reaction is to deny, deny, deny. Our governments can count on this in 98% of the people. Remember, like Sherlock Holmes, in order to crack a crime caper, it is only necessary to disprove *one* of the alibis. After that, the whole tissue of lies falls apart.

Charlie Hebdo. The whole thing stinks to high heaven. Even my Parisian wife is raising her eyebrows: how could they get so many thousands of matching *Je Suis Charlie* t-shirts on people and color placards in their hands, for mass television exposure, *immediately* after the incident? A supposed well trained terrorist just happened to "leave" their ID in the getaway car? How convenient. This is as laughable as Satam Al-Suquami's fake passport "found" in the molten rubble of the 9/11 Twin Towers, which the FBI then conveniently "lost", when even the mainstream media had the temerity to question its validity. But it was enough to "identify" the supposed 9/11 perpetrators immediately after the supposed attack. Ditto Charlie Hebdo.

Why do our governments do this? My extensive research shows that one of the key components of successful false flags is to imprint in the minds of the sheeple exactly who the perpetrators are, as soon as it happens, almost like embedding a social meme across the population. If the sheeple are given any time at all to think about it and ask questions, then the false flag can easily fail. Thus, the 9/11 Nineteen, Lee Harvey Oswald, James Earl Ray, Sirhan Sirhan, the "communists" who burned down the Reichstag, the Spanish who "blew up" the USS Maine, the

North Vietnamese who "attacked" the USS Maddox in the Gulf of Tonkin, the supposed Boston bomber brothers Tsarnaev, Charlie Hebdo, 11/13, San Bernardino, and on and on, were clearly and convincingly identified by the authorities within hours of the false flags. Surely, Nero loudly accused the Christians, as soon as his arsonists were setting fire to Rome, while sending out crisis actors to dramatize these believers' perfidy. He not only got his grand palace, for which the Roman Senators were refusing to give the (now) burned neighborhoods' land to build it, but Nero also got to kill thousands of Christians in the process. The hallmarks of a truly successful false flag.

A few hours of research on Charlie Hebdo makes it glaringly apparent that the deep state was involved. The film footage of the police officer supposedly shot in the head at point blank, while lying on the sidewalk, was quickly extirpated by the mainstream media. With millions of views on YouTube in just two days, it was censored. In the West, our masters have learned that the alternative press is like low grade interference. It is too scattered and diffuse to cause critical mass. But when something like the censored Charlie Hebdo hoax assassination goes viral in a matter of hours, then it can become a threat to the official narrative, and often gets censored behind the GWF. On alternative websites, it's still there. Break out the popcorn and beer, boys and girls, and watch crisis actors help dupe the world.

Well, did he or didn't he? The Deep State would like us to think he did blow the policeman's brains out, but there's no sign of it. See comment below.

[VID 0002] (#2 Video by Youtube)

Page link on YouTube to censored video (Just in case). Those of you with technical ability, make sure to preserve these materials by capturing and downloading to your desktops.

https://www.youtube.com/watch?v=yJEvIKKm6og&has_verified=1&ore f=https%3A%2F%2Fwww.youtube.com%2Fwatch%3Fv%3DyJEvIKKm6 og%26oref%3Dhttps%253A%252F%252Fwww.youtube.com%252Fwatc h%253Fv%253DyJEvIKKm6og%26has_verified%3D1%26bpctr%3D1437 140211&has_verified=1&bpc

The shooter supposedly blasts a bullet at point blank range into the cop's head with a high powered machine gun, yet there is no blood and the "victim's" head stays intact. Had he really been shot, his skull would have exploded like a gangrenous pumpkin. He wasn't shot at all. This is because a combat trained "terrorist" just happens to miss his target from centimeters away. Yet, all the mainstream media are lined up with their propaganda, saying a police officer was viciously and sadistically assassinated by the so called terrorists, while lying helplessly wounded on the sidewalk. Later, a Star News reporter had a colossal slip of the tongue and stated that (fake) blood was put on the ground after the fact, which is obviously true. It goes on and on. The supposed hostage taker, Amedy Coulibaly, at a (surprise, surprise) Jewish grocery store, was obviously already handcuffed, when he was practically pushed outside into a hail of fire. I wonder what his deep state handler inside was telling him in his final moments? We'll never know, because dead men don't talk. Neither can his supposed Charlie Hebdo shooter partners, the Kouachi Brothers, who got cut to pieces the same day.

[VID 003] (Video by YouTube)

https://www.youtube.com/watch?v=I7vscOA78RU

[IMG 0006]

http://youtu.be/OcBF6xlER7E

https://www.youtube.com/watch?v=OcBF6xlER7E&feature=youtu.be

(# 4 Video by Youtube)

[IMG 0007]

The deep state's patsy, Amedy Coulibaly, was already handcuffed, when he jumped into a hail of gunfire, from the conveniently Jewish grocery store, during Charlie Hebdo. (#7 Image by Dolio Kezok, YouTube)

Speaking of important dead witnesses, there was a top cop, Helric Fredou, investigating the Charlie Hebdo hoax. Lemme see if I got this right. The day after the false flag, late in the night while he was writing his report, Mr. Fredou "commits suicide". Whatever he was writing was surely destroyed on the spot. The biggest case of his life, one of the great cases of the decade and he offs himself? Yeah, sure. My research shows that deadly accidents, sudden fatal illnesses and inexplicable suicides happen inordinately often in false flags. Funny how it works out that way. This very important story was largely censored in the West.

There is another Charlie Hebdo story that the West highly censored, A third suspect, Hamyd Mourad, turned himself in, declaring that he had an unassailable alibi – he was in class at high school. Alternative media reported this faithfully, but I found only The Daily Telegraph which reported that Mourad had an alibi. The rest of the MSM (mainstream media) Ministry of Truth omitted this key fact, leaving everyone with the impression that he turned himself in, because he was guilty:

- *The Washington Post* (January 7) "Charlie Hebdo suspect said to surrender; two others at large after Paris terror attack"
- *Die Welt* (Germany), "One suspect has turned himself in to police in connection with Wednesday's massacre at the offices of Parisian satirical magazine, Charlie Hebdo"
- *ABC News* (January 7), "Youngest suspect in Charlie Hebdo Attack turns himself in"
- *CNN* (January 8), "Citing sources, the *Agence France Presse* news agency reported that an 18-year- old suspect in the attack had surrendered to police"

This is not coincidental. There is a concerted effort by the MSM to act as ventriloquist dummies on TV and marionettes in the newsroom, to do the bidding for the West's deep state and elite owners. The MSM is riddled with CIA agents and "intelligence" NOCs (non-official covers) of all stripes, to help keep everybody singing in unison. A journalist with the courage to spill the beans about the pervasive, controlling presence of the CIA in Western journalism, has turned this truth into a best seller in Germany. Former CIA Director William Casey was just stating the obvious, when he went on record saying, "*The Central Intelligence Agency owns everyone of any significance in the major media.*" The Sleuthjournal.com provides this apt graphic summary:

Spoken like a true spy spook.

[IMG 0008]

Another CIA insider has been quoted that a puppet journalist is worth more to the agency than 20 agents actually doing espionage, revealing just how powerful the MSM is, for the deep state to keep the sheeple bleating.

There are many, many videos on the internet exposing the Charlie Hebdo false flag: Here is a French SWAT member opening machine gun fire into the backs of his comrades, obviously shooting blanks. Here are cops setting off explosions in the middle of the swarm of cops surrounding them. Had they been real stun grenades, everybody around them would have been floored by the percussion wave. You can compare all these videos to an "official" mainstream NBC video, to see how the latter one has been expertly edited to excise all the incriminating evidence. [IMG 0009] Winston Smith in 1984's Oceania would feel right at home in the West's "newsrooms", as history is cut, pasted and censored to the requisites of Big Brother. Just like my friend lambasted a communist country for censorship, the West works tirelessly to control its past too.

[VID 005] Paris cops shooting blanks

[VID 006] Charlie Hebdo Hoax - Pyrotechnics & Fake Explosions Exposed

[VID 007] Paris false flag Even World Leaders Photos are Fake

Not surprisingly, the Great Western Firewall has removed this incriminating evidence of censorship from YouTube. Knowing that this happens all the time, the Orwellian MSM flushing the truth down the Memory Hole, I made copies of all these movies to keep on my hard drive and on the cloud. You may want to start doing the same. Like in the movie, *V for Vendetta*, we can all be a virtual version of Stephen Fry's talk show host, Gordon Deitrich. He was bludgeoned to death by fascist government agents for possessing a copy of the Quran.

Like their movie, *The Matrix*, the Wachowski's very prescient *V* is art imitating life, to an all too frightening degree. In the story, the government released its own bioweapon, *St. Mary's Virus* onto the citizens, killing 100,000 people. It was this false flag terrorist attack that shocked the nation into voting the Norsefire Party into power, whereupon the sheeple let their leaders turn the country into a totalitarian fascist state. Any relation to what is happening in the United States, France, Britain and elsewhere in the West, is purely coincidental.

Paris False Flag. Even The World Leaders Photo Was Faked

[IMG 0011] Does it look like one million? *The much ballyhooed world leaders'"Million Man March", in support of Charlie Hebdo, was straight out of Hitler's playbook. Or rather, the Nazis probably got their best PR ideas from behind the Great Western Firewall and its MSM propaganda machine. (#11 Image by Ya Oughta Learn, YouTube)*

[IMG 0012] This bogus photo of Benjamin Netanyahu was published around the world, proclaiming he was waving to the masses at the Charlie Hebdo Million Man March. He was waving to empty buildings on a deserted street. Give this war crimes criminal a Raspberry Award (#13 Image by telegraph. co.uk)

Even the million-man march in Paris, supposedly led by the defiant leaders of the "free world" was a hoax. Benjamin Netanyahu is seen waving, but he is waving to *nobody*. Who needs Kim Jong-un? Heck, he probably gets his best ideas from his Western counterparts. Nobody does censorship and propaganda better than Westerners do. After all, they've been writing the playbook for 500 years.

Apparently, in false flags, there is a psychological slip of the tongue, where crisis actors can't help but smile or smirk, when they get in front of the camera, for the joy of fooling the world. It's called "duping delight" and this website has catalogued a bunch of them.

Numerous visual documents provide proof of this relatively new phenomenon, first developed by Western intel agencies with the support of their media assets. See [IMG 0013] and [VID 008] in online concordance. In these images one of the witnesses *is describing how she just learned about her Charlie Hebdo partner supposedly having his brains blown all over a Parisian sidewalk, the horror of it all, and she's smiling and smirking. No tears, no shock, just a crisis actor's duper's delight smirk on her face, for fooling the whole world. The video shows her fellow actors can barely keep a straight face.* (#15 Image by bbc.com)

As all false flags are used to manipulate the masses after the fact and give a pretext to attack perceived enemies, it is happening in spades, thanks to Charlie Hebdo. France's authorities and thus their mainstream media marionettes are already talking about how Charlie Hebdo is France's 9/11 and the government are passing a Patriot Act law, like the United States. Sayanora to *Liberté, Fraternité, Egalité*. You can kiss your Quiche Lorraine goodbye, *mes chers*. Say hello to persecution of Muslims, indefinite imprisonment, black sites for torture and murder, SWAT teams, military weaponized police replacing cops on the beat, shooting first and asking questions later, while committing what used to be illegal search and seizure. My fellow French citizens, welcome to Angloland's New World Order. Kafka was a fellow European, remember? It's reality imitating art.

It keeps on keeping on. Just Google "crisis actors Boston bombing" and you will see real actors pretending to be injured. The media darling, hoax double amputee, Jeff Bauman, is photoed after supposedly losing both legs, conscious and sitting up, with a phony tourniquet that is loose. The joke is on us. I've worked on major movie sets numerous times in France and China and all these photos and this video look like, well, a movie set. One lady has been interviewed on international TV for at least three different "terrorist acts", and has apparently even been identified. There are many videos showing similar actors before and after the supposed bombing. Also, the private "security" contractors near where the supposed Boston bombs went off, are dressed identically like the two patsy Tsarnaev brothers, replete with carbon copy, oversized backpacks, which is a nice touch. They were working for a company owned and operated at the time by Chris Kyle, of *American Assassin* movie fame, who has mercifully been put out of his psychopathic misery.

[IMG 0014] Boston bombing crisis actors.

[VID 009] Boston bombing crisis actors.

[IMG 0015] **Crisis actress appears 3 different times; 1. Sandy Hook 2. Boston Bombing 3. Police Chase**

[VID 010] **Crisis actress appears 3 different times; 1. Sandy Hook 2. Boston Bombing 3. Police Chase**

[VID 011] "Crisis actress" busted: Adriana Victoria Muñoz

[VID 012] Boston Bombing: Cellphone Captures Actor Late For Work

[VID 013] Crisis actors caught in training exercise

[IMG 0015] *Lemme see, you just had both of your legs blown off by a supposed Boston Marathon bomb, you are fully conscious, sitting up, not bathed in blood, vomit, urine and feces, you still have good skin color, no loss of blood, no shock, and the farcical tourniquet on your leg has a gap in it big enough to run your fist through. The phony bone sticking out of the left leg is a real hoot too. A bomb would have shredded it like ragged meat. Jeff Bauman and all the people around him are crisis actors. (Image by kaotic.com)*

Crisis actors have other defining characteristics. Even though they have just been supposedly traumatized by the most brutal acts of moral deprivation, they invariably are calm and collected, like they are bummed out about getting a speeding ticket. Any normal person who really experienced these acts would be in shock, delerious and beside themselves. When asked by their camera toting handlers what they will do now, crisis actors invariably say, "Well, we'll just get back to normal", or some such nonsense, like they've had a bad case of tummy ache or a skin abrasion. It's ludicrous.

Also, excepting 9/11, where real people died, where are all the funerals being held, for all the hundreds of supposedly dead people? Why aren't the streets being filled with casket toting crowds, showing solidarity with the victims? There are none, because there are few to no real victims to mourn. Palestine's streets are jam packed every day, with solidarity-seeking citizens, bereaving the loss of their loved ones, because these Zionist murders really do occur. Not so, in the false flag West.

If you believe the official, Hollywood version of 9/11, you are saying on that day, the natural laws of physics, chemistry, gravity and matter were miraculously suspended. You are insisting that Newton, Einstein, Bohr, Planck, Lavoisier, Mendeleev and all the foundations of science did not apply that morning in New York City, Washington, D.C. and rural Pennsylvania. No, it was pure *Harry Potter* and *Fantasia*.

You are claiming that for the first time ever, 815°C, burning jet fuel melted thousands of tons of steel, steel that has a melting point of 1,510°C. That's more fantastic than alchemy. You are claiming that tens of thousands of massive, bolted, welded, riveted steel I-beams, girders, piers and supports just miraculously gave way, like hot butter, and collapsed at nearly the same rate as an object falling off the Leaning Tower of Pisa. And not just the two 110-story Twin Towers, but WTC 7, which wasn't hit by an airplane. Yet this massive, 52 story skyscraper (226m/743ft) went down in free fall in six seconds flat. If you had jumped off the top when WTC 7 began to collapse, you would have hit the ground at the same time as the top of its roof did.

[IMG 0016] 30-second reel of building 7 collapse footage

[VID 014] *Three buildings were brought down by controlled demolition on 9/11, not two. It is easy to see in this video where thermite explosives were set off vertically in sequence, to bring down WTC 7, all 52 stories of it, in six seconds flat. (Image by YouTube.com)*

The most likely source of this rapid destruction is the material thermite, which is commonly used for the controlled demolition of steel buildings. Dozens of police and first responders reported hearing series of rapid explosions happening in all three buildings, which is the hallmark of the timed thermite ignitions at each descending level, as the building implodes. Independent investigators also found pools and puddles of still molten steel, several days after the supposed terrorist attacks. Thermite can heat up hardened steel and keep it that hot for that long. Otherwise, the steel would have cooled off and solidified much quicker.

Luckily, they were there early enough to see what they could and gather thermite laced samples. Against every forensic law on the books, all three buildings' physical evidence was immediately hauled off, only to be shipped to China for scrap metal. Your Made in China appliance could very well contain 9/11 evidence inside it.

The other possibility is that micro-nuclear devices were used. Russian intelligence has apparently been discreetly releasing information showing it was Mossad of Israel that organized the controlled demolitions. This would explain why so many first responders were irradiated with beta wave energy, just like survivors of Hiroshima and Nagasaki. Either way, thermite or micro-nuclear devices or both, the three WTC skyscrapers were not brought down by 19 Arabs with box cutters.

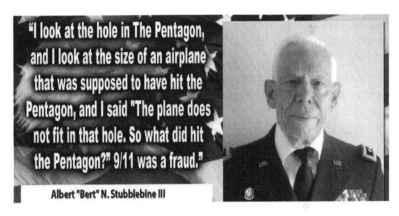

"I look at the hole in The Pentagon, and I look at the size of an airplane that was supposed to have hit the Pentagon, and I said "The plane does not fit in that hole. So what did hit the Pentagon?" 9/11 was a fraud."

Albert "Bert" N. Stubblebine III

[IMG 0017] Major General Albert Stubblebine III knows a false flag when he sees it. You will too, if you watch all the videos and study all the photos in this exposé. (Credit: 369News.net)

Again, you have to suspend the natural laws of the Universe to swallow the guffaw, official story about the Pentagon being hit by a Boeing 757. This was supposed to be a plane with a 38-meter wing span (124ft), still carrying 32,000 liters (8,600 gallons) of highly flammable jet fuel in its wings and two massive jet engines, along with its 47m long (155ft) fuselage, plowing into the outside of the building at several hundred kilometers/miles per hour. Miraculously, that 38m, fuel-filled wingspan supposedly left only a narrow, 19m gash in the Pentagon. Plane wreckage and debris just magically disappeared, no dead bodies, no luggage, no plane seats – it all just evaporated into thin air, like *Bewitched*. Just as damning, all those supposed 32,000 liters of burning jet fuel did not rage into a towering ball of inferno, for hours on end. Nope, all the contents of the offices right next to where the supposed 115-ton plane careened at flight speed

into the Pentagon, were still sitting there. Desks, computers, file cabinets, chairs – even papers and documents were miraculously still sitting on tops of desks right where the fiery "crash" supposedly occurred. A security camera accidentally caught the explosion on film and a massive 757 jetliner never enters the picture, although it looks like possibly a missile on the right came in low for the strike, if it was not blown up from inside. That could explain the damage done. But a careening 757? No way. Where I grew up in Oklahoma, we are fond of saying that you can't stuff ten pounds of manure in a five-pound bag. Well, you can't slam a 38m wide jetliner into a 19m hole. A lesson in just how efficient the GWF's censorship works, this CNN news report right after the supposed terrorist act stated the obvious, that there was no airplane. How many times was this aired? Once, never to be seen or heard again.

Below: More documentation supporting the 9/11 questioners.

[VID 015] The Pentagon was not hit by an airliner.

[IMG 0019] Pentagon security camera on 9/11

[VID 016] Pentagon security camera on 9/11

[IMG 020] Pentagon hit on 9/11-only aired once

[VID 017] Pentagon hit on 9/11-only aired onc

[IMG 0018] Pentagon 9/11 fake attack: there was no airplane.

You have to suspend all the physical laws of the Universe -and your intelligence - to accept the hundreds of inconsistencies of the deep state's 9/11 false flag caper, including airplane wings and engines full of fuel that did no damage.

As far as the infamous heroes who fought those nasty "terrorists" on flight UA93, heck – even a major production Hollywood movie was made about the phantom plane crash – this local Fox affiliate news clip also only saw the light of public viewing one time, before it was cut and censored from the history books, by the Great Western Firewall. China, Cuba, Vietnam, Eritrea North Korea and the rest of the world can only smile in admiration for a Memory Hole job well done.

[IMG 0022] Flight 93 banned newscast.

There you have it, from a helicopter flying over immediately after the fake crash of UA93, a 3-5 meter square hole, where a huge commercial jetliner supposedly crashed. This Fox affiliate footage saw the light of day one time, only to be lost to oblivion in the MSM Memory Hole.

[VID 018] Flight 93 banned newscast

The supposed crash site of the UA93 flight in rural Pennsylvania was nothing more than a small hole about 3-5 meters squared (10-15 feet squared) and paper debris no bigger than a phone book strewn across the countryside. No plane fuselage, no wings, no jet engines, no dead bodies, no luggage, no flotsam from the supposed fiery crash. Three qualified people on the site, immediately after the mythical crash stated,

This crash was different. There was no wreckage, no bodies, and no noise. – Somerset County Coroner Wallace Miller

I was looking for anything that said tail, wing, plane, metal. There was nothing. – Photographer Scott Spangler

I was amazed because it did not, in any way, shape, or form, look like a plane crash. – Patrick Madigan, commander of the Somerset barracks of the Pennsylvania State Police

And then there is just the absurd impossibility of the whole outrageous lie, to quote Paul Craig Roberts,

(In the most tightly controlled air space on Planet Earth) ... According to the official story, a handful of Arabs, mainly Saudi Arabians, operating independently of any government and competent intelligence service, men without James Bond and V for Vendetta capabilities, outwitted not only the CIA, FBI, and National Security Agency, but all 16 US intelligence agencies, along with all security agencies of America's NATO allies and Israel's Mossad. Not only did the entire intelligence forces of the Western world fail, but on the morning of the attack the entire apparatus of the National Security State simultaneously failed. Airport security failed four times in one hour. NORAD failed. Air Traffic Control failed. The US Air Force failed. The National Security Council failed. Dick Cheney failed. Absolutely nothing worked. The world's only superpower was helpless at the humiliating mercy of a few undistinguished Arabs.

All of this is just the tip of the iceberg of what a hoax the official 9/11 fantasy story really is. I have studied it for many countless hours, analyzing all the evidence. I know, I know, I can empathize. I've been there and done that. You want to deny, deny, deny, pretend it's not true, bury it away, go to work, get on with your routine, but the truth is unavoidable. A modicum of homework will easily show that the real conspiracy theorists are the ones who keep denying sound science and patently obvious evidence.

An outstanding, one hour-forty-five-minute documentary, _Zero Hour_, fills out the whole sordid saga. A very comprehensive, 5-hour documentary, _The New Pearl Harbor_, is excellent. On the 13th anniversary of 9/11, the _Corbett Report_ names suspects as a platform for an eventual real, independent investigation and trial. A brave, highly qualified group of 2,400 architects and engineers, risking official opprobrium, has come together, to make the public aware of the greatest false flag in modern times, ever being pulled off. They all deserve our attention.

[IMG 0024]

[VID 019] The New Pearl Harbor

[VID 020] Who was really behind the 9/11 attacks?

And the hits just keep on coming: Sandy Hook, Paris II and San Bernardino. Do your own research on these and you will learn, like me, that they were most certainly false flags. Now I understand how the Western elites operate, in order to maintain their control over the masses and thus, their imperial agenda.

Knowing the truth, it is the first question all informed citizens should ask, when they hear or read about _another_ "terrorist attack": "I wonder if that was a false flag"? It is much, much more probable than we care to admit, because it probably was.

It all goes back to the murder of the JFK, by the Big Banks, CIA and the Joint Chiefs of Staff doesn't it? In fact, in their heart of hearts, Americans know the truth. Yes, I often give my compatriots a hard time, but since the Warren Commission, in its annual Gallup poll, a majority of Americans believe the deep state killed Kennedy. A solid majority believe the same deep state was responsible for Martin Luther King's murder. A solid plurality of Americans thinks there was a cover up about 9/11. This plurality will surely grow to a majority, with the help of groups like AE911. Everytime someone tries to belittle the truth about false flags, I remind them that it is they who are in the minority and the "nuts" in denial of the majority.

[IMG 0025] Assassination of John F Kennedy (Chart by Gallup)

If you believe that JFK was killed by a lone assassin, you are in the minority.

It's not just Americans who recognize rotten fish when they smell it. My high school daughter was fascinated by all the evidence I showed her and my wife about Charlie Hebdo, so she agreed to watch *Zero Hour*. She not only watched it, but took it to school and gave it to her Theory of Knowledge teacher, who in turn showed it to the class. Hats off to the prof. They would surely have been fired had they done that in the United States. The shocking result: my daughter said all of the students already knew that 9/11 was perpetrated by the American government.

And it is their sense of resignation to do anything about that I find so disturbing and shameful. My wife too was just as telling. After looking at all the evidence about Charlie Hebdo and glancing over at the TV screen and seeing millions of sheeple wearing their color coordinated t-shirts and holding up their absurd, color coordinated *Je Suis Charlie* placards, just hours after the false flag, she said, "OK, so what can you really do about it"? It is this feeling of helplessness that is so damning of the West's state of affairs. Our so called democracy is a hollow mirage.

This brings me to the crux of this article. In spite of our evolutionary tendencies to deny and block out unpleasant events, deep down, we know our governments and capital are committing very bloody and disastrous false flags. It is our acquiescence to all these false flags that is giving the Princes of Power a carte blanche to drive the human race towards a dystopian, fascist future. After all, if our leaders can murder their own president and get away with a coup d'état in Dealey Plaza in broad daylight, they can bring down the 9/11 towers and will surely do much worse, confident of humanity's gullibility and even if aware, self-imposed powerlessness. It makes the Iraq's, Ukraine's and all the other false flags just that much easier for them to pull off.

Astute observers have noticed the same problem,

One of the intentions of corporate-controlled media is to instill in people a sense of disempowerment, of immobilization and paralysis. Its outcome is to turn you into good consumers. It is to keep people isolated, to feel that there is no possibility for social change. - —David Barsamian, journalist and publisher

Noam Chomsky said,

The media serve the interests of state and corporate power, which are closely interlinked, framing their reporting and analysis in a manner supportive of established privilege and limiting debate and discussion accordingly.

Until we rise up and protest openly against our leaders' false flags, we will have no freedom in our future and probably no future at all. For our very survival, we must, in mass, get informed of the truth and stop saying, "No, it can't be", because it *is*. False flags are where it all starts and where the nightmare has to end. The Princes of Power are playing for keeps and it's either us or them, now or never. Who knows how long internet freedom and FOIA laws will stay on the books? Another 9/11 sized false flag is inevitable, at which point we can kiss goodbye the alternative media and a still relatively open internet.

OK, I said it. I don't think this piece will be appearing in a mainstream newspaper any time soon. Such is life. But I can live with that.

On this 9/11: why John F. Kennedy was killed by the deep state, in America's first coup d'état

[IMG 0026]

9/11 was America's second coup d'état. JFK's removal from office was the first. (Image by thetimes.co.uk)

A man does what he must – in spite of personal consequences, in spite of obstacles and dangers – and this is the basis of all human morality.— John F. Kennedy - (1917-1963) 35th US President

Today, September 11th, 2015, is the 14th anniversary of America's second coup d'état. The first one was John F. Kennedy's murder.

Listening to JFK give a speech on April 27, 1961, to the American Newspaper Publishers Association, and then watching his commencement address to the American University in 1963, it is easy to see why America's deep state removed him from office in a coup d'état, on November 22nd, 1963.

While the journalists in the crowd of the Newspaper Publishers meeting undoubtedly thought JFK was talking about the Soviet Union, looking back on history since then, one has to believe that he was also talking about his own country's deep state: America's CIA/FBI/NSA/DIA/Joint Chiefs of Staff/Mafia government. After all, he had fired the assassination- and government-overthrow maniac Allen Dulles, as head of the CIA in 1961, promising,

I want to splinter the CIA into a thousand pieces and scatter it to the winds.

Why did Kennedy want to do this? The following is what he said to America's journalists in 1961,

We are opposed around the world by a monolithic and ruthless conspiracy that relies on covert means for expanding its sphere of influence – on infiltration

instead of invasion, on subversion instead of elections, on intimidation instead of free choice, on guerrillas by night instead of armies by day.

It is a system which has conscripted vast human and material resources into the building of a tightly knit, highly efficient machine that combines military, diplomatic, intelligence, economic, scientific and political operations… Its preparations are concealed, not published. Its mistakes are buried, not headlined. Its dissenters are silenced, not praised. No expenditure is questioned, no rumor is printed, no secret is revealed.

Sounds familiar today? Was JFK talking about the Soviets or America's deep state?

<u>Listen to and read the full transcript of Kennedy's 1961 speech to journalists.</u>

As the true puppeteers and heads of the American government, the CIA was not about to let Kennedy threaten the deep state's control of the country. Why else was the deep state ready to kill JFK? He refused to nuke or even bomb Cuba, did not support the Bay of Pigs invasion, compromised with Khrushchev over the Cuban missile crisis, sold the USSR wheat on credit, refused to approve the CIA's and Joint Chiefs' Operation Northwoods, which was a massive plan to conduct false flag acts of terrorism on America's own citizens, to blame it all on Cuba, including blowing up commercial airliners (sound familiar?).

JFK had signed an executive order to remove all US forces from Southeast Asia, which would have ended the Vietnam War in 1964. So, he earned the hatred of the blood thirsty Joint Chiefs of Staff and America's worldwide Wehrmacht. He was also secretly negotiating with Khrushchev and Fidel Castro, in a bid for world peace. JFK was also adamantly opposed to Israel wanting to build nuclear bombs. He was the first and last US president to stand up to Israel, and paid the ultimate price for it.

Even more incredibly, Kennedy signed an executive order which took away the private Federal Reserve Banks' ability to print and loan money to the US government, thereby turning America's minting back to its citizens, something that has been the dream of many, since the administration of President Andrew Jackson in the 1830s. He even had the US government print $4 billion in $2 and $5 bills, all backed by the good faith of silver. I remember seeing those "silver certificates", when I was a kid, and kept a $2 one for the longest time. Little did I know of its true history and import. When Kennedy was murdered by his own government, the Treasury was in the process of printing $10 and $20 silver backed notes, which were not borrowed from the private Federal Reserve Banks. He thus further earned his death sentence for opposing the biggest banking families. As soon as Vice President Lyndon Baines Johnson was sworn in as the new #1, he ordered the mint to stop printing these $10 and $20 silver certificate notes, as well as the incineration of what had already been printed. They were never seen or used by the public.

Not to mention, his Attorney General brother, Robert, was tearing Mafia families new rectums, thus engendering the hatred of the CIA's right hand partners in crime, La Cosa Nostra. In sum, JFK made bitter enemies of too many power-hungry and greedy

psychopaths - banksters, generals, spies and mobsters - who were ready to kill him, to keep him from achieving his system changing, world revolutionizing plans.

During his 1963 commencement speech, JFK pleaded for peace, the way presidents Clinton, Bush I and II and Obama lust for war. He announced sweeping treaty talks with the Soviets in tandem with Harold McMillan, the conservative Prime Minister of Britain at the time. For American Empire, whose domination of the world depends on total war, Kennedy's sentiments expressed in this address were tantamount to treason against the deep state. Eerily, many of the points he brought up in this talk about what the United States would never do around the world, were already happening through the evil offices of spydom, and which have exploded exponentially since 1980.

JFK's Commencement Address at American University, June 10, 1963. The United States experienced its first coup d'état, just five months later, when he was killed by America's deep state

America's 1963 coup d'état had profound implications for the future of the country, and for the entire planet. Emboldened by its success, the deep state (CIA, JCS and the big bankers) committed and continues to cause thousands of assassinations, government overthrows and regime changes across the globe - all of which are changing the course of human history. The CIA oversees the illegal drug trade in Asia's Golden Triangle, Afghanistan and Central/South America, providing it with tens of billions of dollars for black budget terrorism. The American-run Gladio secret armies in Europe are still thriving, murdering, regime changing and making a mockery of the Old Continent's farcical, managed and controlled "democracy". Stateside, it's even worse. Robert Kennedy, Martin Luther King, Malcolm X and thousands more led shortened lives, for opposing the deep state's objectives. 9/11 was just another, more audacious false flag event to scare Americans into accepting a neo-fascist police state and to justify the slaughter of millions of Muslims across our Pale Blue Dot, while stealing their natural resources, colonial style.

9/11 also allowed the deep state to pull off its second American coup d'état. That day, George II was illegally removed from office under the program of *continuity of government* (COG). During this brief military rule, the country radically changed its foreign policy and defense. A rash of freedom stealing laws were passed by fiat during that fateful day. On September 11th, 2001, all members of Congress and their staff were placed under house arrest by the COG military authority, in the government complexes at Greenbrier and Mount Weather, Virginia. Dick Cheney, the avatar of the deep state, was large and in charge. COG is nothing more than martial "law" fascism, a military junta and Americans got their first official dose of the future state, 13 years ago.

John Fitzgerald Kennedy must be crying in his grave.

(WN.com)(cc)

MH370: Gallows humor is universal and timeless - including in China

[IMG 0027]

Why is no one talking about the northern flight path? Just asking.

Who says the Chinese don't have a great sense of humor, even in the face of a minor national tragedy. The inexplicable and it just keeps getting-weirder disappearance of the Kuala Lumpur-Beijing flight MH370, is a Page One obsession in China.

I saw this joke in Chinese on Wechat, which shows a self-deprecating, gallows humor in the face of an informational void. Translated, it says,

If MH370 had 154 Americans on board, the United States would already be taking the Malay government to the international courts; if they were 154 Russians, the Malay government would already be in the grave; if it were 154 Japanese, the Japanese government would have already calculated down to the cent how much Malaysia owes them; if it were 154 Israelis, Israel would have already found the hijackers; if it were 154 Koreans, three missiles would have been already hit the Japanese fishing fleet; but since they are 154 Chinese people, we get candles, protests and poetic lyricism in the media.

This helps explain why Baba Beijing is putting such a huge amount of publicized effort into finding the missing plane. The Chinese citizenry is extremely distraught about what happened to MH370 and Baba has picked up on this popular angst. When there is widespread popular anger, Baba knows that their ability to maintain the Heavenly Mandate and the Communist Party's continued leadership, hangs in the balance. Baba Beijing definitely wants to stay ahead of this perceived national humiliation, to keep it from blowing up in their faces.

What do I think? There are around 100 reconnaissance (read: military and spy) satellites encircling the globe like an octopus, that are powerful enough to say whether my sandwich is being served on rye or whole wheat bread. You can't tell me that the US, Russia and France, even China don't know where MH370 is or ended up. The problem is the people who run these satellites are all the world's bad actors within governments, the deep state, their spy and military agencies. They won't even admit to having this level of reconnaissance capabilities, much less hold a press conference to talk about it. At least in the West, if the Freedom of Information Act (FOIA) still exists - and in today's world that is always questionable - we may find out in 30-50 years, when a FOIA request stumbles upon the truth.

MH370, Chinese Cyberwar Geniuses and the Long Arm of Western Empire

[IMG 0028]

I asked this same question in the previous chapter: why isn't anybody looking towards the North? Now we know why.

Why are the Princes of Power keeping the 99%'s attention riveted on the middle of bumfug nowhere, in the Southeast Indian Ocean, looking for MH370, and why is nobody asking about the second possible escape route – to the North, in Afghanistan and Pakistan?

Everybody I talked to, including journalists based in Beijing, and other bright lights of the intelligentsia, just guffawed at the thought. Chortle no more. I do not have the means nor the tools to confirm all of this. And one thing for sure: if true, the mainstream media won't touch it with a ten-meter pole, as it would implicate their masters and handlers. But as a rational thinker, the following scenario is looking more than credible. This is especially true, given the goose egg laid in the Indian Ocean, finding not even one shred of debris, in spite of a massive, extended, multinational search: no seats, luggage, clothing, bodies – nothing. Then a supposed flaperon was dubiously found a year and half later, all the way over on Reunion island, and which was never confirmed by an independent source. Then, another piece of whatever supposedly washed up on the coast of Madagascar. It saturated the 24-hour news cycle, then disappeared. No investigation, no outside laboratory forensics. *Just take our word for it.* Yeah, sure.

Early on, a journalist friend was pleasantly surprised when I brought up Occam's razor, in looking for a solution to the MH370 mystery. Occam's razor is the law that usually the simplest explanation is the best or correct one. Thus the pilots, for whatever reason, just flew the plane into the deep blue sea. End of story. But this Occam's razor is just not cutting it anymore. Time to look elsewhere to unwind 2014's Gordian knot of the year. The passengers' families obviously smell a rat. They are getting together a $5 million reward, in hopes of enticing someone on the inside to spill the beans - if they live long enough to meet with the grieving. The half-life of informed people like this tends to be measured in days and hours, if there is a whiff of suspicion from on high.

And then as if by divine providence, we learn that in Europe of all places, dozens of commercial airliners went missing off the Old Continent's sophisticated air traffic control screens, due to high tech NATO electronic war games. Well, blow me down, Captain Ahab, I can see far, far away from this here Beijing crow's nest. If they can make fifty Boeing and Airbus jet planes full of thousands of people vanish off radar terminals in one of the busiest skies in the world, then it must be a piece of cake to disappear a solo plane like MH370, right?

In an *Anonymous* news release on YouTube, we learn that there were 20 (Chinese) employees of Freescale Semiconductor on board MH370, bound for where else - Communist China. Four of these employees shared a revolutionary patent on the new "KL Zero" computer chip, which will be used in missile defense (read Star Wars) radar systems. The patent was approved just four days *after* the disappearance of MH370. Therefore, the four Chinese patent holders could not legally pass the wealth and control of this patent on to their heirs. This leaves the fifth shareholder of the patent as 100% owner: Freescale Semiconductor itself. Who owns Freescale Semiconductor? Jacob Rothschild and the Bush Dynasty's Carlyle Group. Either you are a conspiracy theorist or a coincidence theorist, but it's funny how things work out that way.

So, the plot thickens. Why were they in Kuala Lumpur? Why were they all together? Why were they going back to China? Were they defecting *back* to the Motherland? Were they single or double agents?

Who wouldn't want to get their hands on these Chinese scientist patent holders and their vast knowledge of warfare cybertechnology? Or better yet, who would want to make sure these geniuses did **not** help the People's Liberation Army (PLA) use the very same "Western" stealth technology, to defend the Chinese Homeland? This is not primarily about Jacob Rothschild's greed and the Carlyle Group's Bush

Dynasty-Bin Laden bedmates, although filthy lucre is often seen lurking around the stage set. This is more than likely about the United States and NATO making sure these Chinese scientists didn't land in the Middle Kingdom and work for Baba Beijing. How big is a computer chip? The size of your fingernail? It would have been very easy for one of these Chinese brainiacs to hide this new KL Zero war-chip in their suitcase. One or some of these guys could have been PLA (double) agents all along, which if true, would be a John Le Carré-esque-spy-thriller infiltration of the century, into the dark heart of America's most sensitive military technology.

Since the 1970s, Freescale, a military cybertech supplier, has been helping the Western Empire keep its Wehrmacht jackboot on the face of the Dreaded Other (including communists starting in 1917 and in 2001 add Muslims). Of course it would have its share of CIA/NSA minders working on the inside, keeping tabs on its highly sensitive advancements. These 20 Chinese scientists were way too close to something obviously very coveted and extremely compromising to the US/NATO war machine. US/NATO would do *anything* to keep them and "it" from ending up in Baba Beijing's hands.

All of this is bolstered further by the divulgations of a recent _Oped News_ article by Scott Baker. In it, an anonymous Russian (maybe a KGB stringer) reports on the whereabouts of MH370 being on the Afghanistan-Pakistan border, and that "there were 20 Asian specialists on board", who have been taken to a bunker in Pakistan. According to this report, these facts have been collectively corroborated by several intelligence agencies. Given that the United States rules Pakistan's and Afghanistan's skies as much as it does Washington DC's, any denials by these NATO puppet governments can be taken with a grain of salt. Whether these 20 Chinese scientists are being used for blackmail or as bargaining chips to "sell" is debatable. More than likely, US/NATO would prefer to have them offed, now that the West has the coveted technology to themselves. Or do they? If these Chinese scientists were agents of the PLA, then they may have already sent Baba Beijing the blueprints. However, it would have been nice for Baba to hold the Real McWang in the palm its hand, and plug it into the ol' Victrola for some space age *East Is Red* Karaoke.

The only positive outcome of all these high level espionage and warfare power plays is that the 227 passengers and 12 crew members might still be alive. The Russian report says they are alive, divided into seven groups and living in mud huts, southeast of Kandahar. However, if it is true that US/NATO is pulling these nefarious puppet strings, from Empire's standpoint, these hostages would be more of a liability than an asset, and better off dead.

The deep state of US/NATO, along with Russian intelligence, which together have well over 100 military reconnaissance satellites suffocating every square meter of the Earth's surface, know exactly where MH370 ended up. If they know, Baba Beijing surely knows too, and is just holding its cards close to see how events shake out. In any case, except for two pieces of very late on the scene, highly dubious, maritime evidence to show for the massive and exhaustive searches in the Indian Ocean, an Afghanistan-Pakistan change of flight plans is looking more and more believable. You are either a conspiracy or coincidence theorist. Pick you poison.

The face of Western imperialism exposed by Ebola

[0029] Lon Chaney acting in Phantom of the Opera, unmasked, channeling Western Empire

For the 85% of the world's people who are not among Western Empire's sheeple (sheep people), these are trying times in the Age of Colonialism. Like for the last 500 years.

Westerners have a history of using humans as guinea pigs for all kinds of horrific experiments and eugenics. The Spanish Inquisition, Medieval torture of witches, and later the Nazis come to mind. In the days of our lives, the CIA gleefully tortures or teaches others to torture for hire, while many of America's vassal states and proxy entities like Saudi Arabia, Indonesia, and ISIS, take pride in the brutalization of their designated enemies and frequently own citizens.

Not so long ago, upstanding leaders of Western style "democracy" vociferously sterilized hundreds of thousands of unwitting citizens. The United States targeted blacks, Native Americans and Puerto Ricans. All the perpetrators targeted those who are perceived to be inferior races. Some of the programs continued well into the 1970s. This hall of shame includes Canada, Czech Republic, Denmark Estonia, Finland, Iceland, Israel, Japan, Norway, Sweden, Switzerland and the United States, among others.

Australia, Canada and the United States, even into the 1970s, were tearing apart many thousands of native families, by forced removal of children, to be sent to colonial schools, where they could learn the superiority of White Man's culture and Christianity. It was benignly termed cultural assimilation, but in reality it was ethnic genocide.

In 1940s Guatemala, the United States purposely infected thousands of natives with syphilis and gonorrhea, to test these human guinea pigs with antibiotics. Of course, these suffering souls were sexually active for the rest of their lives and unwittingly infected everybody they came in contact with, including spouses. Thus the total number of people who were eventually infected, including children born with these diseases, would total in the many thousands. Lots of lives were destroyed in the process. But for Empire, that's no problem, because dark skinned Guatemalans are less than human.

At Tuskegee, American blacks were treated just as inhumanely. Hundreds of them were allowed to carry syphilis from the 1930s to the 1970s, to act as human petri dishes. This was to track the progress of the disease and observe the eventual macabre deaths that this bacterium is wont to inflict on its victims, in its final stages: insanity, nervous disorders, liver and heart disease.

The United States has a long, illustrious history of using bioterrorism around the world. Cuba has been a favorite target and has seen hundreds of thousands of its people infected with Dengue fever (a close cousin to Ebola), as well as its entire swine herd wiped out by swine fever. Biochemical weapons go way back and since the 20th century, the West has been and continues to be their most avid user. The United States is the biggest user of (bio) chemical weapons in history, including in places like Cuba; Iraq, Syria and Iran (by proxy); Serbia, Japan, Vietnam, Laos and Cambodia, and America has eagerly used them on its own people, apparently more often than we care to admit.

With this lengthy rap sheet and any doubts you may have about the evilness of empire, just take a look at the real story behind the nascent Ebola outbreak.

Did you know that the United States of America holds the exclusive patent on the Ebola virus? Yes, it does sound insane, that there should be a patent on the Ebola virus, but nothing is really off limits to the deranged mind of capitalists and their scientific and intellectual servants. It's right there in the public records: US patent number 20120251502, owned by the American government. Ebola has been Uncle Sam's bioweapon plaything since 1976, when it was discovered in Zaire and shipped 3,500 km by America's bio-warfare lab at Fort Detrick, Maryland, then to West Africa for cultivation and development (via the UK's bio-warfare labs in

Porton Down and with the help of the World "Health" Organization), specifically, to Liberia, Guinea and Sierra Leone, the current epicenters of the Ebola epidemic on the Great Continent.

[IMG 0030] *Ebola virus. US patent number 20120251502. Patent owned and controlled by Uncle Sam*

The United States, in complete contravention of the International Biological Weapons Convention, operates bio-warfare laboratories in these impoverished puppet states, infecting unwitting African human guinea pigs with the Ebola virus, with the purported intent of developing a vaccine. Don't believe me? The study was announced, business as usual, on an official US government website. Tekmira Pharmaceutical, a Canadian company, won the contract and is doing the Western Empire's evil Ebola work on West African human subjects. Tekmira is being paid $140 million of American taxpayers' money to flout international law and all boundaries of human decency.

Why even be working with the deadly Ebola virus and hold a patent on it, just to develop a vaccine? Or is it really a case of genetically modifying the Ebola virus in these two African-American laboratories, to make it even more lethal, as a bioterrorism weapon? American biological warfare researchers have been working in West Africa for years. They don't give a damn about vaccines for humanity's sake, although they are probably creating vaccines to protect themselves, when the genetically modified version is used against America's targeted enemies. The first job of US biowar laboratories is to create ever more powerful, weaponized bacteria and viruses.

But where is the moral outrage at using fellow human beings to create biowar Ebola bombs? Given that the people being sacrificed are poor, nameless black Africans, it is hard to avoid the racial overtones to humanity's total lack of concern, or rather, to be precise, the sociopathic, morally-bankrupt leadership of the West's segment of humanity. (Of course, that is what I have been trying to sketch out in this book for the preceding 70-odd pages.)

The World Health Organization (WHO) and America's Center for Disease Control (CDC) look mighty suspicious in all this travesty. US law professor Francis A. Boyle, who drafted the Biological Weapons Anti-Terrorism Act of 1989 and the American legislation for the 1972 Biological Weapons Convention, says they are fully implicated in the seemingly intentional spread of Ebola and not to be trusted, outright calling them liars. Mr. Boyle says that the CDC works hand in hand with the Pentagon's bioweapons program and that WHO is complicit in these developments as well.

It would be comical if it weren't so serious, reading how now deceased Ebola patient Thomas Eric Duncan was practically used as a vector to spread the disease in a Dallas, Texas hospital. It must be said though, that in America, where every patient is a point of sale, every medical intervention a profit center and where every procedure or regulation that does not generate money is considered a burdensome cost, this Keystone Cop-Looney Tunes gross malfeasance could be chalked up to just plain old corporate greed. However, having discovered that Texas Health Presbyterian Hospital is a non-profit, we can assume that the Duncan case was not due to greed, but was an ex-Africa Ebola epidemiological experiment. This hospital's Nurses' Statement confirmed as much, testifying that the CDC, which had personnel on site, refused to provide an Ebola protocol for them to follow and that the whole affair looked like it was trying to test the infection capabilities of whatever variety of Ebola Mr. Duncan had been inoculated with. These are professional nurses saying this, at great risk to their careers and/or lives. One can assume the CDC representatives had probably already received the Pentagon's vaccine against this particular strain, developed in its West African labs.

The whole sordid story stinks to high heaven. Disaster teams were told months in advance to be ready for an Ebola outbreak in the US, specifically in the month of October. What did they know was on the Pentagon's biowar calendar that we didn't? Also, why did the US State Department buy 160,000 biological hazmat suits in September, specifically for Ebola exposure? What does Ebola protection have to do with State's supposed mission, foreign affairs? It sure sounds like they knew in advance that something was going to happen.

In light of all the evidence presented and referenced in this chapter the ten points brought up in this article just pile the questions and suspicions ever higher. Here are the bullet points,

#1) Obama refuses to halt air travelers from infected countries from entering the United States

#2) Texas family is quarantined in a home that still hasn't been cleaned or decontaminated

#3) The CDC continues to lie about modes of transmission for the Ebola virus

#4) The FDA is openly threatening sellers of natural remedies that might be useful for slowing or stopping Ebola

#5) People entering U.S. customs are not asked where they've been

#6) The U.S. government knew about the outbreak in advance, but didn't warn the public

#7) Even during a global pandemic outbreak, the U.S. government refuses to secure the southern U.S. border

#8) The government's official advice of "don't panic, don't prepare" ensures a greater pandemic emergency during any outbreak

#9) The U.S. watched and waited, doing nothing during the original window of opportunity for halting Ebola six

#10) The U.S. government has held the patent on Ebola since 2010

Does this look like a government bent on stopping Ebola, or wanting to test how the latest version spreads?

And for me, the crown jewel in all this, the bright red cherry on top of this ghoulish, Halloween nightmare is not Lon Chaney unmasked in *Phantom of the Opera*, but that other Cheney - Dick to be exact. **The**

still reigning President of America's Deep State and master of its Continuation of Government (COG), said this on October 13th, 2014,

[ING 0031] COG master Dick Cheney

We're in a very dangerous period. I think it's more threatening than the period before 9/11... I think 9/11 will turn out to be not nearly as bad as the next mass casualty attack against the United States, which, if and when it comes, will be with something far deadlier than airline tickets and box cutters.

Hmm... does Herr Cheney know something we are not privy to? Is he using the classic deep state/CIA ploy of projecting a false flag operation, to validate it all in the minds of the people, once it is perpetrated?

LEFT: The psychopaths with the deep state plans sure seem to be slobbering for a new, bigger 9/11 Cheney and his twisted smirks clearly shows the ugliness inside. (#40 Image by corbis.com)

Unlike chemical weapons, bio-weapons are fiendishly difficult to get to work consistently and repeatedly, in a variety of environments and situations. They are living creatures, after all. So far, we may be in luck. Just studying all the evidence discussed in this chapter, it seems that quite possibly, the perpetrators' hopes were that the newest bred, American patented strain of Ebola would be infectious via airborne vectors, such as sneezing and coughing. This vector may not be working as planned. That's the good news.

The bad news is that America's Fort Detrick, the UK's Porton Down, the CDC's bio-warfare labs in West Africa and heaven help us, what is ongoing in other countries around the world – they are all still working 24/7 to create mass murder on a tactical, regional or global scale. If you think this is preposterous, <u>the US military refuses to promise it will not</u>

weaponize Ebola. As far back as 1995, the US Army was experimenting with lethal Ebola aerosols on Rhesus monkeys. Facts on the ground today suggest that they have not stopped trying to get aerosol Ebola to work. In other words, they are creating an Ebola bomb. This must explain why Obama sent 3,000 US Army soldiers to West Africa to "combat" Ebola. How many of these soldiers have been trained in the use of transporting, handling and delivering biowar vectors? After all, Ebola is America's very own, viral, bioweapon Frankenstein.

Remember that 1972 Biological Weapons Convention that the United States brags about creating and signing? Just another quaint treaty to wipe Uncle Sam's rear end with.

Heck, the 1%, their Princes of Power and mercenary Praetorians could do with a little *lebensraum* these days. Count 'em, 7.3 billion souls. Wiping out a billion or two dark skinned Africans, Asians or Americans would sure do the trick. If this sounds outrageous, remember that Western elites have been barking for reduced world population, since Robert Malthus wrote his *Essay on the Principle of Population,* in 1798. Colonialist Mr. Malthus was not at all worried about privileged elites multiplying. His fear was the poor and uneducated classes in England, and all those exploited, teeming subjects populating Britain's resource rich colonies around the world. Since then, many of the world's mostly white, Western 1% have not been and continue to not be bashful about the desire to see Planet Earth's human population drastically reduced. CNN Founder Ted Turner unapologetically said,

A total population of 250-300 million people, a 95% decline from present levels, would be ideal.

Most of the time, this Western fear of the Dreaded Other – the world's 85% dark skinned citizens - is more subtly conveyed in the mainstream media. Roger Martin in the Guardian, sums up nicely the common refrain of the world's privileged class,

...all environmental (and many economic and social) problems are easier to solve with fewer people, and ultimately impossible with ever more... On a finite planet, the optimum population providing the best quality of life for all,

is clearly much smaller than the maximum, permitting bare survival. The more we are, the less for each; fewer people mean better lives.

Again, Mr. Martin, like Malthus, is not worried about "his people". He's talking about Earth's six billion, mostly dark skinned people, who survive on less than $10 per day. Quotations and their implicit wishes on depopulation, from elite Westerners, are dime a dozen.

Whether America's development of a weaponized Ebola virus plays into this common sentiment among the West's elites, for Planet Earth's owners, what's left of the West's ever shrinking middle class could stand to have its lawn mown too. I can just hear the 1% grumbling,

Heck, just brush hog all that human undergrowth. The 99% are peskier and more parasitic than mesquite and cedar trees on Oklahoma grazing land, just wasting valuable resources. Ebola: a new kind of forced sterilization/population control program on a logarithmic scale... Just think of all the spacious, guarded communities we could have, the country clubs and golf courses! Each of our mansions with square kilometers of privately owned natural park land!

The American Dream on mega-steroids...

Chapter 2

How the West Was Lost and Other Hair Raising Tales of Empire

Many of you readers will either find this section inspiring and hopeful, cheering me on, or angry and polemical about topics you would prefer not to deal with. I fully empathize with both groups, since I have been in both places during my life. Speaking truth to power and calling a lie a lie takes courage and inevitably upsets a lot of people in the process.

I respect whichever side you may currently be on, during your life's journey. For the purposes of this book, my understanding of China, its people and leaders would never have been laid bare, unless I accepted as truth everything that is thoroughly researched and written about herewith.

It took me years to figure it out, but I finally realized that to know China's past, present and future, I had to get to the bare bones of my ancestors' and culture's timeline, past present and future. I'm talking about the dark underbelly of truth that a lifetime of brainwashing and propaganda has kept hidden. It has been one incredible, personal and intellectual journey, to discover it all. Finally, finally, I am at peace with myself.

+++

The most dangerous man to any government is the man who is able to think things out for himself, without regard to the prevailing superstitions and taboos. Almost inevitably he comes to the conclusion that the government he lives under is dishonest, insane and intolerable, and so, if he is romantic, he tries to change it. And even if he is not romantic personally he is very apt to spread discontent among those who are. — H.L. Mencken

A Tale of Two Democracies: What It Is Like to Vote in the United States Compared to France?

Note: the following article is an exposé of just how corrupt the United States' election process is. My ability to vote in two different Western countries is uniquely revealing and a real life example of American decline.

America is an outlier in the world of democracies when it comes to the structure and conduct of elections. Thomas E. Mann

How It All Happened

I recently voted in the French primary and runoff presidential races and just voted in the first and second rounds of France's legislative elections. I have been voting in France's elections since 1990. I have also faithfully voted in every presidential election in the United States, since 1972, as well as most federal legislative, state and local ones since that time, all the way down to the local school board level. Needless to say, I take my right to vote very, seriously and look upon it as an anchor that helps ground society, at least in theory and the ideal.

How is this possible? Well, it is because I am a member of that rarified population of world citizens who are dual nationals, carrying two passports. So, I have the truly unique perspective to compare the voting systems of two countries that take great pride in their sense of democracy and the processes of civil life. On the west side of the Atlantic, the United States, with its founders, freedom fighters, revolution and constitution; and on the opposite shores is France, with some of the greatest political and philosophical minds to ever put plume to paper, its revolution and Declaration of the Rights of Man and the Citizen. And can we not forget that is was France that gave the Statue of Liberty to the United States? Or that it was France, more than any other country that gave active support to the aforementioned freedom fighters and revolution? There is a common bond of ideals that these two countries have shared for over 200 years.

I most recently lived and worked in the United States 2001-2010 and went there from France, where I lived from 1997-2001. I have the bragging rights of being one of the passengers on that United Airlines flight that was the first one to reenter American airspace after September 11th, Paris to JFK on September 15th. And to complete the scenario, I lived in China 1990-1997 and moved back to Beijing in 2010, from the United States. Thus, I have the bizarre baseline of comparing these two proud [capitalist] democracies to a country that has a very different historical perspective and practice on the meaning of "freedom" and suffrage. And the fact that I left the United States in 1980 (I lived and worked in Africa and the Arab World 1980-1990), as Reagan was being elected (I campaigned hard for John Anderson before my departure and even got to meet him), and came back in 2001 to a radically transformed American society and economy, a country I could hardly recognize, was a shocking and sobering experience.

What I have learned over the years of voting in France and the United States is that these two great republics have almost diametrically opposed visions of what the democratic process means, what it has to offer and how much it can truly represent the voices and desires of their peoples.

God Bless America's Corruption

It is enough that the people know there was an election. The people who cast the votes decide nothing. The people who count the votes decide everything. Joseph Stalin

For as long as American history has been written, voting corruption is a staple topic and is benignly accepted as part and parcel of the process, especially at the local and state level. Tammany Hall, the Chicago Machine, Texas heavyweights, good ol' boy politicians in the South and many other big city and state party operations have filled books about how elections are rigged and stolen. Americans love to engage in prideful one-upmanship with their neighboring states' citizens about how much better one state is than the other for political corruption and rigged elections. Get a New Yorker, a Texan and an Illinoisan in a room together over a few beers and they'll be arm wrestling and breast beating in no time that their state is the most corrupt.

Stolen elections and local and state corruption are as much a part of America's political DNA as apple pie and Budweiser. And like torture is spun as *harsh interrogation techniques*, and thousands of dead and maimed Muslim children, women and elderly as *collateral damage*, political corruption in America's most hallowed of democracy's inalienable rights is simply called *irregularities*. How quaint.

Who can forget the 50,000 ballots that magically turned up in Chicago precincts, to assure that John F. Kennedy took Illinois, its electoral votes and the presidential election from Richard Nixon? Or Robert Caro's majestic account in his biographical *Means of Ascent*, about how Lyndon Johnson used every dirty trick in the books to beat *Mr. Texas*, Coke Stevenson, in his bid for a U.S. Senate seat (Coke was stealing votes too, he just got out stolen by LBJ). These two crooked elections helped change the course of American history and depending on your point of view, for better or for worse.

The Corruption Bar Is Raised for the 21st Century

One thing however, is certain. Although we may never know with complete certainty the identity of the winner of this year's presidential election, the identity of the loser is perfectly clear. It is the nation's confidence in the judge as an impartial guardian of the rule of law. John Paul Stevens

Then more recently, as power shifted from Democrats to Republicans at the state and legislative level, these classic American ballot stuffing practices, along with increasing technological opportunities, are being taken to frighteningly bold national levels. The two elections of George W. Bush have filled books, newspapers, magazines and websites with volumes of brazen theft in Florida and Ohio, as well as numerous issues in other states. With America's undemocratic Electoral College, you only have to steal the election in a couple of key states in order to steal the whole country. Herewith is a stream of consciousness litany of America's recent election realities,

- *Bush lost the 2000 election by 500,000 votes.*
- *He was royally appointed sovereign by the Supreme Court.*
- *Democracy was reduced to the farce of hanging chads and confusing ballot columns.*
- *Voter registrations from poor and minority neighborhoods being dumped in incinerators by the thousands.*
- *Robocalls to citizens in these same neighborhoods to intimidate or deceive them into not voting.*
- *Making sure that these undesirable precincts have fewer voting machines and the oldest and most broken down ones, to increase the time to wait to vote, thus sending thousands home in frustration without voting.*
- *Voting on computers and seeing the opposing name of the person they voted for instead of the candidate they desired, thanks to rigged software.*
- *Millions of American citizens disenfranchised, using all kinds of dirty tricks to keep people from voting, including caging and purging.*
- *Medieval laws persecuting felons, and in more and more states, even those who have misdemeanors.*
- *Hard drives with vote counts on them going missing for hours on end.*
- *Voting software so easily hackable that a high school kid on their PC can easily change the results to whatever they want, with a few key strokes and some spare time.*
- *Opaque ballots boxes stored where only (the currently ascendant) Republican operatives could enter.*
- *Photo IDs are now being required, knowing full well that it is the poorest and minorities who have the highest rate of not having a photo ID in the US.*

A quick survey of today's headlines shows that many of these corrupt practices are still being openly engaged in and being universally ignored by America's citizens all across the country. It is all so diabolical and downright disgusting, yet Americans seem to love it and revel in all this anti-democracy dirt.

Two Sides of the Same Trick Coin

We have a presidential election coming up. And I think the big problem, of course, is that someone will win. —Barry Crimmins

I bring up Democratic election malfeasance from a generation or two ago for a reason. This is not a case where the Republicans are uniquely evil and the Democrats being saints. It is a case of spoils to the victor. In war, the victor publicly gets treaty reparations and new national boundaries. But behind this veneer are the spoils of rape, plunder and pillage. Ditto the political cycles we live through.

In politics, the victors publicly get to pass laws and deciding on enforcing or not enforcing laws and regulations on the books. Behind closed doors, the victors get to draw up Picassan-Munchean gerrymandered voting districts and coveting all those stuffed ballot boxes.

In the 2012 movie, *Lincoln*, an important storyline is that America's president and his Secretary of State William Seward refuse to get his anti-slavery legislation, the Thirteenth Amendment, passed the time honored way: bribes to the opposing party, in this case, the Democrats. But they do offer quid pro quo, plum federal job posts to the Dems, in order to get it get it passed. This was 1864. Do you honestly think anything has changed for the better since then?

From 1880-1930, Republicans were King on the Hill and plundered the country and its resources (as they are wont to do), as well as corrupting the election process during the Gilded Age. While pillaging America's resources, they used the raw power of money to buy judges, congressmen, the White House and state governments like so many buckets of minnows and jars of chad to be fed to their mako shark owners.

This ascendancy goes in cycles. Democrats took all this to heart and when they were ascendant from the 1930s to the 1970s, adapted these methods of corruption to their strengths. New Deal Democrats at the state and local level simply paid people to vote for like-minded judges and politicians, who in turn made sure that contracts, construction and employment, with the requisite kickbacks, fueled the corruption. When they couldn't buy the votes, well, it was just a simple matter of stuffing those opaque urns with ballots.

This cycle of ascendancy changed sides in 1980, as Reagan Republicans seized control of America's political process. During this cycle, Reagan's Republicans took to heart their brethren's dominance during the two generations of the Gilded Age, as well as the amazingly successful methods of Democrat's local and state political machines for the two generations of the New Deal. What has happened is truly frightening. Reagan's Republicans have mutated and metastasized into an aggressive, malignant political tumor that is in the process of consuming America's electoral system.

21st century Republicans are buying lapdog politicians in state governments, US congress, the Senate, the White House and the Supremes, just as happened during the Gilded Age. Then, they have flipped the New Deal democrats' modus operandi on its end. If you can't buy the needed votes, then just purge and disenfranchise your enemies *en masse* from the voting rolls.

Let's Get to the Really Bizarre Stuff

Government is a broker in pillage, and every election is sort of an advance auction sale of stolen goods. —Henry Louis Mencken

On top of all this historical and ongoing corruption in America's voting booths, Americans accept with pride and a wry smile the corruption of gerrymandering. This uniquely American practice is another amazing anti-democracy tool used by the reigning party in power and when explained to people outside the United States, elicits reactions of scorn and embarrassment for their American friends.

Ditto the Electoral College. The United States is the only major [formal] democracy that I know of whose president is not elected by the direct vote of the people. They are elected just like China's president and Hong Kong's chief executive, via indirect vote. Again, non-Americans are shocked that such a system is tolerated in a modern, *democratic* society.

And the American system of indirect vote works. Just ask Al Gore, who beat George W. Bush in the 2000 presidential race with 500,000 more votes. Look who ended up being the guy: The Decider, W.

And how to explain Washington, DC's citizens, who have no real representation in America's Congress and Senate? Never mind that WDC has more American citizens than Wyoming and almost as many as Vermont. The fact that WDC is over 50% black may have nothing to do with it, but I bet all the senators from the South, Midwest and Rockies are keeping count. Again, non-Americans are speechless when they learn that 600,000 US citizens have no democratic voice in the legislative process.

And then there is the question of which day of the week to vote. America, for arcane 18th century practical reasons, votes on Tuesdays, a working and school day for the vast majority of its citizens. Gotta go to work, go to school, cook dinner, clean the house AND vote. A few countries also vote on a weekday (Canada, UK, Norway, Netherlands, Denmark and Ireland). But the large majority of democracies vote over their weekend, when people and their families have the freest time to go vote. France votes on Sundays, the day of rest for the entire nation, so its citizens have all day to go to the polls and still have time for a picnic.

Is all this democratic? No. Is it fair? No. Is it good for the vast majority of America's citizens? No. Is it dog-eat-dog Randian libertarianism? We're getting warmer. Is it banana republic foibles, a Peter Falk-Alan Arkin movie script writ large? Sure seems so.

[IMG 0031] Poster: The In-Laws

The American electoral system is not much better. (Image by Wikipedia)

The preceding calls for an elaboration of the term "formal democracy," which is not exactly what most people think it is. The Governance Wiki offers a usable (but not perfect) definition:

Formal democracy is a State system that has in place superficial forms of democracy but is not actually managed democratically. The former

Soviet Union has been retroactively characterized in this fashion since its constitution was essentially democratic, while the state was managed by the bureaucratic élite known as thePolitburo. But the concept was originally introduced in the 1988 book Manufacturing Consent by Edward S. Herman and Noam Chomsky to describe one effect of USA foreign policy and Nation building techniques which created market client states for neo-liberal capitalism.[1]. States identified by Herman & Chomsky as **formal democracies** include pre-revolutionary Iran, Nicaragua under Somoza and the Philippines under Marcos. The United States, from 1980 on, under Ronald W. Reagan, is also said to fit the description, as all levers of government were effectively controlled and often staffed by members of the plutocracy. The process peaked under George W. Bush, who went so far as to undermine the US Constitution itself, but government by manipulated consent is a problem afflicting the entire US political system, regardless of party affiliation, and is likely to continue and worsen until radical democratic reforms are put into effect.

(Formal Democracy, Wikia)

+++

How It's Done Across the Big Pond

The United States brags about its political system, but the President says one thing during the election, something else when he takes office, something else at midterm and something else when he leaves. —Deng Xiaoping

Now that we have had a chance to review America's voting history, trends and colorful highlights, how do elections in another great democracy, France, take place? You remember France, right? Freedom fries, frogs, being steadfastly against NATO for two generations, refusing to aid the US in its invasion and occupation of Iraq, American envy that France gets 80% of its electricity from nuclear power and France having the (now second best, after China) best high speed rail network on the planet; oh yeah, I almost forgot, it was the French who developed and pushed for worldwide adoption of the Système International (metric), which has pretty much isolated America's 5% of the world's population against the rest of the 95% who live by it (OK, the English cannot quit using their *stones*). But that ain't all, as Jimmy Cagney used to say. In WHO's estimation, France also boasts just about the best healthcare system in the world.

The **French health care system** is one of universal health care largely financed by government national health insurance. In its 2000 assessment of world health care systems, theWorld Health Organization found that France provided the "close to best overall health care" in the world.[1] In 2011, France spent 11.6% of GDP on health care, or US$4,086 per capita,[2] a figure much higher than the average spent by countries in Europe but less than in the US. Approximately 77% of health expenditures are covered by government funded agencies.[3] (Health care in France, Wikipedia)

After studying the rest of this chapter, I think you will agree that these two [officially] democratic countries' visions on universal suffrage are like night and day: exclusion against inclusion, fear vs. confidence, electoral Twiddle Dee and Twiddle Dum against a broad spectrum of electoral choice and debate, corrupt vs. clean voting systems, roadblocks vs. convenience and elections bought like show hogs at auction against a fairly level financial electoral playing field.

My personal experiences and this study make a laughable mockery of some *democracy* country rankings. After all, universal suffrage is the bedrock and fertile soil in which the roots of democracy are so firmly anchored or at least on mythical paper. A good example is nationmaster. com, which ranks the US #6 and France #28 in electoral freedom. What solar system are they living in, to make such ridiculous rankings?

France's Electoral Voting System

> We always want the best man to win an election. Unfortunately, he never runs. —Will Rogers

Prisoners and Felons

In France, the judge includes in the sentencing whether or not the convicted person loses their right to vote. For the 2012 presidential elections, France had a total of about 67,000 in jail. Out of these 67,000 prisoners, only about 15,900 have lost their right to vote, leaving about 51,000 detainees who can vote. Those who do so, vote absentee by registering in the location of their prison. While 80% of the French voted in this year's presidential election, less than 6% (about 2,500) of these eligible convicts actually voted. In 2007, a government decree was issued stating that prisoners had the right to leave prison to go vote. This became a culture war cudgel for the far right wing in France, but permission must be given by the warden on a case by case basis, and its use is very limited.

Only two states, Vermont and Maine, allow prisoners to vote, like France. In 13 states, felons can lose their right to vote for *life*. Or, they cannot vote if they are on probation or parole. Ten US states even restrict the voting rights of some people convicted of a *misdemeanor*. With 3.1% of its adult population in prison, on parole or probation (1 in 31, or 7.3 million total, by far the highest in the world), this is a huge number of citizens who are deprived of one of democracy's fundamental rights.

With blacks and Hispanics being locked up at twice the rate as whites in the United States, and with the vast majority of people in the maw of Wall Street's prison industrial complex being poor, it is hard to escape the impression that the United States has found a very effective system to disenfranchise millions of its citizens that the princes of power do not want voting against them.

Permanent Residents

VOTE, n. The instrument and symbol of a freeman's power to make a fool of himself and a wreck of his country. —Ambrose Bierce, *The Devil's Dictionary.*

While the thought of non-citizen permanent residents voting in the United States would send Fox News, Tea Baggers and Republicans into foam-at-the-mouth seizures, France has made efforts for this class of tax paying people to vote in municipal (local) elections. According to recent surveys, the majority of French support this right for foreign residents.

The movement started in 1985. The town of Mons-en-Baroeul, near Lille was the first municipality to establish an associated (shadow) city council of foreign residents. European integration led to a directive in 1994 to allow all European citizens to be able to vote in local and Pan-European elections. And that is the case today. So, a German living in Lisbon and a Greek working in London have the automatic right to vote in all local elections where they reside. Naturally, they can continue to vote in all the federal elections in the country of their nationality.

Even though the majority of French are for allowing non-EU foreigners to vote in local elections, the debate between left and right continues to rage. In December, 2011, the French Senate passed a much heated resolution in support of this cause. In the meantime, ten cities, including big ones like Paris, Toulouse and Lille have set up shadow city councils composed of non-EU foreign residents, so they can have a voice in their local affairs.

While this is pipe dream stuff in America, the trend in France is to allow non-EU foreigners to vote in local elections.

Election Financing

An election is coming. Universal peace is declared and the foxes have a sincere interest in prolonging the lives of the poultry. —T.S. Eliot.

In the United States in 2008, $5,300,000,000 total was spent on all the election campaigns. Of this $2,400,000,000 was spent for president for 132,618,580 votes. This comes out to about $18/vote. In 2012, it is estimated that about $6,000,000,000 was spent on all US election campaigns, of which about half, $3,000,000,000 was paid for the battle between Obama and Romney. With 240 million eligible voters and a 56% turnout, 2012's 134,400,000 votes cost $22 each.

In France's 2012 presidential race, various French newspapers reported that taxpayer spending by all the candidates and their parties amounted to a cost of only €1 per vote, or about 20 times less than it costs per vote in the US. That is probably on the low side and does not include money gotten from citizen contributors. But still, as you will see below, the limits are such that the total cost per vote is probably somewhere in the €2-3 range. But still, how can they do that?

In France, elections are a two-round process. In the 1st round, maximum campaign spending for each candidate is €16,851,000 and in the 2nd round, €22,509,000 can be spent by each of the two finalists. Most of this has to be raised privately, but a good chunk is paid for by the taxpayers.

If a candidate for president gets enough signatures to be on the ballot (amazingly, only 500 signatures are needed among all elected officials), they get €153,000 before the first round, for their campaign. If they get 5% or more in the first round, taxpayers give that candidate 47.5% of the top limit, or €8,004,000. Less than 5%, they get 4.75%, or €800,423.

This considerable sum of taxpayer money for any candidate who garners only 5% of the vote in the first round assures that a broad spectrum of political persuasions is kept in the political media limelight.

In 2012, in addition to the frontrunners socialist Hollande and conservative Sarkozy, three parties got at least 5% of the vote: The far right wing *Front National*, the anti-Wall Street left wing *Front de Gauche* and the centrist, left leaning *Mouvement Démocrate*. Compared to America's Democrats and Republicans, there are more philosophical and ideological differences between the two main parties. There is more of a choice between them. Keeping three other parties in the limelight, two that are diametrically opposed, helps keep the political system honest and the citizenry much more engaged.

In the first round, there were ten presidential candidates. The fact that one half of them got at least 5% of the vote and will continue to make noise in the media and on future campaign trails is indicative of a robust, confident democracy, from the far left, to the center to the far right.

The other five parties that got less than 5%, in descending order of success: the *Greens*, an anti-capitalist *New Party*, the communist *Workers' Struggle*, the conservative Gaullist *Stand up Republic* and a party called *Solidarity and Progress*, which believe it nor not, has connections to Lyndon LaRouche. Go figure.

Needless to say, if you can't find a party to vote for in the first round of France's elections, you are either an anarchist, in a coma or are dead from the neck up.

If a candidate passes to the second round of presidential voting (the top two candidates from round one, this year the socialists, who went on to win the presidency versus the conservatives), they will each get 47.5% of the campaign total paid for by the taxpayers, or €10,691,000.

Individual contributions are a maximum of €4,600 per cycle per contributor per candidate, presidential and legislative in both rounds. These funds must be paid to a registered political party. Corporations, unions and any other legal entity are forbidden to contribute to any candidates, parties or political campaigns. Only real physical French citizens can contribute, to the political party of the candidate, and of course the parties and candidates seek donations from French individuals.

Political parties do get greedy and are caught spending more than these incredibly modest spending limits. There was the Affaire de la Sempap in the early 90s that involved about €15 million.

And in 2010 there was the Bettencourt-Woerth scandal, where the billionaire heir to the L'Oréal fortune said they gave envelopes of money to various politicians, including former president Sarkozy, who unlike George W. Bush, has lost his immunity from prosecution and was charged with fraud. Ditto Jacques Chirac, who lost his immunity when he stepped down as president, and was *convicted* (remember, these are *presidents* we are talking about) for ghost jobs when he was mayor of Paris years ago.

But it is not all as rosy as all that. The French, being clever people and knowing that money is the milk of political success, are getting around these restrictions by creating microparties. A comparison to the United States would be the old political action committees (PACs), before the Supremes unleashed the monster Super PACs on the land. In addition to the €4,600 limit citizens can donate directly to candidates, each citizen can give up to €7,500 per voting cycle to as many political parties as they want.

And twenty years ago, there were about 20 parties. Today? Including all the microparties, there are now around 280.

So, the loophole is to simply establish political parties, usually a party around one politician or a local area in-country. Political parties can legally transfer funds among themselves in France. So, a wealthy donor can give many €7,500 donations to these microparties, knowing that they are aligned to their point of view and that likely, much of this money will end up transferred to the big party targeted and which is supporting their candidate for president.

The conservatives for sure and the socialists, less so, are sitting fat and happy over this debasement of the law, but the smaller parties are screaming bloody murder and the French people are upset by the system. So, Hollande got a majority of socialist/left wing seats during the legislative votes. Since this system is really helping the richer conservatives more than the socialists, it will be interesting to see if Hollande's mandate can stand up to and resist the sweet fruit of bank accounts full of cash to do battle with their adversaries. Money as we know, and the power that comes with it, is intoxicating, even if you are less intoxicated than your enemy.

At the end of the day, especially now that the US has unfettered corporate and secret super PACs, the amounts of money we are talking about in France are chump change compared to the US's multi-billion-dollar campaign colossi.

And as everywhere else on Earth, the US, Japan and in all pluralistic democracies, France has its fair share of corruption, in the name of crony contracts and kickbacks. But unlike the United States since 2000, people do get caught and do go to jail. Reagan's administration was the most indicted, convicted and imprisoned in US history and some big fish got grilled over the savings and loan corruption in the 1980s. But since then, there is merely an outside chance that an American political crook may have to pay a token fine, while never having to admit guilt.

For the record, according to Transparency International, in 2011 France is rated #25 in overall corruption and the United States #24, no statistical difference (unfortunately, the US has been dropping rapidly on the world list since 2000). Clearly, corruption is a problem in both countries, but it seems remarkably absent in the election process in France.

Overseas citizens

People never lie so much as after a hunt, during a war or before an election.
—Otto von Bismarck

One million French voters live outside France. This is 2.2% of the 46 million French who are eligible to vote. In the recent presidential election, 400,000 overseas French voted, or 40%. This level is half of the 80% of French voters who passed the urns in France to vote for president in 2012. This could be due to a greater sense of apathy among French expats or the fact that you have to get to the French embassy or closest consulate in your country of residence to vote, or someone has to get there for you, if you decide to vote by proxy. Absentee voting in France is illegal, so that means someone, you or a proxy friend have to show their face to vote. Obviously in some less developed countries, getting there may be very difficult, if you live far from the embassy/consulate.

Like in France, expats vote on Sunday, except in North America, where they vote on Saturday. I suspect this difference is to respect America's sense of impropriety about voting on the Sabbath day (unless you are Muslim or Jewish.). But Saturday sure beats the heck out of Tuesday, in terms of convenience, and Sunday is great too.

And things are looking up for this group of voters. For the first time in France's history, ten members were added to the lower Chamber of Deputies (like the US's House of Representatives) to represent French citizens living outside France. The world map was divided up into ten voting districts according to French expat population numbers.

And another first for 2012: overseas French could vote for their new legislator by internet. So, from the comfort of my home, after registering with the French consulate, receiving a user name and password by mail and SMS, I voted. The whole thing takes about three minutes, assuming you already have studied the candidates. You even get a 10-digit code when you finish, which you can input on the federal government voting website to confirm your vote was counted. You are implored to keep this code handy in case of a recount. Impressively, 57% of the expat French voters used this brand new internet system for the first round of voting for legislators.

So, I now have a French congressperson representing my interests as an expat citizen living in China. What a cool concept. Can you imagine the United States having the foresight to add members of Congress to represent its 5,000,000 plus expat citizens? I didn't think so. Can any French person imagine their government farming out this website and voting system to private vendors in order to lower costs and avoid hiring government employees? *Je ne croix pas*.

Voting day system and controls

It's not the voting that's democracy, it's the counting. —Tom Stoppard

---

Here is how voting day went down at the French Embassy, in Beijing:

Before Election Day, some of the taxpayers' money to finance the elections goes to sending out campaign flyers to the voters. I got envelopes for both rounds of the presidential, as well as the first round of the legislative elections. Inside each envelope were nice color A4 folded brochures, where each candidate laid out why I should vote for them. I did not get all ten of the presidential brochures, so I suspect the candidates must need to send them to each city hall or embassy, at their choosing. I also got close to ten different one-page color flyers for the first round of the legislative elections. As well, there are government and journalistic websites where you can consult and see the complete platforms of all the candidates.

[IMG 0033] French ballots, campaign brochures, etc.

Hollande's and Sarkozy's back pages of their 4-page campaign brochures received in the mail, along with most of the others' from the smaller parties. Hollande promises change. Sarkozy a strong France. Change won over strength. (Image by 44 Days)

[IMG 0034] La France forte—Sarkozy/ Hollande poster

By law, each voting station must have the mayor present during the entire proceedings, acting as president of the *voting office,* or the mayor can designate someone from their office or within the community. In embassies, the consul takes the place of the mayor. In addition, there must be at least two *assurers,* who are designated by the candidates (parties), as well as someone acting as a secretary. So, there must be a minimum of four persons witnessing and processing the voters and their ballots. This is a minimum. Any candidate can put a representative at any voting station to witness the entire operation, including the counting of the ballots. In fact, I saw about 15-20 people watching the entire operation. Little chance of any shenanigans with so many eyeballs on the scene.

I went to the (brand new) French Embassy in Beijing to vote, about 20 minutes from where I live in the suburbs. Once you show your picture ID (they even accept expired passports and national ID cards, as long as the photo is your resemblance), you pass through embassy security and line up to vote in the consulate. It is a very sociable and light hearted atmosphere. Friends are saying hello, giving each other the famous French *bises* on the cheeks and warmer, longer hugs, depending on the relationship. A few have not seen each other in ages and catch up on news. Of course, people are texting and going online with their mobiles, or calmly reading ebooks.

As you stand in line, ten big color campaign posters of the candidates are hanging on the walls of the foyer. So you have this eerie feeling of these people watching you and reminding you, *be careful who you vote for*, as you wait your turn. They are the same covers of the color brochures I received in the mail.

[IMG 0034 ff] The posters and brochure covers of the two leading presidential candidates. Is it just me, or does Hollande look like the cartoon character Droopy? I also find the psychology of Sarkozy not looking directly at his constituents interesting. (#43 Image by 44 Days*)*

There were two lines to queue up, A-M and N-Z. So, everything being described is doubled, with two urns, two sets of voting booths, etc. Thus, there were a minimum of eight witnesses, and by law, these are people of competing political interests. And on top of that, there were many witnesses observing to keep everybody honest.

For each urn, four people control the voting operation. The first person looks at your ID, finds you on the voting rolls, marks your name on the big list and puts a small piece of paper with the page number and line number inside your passport or with your national ID. The next step is to get your ballots.

Government printed ballots on low quality notebook paper, about the size of an index card, are laid out on a long table, one for each candidate. So, in the first round of the presidential election, the ballot table had ten stacks of ballots, one for each candidate. There is also a stack of government printed envelopes, cerulean blue, with the state seal on the outside. Voters can take all ten (to be discreet) or can only pick up the ballot of the candidate they intend to vote for. Most voters choose the discreet option.

[IMG 0035] French paper ballots *The paper ballots of the two front runners. The paper used is like the slick kind used to wrap dishes when moving. (Image by* 44 Days*)*

Once inside the private voting booths, the voter folds their chosen ballot in half, puts it in their small, greeting card-sized envelope and slips the envelope tongue inside the envelope, without using any glue, so it stays closed but can be easily opened when the ballots are counted.

Inside the booth is a trash can where the voter can dispose of their unused ballots.

Once the envelope is prepared, you pass to a second recorder/witness who again checks your ID against the same voter roll and double checks that the first recorder got the voter name, ID, page and line number correct, using that slip of paper given before going into the booth. They announce to the urn manager *they are good to go.* You then step up to the urn, the urn manager flips a spring loaded chute handle to open the slot, you drop your ballot-filled envelope in the big, clear, Plexiglas urn and watch it drop on top of all the other ballots in the box. The urn manager says loudly, for all the world to hear, "Sir, you have voted" (*Monsieur, vous avez voté.*), who is in fact the Consul (or mayor back home).

I think the transparent urns are a statement, a real symbol to the citizens that *our elections are truly open and honest.* I can only speculate they used glass before plastic was invented.

Then a fourth control, another witness, using the same voting roll, has a small, mask like template that they put over your page, and asks you to sign in the little box on your line. You cannot accidentally sign in the wrong box (unless this controller makes a mistake, of course, but they've been told by two different people where to find your name, so I suspect it doesn't happen very often.) because the template only exposes your box to sign. Everybody politely says, "Thank you, good day," and you move on.

At the end of the day, the four members of the voting office and any and all candidate witnesses, who, based on what I saw in Beijing, there were quite a few, go to a room to count the votes. The transparent urns are placed on tables in the middle of the room so that anyone can circulate around them to witness the counting. The total envelope count is first verified against the number of signatures on the voter roll.

Then, for each urn, each candidate is to have two witnesses each. One opposing pair (left wing and right wing) verifies the voting roll and the other opposing pair, left wing-right wing witnesses the ballot count. The remaining candidate witnesses are free to circulate around the tables to verify, but law stipulates that a minimum of four persons are seated at each urn table to witness the ballot count, with an equal number of competing party members in the mix. Each envelope is opened, and one of the witnesses unfolds the ballot to read it and hands it to their competing party partner, who reads out loud the ballot's name. The other two competing witnesses each have the same ballot control sheet and upon hearing the name called out, mark their respective ballot tallies. Naturally, at the end of the day, these two ballot tally sheets need to be identical, or the count starts over.

Any irregular ballot is placed off to the side with its envelope attached, to be decided upon by the persons in attendance. Ballots do get disqualified: hand writing on the envelope or ballot, having more than one ballot in the envelope, voters trying to put their own ballot inside, obviously empty envelopes, etc. In the second round of the French presidential election, there were two million disqualified ballots, which was taken as an indication of a certain level of dissatisfaction about the two finalists, at least for some citizens. But they showed up to voice their opinion to the Princes of Power about how they feel.

Once the two ballot tallies match up, the two competing controllers sign these registers. Then, with all witnesses on hand, a *Minutes of the Vote* is written up, with the results noted and everyone duly putting their signatures upon it.

Reflecting on the lengths the French go to in order to assure fair, open and transparent elections, the system is awfully fool proof. So, pretend you are a political party operative hired to steal an election in France. Where do you see the weak links?

Flashback to America: Hanging chads, using the wrong kind of pencil, marking the wrong box, (rigged) electronic voting machines sold to sucker citizens by politically motivated CEOs, one party hacks disappearing with opaque urns or the voting software for hours on end? Handing over democracy's most precious right to Wall Street and political goons that Stalin or Hitler would be proud of?

In France? Are you kidding? What I witnessed in Beijing is repeated thousands of times across France and around the world, using the same exact system, the same ballots, envelopes, transparent urns, voter rolls and double competing, open air, multi-witness counting procedures. It is controlled and duplicated at the federal level, 100% by the French government, managed by the mayors and witnessed by umpteen mutually suspicious political party representatives. And it is all paid for by French taxpayers.

This sense of probity extends beyond the urns. In France, no campaigning or advertising is allowed during the final 24 hours before the voting booths open up. This is a time for sober reflection and earnest discussions with those whom you respect, not last minute stadium appeals from wily hucksters. Exit polls are also forbidden to be released or discussed in the media, until all the voting booths around the world have finished voting. France, like America's Hawaii or Guam, has departments (states) and territories that extend to North and South America, the Pacific and the Indian Ocean, so this information has to wait a while on Election Day. However, this ban is getting harder to enforce, what with Twitter, blogs and Facebook.

Voter participation

An election cannot give a country a firm sense of direction if it has two or more national parties which merely have different names but are as alike in their principles and aims as two peas in the same pod. —Franklin D. Roosevelt

I guess the MBA way to look at which system has the best performance is voter participation. In France's 2012 presidential election, 80% of all French voters went through the urns to vote, which is impressive indeed. And no, not just in the first round when there were ten different candidates. Eighty percent also voted when there were only Hollande on the left and Sarkozy on the right in the second round. Now that is jaw dropping.

In 2008, everybody was giddy that Obama helped draw out over 56% of all voters, the highest level since 1968. Traditionally, Americans vote in the low fifties to choose their president. In 2008, if 80% had voted like in France, *52,000,000* more Americans would have been enfranchised.

And that is the whole point. Let's be honest. Wall Street and their lapdog minions in Congress, the Senate, the White House, the Supreme Court and more and more state governments and judges don't want all these Americans voting. Because if they did, the United States would more than likely look a lot different than it does now, and not in favor of these power elites.

+++

The next time they give you all that civic bullshit about voting, keep in mind that Hitler was elected in a full, free democratic election. —George Carlin

Americans revel in and brag about their crass, corrupt electoral process because it is an expression of their libertarian political DNA. In Morris Berman's political trilogy, he lays out convincingly that at heart, America is a nation of hustlers: Fast Buck Freddys, Easy Money Eddys, Laissez-Faire Looky-Loos and Me-Me-Mes Gonna Be a Millionaire, who populate our churches, institutions of government and corporate boardrooms (my made up names, not Mr. Berman's).

If there is one aspect of American culture that is emblematic of this political phenotype, just take a look at its electoral process. And for a baseline, compare it to a truly pluralistic, openly democratic, proud and fearless-of-the-populous-masses country, like France.

We like nonfiction and we live in fictitious times. We live in a time where we have fictitious election results that elect a fictitious president. —Michael Moore.

The West's Russell Brand vs. Sinoland's Rushe Wang: A Conversation in Commonalities and Key Contrasts

The Princes of Power and Lords of the Loot

The Princes of Power are a prickly lot, be they Western or Eastern, Northern or Southern. They know they are one spark of popular outrage away from economic re-equilibrium, or if the 99% get really radical and revolutionarily randy, they can pay with their hubristic heads. Just ask the ghost of Robespierre. It says a lot about how rigged the roulette table of civilization actually is, when there is only one significant example of the former in recent times: Franklin Roosevelt's New Deal and its very ephemeral 50 years of a chance of a better life for the common people. That sure didn't last long. From the perspective of deep history, which consumes Baba Beijing (China's leadership), a half a century is a fleeting moment along the Arrow of Time's trajectory. The world's shadow fascists, who have been calling humanity's shots on Mother Earth since the glory days of Babylonian Big Boss Hammurabi 4,000 years ago, and surely long before that, don't take too kindly to sharing our Pale Blue Dot's natural resources - not even a teensy-weensy bit - 101% will do just fine, thank you. And while we 99% are at it, busy beavers all, we can work for free and be grateful for the time spent maintaining the glories of the *official narrative*, which for the last 500 years has been and continues to be Caucasian conquest, colonialism and cupidity. Post World War II, it's now fawningly called the *Washington-London-Paris consensus*, since these three countries, more than any others, set the tone and message in the Western mainstream media. The US Marines' finest have the Few and the Proud. The 99% have their Meek and their Many. Sitting here in Buddha World Beijing, and with all due respect for Jesus Christ, I don't see us inheriting the Earth anytime soon. About the only time America came close to living up to Christ's prophesy, was during the 50 years of Roosevelt's New Deal and in reality, it was a pretty tepid affair for the common man and woman.

The Lords of Legal Loot also get very tetchy when someone is clever enough to gin up a simple message of outrage, a sound bite that resonates in the rapidly emptying pockets, stomachs and under the disappearing roofs over the heads of the masses. Short and sweet, pungent and powerful. Such was the case with the pithily named *Occupy Wall Street* (OWS). Too clever by half, so it just had to go. Those kinds of quickly coined phrases are so easily remembered, can circulate like wildfire and thus must either be sucked into the upward vortex of Newspeak and bastardized, or with great and extended effort, sent in the opposite direction deep down Orwell's Memory Hole, just like the Palestinians' Al-Nakba, never to be acknowledged, mentioned, reported on or referenced again.[1] The one percent's infanticide of OWS has been remarkably and ruthlessly efficient, like the gas chambers of Auschwitz.

Would the 99% please just shut up?

But these silly and feckless nuisances just keep coming. Will they ever learn? The 1% have again been forced to budge just a little bit in their Pininfarina Aresline Xten designer chairs,[2] because of a smarty pants by the name of Russell Brand. And smart he is: well spoken, a man of letters and possessing a rapier wit with words. Just ask BBC's hapless errand boy for the official narrative, Jeremy Paxman, who interviewed this wily whippersnapper during *Newsnight 2013* on the 23rd of October. Paxman surely thought that our curly coiffed, nouveau rich British comic should know better than to turn on his new high class fan base, the uber-wealthy. In fact, Russell could make many more millions as a neocon comedian, like Dennis Miller, the right wing's poster pundit in laugh land. Miller confirms with a condescending smirk what his financial brethren already smugly know: they own the world. And you know what the Russians say - tough shitsky.

Russell Brand: fracking vs twerking. (Image by kateausburn) **[IMG 0036]**

But no, this ungrateful former poor boy parvenu, Brand, who has cleaned up his drug addicted soul, gave a very simple political manifesto, as the guest editor of the venerable Fabian Society liberal magazine, *The New Statesman*. Paxman couldn't resist the bait and had Mr. Brand on British national TV. It has now gone viral on planetary TV cum YouTube and the rest is history. The leaders of the Unfree West cringed - no not Obama, Cameron and Hollande, they are the chattel property of the Gods of FIRE (Finance-Insurance-Real Estate). It is these latter who squirmed, as this very passionate and articulate man stated what is obvious to all of the 7,133,000,000 members of the human race, except the few thousand families who own *them*, that:

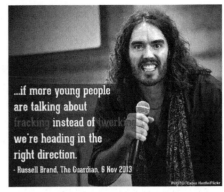

...if more young people are talking about fracking instead of twerking we're heading in the right direction.
- Russell Brand, The Guardian, 6 Nov 2013
PHOTO: Eston Hustle/Flickr

You yahoos at the top of the money mountain shouldn't destroy the planet,
You shouldn't create massive economic disparity,
You shouldn't ignore the needs of the people,
And since your servants in the whoredom halls of statecraft only serve the interests of your legalized world resources chop shops, namely corporations,
It's time for a revolution.

Talking revolution can get you killed. Just ask John Lennon, Martin Luther King, Jr. and Malcolm X. Hopefully, Mr. Brand has well paid, loyal bodyguards.

Memories of Ol' Kingfish and the Great Depression

Hmm. Brand sounds pert near a 21st century meme of Depression-era, Louisiana's US Senator Huey "Kingfish" Long, who was running for president against the venerable incumbent, FDR in 1936, on his <u>Share Our Wealth</u> program, and gaining a serious groundswell of popular support. The disgusted 99% were ready to seriously realign the country's human and natural resources - the New Deal in hyper drive. We're talking about radical, socialist redistribution of wealth from the 1% to the 99%, a platform that Father Oscar Romero Martin Luther King, Jr., Jesus Christ and Pope Francis would all heartily endorse. Here it is,

1. No person would be allowed to accumulate a personal net worth of more than 300 times the average family fortune, which would limit

personal assets to between $5 million and $8 million. A graduated capital levy tax would be assessed on all persons with a net worth exceeding $1 million.

2. Annual incomes would be limited to $1 million and inheritances would be capped at $5.1 million.

3. Every family was to be furnished with a homestead allowance of not less than one-third the average family wealth of the country. Every family was to be guaranteed an annual family income of at least $2,000 to $2,500, or not less than one-third of the average annual family income in the United States. Yearly income, however, cannot exceed more than 300 times the size of the average family income.

4. An old-age pension would be made available for all persons over 60.

5. To balance agricultural production, the government would preserve/ store surplus goods, abolishing the practice of destroying surplus food and other necessities due to lack of purchasing power.

6. Veterans would be paid what they were owed (a pension and healthcare benefits).

7. Free education and training for all students to have equal opportunities in all schools, colleges, universities, and other institutions for training in the professions and vocations of life.

8. The raising of revenue and taxes for the support of this program was to come from the reduction of swollen fortunes from the top, as well as for the support of public works to give employment whenever there may be any slackening necessary in private enterprise.

Go, Kingfish, GO! **[IMG 0037]**

Oh yeah, I almost forgot, Kingfish got shot in the guts on Louisiana's capitol steps in Baton Rouge, in 1935. Minor detail that. Serves him right too, depending on your point of view, but I know one class of people, America's shadow fascists, who were mighty relieved that their dirty deed was done cheap, for the price of a .38 caliber lead bullet. That was an investment in metals commodities that makes rigged IPOs look like passbook savings returns.

The gold plated glutei maxima lounging in those million dollar XTen's are clinching up in quiet queasiness, as Russell's video interview is going around the world, and we know their *modus operandi* like a well-worn playbook. The Princes of Power, are and will at first ignore Brand in stony silence, or with well-coordinated, manufactured media mewing, mocking him for his childish naiveté. Denigrating chuckles of belittlement are de rigueur, in hopes that the Lords' contempt is imprinted on the minds of the masses, and let's face it, it almost always works. Otherwise, reality would be radically and positively different than what it is and I could find something else to do besides write about it.

And now over to you Beijing.

It's not much better over here in Sinoland. Baba Beijing would rehearse the first act of this playbook to perfection. If an oriental doppelganger called *Rushe Wang* did the same thing here and crossed the Obaman red line of blaming the Communist Party of China (CPC) for what ails the 99%, the truth of the matter is he would likely be harassed and/or arrested on trumped up charges of tax evasion or some such, by the Chinese authorities. But unfortunately, this also happens all too routinely in the United Stasi of America. A case in point: just ask the ex-governor of Alabama, Don Siegelman, ex-New York Attorney General Eliot Spitzer, or Karen Silkwood, Marin Luther King, Jr. and the Kennedy Brothers for that matter.[6] Try to suggest taking even a teensy weensy bit of the Princes of Power's 101% and you can end up paying a very heavy price indeed.

The parallels between Baba Beijing and the FIREmen only go so far though. Yes, Baba Beijing considers the CPC to be above criticism, just as the West's owners consider deregulated, rigged for the superrich, libertarian jungle capitalism to be beyond reproach. To speak out against capitalism is heretical and public protests against the West's rapidly declining day-in-the-life are now criminalized. If Mr. Brand's message takes off and lights that spark the Princes of Power have nightmares about, they will crush him and his followers, just as they did Occupy Wall Street and as Baba Beijing did to the Falun Gong movement. But if our oriental Rushe Wang was clever, kept his criticisms void of name calling, to save Baba's face, and stuck to targeted vitriol against the 1%

Chinese, here is where today's vacuous excuse for Western leadership and the savvy, ears-to-the-streets Baba Beijing would likely diverge: Baba would not hesitate to take a pound of flesh and more out of the gold plated backsides of the Sino-superrich and probably seize their Pininfarina Aresline Xten designer chairs to boot, in order to maintain credibility with its restive citizens. All this, to honor China's 2,200-year old Heavenly Mandate, which weighs so onerously on their collective, historical shoulders.

The West's political class just helps itself

In the West? They couldn't be bothered with such face saving niceties, not to mention the finer points of running a country. As Russell Brand so eloquently declared, our bought and paid for political class serves only one interest: its owners. I don't know about you, but I'm starting to hum over and over in my head that Beatles' riff,

You say you want a revolution…

http://aljazeera.com/programmes/specialseries/2013/05/201356123487
74619.html
Rock on.

1- As an example, try to find Al-Nakba in Encyclopedia Britannica, complimentary electron microscope and zigapixel CCD camera included. Its non-existence in Western thought is one of the modern era's greatest triumphal Memory Holes, an Orwellian pièce de résistance that George would duly appreciate.
2- Cost per pampered poof is a trifling $1,500,000, http://most-expensive. com/office-chair.
3- https://youtube.com/watch?v=xGxFJ5nL9gg. Eight point five minutes of principled mirth.
4- Great stuff this. No wonder they killed him: https://en.wikipedia.org/wiki/Share_Our_Wealth. America's shadow fascists were already retching over the New Deal.

5- *Paxman was so desperate, he was even reduced to calling Brand,* "A trivial little man".

6- *Don Siegelman's sad tale is the tip of America's injustice iceberg:* http:// donsiegelman.org.

Reflections from Sinoland on the West's Veterans/Armistice Day

While Ushering in the 20th Century, The West's Colonial Princes of Power Cranked Up Their Worldwide Wehrmacht. This is their Official Narrative.

China

US Marine Sergeant Clarence Edwin Sutton was born 18 February 1871, in Middlesex County, Virginia. On 13 July 1900, near Tianjin, China, his unit was under heavy fire from *the enemy*. Sutton assisted carrying a wounded officer from the field of battle and was killed that day. For his bravery in defending the honor and glory of the United States, Sgt. Sutton was awarded the US Marines Medal of Honor. He lived to be 28 years old. **[IMG 0038]** China—Colonialism, US Marines invading China in 1900 during Boxer rebellion.

Europe

Charles F. Hoffman (aka Ernest Janson) was a Gunnery Sergeant in the US Marine Corp, 49th Company, 5th Regiment, 2nd Division. He was born on 17 August 1878 in New York, N.Y. Entering service in Brooklyn, he gave the last full measure of his devotion on 6 June 1918, near Chateau-Thierry, France, during WWI. He received a US Marines Medal of Honor and also the Navy Medal of Honor. Immediately after the company to which he belonged had reached its objective on Hill 142, several hostile counterattacks were launched against their line before the new position had been consolidated. G/Sgt. Hoffman was attempting to organize a position on the North Slope of the hill when he saw 12 of the enemy, armed with light machine guns, crawling towards his group. Giving the alarm, he rushed the hostile detachment, bayoneted two leaders and forced the others to flee, abandoning their guns. His quick action, initiative, and courage drove the enemy from a position from which they could have swept the hill with machine-gun fire and forced the withdrawal of the American troops. He was 38 years old that day, when he took his last breath.

[IMG 0039] *World War I was very deadly modern warfare indeed. (#48 Image by State Library of South Australia)*

Latin America

Donald Leroy Truesdale was a corporal in the US Marines. He was born on 8 August 1906, in Lugoff, South Carolina, where he enlisted. He received a Marines Medal of Honor when he was second-in-command of a Guardia Nacional Patrol in active operations against armed *bandit forces* in the vicinity of Constancia, near the Coco River, in Northern Nicaragua, on 24 April 1932. While the patrol was in formation on the trail, searching for the *bandit group*, with which contact had just been made, a rifle grenade fell from its carrier and struck a rock, igniting the detonator. Several men close to the grenade at the time were in danger. Cpl. Truesdale, who was several yards away, could easily have sought cover and safety for himself. Knowing full well the grenade would explode within 2-3 seconds, he rushed for it, grasped it in his right hand and attempted to throw it away from the patrol. The grenade exploded in his hand, blowing it off and inflicting serious multiple wounds about his body. Cpl. Truesdale, in taking the full shock of the explosion himself, saved the members of the patrol from loss of life or serious injury. Until that fateful day, Donald Leroy lived for a brief quarter of a century.

[0040]

So many Latin American invasions, occupations and coups, so little time. (Image by swanksalot)

The Pacific

Clyde Thomason was a WWII US Marines Sergeant, born on 23 May 1914 in Atlanta, Georgia, where he enlisted. He received the Marine Medal of Honor for conspicuous heroism and intrepidity above and beyond the call of duty. During a Marine Raider Expedition against the Japanese-held island of Makin, on 17-18 August 1942, he was leading the advance element of the assault echelon. Sgt. Thomason disposed his men with keen judgment and discrimination and by his exemplary leadership and great personal valor, exhorted them to fearless efforts. On one occasion, he dauntlessly walked up to a house that concealed an enemy Japanese sniper, forced the door, and shot the man before he could resist. Later in the action, while leading an assault on an enemy position, he gallantly gave his life in the service of his country. His courage and loyal devotion to duty in the face of grave peril were in keeping with the finest traditions of the U.S. Naval Service. He was 28 years old that day.

[IMG 0041]

Korea

Frank N. Mitchell was a First Lieutenant in the US Marine Corps, Company A, 1st Battalion, 7th Marines, 1st Marine Division. He was born on 18 August 1921 in Indian Gap, Texas, and entered military service at Roaring Springs, Texas. During the Korean War, he received the Marine Medal of Honor for conspicuous gallantry and intrepidity, at the risk of his life above and beyond the call of duty. He was the leader of a rifle platoon in Company A, in action against the enemy aggressor forces. Leading his platoon in point position during a patrol by his company, through a thickly wooded and snow-covered area in the vicinity of Hansan-ni, 1st Lt. Mitchell acted immediately when the enemy suddenly opened fire at pointblank range, pinning down his forward elements and inflicting numerous casualties in his ranks. Boldly dashing to the front under blistering fire from automatic weapons and small arms, he seized an automatic rifle from one of the wounded men and effectively trained it against the attackers, and when his ammunition was expended, picked up and hurled grenades with deadly accuracy, at the same time directing and encouraging his men in driving the outnumbering enemy from their position. Maneuvering to set up a defense when the enemy furiously counterattacked to the front and left flank, 1st Lt. Mitchell, despite wounds sustained early in action, reorganized his platoon under the devastating fire, and spearheaded a fierce hand-to-hand struggle to repulse the onslaught. Asking for volunteers to assist in searching for and evacuating the wounded, he personally led a party of litter bearers through the hostile lines in growing darkness and, although suffering intense pain from multiple wounds, stormed ahead and waged single-handed battle against the enemy, successfully covering for the withdrawal of his men before he was fatally struck down by a burst of small arms fire. Stouthearted and indomitable in the face of tremendous odds, 1st Lt. Mitchell, by his fortitude, great personal valor, and extraordinary heroism, saved the lives of several marines and inflicted heavy casualties among his aggressors. His unyielding courage throughout reflects the highest credit upon himself and the U.S. Naval Service. He gallantly gave his life for his country. Frank N. Mitchell lived to be 29 years old.

[0042]

Southeast Asia

Jimmie E. Howard was a US Marines Gunnery Sergeant, Company C, 1st Battalion, 1st Marine Division. He was born on 27 July 1929 in Burlington, Iowa, where he enlisted. During the Southeast Asia War, he was awarded the Marine Medal of Honor for conspicuous gallantry and intrepidity, at the risk of his own life above and beyond the call of duty. G/Sgt. Howard and his 18-man platoon were occupying an observation post deep within enemy-controlled territory. Shortly after midnight on 16 June 1966, a Viet Cong force of estimated battalion size approached the marines' position and launched a vicious attack with small arms, automatic weapons, and mortar fire. Reacting swiftly and fearlessly in the face of overwhelming odds, G/Sgt. Howard skillfully organized his small but determined force into a tight-perimeter defense and calmly moved from position to position to direct his men's fire. Throughout the night, during assault after assault, his courageous example and firm leadership inspired and motivated his men to withstand the unrelenting fury of the hostile fire, in a seemingly hopeless situation. He constantly shouted encouragement to his men and exhibited imagination and resourcefulness in directing their return fire. When fragments from an exploding enemy grenade wounded him severely and prevented him from moving his legs, he distributed his ammunition to the remaining members of his platoon and proceeded to maintain radio communications and direct air strikes on the enemy with uncanny accuracy. At dawn, despite the fact that five men were killed and all but one wounded, his beleaguered platoon was still in command of its position. When evacuation helicopters approached his position, G/Sgt. Howard warned them away and called for additional air strikes and directed devastating small arms fire and air strikes against enemy automatic-weapon positions, in order to make the landing zone as secure as possible. Through his extraordinary courage and resolute fighting spirit, G/Sgt. Howard was largely responsible for preventing the loss of his entire platoon. His valiant leadership and resolute fighting spirit served to inspire the men of his platoon to heroic endeavor in the face of overwhelming odds, and reflect the highest credit upon G/Sgt. Howard, the Marine Corps, and the U.S. Naval Service. In fighting for his country, he almost lived long enough to see his 37th birthday.

[0043]

The 21st Century Continues the Stars and Stripes' Shock-and-Awe Show; Stay Tuned

Afghanistan

US Navy Lieutenant Michael P. Murphy was born 7 May 1976 in Smithtown, New York. He was a member of ALFA Platoon, SEAL Delivery Team One. He entered service in Pensacola, Florida. He was awarded the Navy Citation of Merit for conspicuous gallantry and intrepidity at the risk of his life above and beyond the call of duty. Lt. Murphy was the leader of a special-reconnaissance element with Naval Special Warfare Task Unit, near Asadabad, Konar Province, Afghanistan, on 28 June 2005. While leading a mission to locate a high-level anti-coalition militia leader, Lt. Murphy demonstrated extraordinary heroism in the face of grave danger. Operating in an extremely rugged, enemy-controlled area, his team was discovered by *anti-coalition sympathizers*, who revealed their position to Taliban fighters. As a result, between 30-40 enemy fighters besieged his four-member team. Demonstrating exceptional resolve, Lt. Murphy valiantly led his men in engaging the large enemy force. The ensuing fierce firefight resulted in numerous enemy casualties, as well as the wounding of all four members of the team. Ignoring his own wounds and demonstrating exceptional composure, Lt. Murphy continued to lead and encourage his men. When the primary communicator fell mortally wounded, Lt. Murphy repeatedly attempted to call for assistance for his beleaguered teammates. Realizing the impossibility of communicating in the extreme terrain and in the face of almost certain death, he fought his way into open terrain to gain a better position to transmit a call. This deliberate, heroic act deprived him of cover, exposing him to direct enemy fire. Finally, achieving contact with his headquarters, Lt. Murphy maintained his exposed position while he provided location and requested immediate support for his team. In his final act of bravery, he continued to engage the enemy until he was mortally wounded, gallantly giving his life for his country and for the cause of freedom. By his selfless leadership, courageous actions, and extraordinary duty, Lt. Murphy reflected great credit upon himself and upheld the highest traditions of the U.S. Naval Service. Michael P. Murphy was just able to celebrate his 29th birthday on the battlefields of Afghanistan, before perishing.

A glimmer of hope. **(0044 Image by _tEdits_)**

Iraq

Michael A. Mansoor was born on 5 April 1981 in Long Beach, California. He enlisted in the U.S. Navy in Garden Grove, CA, and was Petty Officer 2nd Class in the Navy Division Seal Team 3. On 29 September 2006, in Ar Ramadi, Iraq, he was an automatic-weapons gunner for Naval Special Warfare Task Group Arabian Peninsula, in support of Operation Iraqi Freedom. As a member of a combined SEAL and Iraqi Army Sniper Overwatch Element, tasked with providing early warning and standoff protection from a rooftop in an insurgent-held sector of Ar Ramadi, P.O. Mansoor distinguished himself by his exceptional bravery in the face of grave danger. In the early morning, insurgents prepared to execute a coordinated attack by reconnoitering the area around the element's position. Marine scout snipers thwarted the enemy's initial attempt by eliminating two insurgents. The enemy continued to assault the element, engaging them with a rocket-propelled grenade launcher and small arms fire. As enemy activity increased, P.O. Mansoor took position with his machine gun between two teammates on an outcropping of the roof. While the SEALs vigilantly watched for enemy activity, an insurgent threw a grenade from an unseen location, which bounced off Petty Officer Mansoor and landed in front of him. Although only he could have escaped the blast, Mansoor chose instead to protect his teammates. Instantly and without regard for his own safety, he threw himself onto the grenade to absorb the force of the explosion with his body, saving the lives of his two teammates. By his undaunted courage, fighting spirit, and unwavering devotion to duty in the face of certain death, Petty Officer Mansoor gallantly gave his life for his country, thereby reflecting credit upon himself and upholding the highest traditions of the U.S. Naval Service. In dying at 25 years of age, Michael A. Mansoor was awarded the US Navy Medal of Honor.

[0045] Wall Street cannon fodder

...The Reality of War and Empire Is Lying on the Memory Hole Cutting-Room Floor

When reading these incredible stories of Americans who died while fighting in the military, it is hard not to be overwhelmed with emotions and amazement. Incredibly, they are not unique. There have been millions of others just like them, from the time of Menes, in 3,000 BC Egypt, surely even before, when Homo sapiens began its millennial stab at sedentary civilization. Slowly, humanity had surplus agricultural production and infrastructure to fight for and protect, as well as their neighbors' same said assets to attack and seize. There was wealth to be had with the use of all those arrows and spears. And in every population, there were and are psychopaths and megalomaniacs who wanted to control it all.

Every human on Earth should read Canadian Gwynne Dyer's majestic and sweeping history of the human race, 1985's War, or for the more visual learner, watch the eight-hour mini TV series of the same name.[1] In a nutshell, for war to be waged among a population, two mind games must be perpetrated by the Princes of Power on the 99%. The one percenters must first completely psychologically break down the man, destroy his individual identity and empathy, and rebuild him into a fighting machine, a real live Myrmidon, ready to sacrifice his life and kill upon command for God, Country, and King, the sugar-coated flipside of Fundamentalism, Nationalism, and Fascism. It's a story as old as fairy tales and the Knights of the Round Table.

[0046]

Step Two is to brainwash history's millions of Myrmidons. The goal is to dehumanize *The Dreaded Other* into mere animals, or better yet, insects to be eradicated or exterminated. The targeted group is of course those who occupy the land or have the human and natural resources that the Princes of Power want to exploit for their own enrichment and aggrandizement, and at the expense of everything and everyone else. While there are variants to this well-worn playbook, the modus operandi and *raison d'être* of war, and, by extension, genocide and ethnic cleansing, are as predictable as the motions of the planets, the Sun, and the Moon. Banally so.

Westerners celebrate their *glorious* wars on Veterans/Armistice Day, which were and are still mostly economic policy in support of colonialism and empire. The Princes of Power, philistines all, piously honor their millions of 99% Myrmidons, whose souls grace countless cemeteries and memorials around the world. They also pay self-satisfied tribute to the brave survivors, most of whom return home psychologically fractured and socially handicapped. But the *Dreaded Other* have their own versions of history to recount, no matter how contrary to the Washington-London-Paris consensus.

To wit, the aforementioned, historically true, stories, are explained below, from an alternative, anti-empire point of view…

[0047]

China

This was known as the Boxer Rebellion. The *enemy* was Chinese citizens who were sick and tired of being exploited like dogs by the United States and seven other countries - Austria-Hungary, France, Germany, Great Britain, Italy, Japan, and Russia. These colonial powers all had what were euphemistically called *interests* in China, i.e., corporations, banks, and insurance companies, which were helping to keep one-fourth of the country's people addicted to British and American imported opium and hauling out billions in exploited resources, human and natural. The West's colonialists thrive on euphemisms, calling this racket their *open-door policy* and China as a *sphere of influence*, later to be *lost* to Mao

Zedong and the communists. It was not the first time the US military was dispatched to the four corners of the planet to play the role of taxpayer-funded Pinkerton goons for the 1%. Sadly, Sergeant Sutton was one of the first US soldiers in the 20th century to die for their profits. He was just following orders, one of the few, the proud, who believed he was defending America's freedoms 10,000 km away from home, halfway around the world, with honor, valor, and faith in the righteousness of his government, its leaders, and its mythical ideals. His death was only the beginning of what would turn out to be tens of millions who joined the swollen roles of maimed and killed last century, for the benefit of Western capital.

[0048] Cartoon on the Boxer rebellion.
[0049] Boxer rebel being beheaded by European conquerors.
[0050] Foreign armies assembling inside Forbidden City, 1900
[0051] Japanese soldiers executing Boxer rebel.

The tragic uprising was naturally glamorized and glorified by Hollywood, always happy to whitewash imperialism, in the blockbuster *55 Days at Peking (1963)* with plenty of star power, including Charlton Heston, David Niven, Ava Gardner and others.

The day after Sgt. Sutton's death, during the same American invasion, Lieutenant Smedley Butler was heroically injured and also received a Medal of Honor. He would later climb the ranks to Marine Major General and become the most decorated soldier in US history, retiring in 1931. But a funny thing happened. Thereafter, with the wisdom of hindsight and a moral consciousness that brought clarity and compassion to his perceptions (he was ironically

descended from a prominent Pennsylvania Quaker family), Butler had an epiphany. In a little known, historically important 1933 speech, he said,

War is a racket. It always has been. It is possibly the oldest, easily the most profitable, surely the most vicious. It is the only one international in scope. It is the only one in which the profits are reckoned in dollars and the losses in lives. A racket is best described, I believe, as something that is not what it seems to the majority of the people. Only a small 'inside' group knows what it is about. It is conducted for the benefit of the very few, at the expense of the very many. Out of war a few people make huge fortunes.

Butler's *War Is a Racket* speech would later be printed up in a short book and has become an antiwar classic.[2] But that very same year, the general's former Wall Street paymasters, and its fascist front, the American Liberty League (ALL), headed by Prescott Bush (H.W.'s daddy and W's grand pappy), enlisted Butler to march 500,000 veterans on the White House, to overthrow Franklin D. Roosevelt and the hated New Deal, to, according to the BBC, "Adopt the policies of Hitler and Mussolini to beat the Great Depression."[3] In order to find out who was behind this fascist putsch, Butler, who was pegged to be the stooge Caesar taking corporate orders, played along with Wall Street's finest. ALL included families who owned DuPont, J.P. Morgan, Heinz, Colgate, Birds Eye, and General Motors, among others, as well as, amazingly, democratic presidential candidates Al Smith and John W. Davis, which would make them turncoats to FDR's New Deal. A true patriot, Butler went to America's historically celebrated, congressional House Committee on Un-American Activities, with the list of names. None of these traitors from Bush on down were ever questioned and Smedley's testimony was stricken from the record. When you can buy an army of a half a million, it's just as easy to purchase a House and Senate full of slavish satraps, to keep things clean. It's so much more profitable for the Committee on Un-American Activities to hunt down and destroy communists and socialists, instead of fascists, especially one percenters paying for their reelections and buying their votes, cash on the table top.

[0052] Smedley Butler: War is a Racket
[0053] *Straight from the horse's mouth*

One basic definition of fascism is the marriage and mutual support of government and corporate interests. American shadow fascists have their roots and origins in the very corrupt 19th-century Gilded Industrial

Age, where they coalesced into a force in the 1880s. This American shadow government has been the behind-the-scenes puppeteer ever since, quietly filling up cubicles and seats of power in the corporate world and government. They were attracted to Truman's CIA like bugs to light, then into the alphabet soup of America's military-industry-government/security apparatus. Starting in 1980, with the neocons taking over the White House, they effortlessly began moving directly into the bright lights of day-to-day statecraft and as corporate CEOs and board members. The1980s mainstreamed the deep state. These rightwing extremists and neo-fascists could now flaunt and flex their power to the American public – and to the rest of the world.

Europe

As Barbara Tuchman so splendidly and pithily detailed in her Pulitzer Prize-winning masterpiece, *The Guns of August* (1962), there was nothing honorable or noble about World War I. It was in fact one of our species' greatest examples of how stunted and antediluvian our brains have socially and psychologically evolved, juxtaposed next to our breathtaking technological prowess in creating more and more lethal ways to destroy each other. With all due respect to the 16 million people who perished and the 20 million who were injured during *The War to End All Wars* (talk about a PR fail of galactic proportions), an alternative interpretation is that it was essentially an extremely deadly slaughter between feuding colonial powers, who were out to control as much of the world's dark-skinned peoples and their natural resources. The final result? Germany lost its colonial territories in Africa to Britain and France. In China, Japan got Shandong Province.

In spite of a public largely against external intervention, in spite of an official election platform of neutrality and the campaign slogan of *He kept us out of war*, no sooner was Woodrow Wilson reelected in 1916 that he performed one of American history's greatest political deceptions. Bowing to the hubris of the human condition and satisfying the money lust of American capitalists, who were panting like dogs in heat, to crank up their factories of war profit, Wilson plunged the United States into its second big imperial war, after the 1898 Spanish-American version.

Sad to say, but for Gunnery Sergeant Charles F. Hoffman, along with his 116,000 Americans killed and 204,000 wounded, it was a tragic and senseless waste for the United States. A whole generation of affected families and communities suffered tremendous losses, all in the name of vainglory and profit. G/Sgt. Hoffman's Hill 142 was there to be conquered again in World War II, as it surely has been countless times before, in the bloody annals of European geopolitical history.

We can also thank World War I for the millions of veterans returning home infected with deadly influenza, spreading it all over the country and killing 675,000 Americans, more than World War I, World War II, the Korean and Southeast Asian Wars *combined*. Wordsmiths are wont to call something like this as *unintended consequences*. Regardless of how the history books are written by the victors, wars are never neat, clean and glorious.

Latin America

Every American incursion, invasion, occupation, and perpetrated coup in Latin America has been and continues to be in service to the 1% and their corporations, who continue to exploit this region's dark-skinned peoples and their rightful resources. In addition to Nicaragua, before the Cold War, the United States militarily invaded or occupied Argentina, Colombia (under manufactured pretexts it amputated its Panama province), Costa Rica, Cuba, the Dominican Republic, El Salvador, Guatemala, Haiti, Honduras, Mexico, Panama, and Puerto Rico, and postwar, added Bolivia, Chile, Grenada, Uruguay, and Venezuela - all for the Princes of Power, banksters, and FIREmen (Finance, Insurance, and Real Estate).[4] Not to mention instigated coups, as the one that put a brutal military junta in power in Brazil on March 31, 1964, thereby toppling the leftwing administration of Joao Goulart. A very mildly worded account is posted on the Wikipedia tipping us off about the real reasons for Goulart's abrupt departure:

"President João Goulart was not favorably viewed in Washington. He took an independent stand in foreign policy, resuming relations with socialist countries and opposing sanctions against Cuba; his administration passed a law limiting the amount of profits multinationals could transmit outside the country; a subsidiary of ITT was nationalized; he promoted economic and social reforms." (João Goulart, Wikipedia)

Gee, did we leave any countries out?

Sorry Corporal Truesdale, and with all due respect to his brave military brethren, but those *bandits* you killed and their hundreds of thousands of brothers and sisters, mothers and fathers, who were slaughtered, were and are defending their rights for independence, freedom from exploitation, and the rape of their natural resources. Most of them were and are Native Americans. Thus, all the American soldiers in Latin America, from Smedley Butler on down, were taxpayer-funded thugs for Wall Street, pure and simple. Not protecting the home front, not maintaining Americans' freedoms, and not making the world a safer place for democracy. Sad, but true.

The Pacific

For a brief time, it gets better. Out of all of America's post-independence wars, there is a reason that Studs Turkel called World War II *The Good War* (1984). It is the *only* war that the United States has participated in the last nearly 200 years (not counting the Civil War's internecine fratricide) that could conceivably be regarded as a noble cause. The United States liberated the Pacific Basin from the military and strategic overreach of Imperial Japan, island by island. It is unfortunate that because of America's ever-increasing hubris and naked fear of international communism exposing capitalism's screw job of the 99%, Hiroshima and Nagasaki got the nuclear-annihilation treatment as a show of force to Stalin and the Soviets.

Speaking of Stalin, I lived for five years on the Normandy beaches and owned a business in France's first post D-Day liberated city, Caen. The Anglo-Saxon invasion conducted by the Americans, British and Canadians was a then technological and daring marvel and it did hasten the end of World War II, but it was not at all necessary to bring it to a close. D-Day could have never happened and the Germans and Italians would have still been ground to a pulp in the Red Army's bloody maw. The European theater was truly Stalin's War. His strategy was simple: one Russian goes down, put two in his place, while pushing relentlessly to the West. The Soviets had up to 491 divisions on the ground and lost up to 12,000,000 soldiers. The Anglo forces had 115 divisions on the European theater's map and lost a total 615,000 men.[5] Not the same thing. What we can say is that the Anglo forces stopped Stalin's communist tsunami from driving all the way to Lisbon, Portugal. Thus, in reality, what the Anglos really did was keep half of Europe firmly in the grip of colonialism's historic 1%. Come to think of it, I have D-Day to thank for meeting my French wife.

Korea

Post WWII, for the American 1%, the specter of international communism infected them with white-knuckled, crazed fear. This is because communism offered an attractive succor and level playing field in the eyes of the West's 99% have-nots. Communism also guaranteed a Robespierre-esque annihilation of America's slave-driving Princes of Power. It was Korea's over-the-top, foaming at the mouth, anti-red war that started the corrosive acid drip on America's mythical aura. As already mentioned, today's shadow fascists openly and brazenly ply the halls of power, sacking and pillaging the commonwealth and hastening the destruction of the 99%'s rapidly disappearing American Dream, which, truth be told, was purely a short-lived manifestation of the semi-socialist New Deal.

The Korean War was the United States' first big military-industrial-government/state security complex's folly (or Nuremberg-class crime, to be precise), in the name of fighting communism, with a capital C, around the globe. It was a warm-up exercise for Southeast Asia and exactly what Dwight D. Eisenhower was talking about, in his now famous and prescient presidential farewell address on January 17, 1961.[6] Good man that Double D. It was in this speech where he warned about the risk of the military-industrial complex taking control of the democratic process, to commit the country to endless wars and the manufacture of all the war machinery to keep it going. His dire predictions have come true, in spades.

While First Lieutenant Murphy served courageously, as did the other 36,516 dead, 92,134 wounded, and 4,759 missing in action, it was surely not for Americans' freedom or for their God, Country, and King.[7] It was to continue Uncle Sam's encirclement of communist China. The Vietnam genocide was not far behind.

Southeast Asia

After the Korean War, America really started drinking the *kill a commie* Kool-Aid - by the oceanful, turning Uncle Sam into a frightening Mr. Hyde cum Heath Ledger's heinous Joker in the movie, *Batman*. This sugary poison became Agent Orange, and its nearly three kilograms of dioxin sprayed on every Vietnamese standing. This does not include the three million or so Southeast Asian civilians, you know, grandmas, grandpas, kids, and mothers, who were bombed, gunned, napalmed, and raped to death. They did not live to see the hundreds of thousands of their future family tree afflicted with the most horrific of mental and physical birth defects, from dioxin-induced, recessive mutations, which are now endemically being carried by the survivors from one generation to the next.[8] The Viet Cong were only fighting an invading, pitiless, soulless, and faceless American army, whose official mantra was *burn all, destroy all, kill all*.

The more things change: Japan's official policy in China was "Senko-seisaku", meaning the *Three Alls - kill all, loot all, destroy all*. Before that, the Japanese were inspired by another genocidal psychopath. General William Sherman, who was charged with punishing the South, at the end of America's Civil War, devised a similar strategy against his own citizens, as his Yankee army burned and plundered its way across the former Confederacy.

War, if nothing else, suffers from a lack of imagination and is sickeningly redundant. Thus in Southeast Asia, with a game plan writ large by Joseph Conrad's Mr. Kurtz, in his masterful anticolonial book, *Heart of Darkness*, life was savagely imitating the literary arts. My heart goes out to all these millions of *Dreaded Others*, who gave their last full measure of devotion, as well as US Marines Gunnery Sergeant Jimmie E. Howard, his 58,220 dead brothers. 303,644 wounded, and the millions who came back destroyed by alcoholism, drug addiction, and post-traumatic stress disorder (PTSD).[9] I also mourn my native country, which was exposed for what it truly and sadly was and is: a colossal, worldwide colonial hegemon. Southeast Asia was merely a modern continuum of 300 years of American slavery and the genocide of 15,000,000 Native Americans, except it had now gone international. The Korean War was the canary in the gold mine about America's defective empire and impending, 21st century collapse. The Southeast Asian War was simply a continuation of the United States' arc of decline. Not a pretty picture.

Iraq and Afghanistan

Cut to the nineties, the fall of the Berlin Wall, and the eventual collapse of international communism. Peace dividend? Hah. The West's 1% needed a new bogeyman to keep the war-machine lucre flowing and they got a double payday by pinning Muslims on their geopolitical dart board. First, the West already had firmly installed their proxy shock troops in colonially created Israel, a dagger in the heart of the Islamic world. Secondly, the Muslim world nominally controls some of Earth's greatest reserves of natural resources, especially of the black-gold and natural-gas varieties. Forming a huge swath of territory, the Islamic world is composed of the northern half of Africa, the Near East, Middle East, and the largely Turkic-Dari-speaking belt of nations stretching across the southern flank of Eurasia and on into Xinjiang, China, where it hops down to Southeast Asia and Indonesia. It is essentially a world map of the Muslim world, a huge, resource-rich prize all one percenters can appreciatively drool over, and they want it all.

Going back to Nero torching Rome and proving the 1%'s adage that false-flag operations almost always succeed in manipulating the 99%, the American shadow fascists' blatant 9/11 false flag worked beyond their wildest expectations. The neocon Project for New American Century officially declared they needed a new Pearl Harbor, to push their radical agenda, and 9/11 gave them that and more. It ushered in Homeland Security's militarized, fascist police state and endless wars in resources rich, Muslim countries around the planet.[10]

Lieutenant Michael P. Murphy, Petty Officer 2nd Class Michael A. Mansoor, and his hundreds of thousands of Western military brethren around the world, sadly continue to carry the torch of warrior colonialism, exploitation, and resource extraction to humanity's 1.5 billion-plus Muslims. And why not? The money's beaudaciously abundant, the profits are usurious, and the lives of the fighting 99% and the dehumanized, dark-skinned *Dreaded Others* are a dime a dozen.

One can only wish for as quickly as possible, the *Fall of the Western Empire*. It was probably the same about 2,000 years ago for the oppressed 99% in Europe, North Africa, and the Near East, who were sick of being dominated by the 1% of Rome. You can just hear them gathering and singing,

Break out the wine and lutes boys and girls, let's get down and celebrate the fall of the Empire!

For the sake of the human race's survival, a new international order needs to be ushered in, and it must decidedly be un-Western. All indications are that China is going to be the one wearing the world champion belt in the decades to come, what with its dynamic economic growth and exploding middle class. As a world leader, will Baba Beijing be a hegemon colonialist, like the West? Or will the Chinese be different? To be continued.

As usual all these links appear live on the audiovisual digital concordance of this book, as explained in the front pages. .

1- *http://GwynneDyer.com*.

2- War Is a Racket, *by Smedley Butler, can be bought at your local book store or checked out at the library. A must read.*

3- *All about the Wall Street fascist overthrow plot:*
http://coat.ncf.ca/our_magazine/links/53/53-index.html.

4- *http://yachana.org/teaching/resources/interventions.html*. *History of US Interventions in Latin America. Quite a list.*

5- http://angelfire.com/ct/ww2europe/stats.html. (World War II Statistics (also WWI)

[VID 019]

6- http://youtube.com/watch?v=CWilYW_fBfY. Eisenhower originally included the government in his complex, along with the military and industry, but took it out of the speech. Ever the gentleman, he did not want to be disrespectful of the Hill, after working with them for eight years, but he knew what he was talking about. He saw our world today coming, like a freight truck: the military-industrial-governmental complex. (#57 Video by YouTube). Today we have to add another component to the lethal brew: the corporate media, the great enabler of American government crimes.

7- http://en.wikipedia.org/wiki/United_States_military_casualties_of_war.

8- A number of YouTube videos on Vietnam's postwar, Agent Orange/dioxin-induced genetic mutations are so shockingly grotesque, that you have to sign that you are over 18 years of age: https://youtube.com/watch?v=XEFtAezgTso. (Video by YouTube)

9- http://en.wikipedia.org/wiki/United_States_military_casualties_of_war.

10- http://ae911truth.org and https://en.wikipedia.org/wiki/Project_for_the_New_American_Century

The dollar's diminishing dictatorship spells the end of Western financial fascism

Sitting here in Sinoland, eating popcorn, drinking an ice cold Yanjing beer and watching the world changing at warp speed. I can see for miles from my 10th floor Beijing apartment.

[IMG 0021]

In Chapter 38 of *44 Days*, I wrote about the fact that Iraq, in switching all of its international settlements, including oil, from US (petro-) dollars to euros, and being invaded and destroyed, was no mere coincidence. Nor was Saddam Hussein being hanged, filmed for all the world to luridly see. Symbols matter in the cold cruel world of Empire and Realpolitik. Anybody with a glint of the statistician in them can find what these scientists like to call a trend, by looking no further than Iran, Libya, Russia and China.

Muammar Gadhafi thumbed his nose at Uncle Sam's feudal monetary system. Instead of dollars, he opted for selling his country's petroleum products, using Gulf Kingdom currencies backed by the full faith of gold. Gadhafi had big plans to roll out this Pan-African petro-dinar, as a way of unifying the Great Continent. In the greedy eyes of the Bretton Woods dollar central banks La Cosa Nostra, his even bigger sin was campaigning around Africa and the Middle East, to promote this new gold backed currency, like a salesman barnstorming the countryside. It was so credible and doable and with Libya's reported 150MT in gold bullion to seed the kitty, it was bound to be realized, so he had to be stopped. No need asking where the Libyan people's gold vault ended up: in the West's hands, stolen, good and proper.

Making the US dollar purely fiat is something Richard Nixon and the United States did on back in 1971, when they uncoupled the US dollar from the gold standard. This is often attributed as the beginning of America's incurable addiction to green ink photocopiers, printing trillions of dollars in the process.

We all know what happened to Libya. British and French jets, with the full backing of the United States, bombed Libya back to the Middle Ages and the West assassinated the once-good-now-evil Colonel. He died ignominiously, Mafia style, at the hands of CIA/MI6/DGSE proxy terrorists. They were perverts too, sodomizing Gadhafi with a bayonet, all preserved for posterity, on film. The message was clear to all of the Dreaded Others' leaders across Asia, Africa and Latin America: this is what will happen to you, if you fancy disturbing the West's financial dollar dictatorship.

Both Iraq and Libya were modern, prosperous countries, with free or heavily subsidized medicine, education and housing, where women were afforded rights and job opportunities that even Westerners could be envious of. Not anymore.

ABOVE: *Zbigniew Brzezinski: Polish nobleman emigré, "foreign policy advisor" to the empire, visceral anti-communist and Russophobe. A tireless engine of evil in modern history.*

Iran, one of George W. Bush's Axis of Evil nominees, along with North Korea and Iraq, has been relentlessly destroyed by the West, since 1979, never forgiven for overthrowing the West's finger puppet Shah Pahlavi, as well as humiliating the United States, with the 444-day occupation of its embassy in Tehran. Empires don't take lightly being slapped in the face like that. Time to get even. The result was revenge by proxy slaughter, during the eight year Iran-Iraq War. President Jimmy Carter and his blood lust warrior, National Security Administration Director, Zbigniew Brzezinski, goaded Saddam into the conflict with promises of the Moon, and the US and Europe gleefully supplying him with chemical weapons and tactical support to gas-massacre an estimated 100,000 Iranians. Iran, true to its Islamic revolution and respecting the Ayatollah's fatwa against nuclear, chemical and other weapons of mass destruction, never reciprocated.

Since then, absurd and cruel economic sanctions have been enforced, causing great suffering among the Persian people, women, children, the elderly and infirm alike. This is after all, what Empire does as a matter of course. To get around this barbarity, Iran has cleverly circumvented much of the US dollar's diktat, by dealing in gold and neighboring currencies, with Turkey, Russia and India.

And now we come to China and Russia. Without coming out and saying it, they are going out of their way to bring the world's US dollar dictatorship to its knees. First, China has been signing so many international trade settlement deals with other countries the last couple of years, to use the renminbi (RMB) and/or the other countries' national currencies, in order to circumvent dollar conversion, that it is no longer news. Cross border yuan trade has already hit a staggering ¥8.6 trillion, which is over a trillion dollars, or euros for that matter. This is not chump change and will continue to grow exponentially in the years to come.

Then, Russia and China pushed their twin scimitar and long knife closer to the heart of Western darkness, by signing a staggering $400 billion, 30-year natural gas deal, plus tens of billions in construction and manufacturing projects into the 21st century, etc. But even calling this bilateral deal "$400 billion" is misleading, because the whole kit and caboodle is going to be transacted in Chinese yuan and Russian rubles. Ouch. Sorry about that Uncle Sam. So, we might as well start saying *2.4 trillion renminbi* or *14 trillion rubles*, and get used to it, because this is the beginning of the end of Western Empire's US$/World Bank/IMF financial fascism.

The unraveling of this post World War II, Bretton Woods system of extortion and human and natural resource extraction is now reaching warp drive speed. Gazprom, Russia's natural gas giant and Sumo sized supplier of Europe's energy needs, has signed agreements with 90% of its customers, to circumvent the US dollar and be paid in euros instead. Remember what happened to Iraq and Libya when they tried this. But Russia is a tad more to destroy and destabilize than these two relatively pint sized, resource rich lands. Ditto colossus China.

The agreement goes on to say the ultimate goal is for Russia's customers to phase in settling all their purchases in rubles. This concept already got the ball rolling, with Belarus now paying in the Russian currency. Other countries will surely follow. And why not? Russia has the world's fifth largest forex reserves, weighing in at a half a trillion dollars, er, 17.5 trillion rubles or RMB3 trillion, thank you. Russia still has a long way to go to recover from the 1997-98 Western financial gang bang of Asia and Russia, but clearly is headed in the right direction. Want proof? Japan's 2014 government debt is 242% of GDP, the US's is 107% and France's and the UK's weigh in at 90%. And Russia's? Fourteen percent, with ally China's a very manageable 21%.

Thanks to Western Empire overthrowing the legally elected government in Ukraine and installing a fascist junta on Russia's doorstep, Russia is making it a top priority to create its own national payment system and credit card, to compete against the West's Visa and Mastercard duopoly. They are looking at China's very successful Union Pay card as a model, which has surpassed Mastercard, to become the world's second largest bank card on the planet. In the not too distant future, it will surely pass Visa to become the world's #1 card. China now has four of the ten largest banks in the world: #1 Industrial and Commercial Bank of China (ICBC), #5 China Construction Bank (CCB), #9 Bank of China and #10 Agricultural Bank of China (ABC), all 100% Chinese, and more amazingly, all state owned. Who says you need private banks? Take that Wall Street! And to think that only 30 short years ago, China didn't have much in the way of an integrated banking system at all.

Next, look to the BRICS to start poking gaping holes in the fiat paper tiger dollar, by creating its own reserve fund, thus circumventing the need for IMF emergency loans, which are nothing more than a Mafia style extortion racket to impoverish developing nations' already struggling peoples, and strip out their natural resources and manufacturing base at pennies on the dollar. Next, we will see the BRICS create their own trade settlement currency, affectionately being called the *brisco*. These five countries are sitting on a mountain of cash, about $5 trillion, while Eurmerica is drowning in sovereign debt: $17 trillion in the US and €10 trillion in Europe, not even counting credit card, personal and student debt in the US. Eurmerica, along with Japan, cannot print funny money fast enough to extricate themselves from the inevitable fiscal implosion.

For five centuries, the tiny Western tip of Eurasia and its gluttonous spawn, the United States, have been gang raping the world's Dreaded Other – the 85% of humanity who have been enslaved, exploited and fleeced by the Great White Race. These dark skinned peoples are the ones who survived their hundreds of millions ancestors who were exterminated, via colonial genocide and slavery - they ostensibly got their political independence in the 20th century, but are still under the brutal jackboot of Eurmerica's banking and financial system.

Now it is payback time, boys and girls, a *Carrie* cum *Chucky* vengefest, real horror show like. It is never discussed in the West's mainstream media, but its empire is collapsing. Societal and economic collapse are simply the last stage of every civilization which has existed in human history.

As so methodically explained by Joseph Tainter in his well-researched tour de force, *The Collapse of Complex Societies* (1990, University Press), America and the West are following an all too predictable and unstoppable process, as regular as a subway schedule. Jared Diamond's *Collapse: How Societies Choose to Fail or Succeed* (2005) is equally as revealing.

Mr. Tainter finds that ever increasing societal complexity and specialization bring down civilizations, be they as small as Easter Island or as huge as China. This is because specialization costs more and more and gives fewer and fewer positive results to society, in terms of the cost-benefit ratio. Dr. Diamond takes a more holistic, systemic approach and suggests that a variety of reasons cause collapse: militarization and war, environmental destruction, unfavorable natural cycles in the climate over time and invading competitors, a disruption of trade with neighboring countries, among several others.

In both books, the authors quite matter-of-factly say it: all evidence suggests that American/European civilization is showing clear signs of collapse.

Through China's long history, it has had several societal collapses of its very own: the Han and Tang Dynasties collapsed and reverted to smaller, more primitive states. The Qin, Song, Mongol and Qing reigns where all absorbed by other groups, ready to fill the breach, including Mao Zedong's communists in 1949, when they relegated the Qing dynasty to the dust heap of history, by finally deposing the emperor, Pu Yi, sending him to a labor farm. These national collapses are episodes in Baba Beijing's Heavenly Mandate that eat like acid on the current leadership's sense of place in China's history books. President Xi Jinping, Premier Li Keqiang, their all-powerful 7-man Politburo Standing Committee and their attendant 300-person Central Committee, definitely do not want to end up being the latest entry on this list of Chinese civilization's catastrophes.

[IMG 0057] *What were the Rapa Nui natives thinking, as they were cutting down Easter Island's last tree, thus dooming their people to inevitable collapse? (Image by wikipedia.org, tagline paraphrased from Jared Diamond's book, Collapse.)*

While the West is doing what long term civilizations do best – collapsing - BRICS and NAM are building institutions and alliances to brace against this eventuality, because history also shows that neighbors of the declining power are rarely unaffected. There is blowback in all directions and in the West's case, its empire is worldwide. Thus the blowback will likely have a negative impact on countries around the planet.

It is for this reason that as much as BRICS and NAM would love to see a different world order in place, with Western colonialism and financial suzerainty still dominating them, when the collapse happens, it's likely to very traumatic for everyone involved.

Thus, BRICS and NAM keep building alliances, institutions and infrastructure, preparing to be as strong and as immune as possible for when the time comes.

After all, it they wanted to today, BRICS and NAM wouldn't even have to fire a shot to win a war against the Western Worldwide Wehrmacht. They would just need to use Euramerica's financial system against itself: stop using the US dollar as their trading and reserve currency. It would be the ultimate Hollywood thriller plot: hoisting Planet Earth's Western Axis of Evil on its own petard. Many of the world's people would simply call it karma, while beaming smiles of schadenfreude. Curtains up. On with the show!

I know I'm smiling. Heck, it's a blast to watch. Think I'll cook up some popcorn, have an ice cold Yanjing beer (640ml, cost RMB3.00/RUB17.00), gaze out my 10th floor Beijing apartment window and soak in all the action. To coin that great Who classic rock song, *I Can See for Miles*, I'm sitting here in Sinoland, in the belly of the New Century Beast, taking in the long view of the world and current events.

[IMG 0058] *It's going to be scary fun, boys and girls, a real Carrie x Chucky vengefest, when the Western Empire starts to implode (Images by fanart.tv and images.sodahead.com)*

Operation Rescue Russia and a big "F.U." to Eurangloland

A funny thing happened on the way to the last 500 years of Western Empire and colonialism. Russia has boycotted Eurangloland's (The EU, US, Canada, Australia and New Zealand, but the Kiwis were spared by Russia this time) food and agricultural products, which in itself is very telling about ongoing trends. This was in response to incessant Western sanctions being heaped on Russia; first for its supposed involvement

in the Western backed fascist junta in the Ukraine and secondly, for Crimeans voting to rejoin the Russian Federation. Thus, unsurprisingly, the Great Bear has struck back.

But there's more. The oppressed, the 85% of the world's citizens who are not from the West, I call the *The Dreaded Other* or the *Moral Majority,* and they are helping Russia to poke a big stick in the West's eye. Until recently, the ongoing reaction of the world's Moral Majority governments to Russia's anti-Western boycott, would have been unimaginable.

In all fairness to the proud, non-Western Dreaded Other, you must remove the peoples of Japan and South Korea and add them to Eurangloland's empire. Like Europe, they are militarily occupied, supine satraps to the Princes of Power in Washington. Like Europe, groveling like dogs, they actually take their barking orders from America seriously. It's really hard to stomach. Throw in a few more countries that cower at the feet of the Western Empire and we can say that approximately 20% of the world's people rule the remaining 80%, not much differently than the pharaohs did over their subjects and slaves in Ancient Egypt. A reverse version of the Pareto principle applies here too: 80% of the world's masses are fighting the 20%'s hegemonic, colonial empire.

This secondary list of client states waxes and wanes, depending on how recently the CIA/MI6/DGSE/BND deep state has installed a whore government in their puppet, local halls of power, or as in the Philippines, which prostrated itself to America's Worldwide Wehrmacht, by accepting to be occupied by American soldiers – again, Ukraine is the most recent prom slut for Western servitude and so far, Venezuela is holding out admirably against the West's internal efforts at regime change, as is Ecuador, Argentina, Bolivia, Kyrgyzstan, Eritrea and many others. [Note: As we go to print (March 2017), the situation in Argentina has deteriorated amrkedly and a new pro-Washington regime was installed, with a similar soift coup in Brazil; in Ecuador the popular left-wing Correa government is being challenged by a powerful rightwing coalition supported by the US.)

Kudos to Russia for its genius to pick agricultural products as a punch in the solar plexus of power. As Deena Stryker recently pointed out in a recent article,

Anyone who has witnessed European farmers drive their tractors into the center of Brussels and dump crops in front of EU headquarters, knows the hold they have on legislators. Much of European agriculture takes place on family farms and the EU has had to create special rules and subsidies to keep its food producers happy.

And now, these disgruntled EU farmers are going to have mountains of agricultural products with no immediate export market, and which have historically been grown for Russia.

Back in the United States, I hear how stupid Putin and Russia are to ban food imports, since "the grocery shelves there are empty and Russians have nothing to eat." Really? This just confirmed to me how insulated Americans are in their *Fox-CNN-Wapo-NYT* propaganda bubble. Herewith is a list of all the agricultural products, where Russia ranks at least in the world's top four. Thank you FAO:

[IMG 0059] Russia: World food production rankings chart. (Russia occupies #1 spot in many categories)

Wow, a pretty impressive food dossier, if you ask me. Given that much of Russia is in permafrost and the rest of the country has to deal with the world's shortest growing seasons, it is not surprising that Russians want to import what they cannot meteorologically grow, such as temperate fruits and vegetables. Clearly, as the table above demonstrates, Russians don't need to import a damn thing agriculturally, in order to be nutritionally self-sufficient. They are now simply much richer and can afford to pay for a more varied diet. Like any trading people, be they African or Asian, variety is the spice of life. Food trade has been going on for at least 8,000 years of sedentary civilization, probably much earlier,

Hey, Neanderthal Nate, I'll trade you this here skin full of mastodon liver for that hindquarter of sabretooth tiger, wadda ya say, bub? N' if you don't mind me saying so, pal, gawd youz iz ug-i-ly!

For our pre-civilization ancestors, trade offered the possibility of direct mutual benefit. Much of the West's five centuries of resource extraction around the world has been to take nutritious and tasty foods and spices from the lands of brown skinned peoples, those 85% just discussed, and bringing it back to home base for obscene profit and culinary pleasure, most of it too expensive except for the wealthiest members of society. So it goes.

Even funnier for the uninformed, Russia does not even rank among the world's top ten food importers. If not then, who are the people so starving to death, that they must resort to importing food, in order to keep their grocery store shelves from being barren?

[IMG 0060] Countries by agricultural imports

Hmm. Times must be tough in the United States, Western Europe, Japan and for <u>all those obese millions in China, where diabetes, the scourge of modern, sedentary society, is now rampant</u>.

Contrary to Western propaganda, picking agricultural products was pure genius on Russia's part. Not only have they got millions of politically well-connected small farmers in Eurangloland, who are pissed off as mad hornets, but these are the kinds of commodity products that *We Hate the West* countries can readily and happily supply, thus enhancing Russia's relations with BRICS and NAM.

<u>Russia is threatening to ban car imports, which would be a dagger in the heart of Western Europe's industrial heartland of Germany, Poland, France, Italy, etc.</u> Russia's car

import numbers are not huge, so it would mostly affect BMW and Mercedes-Benz, since Ford, Volkswagen Renault, Toyota and Hyundai have invested $5 billion in automobile manufacturing inside Russia. Still, if you don't think the Russians know what they are doing,

We are seriously concerned. We hope that the Russian government will think twice before taking any such measures as they would hurt all manufacturers,

<u>Said Joerg Schreiber, chairman of the Association of European Businesses' Automobile Manufacturers Committee,</u> *All* manufacturers, my dear Herr Joerg? Or mostly European ones? The Russians would of course continue to only allow in the components or materials that are needed to keep their domestic auto industry humming.

Car manufacturing, like many other modern conveniences, has a web of thousands of secondary and tertiary suppliers who ripple across the economy. They would all be adversely affected. And which countries could fill the breach? Why, China and Korea of course. China's Great Wall and Chery cars, as well as Korea's SsangYong brand would love to take advantage of Europe's suffering. Although it's doubtful obedient Korea would go against its American master's wishes and do so. When a small country like South Korea, about the size of Iceland or Portugal, has been militarily occupied by almost 30,000 American soldiers for almost 60 years, and with no intention of ever leaving, it's hard to be free on the international stage. <u>To make matters even more humiliating for the Koreans, all of their own troops will continue to take orders from an American general, not a Korean one.</u>

Remember, the first rule of the 1% is,

When they are down on the ground, stomp them as hard as you can in the face.

So, for the 99%, turnabout is fair play…

Thus, the world's economically oppressed are starting to rise up. It only took hours after Russia's announcement to boycott Western food, that The Dreaded Other were happy to give a cheeky kick to the world's occidental mandibles. Latin America, which for 250 years has more or less been a Monroe Doctrine economic and political prostitute for Washington, was the first to go to the media (there are still poor Guatemala, Honduras and El Salvador, that are US client states – is it a coincidence it's from these countries where all the tens of thousands of children are fleeing local American "democracy" and capitalism – and not socialist Nicaragua?). Ecuador, Chile, Uruguay, Paraguay, Argentina and Brazil came out to proudly say they are ready to help Russia. The EU's attempts to threaten these proud, now mostly independent countries are pathetic and denigrating to Latin America, but it fully confirms the West's ongoing imperial attitude to their former colonies around the world. And since the servile EU cannot pass gas without Washington's permission, the US is implicated too. Sorry Eurmerica, but your genocide of 100 million Native Americans ended some time ago. Take that Cortez! And you Jackson!

Among the Latin American countries who offered to help Russia, Argentina is a major meat and grain producer. Its official government press release made it clear that, *Hell yes Eurangloland, we'll increase our food exports to Russia,* saying,

(Argentina) is reaffirming its status as food supplier to 400 million people at present and the world's fifth-largest (food) exporter.

And then there is Brazil. Is there anything agricultural that this BRICS behemoth doesn't grow? After all, it's bigger than the continental United States and has the tropical climate to grow crops year round.

Next, the Chinese sounded their Buddhist long horns, announcing that they would move into high gear to build a huge, 100,000m^2 special cross-border customs zone food market and warehouse complex on their northeastern border, in direct cooperation

with their Russian colleagues. When the Chinese decide to do something, it will take them merely months to finish the project and get it launched.

At that point, even Eurangloland's supposed allies began to pile on. Turkey, a key member of colonial NATO and an EU pretender, vocally announced,

We're ready to increase food exports to Russia.

Ouch! Egypt, a loyal Western client state that merrily helps Israel in the genocide of the Palestinians, is ready to go. Ditto Africa, with Kenya, Uganda, Tanzania, Zimbabwe, Zambia and South Africa making it public. Just to let Eurangloland know on which side their rye bread is buttered, Belarus and Tajikistan lined up to open the food flood gates to their colossus neighbor. Even Serbia, which is trying to gain ascension into the EU, came out swinging at the West. This, in spite of explicit threats from Brussels. Tee-hee-hee. Maybe all those thousands of deformed babies and locals dying from cancer, due to NATO's 50,000 rounds of depleted uranium laying around Serbia, is starting to get to them, a high price indeed to pay for servitude to the West's Princes of Power. Ahhh, uranium 238, the gift that keeps on giving – for 4.5 billion years.

[IMG 0061] *More and more of the world's 85% are happy to give Eurangloland a big, public raspberry – and loving it (#63 Image by busyminds. ae)*

In addition to this impressive list of countries now unafraid to give Eurangloland a huge, slobbery raspberry in the face, Russia is also contacting Colombia, Kyrgyzstan, Mauritius, Mexico, Mozambique, Paraguay, Peru and Sri Lanka, to sign food import contracts. Now that Russia has become the world's sixth largest gold owner, even surpassing voracious China, as well as sitting on the world's fifth largest pile of foreign cash reserves, more than the United States or any EU country, we can fall back on that ever-so-true adage of American capitalism,

Money talks and shit walks.

Then there are all the numerous, unnamed countries, too timid to give Eurangloland a public kick to the *cojones* (Spanish for *gonads*), but will happily and quietly fly to Moscow, food export contracts in hand.

In sum, Russia's choice of food and agriculture products to boycott was a brilliant stroke of win-win diplomacy and economics for the world's Moral Majority, and a superb strategy to rally them to help join in standing up to the Western Empire. This would have all been unimaginable 15-20 years ago, and looking back, maybe even ten years. Today it's food, tomorrow automobiles and next? Americans: continue watching Fox and CNN. Keep your faces buried in the New York Times and The Washington Post. Europeans, keep licking Uncle Sam's blood spattered, Gladio-NATO boots with spineless servitude. It's all coming undone under your noses faster than a speeding Chinese bullet train.

Europe's inglorious, ignominious infamy

[IMG 0062] *The new true blue and gold flag of the EU. Fascism is back with a vengeance across the Old Continent, because the Princes of Power and Profit want it that way.*

I will never forget the day in 1990, when at a French Embassy public reception in Beijing, a diplomat asked me why I had not applied for French citizenship. I had married my French wife in September, 1988 and had no idea about the possibility of doing so, although my friends over beer will razz me otherwise. We're still together after 26 years, so it must be love. I was immediately intrigued and honored. Even that far back, my sense of patriotism and support for the United States, my birth country, was already starting to be challenged. Something was not sitting right in my soul. Something about America's actions around our Pale Blue Dot was sticking in my philosophical crawl. Compared to my knowledge today of Western history, with its 500 years of false flag operations, war, slavery, colonization, genocide and human and natural resource expropriation around the world, I was bone dead ignorant.

The internet in 1990 was very primitive and resources in general were limited. I was even subscribing to *The Nation*, *The Oklahoma Observer*, rotating *The Utne Reader*, *Harper's* and *The Progressive* into the mix. All this at no small cost, due to international shipping costs. I also subscribed to *The International Herald Tribune* and *The Economist*, which at the time I took for enlightened, cutting edge journalism. I held my nose when they endorsed George I in 2000 and never resubscribed, when they again endorsed Bushy Boy in 2004.

I was still living in an age of innocence, where I always gave America and Europe the benefit of the doubt: the "noble" cause of anti-communism, the wisdom of the West's democratic principles and their sincere wishes and efforts to help the downtrodden around the world to achieve a better life. Over the next 35 years, those ideals I held so dear for the United States, and the West in general, were smashed to nanometer dust, as I stopped reading so much fiction and literature, and moved towards reading history and current events books, as well as getting very adept at researching on the Internet.

Mind you, I was way ahead of the curve, compared to most Westerners. I had lived in Africa and traveled all over this vast and (Western-) tortured continent, as well as three years in almost all the countries in the Middle East. I spoke Arabic fluently, thanks to two years in the Peace Corps in Tunisia, 1980-82, as well as French, so my ability to get up close and personal with many of the locals was linguistically made easier. Also, my jobs after the Peace Corps, 1982-90, were agricultural in nature, so I was not one of those crass traveling salesmen who get a room at the Intercontinental in the capital and go to a few meetings around town, before jumping back on a plane to the next capital. No, I would rent a car at the airport, drop by a shop and buy a bagful of cassettes of all the local music stars, African and Arab, and drive for thousands of kilometers, music blasting away, going from region to region and farm to farm. I saw many vistas, social and cultural scenes, that were so moving, I would cry with joy. I would not trade my ten years in Africa and Middle

East for any other experience in the world. It defines who I am today as a citizen of Planet Earth.

In Beijing in 1990, I remember reading an article about the Iran-Iraq War, with credible evidence that the United States was heavily involved with Iraq's use of chemical weapons on the Iranians. It is now such commonplace knowledge that all the genocidal details are described on Wikipedia and such establishment sources as Foreign Policy. So much for moral outrage in the "morally superior" West. That raised warning signs in my conscious. How could the "Beacon on the Hill", the "Land of the Home and the Brave", commit such a horrific act of genocide? It went against all that I was taught when I grew up in Oklahoma, about all that "great and good". Of course, thirty-five years later, we now know that the United States is the world's biggest user of chemical weapons, and with NATO, nuclear weapons in Iraq and Serbia, using depleted uranium.

Then I read articles about how the United States duped Saddam Hussein into seizing Kuwait, as a pretext to invade his country. The entire text of Saddam's meeting with US Ambassador to Iraq, April Gillespie, has since been released. For all intents and purposes, Ms. Gillespie gave Mr. Hussein the green light to invade Kuwait. It's a diplomatic version of Paul Newman's and Robert Redford's film, *The Sting*. Again, there was this angst in my soul, a terrible cognitive dissonance between all the perfection and self-sacrifice that Uncle Sam has supposedly nobly committed himself to, and upon which I was nurtured, versus this glaring evidence to the contrary.

Over the ensuing years, I learned that false flag operations are de rigueur for any government, large and small, from deep history (Ancient Rome) to today (Ukraine, Venezuela, Georgia, Russia, and all the cookie cutter "color revolutions"). They are so common as to be banal. At the top of the list in modern times, the kings of false flag operations are the United States, NATO and Israel. It's the only way they know how to "conduct foreign affairs", or rather control the precious natural and human resources of the world's dark skinned people, the 85%, the ones I call the True Moral Majority.

But in the nineties, I was still making an innocent distinction between Europe and the United States. The US had already sold its soul to rigged markets and greed is good capitalism, and outside of embarrassing Maggie-Mini-Me Britain, I thought Europe was morally superior to America, especially France. I always admired Charles de Gaulle for leaving NATO in 1966 and the country did not join back in until Monsieur Mini-Me Nicolas Sarkozy, renounced his country's sovereignty in the process, officially letting the CIA/MI6 Gladio secret armies back on French soil.

Back when I applied for French citizenship in 1990, François Mitterand was President of the Republic, a socialist who governed like one. The US had just suffered through a decade of Reagan and George I, so the contrast was superficially remarkable. I truly believed France was committed to *Liberté, Egalité* and *Fraternité*, not just at home, but around the world. I felt after Vietnam, Algeria, along with its string of DOM-TOM territories encircling the planet (these are like America's Hawaii and Guam), not to mention two savage, bloody world wars across Europe, when fascism was on the march, that France and (continental) Europe had learned their lessons about colonialism and exploitation. I deluded myself into thinking that the EU was different than Uncle Sam and knew better.

Thus, sincere pride was felt when I got my French passport less than a year later. Being married to a French woman and speaking fluent French surely accelerated my approval, and cynics can say that because I'm a white person, this probably didn't hurt my cause. I demur. Without going into all the details, I began declaring I was French-American and whenever I could, I would travel on my French passport, especially in Europe. I was using my French passport as a political and philosophical statement: I was different than those gluttonous, money crazed, credit laden, materialistic Americans back home.

When we came back to China in 2010, I used my French passport for my Chinese resident visas and always tell the Chinese I am French. The difference in their approach if you tell them you are American is remarkable. With Iraq, Afghanistan and on and on around the world, the Chinese get more of the truth about America than Americans do, and they still cut France some slack, for being the first Western country to recognize the People's Republic in 1964, again, thanks to de Gaulle, who, like Vladimir Putin, always put the interests of his citizens first, damn Uncle Sam.

Over the ensuing years, I continued to give the EU the benefit of the doubt, that is, until Ukraine. Now, all bets are off. Scores of millions of Europeans and Asians died at the hands of the fascist Axis before and during World War II. It is incredulous that the NATO countries in Europe, as well as Angloland (the US, Canada, UK, Australia and New Zealand) are openly supporting, financing and lying for a blatant Nazi government and fascist junta. The whole kit and caboodle has been meticulously planned since 1990 by US/NATO, paid for to the tune of at least $5,000,000,000 (according to Department of State's Victoria Nudelman/Nuland), in a country that was at the vanguard of fascist genocide, thanks to Hitler's right hand Ukrainian psychopath, Stepan Bandera.

You can always add Israel to these Western regime change schemes. Counterintuitively, Israel's government is supporting Jew-killing fascists in Ukraine, because Ukraine's numerous Jewish oligarchs are among the 1% elite in Israel controlling its government. Incredibly, only twenty Israeli families control around 50% of the country's stock market and one-fourth of the largest corporations, especially media, banking and IT. They hate their ancestral motherland Russia more than they hate Jew-hating fascists.

Turning Ukraine into a fascist hellhole also serves Israel's needs for increasing immigration of new citizens, to replace the disgusted thousands who are leaving the Jewish state in droves. It is working. Immigration to Israel from war-torn, fascist infested Ukraine has surged 215%.

So, in honor of Europe's inglorious, ignominious infamy in Ukraine, Greece and all the secret Gladio armies puppeteering Europe's controlled, Potemkin democracy, today I raise the true blue and gold flag of the EU, which proudly flies the fascist Svoboda Party's insignia, the *Wolfsangel*. It has glorious roots in European history. It was proudly flown in Nazi Germany by:

- The 2nd SS Panzer Division Das Reich
- The 4th SS Polizei Panzergrenadier Division
- The 34th SS Volunteer Grenadier Division Landstorm Nederland
- The Sturmabteilung „Feldherrnhalle" Wachstandart Kampfrunen (Assault Unit—SA--"Warlord's Hall" Guard Regiment)
- The NS-Volkswohlfahrt

My fellow Europeans, it makes you break out with goosebumps of pride, doesn't it, to know the *Wolfsangel* is now back up on flagpoles in your homeland? Just being sarcastic. Unlike the very moving scenes I experienced in Africa and the Middle East, I am moved by tears of shame, not joy.

[IMG 0063] *The West and Israel intentionally and willfully ignore that Western Ukraine is under the control of Nazis.*
(Images by thetruthspeaker.co and globalresearch.ca)

It is illegal to display this Nazi symbol in Germany. But no matter. Today, Angela Merkel, François Holland, David Cameron and the 500 million citizens of Europe have come clean: fascism is as European as apple strudel, linguini and Camembert cheese. If Ukraine's fascism spills over into other parts of Europe and infects the body politic, it looks like the Russians may have to do the bloody, dirty work of killing off Nazism one more time, less than a century after the last time they saved Europe and the world from Hitler's Wehrmacht. And they will do it, even if it means war with the West.

The Communist Party of China fought Japanese imperialism and Chiang Kai-Shek's gangster fascism (lavishly supported by the US), with the whole nation losing 35 million citizens in the process. While Europeans beam with pride at their new flag, it is raising eyebrows of the severest consternation in the halls of power in Beijing and among its nation of 1.3 billion souls, who are well schooled in deep and modern history. If it means keeping fascism out of the People's Republic, and that is what would happen if America were successful with its Asian Pivot, and its carbon copy balkanization plans for Russia, then the proud Chinese people would go to war with the West, to keep it from happening.

In the eyes of the world's 85% - the True Moral Majority - the West crossed a demented, odious Rubicon in Ukraine. There is no turning back in the eyes of Russians and Chinese. If Ukrainian fascism spills over, only the United States and its supine, satrap Eurangloland, can turn back the Arrow of Time and stop World War III. The 2nd Law of Thermodynamics demonstrates that the Arrow of Time cannot be reversed or deviated. Yet, somehow, some way, Eurangloland had better figure out how to defy the laws of universal physics and pull a political rabbit out of the bag. The fate of humanity may hang in the balance.

Our Bipolar World

Sitting here halfway between the United States and Europe, in the belly of the New Century Beast, affords a unique view of the world. As I peruse the mainstream media of the West, which only represents (at most) 15% of our planet's people, and put it up to the mirror of the True Moral Majority's global viewpoints, the other 85%, it is easy to parse a bipolar world. Yes, countries outside the West control their media just as much as the West controls its own, which is exactly why the conflicting messages are diametrically opposed.

The West portrays a unipolar world. This is the West's version of history, starting in 1492, where they are the absolute masters of our Earth, its peoples and natural resources. This hegemony over what the West calls "minorities" and their lands, has and is continuing to be maintained by genocide, forced famines, war, false flag operations, covert and overt assassinations and regime changes across the planet. The original crusaders who lusted for gold, silver, timber, ore, food, spices and slaves, hid behind a sanctimonious shield of Christian righteousness: Britain, France, Spain, Portugal, Netherlands, Germany and Italy, principally. With the inevitable decline of their empires, Europeans bequeathed their bloody rapiers, escutcheons and crosses to the United States, and have been cravenly helping Uncle Sam in his continued terrorism around the world. For Eurangloland and its satrap states, the world is *unipolar*, and the United States is the avatar master of the world, the logical culmination of 500 years of Western capitalist greed and exploitation.

Not so fast, Jezebel. For five centuries, the True Moral Majority, those dark skinned 85% of humanity who populate the vast majority of Earth's topography, are finally finding a voice. They are calling it a *multipolar world*. Most of the liberation struggles for independence in the 1950s-60s and 70s were covertly and overtly overturned, manipulated and corrupted by the West, through assassinations, false flag operations, black ops propaganda, coups d'états, wars, rigged elections, proxy wars, genocides and military incursions. Just in assassinations alone, the list is long: Mosaddegh in Iran, Lumumba in Congo, Allende in Chile, Armas in Guatemala,[1] Rafael Trujillo in the Dominican Republic John F. Kennedy,

Robert F. Kennedy, Martin Luther King, Malcolm X in the US, Aldo Moro in Italy, Hussein in Iraq, Gaddafi in Libya, plus thousands of second tier politicians, labor unionists, religious leaders, journalists, witnesses and other perceived undesirables. Since 1963, France's secret services (DGSE) are said to have assassinated 23 independence minded African heads of state, who would not do the West's bidding. Throw in Mossad, MI6, BND and all the other alphabet permutations of the deep state, and you have a seriously large database. Much of this is spelled out in gripping, irrefutable detail in William Blum's majestic book, *Killing Hope*.

[1] Some of these assassinated leaders were not exactly shining democrats or leftwingers, but convenient US stooges the CIA was instructed to "remove" when their usefulness was over. Such is the case with Carlos Castillo Armas, a Guatemalan military officer who seized power in a United States-orchestrated coup in 1954 after helping to topple the legitimate president, Jacobo Arbenz, a progressive nationalist. Ditto with the Dominican Republic's Rafael Truijillo, a notorious crook and despot in his small nation, tolerated by the US while his rule was seen with approval by the American ruling elites, but quickly dispatched when the man became an albatross about the neck of Washington's policy planners. A similar cynical calculus applies to the killing of Italian PM Aldo Moro, an establishment Christian Democrat, and thereby an ally of the US, executed by the Red Brigades, a leftwing group heavily infiltrated by the CIA and Gladio elements.

Like the great, hopeful song by the Beatles, *Getting Better*, it finally took the economic and political might of Russia and China to join hands in the 21st century, to provide a serious challenge to counterbalance the West's traditional arrogance of superiority. The world's 85% can now stand side by side with BRICS and NAM, shoulder to shoulder, to proudly begin to replace their imposed, historical inferiority with a new page in humanity's annals. It won't be easy, nor happen overnigh, and there will be zig-zags and backslides. (As we write these lines [June 2016] BRICS is under heavy pressure, and the empire—ever resourceful and relentless—has already scored important strategic victories in Brazil and India, where pro-West regimes have replaced those nations' more progressive leaders.) When you've been told for 500 years you are less than dirt, it takes time to reach a critical mass of dignity and purpose. But it is happening and gaining speed, at a rate I never would have imagined, since arriving back in China in 2010.

The true Moral Majority can laugh in derision when the West pontificates that its sanctions are "isolating" Russia. They equally scoff at NATO's lame attempt to control China's regional relations by implementing America's Pivot to the Pacific (which also threatens Russia's eastern flank). The overwhelming majority of the world's 85% support Russia and China in their fight against Eurangloland. Thus, we truly live in a bipolar world: The unipolar West completely ignores the multipolar dreams and aspirations of the true Moral Majority.

[IMG 0064]

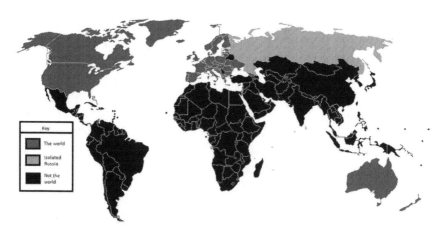

"Isolated" Russia in green and the West's invisible peoples in the countries marked in black. Together, they make up the True Moral Majority, 85% of humanity. Eurangloland is marked in cerulean, the remaining 15%.
(#66 Image by zerohedge.com)

Merkel is my sweetheart now, a veritable Obama slayer

I've got a crush on her now. She's my sweetheart for a day.

[IMG 0065]

Amazing. Only one news source is reporting the most earth shaking news about the US financed Ukraine fiasco - not the *BBC* and of course not the *New York Times* nor the *Washington Post* – all three ever faithful factotums to the Western Empire, but heck, even the somewhat liberal, mildly rebellious *Guardian* and *Al-Jazeera* are lining up to save the Imperial West and their black Caesar from the most humiliating revelation since the Crimea voted to skedaddle back into the embrace of Mother Russia: Angela Merkel has gone public that she refuses to support economic sanctions against her behemoth Eastern neighbor.

Only RT has the scoop of the year, along with another Western Memory Hole beauty, former German chancellor and cold warrior Helmut Schmidt, siding with Crimea's return to the warm embrace of Red Mamma. This of course after the brown shirt in the White House made a total fool of himself, barking at the moon that "we", meaning all of America's poodles in NATO, Germany included, were behind ever more severe economic sanctions against Russia. Well duh: natural gas, automobiles, and tens of billions of euro-rubles in reciprocal Russia-Germany trade, not to mention massive investments by Germany's leading industrialists across the great expanse in the Land of Bears.

This while Michelle and the girls are practicing taichi and feeding the Panda bears in Beijing, leaving POTUS (President of the United States) playing with his putz on the world stage. Clearly, Ms. Angela was waiting for the nuclear arms meetings to end and send Barak-O-Baby back on Air Force One before she dropped her diplomatic neutron bomb, to deftly deliver the proverbial knife in the back. This is so damning and such a monstrous humiliation for the executive fascist on Pennsylvania Avenue, exit stage right for every media outlet to the west of the Ural

Mountains, putting up their own Berlin Wall of silence and Newspeak for Empire. Shameful doesn't even begin to exonerate them for their craven cowardice. The problem is that for centuries, the West has been infected with a serious case of Russophobia and fear of its military and diplomatic potential around the world. Throw in communism in the USSR and it is hard to find a sane head in the West who can talk rationally about Russia, including liberals.

You can bet your bottom RMB that Chinese President Xi Jinping got a smoking hot diplogram put into his busy little hand, which must be plum worn out by now from all the billions in trade deals he's signed during his travels in Western Europe. This while BHO was simultaneously barnstorming Empire's European capitals to whip his vassal centurions into a rabid, mouth foaming rage of hatred against Vlad *The Hammer* Putin and mighty Russia. Well, Mighty Merkel just popped that Wizard of Oz hot air gas bag in a hurry.

I'll have to look up *schadenfreude* in Mandarin, because I know Xi will have a hard time sleeping, being overcome with joy. Not to mention keeping from rolling out of bed with gales of guffaws, for what happened in Berlin. Come to think of it, I'm feeling pretty giddy myself.

What Jeff J. Brown reads and researches to write
Reflections in Sinoland

[IMG 0066] *Deng Xiaoping is credited for saying "Seek truth from facts" (实事求是; shí shì qiú shi). He actually borrowed it from Mao Zedong, who in turn borrowed it from the façade of his alma mater, Hunan's First Teachers Training School, which in turn got it from the "Book of Han". When was this noble tome written? The year 111 AD. Sage advice from long, long ago. (#68 Image by doctordebee.com)*

People often ask what I read and research to write *Reflections in Sinoland*. Below is a list of all the internet resources I *currently* use. I say currently, because it is always evolving. Some drop off, some come (back) on the list. For example, I used to have <u>Consortium News</u>, it dropped off in the never ending ebb and flow of searching and researching the truth, as others came to the fore. Then just recently, an article cited column a couple of times. Now I'm putting it back on my list to see how it stacks up with what I'm currently looking at.

Naturally, I look at links within the articles I read, as well as using a search engine to find specific information. As can be noticed, I don't actively refer to many mainstream media (MSM) sources, but will refer to them when they are cited in articles. I'm more interested in learning how the world's people *outside* of Eurangloland (EU, US, Canada, Australia and New Zealand) perceive reality. After all, Eurangloland only represents 15% of humanity. All those dark skinned people outside of Western Empire are a staggering 85% of the human race. They are humanity's historical Moral Majority. In George Orwell's semi-autobiographical novel, *Burmese Days*, it was explained that all over Britain's empire across the globe, the world's non-white people were called niggers, be they Asian, African or Latin American. Another popular Western slur for the colored races was proudly shouted out by Joseph Conrad's metaphorical Kurtz, in *The Heart of Darkness*, divulging Western Empire's Final Solution,

Exterminate all the brutes!

It is these Dreaded Others' aspirations and voices that are driving the 21st century to a different place, rather than where the world has been for the last 500 years of racism, colonial exploitation, slavery and genocide. We have to hope they will be victorious. Otherwise, the Western Empire will surely drive the human race over a cliff of nuclear war and ecosystem meltdown. Sadly, the West's and especially America's model of grotesque, excessive resource consumption is being aped in middle class countries like China and Russia. For the sake of humanity's survival, we can only hope that BRICS and NAM can envisage more sustainable models of development and lifestyle.

This real possibility of a Moral Majority victory is much to the increasingly desperate chagrin of the 1%. This can be seen by their dictatorial excess with NATO and the CIA/MI6/DGSE/BND deep state in Ukraine, Venezuela, the Middle East and Africa, and the bellicose Pivot to China and Russia's eastern flank. Not to mention, it all being financed with staggering Mt. Everests of funny money sovereign debt that will*never* be paid back. In almost every case, it's all about controlling human and natural resources, principally pennies-a-day labor and hydrocarbons. Most of the Mainstream Western Media (MWM) works tirelessly and slavishly to protect the Princes of Power, by creating a propaganda bubble for all of us to suffocate in. Only by escaping this stifling Western disinformation fog machine can we discover the true reality of the world and its majority peoples.

Mind you, I have friends and colleagues who work in the MWM. They are good, intelligent people who do their jobs well. I like them and have a lot of respect for their talents and craft. But as in any corporate environment, their bosses and business owners send a clear message from on high, down the employee-departmental flow chart,

These are your boundaries. Do not go outside of them, if you wish to keep your job.

Or, as Upton Sinclair so pithily observed,

It is difficult to get a man to understand something, when his salary depends on his not understanding it.

My MWM friends have spouses and children, as well as medical and education costs to cover. Even as an international educator it is no different, there are limits to what I can teach. But, the main reason I got out of the corporate world, was to be able to write books like *44 Days* and a column like *Reflections in Sinoland*. At least up to now, it has not impinged on my job keeping ability, but that could always change.

In any case, whatever doubts one may have about the West's *Fox-CNN-NYT-Wapo* propaganda bubble can be dispelled by living outside it, as I have for most of the last 34 years, and then going back to the United States and talk to the people. **It is frighteningly surreal and shockingly evident how disinformed the overwhelming majority is, not only of the world outside America's boundaries, but in their own backyards.** It's only marginally better in Europe, where I also lived for years. It is not that they are uninformed. **It is that they are actively and aggressively disinformed by myriad intentional** omissions, wholesale distortions and outright lies, to keep everybody in line with the official Washington-London-Paris narrative, or as Noam Chomsky calls it, manufactured consent. An excellent example is the bull horn echo chamber about all the ersatz Russian invasions into Ukraine, replete with ridiculously phony photos or zero evidence at all. Ditto MH17, which all on-the-ground evidence indicates it was shot down by Ukrainian fighter planes. But in the West, it's all Putin-Russia-Putin. The headlines get blasted all through the MSM fog machine for a few days and it becomes the perceived truth, with more sanctions and war preparations based on lies. It happened for Iraq, World War II, the Spanish-American War and on and on, throughout history. The whole propaganda process is controlled with an iron fist by the Princes of Power, in obedient collusion with the MSM of the day. It was Nazi Joseph Goebbels who proved it right and said,

If you repeat a lie often enough, it becomes the truth.

It works with brutal efficiency and has been for millennia.

George Orwell did not write about the future in *1984* and in his many essays and journalist articles. He was writing about Western Empire's stranglehold on its people and control of the planet's natural and human resources with Perpetual War, as it was happening in *real time*. The ruling elite has greatly enhanced its control over us, since Orwell's death in 1950. People thought he was writing fiction. No. He was writing reality based, expository and descriptive pieces using fictitious settings. Orwell saw very clearly that 1984's Big Brother and Emmanuel Goldstein have been around as long as organized civilization itself. He had *no* idea just how far it would degenerate, thanks to technological advances being coopted by the 1%, those sociopaths and psychopaths who seize and keep power over everyone else. Again, this cooption of technology by the Princes of Power has been true since the dawn of humanity.

I predict that if the 1% are victorious in the 21st century, we will be looking back on another supposed fictitious novel, which in reality is a deadly accurate depiction of the present world. Whatever is left of humanity after environmental implosion and nuclear war, if there is anybody left to tell the story, they will not only recount *1984*, but Suzanne Collins'

Hunger Games trilogy as well. On a global scale, Eurangloland is Planet Earth's Capital and the world's majority 85% living across the globe, are the Capital's impoverished Districts, many of whose boundaries were drawn by the Capital itself during colonial times, and even today, in Palestine, Serbia, South Sudan, etc.

Too few people realize it today, but our Katniss Everdeen's, Peeta Mellark's, Gale Hawthorne's, Haymitch Abernathy's and Cinna's are Daniel Ellsberg, Karen Silkwood, Sibel Edmonds, Chelsea Manning, Julian Assange, Edward Snowden, Glenn Greenwald (and many, many more), as well as truth seekers such as John Pilger, Amy Goodman, Seymour Hersh, Naomi Klein, Ilan Pappé, not to mention countless others who toil in obscurity, I guess including myself.

Be smart. Study hard. Stay hopeful. Live real. Seek truth from facts.

Postscript: The United States just weighed in as having the 49th freest press in the world, behind Malta, Niger, Burkina Faso, El Salvador, Tonga, Chile and Botswana. You can rest assured this story will not see the light of day in the mainstream West. Stand tall, Americans, stand proud.

Alternative News, Information and Research Sources: Operation Get Smart

In 1807, Thomas Jefferson wrote,

Nothing can now be believed which is seen in a newspaper. Truth itself becomes suspicious by being put into that polluted vehicle. The real extent of this state of misinformation is known only to those who are in situations to confront facts within their knowledge with the lies of the day.

Great advice to us all, two centuries later, President Jefferson. The disinformation, propaganda and myth making have never stopped. So, quit flagellating yourself by wasting time accessing the mainstream media. You know they are marionettes for the One Percent, and that includes besides the Great Warhorses—CBS, NBC, ABC, and Fox—the supposedly more reputable PBS, NPR and BBC. When I stopped, I felt like I got off bad drugs. My mind cleared and I could think objectively again. At the end of the day, whose voice has the most credibility: the world's victimized 85% or the West's aggressor 15% (20% if you throw in vassal Japan, South Korea and the other usual suspects)?

Instead, use that time to read the following books, as weapons of truth to combat the Western Empire mind disease. All three are exhaustively researched and referenced. Like William Blake's cleansed Doors of Perception, they literally changed my life:

- *JFK and the Unspeakable*, by James W. Douglass. This was the American deep state's first great, home grown false flag, a coup d'état that changed the world for worse, much worse. Our slippery slope started here.
- *NATO's Secret Armies: Operation GLADIO and Terrorism in Western Europe*, by Daniele Ganser. A gripping, sordid account of how NATO has killed, assassinated, maimed and terrorized thousands of their own European citizens and leaders, while overthrowing a few more, and most assuredly still are.
- *Killing Hope*, by William Blum. It's all here, a detailed dirty laundry list of the CIA's endless coups, assassinations, psyops, (mainstream) propaganda, destabilization, running drugs, partnering with the Mafia, ad nauseam, across the four corners of the planet. The heart of the deep state.

My daily dose from A-Z is *Global Times, The Greanville Post, People's Daily, Press TV, RT, The Saker, teleSUR* and *Press TV*. For several, like *Paul Craig Roberts, American Conservative* and *ICH*, I get email alerts. They all get looked at in cycles, over the weeks and months. I'm still looking for alternative Indian and Brazilian websites in English, and I'm committed to finding one in South Africa, to fully cover BRICS. (All the following links are live on our online audiovisual concordance file, as explained earlier.)

Al Jazeera English – Live US, Europe, Middle East, Asia, Sports, Weather & Business News
The American Conservative
Antiwar.com
China Daily Website – Connecting China Connecting the World
China | South China Morning Post

chomsky.info : The Noam Chomsky Website (his website is always outdated, but he's all over the internet)

Chris Hedges, Columnist – Truthdig

ClubOrlov

http://www.commondreams.org/

https://consortiumnews.com/

CounterPunch: Tells the Facts, Names the Names

Deena Stryker

http://www.democraticunderground.com/

Fort Russ

Trends Monthly – Trends Research Institute

Fire Dog Lake (I contribute to this website)

http://www.4thmedia.org/

Globaltimes.cn | Latest China, world news and business stories, comments from the GlobalTimes

Global Research

The Greanville Post (I am a senior contributing editor)

Hidden Harmonies China Blog | 中国博客 探索和谐

INFORMATION CLEARING HOUSE

Russia & India Report: Top Stories

The Intercept

www.theinternationalreporter.org

http://landdestroyer.blogspot.com/

The Journal | Articles & Archives | Life+Outdoors | Field Notes (great site for science, history, etc.)

MintPress News | Independent, non-partisan journalism

The Nation

New Eastern Outlook

Oped News (I have contributed to this website)

Oriental Review | Open Dialogue Research Journal

Outlookindia.com

Paul Craig Roberts – Official Homepage

People's Daily Online – Home Page

www.thephaser.com

Asia Times Online :: the best of Pepe Escobar

Press TV

Réseau Voltaire (in French, the English version is below)

RT

Russia Insider: politics and news
Sputnik international
teleSUR
This Modern World
TomDispatch
Truthout
The Vineyard of the Saker (I write a monthly column here)
Voltaire Network
Worldbulletin – News on Turkey, Middle East, Muslim World, Latest News, Culture&Islamic History Worldbulletin News
World Socialist Web Site – Marxist analysis, international working class struggles & the fight for socialism
Xinhua – English.news.cn
新华网_传播中国报道世界
http://www.zerohedge.com/

While it is not strictly politics, to keep up on the latest in Science and Technology, I read ZME Science almost daily.

Chapter 3

China vs. the West: Planet Earth's Titanic, 21st Century Wrestling Match for Humanity's Future

[IMG 0067]

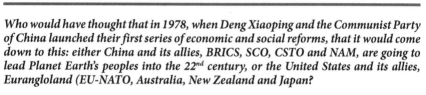

Who would have thought that in 1978, when Deng Xiaoping and the Communist Party of China launched their first series of economic and social reforms, that it would come down to this: either China and its allies, BRICS, SCO, CSTO and NAM, are going to lead Planet Earth's peoples into the 22nd century, or the United States and its allies, Eurangloland (EU-NATO, Australia, New Zealand and Japan?

Never could two overarching visions be so diametrically opposed. This titanic duel between two broadly different systems of governance, social criteria, economic and financial policy will determine the fate of our species. May the best side win.

Be careful what you wish for boys...

I sent a copy of my first book, *44 Days* to an old author friend of mine. For the life of me, I do not know how we have kept in touch since about 1983, when we were marooned together in the Nairobi airport for the better part of a 24-hour news cycle, playing chess and drinking beer. We've only seen each other one other time, in Paris a few years later, as I recall, when he was teaching or doing research there. Yet, after those quirky coincidences and more than a generation later, I have this innate feeling that if we do ever see each other again, that it would be like Chronos reaching down from Olympus and turning off the cosmic pause button; we wouldn't miss a beat.

I emailed him and jokingly said,

44 Days has departed the center of the Universe.

I went on to explain that China's Post Office only tracks to the border and would he please do me the courtesy of letting me know it made it across the big pond safely.

He just as humorously replied back,

Thanks for sending. I'll let you know if it makes it out to the bankrupt provincial periphery of the Chinese universe

I was impressed because it sounded like he had some understanding of China's historic perception of the world, with ever more distant concentric circles from the Middle Kingdom, something I discuss in <u>44 Days</u>. Here was my response,

Funny you should mention that. While China's perceptions of its place in the Universe are surely hyperbole, your personification of America is sadly not. Sovereign debt is the cancer, the hubris and the hallmark of overreaching empire, from the Romans to Napoleon to the 21st century. Our pint sized

French general said creditors call the shots and debtors do their bidding. One of these days in the not too distant future, the US will get that Sinocall on the White House red phone - to the financial frequency of 1.2 terabucks - Tomahawk missiles and the DOD's Air-Sea Battle[1] plans be damned.

Meanwhile, back in Middle America, your average citizens are getting ready to watch television,

Hey Buford, go microwave the buttered popcorn. Bubba, ice down the brewskies and brothers, let's gather around the Jumbotron, 'cuz we're ready to rumble! It's time to buckle up for another anus clenching trans-Pacific adventure, big dogs. To use the vernacular of A Clockwork Orange, Time *for some reality based, realpolitik* Rollerball *me droogs, real horrorshow like. China versus America in a 21st century throw down.*

Be careful what you wish for boys…

[IMG 0068]

Is the West really ready for a 21st century rumble with China? (#69 Image by Wikipedia)

1- http://yalejournal.org/2013/06/12/ who-authorized-preparations-for-war-with-china/

BRICS and NAM or Soylent Green?

A sci-fi classic, Soylent Green. *In a hellish, overpopulated dystopian world, humans are killed and processed into the staple diet for the citizens, to stave off mass starvation. As with many creative expressions throughout history, life imitating art is often incredibly prescient* **[IMG 0069].**

History will look back on 2014 and consider it as one of the most momentous in modern history. Two thousand fourteen is the centennial anniversary of the March of Folly, the great European colonial war that the US just couldn't miss out on – World War I, which does not escape my attention. This year will go down in the history books as the Anti-World War, the Great Eurmerican Unraveling. It may be looked upon as the starting point when, after 500 years of relentless, Western colonialism, with its and human and natural resource exploitation, began to come undone. Call it the Grand Awakening.

Mind you, it is not going to happen overnight, and the suzerainty of the 1% over the 99% is as old as organized civilization itself, maybe even going back as far as 8,000BC, with the salt marsh Arabs of the Tigris-Euphrates delta. But for sure, this social stratification and exploitation started one fine day in Mesopotamia, China or the Indus Valley, around 5,000BC, when there was surplus agricultural production to be *managed*, or more to the point, appropriated by the cleverest of the A-Type personalities in the crowd (let's be honest, they are the sociopaths and psychopaths amongst us). These megalomaniacs became and still are to this day, the vast majority of humankind's political leaders. Everything was fine as long as there were surpluses. But the inevitable drought, damaging flood, fire, other natural disaster or human foible, like war, created a food shortage. That's when the ugliness, the evil side of civilization began to manifest itself – and it has continued to do so millions of times over the vast panoply of human history. It's the old, *what's mine is mine because of who I am and because of who you are, what's yours is mine too.*

This is an ancient and well-worked system of 1% vs. 99% exploitation, going back for millennia,

The Goddess Inanna brought the arts of civilization from the God of Wisdom, Enki of Eridu, but it was like a Pandora's Box:

(Inanna said) Here are the delights of society, exquisite craftsmanship, beautiful clothes, the arts of sex and music. But civilization has a darker side, which has to be accepted along with the good. The art of being mighty, the art of being kind, the art of straightforwardness, the art of deceit; the art of kingship, justice and the enduring crown; the resounding note of a musical instrument, the rejoicing of the heart; the kindling of strife, the plundering of cities, the setting up of lamentation, fear, pity, terror - all of this is civilization - and you must take it all, you cannot refuse any of it. And once taken, you cannot give it back.

This is quoted from *The Epic of Gilgamesh* (circa 2,700 BC, and humanity's oldest extant book), as recited in the movie documentary, *Iraq: the Cradle of Civilization* and narrated by Michael Wood, Legacy Films, telecast by BBC in 1991.

Needless to say, the great Mesopotamian cultures cyclically rose like a Phoenix to greatness, only to crash into burning oblivion. By 300AD, the Fertile Crescent was turned once and for all into sand dunes and desert.

Mr. Wood goes on to observe in this excellent thought provoking six-part series that,

There is a growing and profound disquiet in the West, a feeling that the Western way of life itself is no longer supportable, morally or practically, because of pollution, environmental destruction and the continuing exploitation of the mass of humanity.

The great question for the next generation is: are the values of the West alone, enough to guarantee the continuing health of the planet? For these (values) are individualistic, competitive, acquisitive, always pushing outwards, never happy in an empty room. And yet, they hold in their hands the future of the planet. The West seems to have reached that point in its development when, if a civilization is not to decline, it must transform itself by learning from others.

Obviously, this penetrating documentary series is not going to be used as lesson content in the vast majority of the West's high schools and universities. Heaven forbid if the next generation might dare to envision a saner, more rational and equitable paradigm, than the West's rapacious, global colonialism.

The *empty room* bit is based on a quote from the great French philosopher, Blaise Pascal, that the problem with Westerners (the only people he knew), is that they cannot just sit in a quiet room and be happy, i.e., they have to fill it up with materialist *Fluff and Stuff* to achieve life's contentment. If you are American, this is the truth on resource-inhaling steroids: expand that quiet room into a vacuous, suburban McMansion and fill it with jet skis, gas guzzling SUVs and an endless mountain of soulless, plastic contraptions, to reduce one's physical exertion to the absolute minimum possible. Don't forget the All You Can Eat Buffets. And what the heck, now that we've spent our home equity loan on tons of mindless toys, it's time to max out the MasterCard.

Western Europe and Angloland are not much better. Replace the McMansion with a McFlat or a McHouse and the SUV with a Berliner. OK, we'll let the Israelis, Empire's military garrison in the Land of Islam, do their version of the very same, as well as America's occupied lands, Japan and South Korea. But the other 85% of the world's masses, those Dreaded Other 6.1 billion people in Asia, Africa and Central/South America? They are still White Man's World Bank/IMF/US dollar colonies. Sorry tawny skinned boys and girls, you know what the French say: *allez-vous faire foutre*, meaning, *go screw yourselves*. (You give and we take).

Which is why 2014 is shaping up to be so momentous and worthy of Mr. Michael Wood's comment that,

The West seems to have reached that point in its development when, if a civilization is not to decline, it must transform itself by learning from others.

Enter China and Russia specifically, the five-nation BRICS and more generally, the 120+17 country Non-Aligned Movement (NAM). Within NAM is a whole constellation of anti-Western hope: BRICS, SCO (Shanghai Cooperation Organization), CSTO (Collective Security Treaty Organization), EAEU (Eurasian Economic Union), OAU (Organization of African Unity), ALBA (Alternativa Bolivariana para las Américas) and CELAC (Community of Latin American and Caribbean States). First, we celebrated the fall of classic colonialism after World War II. Unfortunately, the 1% are a crafty, tenacious bunch and nothing less than 101% of the Pale Blue Dot's wealth will do. Thus Empire's Crown Jewels and Dutch East India Companies of the world have thus been replaced by Western financial and corporate neocolonialism.

However, the Dreaded Other - these countries and their peoples (essentially, everybody on Planet Earth except NATO, Angloland and the US client state Asian Tigers) are starting to figure things out. Yes, they are shamelessly chasing capitalism's untenable business model of *Unlimited Extraction for Unlimited Consumption for Unlimited Growth*. There is no other model to consider, because the West has ruthlessly destroyed any world leader and their country's socialist/non-capitalist system, before having a chance to prove its viability. About the only country which has manage to pull it off long term is Cuba. I'm convinced the only reason they have been able to survive Western Empire's 55-year (and counting) onslaught of attempted destruction and sabotage, is because it's a large sized island. Even Hitler took pause to try to invade Britain. Islands are special. More recently, Eritrea in Africa, as well as Venezuela, Ecuador, Bolivia, Argentina and Nicaragua in Latin America, are carrying the torch.

It is from among these Dreaded Other, landlocked and otherwise, with their millennia of pre-Western, pre-capitalist experiences - and yes, we have to consider their good, bad and ugly - for us to find new ways to save humanity from itself. Given that the Western Antarctic ice sheet is a goner and all that it implies for the future (much of Earth's coastal cities will be flooded), I'm not too optimistic for my children and grandchildren. But clearly to all who want to see, if Mother Earth's 1% wins the probable World War III for water, energy and food resources, the entire human race will be subjected to a life-imitating-art, panglobal hellhole of *Hunger Games* cum *V for Vendetta* cum *1984* cum *A Clockwork Orange*.

One only has to read the tea leaves. Case in point: the West's Assassin-in-Chief, Obama gave his May 23rd, 2014 *Drone Speech* (yes, that's what they are calling it) at the National Defense University, where they eat, drink, sleep, dream and plan for world domination. Less than a week later, we had the Big O's May 28th US Memorial Day talk at West Point Military Academy (It's being called his *Post-Iraq/Afghanistan Foreign Policy Speech*), whose graduates will fight the Dreaded Other from one of America's 1,000 military bases overseas, or join one of Obama's 134 secret armies, euphemistically called Special Ops. Then there is of course the option of destroying BRICS and NAM countries via the CIA, NSA, MI6, DGSE, BND, USAID, NED, and the whole Western alphabet soup of espionage, sabotage and what is euphemistically called *regime change*, i.e., installing pliant puppet governments that will sell out to the 1% and the West's neocolonial system of resource extraction.

It is clear as crystal where the West and its satrap states are taking us. Empires throughout history reach a point where every question, every problem, every rebuttal, can only be answered by aggressive and expansive militarism, and the West already crossed this Rubicon of Oblivion years ago. Just the location of President *I'm really good at killing people* Obama's two speeches says it all: military schools. The West is determined to subjugate the world's human resources and dominate its natural ones, through military might and violence, on an unprecedented, global scale. During the centuries of Roman Empire, a behind-closed-doors shibboleth became common currency among the ongoing succession of tyrannical despots, including Cato, Caligula and Justinius,

Let them hate us, so long as they fear us.

We can look back at previous emperors, be they Egyptian pharaohs, Mesopotamian, Mesoamerican, European, African or Pacific Island royalty; Roman Caesars, Mongolian Warlords and Chinese Keepers of the Heavenly Mandate. They all only had influence over their geographical spheres, but no further. Since Christopher Columbus opened the floodgates of genocide, slavery and colonialism of the world's dark skinned peoples, Eurmerica came close to developing a worldwide model of resource exploitation. But the Great White Race could not manage or afford to militarize three-fourths of the world's surface area, nor like today, did they have the technology to do so. As soon as all the dark skinned peoples of the world began to rise up after World War II, the days of classical resource extraction colonialism were numbered. Again, the 1% are a relentless and greedy bunch. When the colonialist model collapsed in the last half of the 20th century, they just moved up the food chain. Instead of "owning colonies", they are keeping their system in place via the levers of financial power, with the World Bank/IMF/US$ FIRE (Finance-Insurance-Real Estate). The other tactic replacing good old fashioned colonialism is the violence of militarism, coupled with the sabotage and subterfuge of Deep State machinations (coups, assassinations, color revolutions, regime change). This happens in a heartbeat to any country that so much as hints at a possible non-capitalist, non-aligned way of taking care of their people and international relations more equitably. One only has to look at Greece, Serbia, Venezuela, Cuba, Ecuador, Bolivia, Ukraine, Syria, Libya, Iraq, Afghanistan, Nigeria, Tibet, Xinjiang and on and on, to see all methods in action.

Xi Jinping and Vladimir Putin are far from perfect and just as susceptible to the hubris of unrestrained power, but what we are seeing happen between Baba Beijing, Russia and slowly joining them in the fray, India and Iran, is encouraging. The Chinese have an old saying: the only way to kill a snake is to cut off its head. For the Western Empire, with NATO, Angloland and its numerous client states such as Japan, South Korea, Israel and the Gulf Kingdoms, its reptilian head rests in Washington, DC.

Everybody knows that BRICS and NAM could decapitate this Western Hydra in a New York City minute. All they have to do is collectively replacing their use of the US dollar as the world's reserve currency and stop using it for cross border settlement. It is commonly acknowledged in the mainstream media and by consensus experts, that America's ability to maintain its global empire is predicated on the US dollar being the preeminent world currency. History supports this with facts. Empires do not survive long when their currency becomes debased: Roman coinage, the Italian fiorino, Dutch gulden, Spanish real, British pound and since the 20th century, the US dollar.

[IMG 0070] *A timeline of the world's dominant trade currencies. What goes up, always comes down (#71 Image by zerohedge.com)*

World history has also shown countless times, when an empire feels backed into a corner or believes that it has no other options to maintain its control, it often resorts to war. It is very conceivable that Western Empire and Israel might make a final lunge to maintain their global hegemony, by starting World War III. In that case, nuclear war is a real possibility and it would spell the extinction of the human race, even if H-bomb equipped BRICS and NAM countries don't even fire a shot. This is because even if the American military is right and it can destroy Russia's biggest cities in a lightning strike, the whole human race will still die anyway, due to photosynthesis shutting down, in a decades-long, post holocaust nuclear winter. The human race will end up like the survivors in Cormack McCarthy's book, *The Road*. Those who survived the nuclear war

are reduced to scavenging for seeds and leftover food in abandoned houses, as well as feasting on each other as cannibals, in order to stay alive.

[IMG 0071] Soylent Green's grim truth

So, we are currently seeing China, Russia, BRICS and NAM delicately playing an historical game of Chicken Chess, riding out the curve to reach their point of diminishing marginal returns, getting stronger, while the Empire slowly rots from the

inside. That rot is based on photocopying mountains of fiat money, to keep its Worldwide Wehrmacht running. But eventually, this house of cards is going to come crashing down, as all Empires have, from the Fertile Crescent to Pre-Columbian Mesoamerica, the Qing Dynasty and in between. And we all know that will be when WWIII gets *justified* by sundry false flag operations to ignite the flame.

The only middle road scenario that might play out, our only hope really, is that a significant American satrap state, such as Japan or Germany, swallows the truth pill, stands up and tells the world they want to get off the West's high speed rail to Hades. This might cause enough of a wakeup call among the rest of the Empire client states, to settle on a solution which is less than panglobal war. Sort of a,

OK, we the Western Empire admit our addiction to racism, colonialism and empire, and are ready to go through the 12-step program to achieve rational resource utilization.

Unfortunately, this is highly unlikely, knowing that the Western Empire's *Lunge to Hell* is racing at breakneck speed, and no country wants to get crushed in the process of trying to jump off, or be blamed for starting WWIII. Not to mention the historical pattern is not good: scores of empires have run off the civilizational cliff over the last 5,000 years, in fact they all have eventually.

But in the 21st century, we can still hold out for hope. The main reason is that all of us, the 1% and 99% alike, even without a cataclysmic nuclear war, are rapidly facing the prospects of an uninhabitable planet, as Anthropocene Era climate change rapidly brings down Gaia's earthly ecosystem. Then again, the destruction of Mother Earth is of no real consequence to the 1%, because they can pay for their own safe haven islands of environmental balance, while the rest of humanity cannibalizes itself.

In another instance of life imitating art, we can all ponder the wonderfully dystopian, futuristic movie, 1973's *Soylent Green*, previously mentioned, where in 2022, heavy machinery scoops up mobs of starving, overpopulated masses, only to be turned into health food to feed the very same masses. I can close my eyes and envision later in the 21st century, Charleston Heston's hero, *Detective Thorn*, Thorn being a great metaphor for pricking or deflating an overextended gasbag, à la *The Wizard of Oz*. He has seen the good life behind the guarded and armored walls of the murdered one-percenter, Joseph Cotton's *William R. Simonson* (eerily close to the real life vulture capitalist, William E.

Simon). As the story reaches its final scene, my heroic Agent Thorn runs down Pennsylvania Avenue, screaming,

Soylent Green is people, Soylent Green is people!

[IMG 0071] *The 1% would happily dispose of a big chunk of the 99% and turn them into to Soylent Green food, if they could, and if it was necessary to maintain their grip on Mother Earth's human and natural resources. Pictured here from the same said movie is a "riot control" team, harvesting 99% flesh to feed back to the survivors (#72 Image by files.abovetopsecret.com)*

In my version of the climax, Thorn can't shout it long enough. Smart, robotic *facebomb* drones, the 21st century's answer to the French guillotine, are monitoring the masses below. They overhear his frightful disclosure of lamentation for the human race; the closest *aerobot* swoops down on Thorn at supersonic speed, cleanly atomizing his head from the neck up.

Empire's Judge, Jury and Executioner.

The End.

Baba Beijing's Belly Laugh Felt Round the World

The Smart Money's on China's Seat at the Head of the 21st Century Roundtable

China's leadership includes the Communist Party of China (CPC) and the many thousands of government representatives, from the 300-person Central Committee, which is at the pinnacle of a very broad hierarchal administrative pyramid, down to the level of village mayors in rural areas across this vast, continent sized country. Because this massive system of governance maintains a firm, patriarchal mein, due to 2,500 years of Confucian thought imbuing all levels of Chinese society, I affectionately call this powerful, mindful system *Baba Beijing*. *Baba* in Chinese, as in many other languages means *father*.

[IMG 0072]

The image that drives American pundits, policy makers and Princes of Power to foaming-at-the-mouth rage: The emblem of the People's Republic of China.

Caucasian pundits and the usual gaggle of media toadies are kowtowing like the craven Mandarins they innately are, to help the Princes of Power maintain the Washington-London-Paris consensus. We the people are supposed to cower under the shock and awe of this *Official Western Narrative*. This system of crowd control has worked like a hypnotic talisman for the better part of 500 years: slavery, colonialism, wars of lust for lucre, fascism, corporatocracy, market bubbles and the gang rape of Mother Nature. This rigged casino table that guarantees usurious house profits for the 1% has recently and forever been tilted in the opposite direction towards the 99%. It was done with the stroke of an oriental calligraphy brush and there is no turning back now.

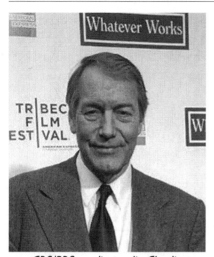

CBS/PBS media toadie Charlie Rose has made a career putting an authoritative face on the lies and crimes of the empire.

The usual Western denial, rationalization and official silence are surrounding the October 13th editorial in China's official press organ, *Xinhua*: _U.S. fiscal failure warrants a de-Americanized world_. It is a damning, honest and unvarnished account of the West's shameful and cowardly conduct. This commentary justly lampoons the buffoonish, Ho-Ho the clown antics inside the Washington beltway, with the neocon White House and its corporate Hessians in the halls of statecraft, making utter fools of themselves. Tang Danlu is the editor of A De-Americanized World. In true Chinese fashion for the appreciation of deep history, Mr. Tang harks back to the United States' long suffering Pax America. We can add to this perceptive comment on what ails our Pale Blue Dot, that this global Monroe Doctrine is nothing but a geopolitical battering ram. It was handed over to the United States by the United Kingdom's Pax Britannica. In both cases, it was and is a grand plan for exploiting the Earth's resources and majority dark skinned peoples. All those natural resources are rightfully owned by this global majority, not the power elite's.

The Chinese know a thing or two about historical Western and Japanese fascism. The West's 1% and their satraps, who pass and sign their pre-packaged laws and regulations with Mont Blanc, 18-carat, diamond studded styluses, in order to justify their pillaging. China to this day bemoans their *century of humiliation*, when, from the 1840s, until liberation in 1949, American, European and Japanese colonialists plied the Middle Kingdom with opium, and tapped her resources and impoverished citizens like an overworked, underfed whore. Mr. Yan Fu was a turn-of-the-20th century Chinese scholar and celebrated translator of Charles Darwin, Thomas Huxley, Adam Smith, John Stuart

Mill and Herbert Spencer. He later was a political activist in the 1895 Gongche Shangshu movement, demanding, in part, a China rid of foreign exploitation. Yan Fu summed up bitterly what billions of people around the world empirically already know all too well,

The European race's last three hundred years of evolutionary progress have all come down to nothing but four words: selfishness, slaughter, shamelessness *and* corruption.

[IMG 0073] *The West forced opium on China for a hundred years, creating endemic poverty and starvation, while bringing the country's population growth to a slow crawl.*

Sitting here in China, thousands of kilometers from and midway between the bipolar lunacy of the United States and its shamefully spineless NATO allies in Europe, it is a sad spectacle to watch, like some nightmarish Beijing opera with a libretto written by Hades. Westerners' blind, official denial of *A De-Americanized World* is just another manifestation of their five century history of hubris and megalomania. Journalist Tang Danlu did not write his editorial all by himself in a dark corner down in the basement of Xinhua's headquarters. Baba Beijing would not have allowed it to be released, unless it was tacitly acknowledged at the highest levels of governance. Baba Beijing is too paternal and perceptive about its international relations to do otherwise.

A few years back, Baba Beijing, through various press releases and commentaries like *A De-Americanized World*, began a subtle campaign to reduce their dependence on the US dollar for trade, and to beef up the credibility of the RMB, China's currency, in international markets.[1] Royal Flush Russia, being a natural resources behemoth, was keen to get the ball rolling too, not to mention Big Kahuna agricultural commodities baron, Brazil. For the last five years, the Official Western Narrative has been pooh-poohing and scoffing at the notion that the West's ace of spades, the US dollar as the world's reserve and trade settlement currency, could ever be considered anything but.

The world's dominant narrative, the Washington-London-Paris consensus, got out its media dog whistle to call their pompom press posse to attention. The West's mainstream media (MSM) went to work to relegate this heinous, heretical idea straight down Orwell's Memory Hole (this is the chute in the novel, *1984*, which delivered all embarrassing news and information into a giant incinerator, where it would be permanently expunged from the collective consciousness).

The United States bullied and bought off allies to refrain from signing non-dollar, cross border, currency swaps for trade settlement. Others were more than ready to head east. These accords were signed with Baba Beijing, behind closed doors and with little fanfare, in order to avoid Washington's wrath, the world's supposed unipolar, superpower. My-oh-my, how fast the geopolitical zeitgeist can change. The King of the Jungle was and is turning into a paper tiger and friends and foes alike sense it. The West talks the talk and the rest of the world is rolling up its collective shirt sleeves and walking the walk. Over the last few years, these RMB currency swaps have become all the rage, even with America's most subservient European, Asian and Middle Eastern vassals. What used to be done furtively is now splashed on the front pages of Western newspapers, since years of official and media denial have failed miserably. Baba Beijing's persistent, patient diplomacy has normalized currency swaps into the mainstream and these deals are just too big to ignore.

[IMG 0074] *A rainbow of Maos is rapidly gaining trade settlement status at the expense of greenback Franklins.*

Iacta alea est (the die is cast) and the West still does not get it. Tang Danlu was the one who picked up his calligraphy pen and wrote one of the most important realpolitik editorials of the decade, a veritable shot across the bow of the Washington-London-Paris consensus, and like the ghost of Yan Fu, he had plenty of historical and timely reasons to write it. But rest assured, ever paternalistic Baba Beijing was standing there in his office, glowing with pride, like a gentle, Confucian *laoshi*, or teacher, chuckling with a belly laugh, and giving him a smiling, encouraging pat on the back.

The 21st century marches on. Head East and hop on board. You can't miss the signs if you care to look.

1- *BRIC summit may focus on reducing dollar dependence:*

2- *http://chinadaily.com.cn/bizchina/2009-06/16/content_8287812.htm.*

Baba Beijing Is Sitting in the Senkaku Islands Catbird Seat

Note: a catbird seat is slang for being in an enviable, unrivaled position, usually in a competitive situation.

The Usual Mainstream Media Suspects

You've come to the right place to get the real lowdown about Baba Beijing claiming an air defense identification zone (ADIZ) over the Diaoyudao (In Chinese)/Senkaku Islands (In Japanese). Under the iron fist of the Washington-London-Paris consensus, the mainstream media's (MSM) pusillanimous reporting is right on cue, with their very selective spoon feeding around exactly what the Princes of Power don't want you to know. When headlines from supposedly hard hitting journalistic websites like Al-Jazeera are shouting, *US trying to cool East China Sea dispute* - yeah right, with gasoline - it's a disgrace to civilized society. [1]Al –Jazeera suggests that the US stepping in and getting in China's face over a Sino-Japanese dispute, is an act of "keeping it cool".

These specks of land go way back. China claims them from the 14th century, as they do much of the South China Sea, based on ancient ship wrecks in these expansive waters. Fair enough, this is accepted evidence when countries arbitrate through the United Nations Convention on the Law of the Sea (UNCLOS). Japan controlled them from 1895 until its defeat in WWII. The US then administered them until 1972, whereupon it "gave" control of the Diaoyudao/Senkakus "back" to Japan. This evidence can of course also be used during negotiations to present under the UNCLOS framework. About the same time, it was discovered that this tiny archipelago of eight islets might have some serious oil reserves. Thus, the manifest interest in who controls their resources.[2] Just follow the money. A key point unmentionable in Western newspeak is that Japan long ago established an Air Defense Identification Zone (ADIZ) over these disputed islands, which even China respected. An ADIZ is where a country publically states that a certain airspace is of strategic interest to it, and it requests that any other country flying through it, radio to identify themselves. Since Japan and China both stake a claim to the same territory, then Baba Beijing is only doing what any country's leadership worthy of the name would do: they are adding precedent to their arbitration dossier for the UNCLOS.

And it's not just China and Japan. Taiwan also claims them, but they are staying out of the fray for right now. China yearns for the day Taiwan returns to the motherland, thus fulfilling a huge geographical lacuna for China's Heavenly Mandate. The United States is of course goading Japan, its biggest Asian vassal state, to stake its claim. This is in tandem with the 1954 U.S. and Japan Mutual Defense Assistance Agreement.[3] If Japan gets attacked, then for the US, it's tantamount to an attack on American soil. Ditto for South Korea.

[IMG 0075] Map of Senkaku Islands / South China Sea

China's official map of the Diaoyudao, encased in the red box. They are nested between China, Taiwan and the chain of Japanese islands called Ryukyu.

Air-Sea Battle, aka The Pivot, aka Rebalancing America's Military Resources

Why, you might ask, is Uncle Sam looking to spit in Baba Beijing's eye? Well, hadn't you heard? You may want to sit down or pull over the car before you read on. *The United States is preparing for war against the world's second biggest economy*, and no, that's not hyperbole. America's fascist neocons, like termites in rotted wood, have infiltrated every root and branch of America's bureaucracy, including the Pentagon. War preparations began percolating in the 1990s and in 2009 it was made official policy. It became White House Cabinet level policy in 2010, when it was given the imprimatur of Robert Gates, the Bush/Obama Secretary of War, and further reinforced in 2010 by his replacement, Leon Panetta. The Joint Chief of Staff's war preparations are officially called *Air-Sea Battle* (ASB).[4] Through all this, Obama, as Commander-in-Chief, has completely let the US military run rabid with these now concrete war plans, and has not bothered to conduct a review, nor has asked Congress to do the same. This is default by the highest levels of willful neglect.

The only finger the White House has lifted was to announce *the pivot*, in November 2011, Orwellian Newspeak for the much more martial Air-Sea Battle (ASB). America's pivot is the plan to move 60% of its entire blue water navy off the coast of China. Air Sea Battle is a plan of war officially sanctioned by the US military to attack China from the air and from the ocean. ASB is not a deterrent, but a real live plan to defeat China in a hot war. As a result, the Pentagon's budget is being reallocated in real time, taking away money from the Army and actually building a fleet, two to date, of 55 planned Littoral Combat Ships (LCS), to be able to invade the shallow waters of the People's Republic of China.

I attended the US Embassy Marine Ball in Beijing on Veterans Day. US Marines Lieutenant General Terry G. Robling, Commander of the Pacific Marine Forces was the honored, ranking host. He talked about *a rebalancing of our military resources* to the Pacific, which is now the newest Newspeakian permutation for Air-Sea Battle, since even *the pivot* sounds too dramatic, too precipitous. Listening to Lt. Gen. Robling, he described the Air-Sea Battle plan, like so much as moving yard fertilizer from one wall of the garage to the other. This, while the United States is bringing in the majority of the world's mightiest naval war fleet to the shores of China and along Russia's eastern flank, to back up the ASB invasion,

Hey guys, no big deal, really, it has nothing to do with our plans to attack China… Seriously.

While attending the US Embassy Marine Ball, all the invited Chinese and Asian military officers in the large audience kept a stiff upper lip, but like me, they surely knew every detail of America's pivot and ASB. These green, blue and brown uniforms had to show no reaction, but I savored a wan Cheshire smile on my knowing rictus. While General Robling was explaining it all, it was like some cartoon moment in Dr. Strangelove's war room, but all the adversaries were sitting together, notebooks and sterling silver Sheaffer fountain pens in hand, busily writing it all down, so they could explain it all to their generals back home. Talk about sticking it in someone's face for a big whiff.

[IMG 0076] Dr Strangelove movie poster.

Only this time it's not the USSR, but China. wikipedia.org

Everybody and their dead dog knows about Air-Sea Battle, except 99% of Americans

Of course Baba Beijing doesn't need Edward Snowden's good offices to know all this nutty, nincompoop nonsense. They surely have the formerly top secret ASB plan in PowerPoint and Prezi presentations, on every computer and server in the People's Liberation Army (PLA). Talk about a bugle call. The Pentagon is if nothing else incompetent. You would be too if you were one of the planet's biggest bureaucracies, apparently answerable to no one, spending more on war than the next ten countries combined. The US war machine is a law unto itself. This is not a criticism of America's military, just a statement of observable fact.

Air-Sea Battle and its variant synonyms have gotten scant attention in the West, which is exactly how the Lords of Loot want it. Haven't read much about it? I think I remember seeing it once in a New York Times article, bottom of page 57, sandwiched between the Prozac and Wellbutrin ads. Sorry you missed it. But make no mistake, it's happening, and Obama will not bring his war-mongering Joint Chiefs of Staff to heel. This latest trickery is a one-percenter's double digit cash cow, hedge fund dream, and Mr. O is their loyal butler. Anyway, what the hell, after America's smashing victories in Southeast Asia, Lebanon, Iraq and Afghanistan, why not make it a full house of failure? *Defeat*, of course being the word no one dares utter, in spite of the painfully obvious possibility.

A Changed Perspective

All this critical historical and background information really changes one's perceptions, doesn't it? Thank goodness for alternative news venues like *The Greanville Post, The Saker, Press TV, RT and teleSUR*. With these information sources and other similar ones, one can talk intelligently about current events at the dinner table and around the water cooler, the latter applying only if you're lucky enough to have a middle class job in the West these days. Yet, there is nary a Western word about why China is feeling the need to push back in the face of such unprecedented military buildup. Peruse the Western media and it's all about Baba Beijing *being rash, not thinking things through* and *biting off more than they can chew*. Other denigrating sound bites talk of *diplomatic fallout, questions over China's capabilities* and *having miscalculated*. Seriously? Three thousand years of continuous history, the world's pending economic and political superpower of the 21st century and Baba, who spends sleepless nights fretting over the Heavenly Mandate, is *just winging it*? The West's bought and paid for satraps in Europe and Asia may be fooled, but the vast majority of the world's people, from BRICS on down, know the score, and who's winning this percolating, tactical and strategic battle royal.

For China, part of it is, of course, posturing for the public, both at home and abroad. Baba Beijing is campaigning hard to promote and see through to success China's just announced 3rd Plenum platform. Since the dawn of written history, nationalism has proven to work like a charm in the *God, King and Country* department - East or West. Thus, splashing all over the national press that Baba is giving a poke in the eye to the world's self-designated policeman is just what the doctor ordered, to help rally their 1.3 billion citizens to support their new and ambitious development and economic programs.

[IMG 0077] *Was Bob Dylan's song, Neighborhood Bully, a prescient, subliminal reference to the USA?*

Dylan's Neighborhood Bully and the World's Godfather, Marlon Brando Style

The world's policeman: When Bob Dylan's *Infidels* album came out in 1983, I always thought his song, *Neighborhood Bully*, was a stinging denouncement of Israel's colonialist genocide of the Palestinian people. Come to find out, I was off key to the tune of 180 degrees. *Neighborhood Bully* is actually Mr. Zimmerman's stinging denouncement of anybody on planet Earth who has the temerity to criticize Israel's colonialist genocide of the Palestinian people. Sorry about that Bob ol' boy. Writing this chapter got me to thinking about this song and how it relates to the here and now. Today, Dylan's lyrical refrain perfectly colors America, writ large on the global stage. For sure the *world's policeman* is a total whitewash of geopolitical reality. Even *bully* these days can't begin to articulate America's slaughter of millions of Muslims, starting in the 1990 Gulf War. No, the United States incarnate these days is more like Francis Ford Coppola's *The Godfather*, Marlon Brando playing Don Vito Corleone, who masterminded a ruthless criminal organization behind a bonhomie facade of brotherly love. The Godfather always reacts with his lizard brain towards any perceived threat to his ironclad authority, and it must be publicly rebuked, or even worse. Thus, South Korea and Japan sending military planes into China's Diaoyudao/Senkaku ADIZ, within hours of its establishment by China, is nothing more than James Caan's Sonny Corleone sending a couple of burly thugs into the quarter next door, as a public show of force.

[0078] *The Godfather. America incarnate. The* World's Policeman *and* Neighborhood Bully *just don't cut it anymore.*

The Washington-London-Paris consensus underestimates Baba Beijing – again and again

The Washington-London-Paris consensus wants to hear nothing of it, but sitting here in Sinoland, it's clear as crystal that Baba Beijing is on a geopolitical sweet spot, while sitting high and dry in a Senkaku Islands catbird seat, which means being in an enviable, advantageous position. First, they have time on their side. Baba thinks in terms of millennia, centuries and decades. Sorry to say it, but the West, especially the US, thinks in terms of now and immediate future. (In fact, it might be argued that short-term thinking has become endemic in late-stage capitalism, the trademark of the corporate executive class, the Wall Street variant. **Of course, proudly anti-intellectual, "pragmatic" America has always been a country in a hurry, and this has also infested its politicians and naturally the culture at large)**. Just looking at the complete and total chaos the West has rained across our planet (I'm exhausted listing all the countries, so you get a pass this time), would strongly suggest this is true – from one chaos to the next.

Secondly, Baba Beijing has brilliantly put China in a win-win realpolitik tactical game. The United States and its client states, Japan and South Korea, are damned if they do and damned if they don't. If the US and its lackeys comply, Baba Beijing can show to its citizens and the world's people that China is getting the respect it deserves. This has already happened. President Obama publicly requested to all airlines that they should submit their flight plans to the Chinese, if they are flying in its ADIZ. The reason given was to avoid any potential accident or misunderstanding. [5] On the contrary, if America and its servants in Asia do not comply with China's demands, they come out looking

childish and obdurate, since before China's move, everybody did the same for Japan and its similarly overlapping ADIZ. If it's good for the Wasabi Japanese goose, then why is it all of a sudden not good for the red Chinese gander?

Thirdly, and all of humanity can see the obvious: I think it's been at least a while since Baba Beijing sent war planes to buzz around the Aleutians, Hawaii and the West Coast of North America. Nor have I ever heard of the Russians and North Koreans doing the same thing, at the behest of China. So, it begs the most obvious of questions: what the hell does the United States think it's doing, getting another war on against China, Air-Sea Battle style?

[IMG 0079] Chinese fighter jets? *In Hawaii, Alaska or along the West Coast, "Honey, is that a squadron of Chinese fighter jets I see flying outside our window"?*

1- *Al Jazeera does some great journalism, but maybe trying to get their new US cable channel going is starting to compromise their principles:*

2- *http://aljazeera.com/indepth/features/2013/12/us-trying-cool-east-china-sea-dispute-20131256434384455.html.*

3- *http://en.wikipedia.org/wiki/Diaoyu.*

4- *http://learner.org/workshops/primarysources/coldwar/docs/usjapan.html.*

5- *Read it and you will lose sleep over its implications:*

5- *http://icps.gwu.edu/files/2013/06/Who-Authorized-Preparations-for-War-With-China.pdf.*

6- *http://nytimes.com/2013/11/30/world/asia/china-scrambles-jets-for-first-time-in-new-air-zone.html?_r=0*

Uncle Sam Hands Baba Beijing Its Own Head on an Afghan Platter

Unless You Are Baba Beijing Looking on, It Doesn't Get Any Worse than This

In one of the most damning forensic pieces of evidence that the Western Empire generally, and the American flavored one, specifically, is going to Hades in a hand basket, look no further than the interview no Americans ever saw: Le Monde's geopolitical chitchat with Afghanistan's President Hamid Karzai. Don't let the fact that *Le Monde* is a French newspaper (and one of the last great ones in the mainstream media). The interview is in English. Karzai's interview will be discussed in full here.

The Lords of the American Loot, who spoon feed us what they want us to see and read, kept this canary in a goldmine buried in their vassal state of France, making sure it stays sucked deep inside Orwell's Memory Hole. Damn those contrary French! I'm sure the London part of the Washington-London-Paris consensus gave it zero interest as well. Two out of three ain't half bad, as they say on Broadway.

[IMG 0080] *George Orwell's 1984 Memory Hole: The Princes of Powers' favorite place for the truth and nothing but the truth.*

But this interview is not just a canary in the goldmine. It's an archipelago full of dead dodos. After 500 years of being masters of the world's resources, both human and natural, the Eurmerican geopolitical gig is unwinding much faster than our human brains are registering, with their amazing ability to compartmentalize unpleasant news, cognitive dissonance and the obvious.

Reading Karzai's excoriating account of America and NATO's 12-year criminal folly, three times as long as World War I and World War II, is akin to getting battery acid thrown in your eyes. Each quote is like a chemist's laboratory titration drip,

Hamid Karzai (HK): *My position has not changed for the past 8 years: the war on terror can't be fought and must not be fought in Afghan villages, in Afghan homes... Afghan civilian casualties are the main problem. There is also a lack of visible and genuine effort on behalf of the USA to help us with the peace process. Neither myself nor the Afghan people are opposed to having a good relationship with the USA or NATO. The Afghan people approved the BSA [Bilateral Security Agreement] at the recent Loya Jirga [This is like a meeting of the country's movers and shakers, an assembly of personalities] on November 24th. I'm in favor of the BSA. But I want this agreement to bring peace to Afghanistan and to put an end to attacks on Afghan homes. And the Afghan people must notice that these attacks have stopped.*

The heavy handed hegemony of America's so called diplomacy can be felt at Karzai's meeting with James Dobbins, the American special representative for Afghanistan and Pakistan, on December 5th in Kabul,

HK: (Dobbins') remarks can be interpreted in several ways. In a positive way: once you sign the BSA, there will be peace. If they can reassure us, provide the trust we need, this is a good thing. You can also interpret his comments in a different way: "If you don't sign the BSA, we will cause you trouble and provoke disturbances in the country".

In other words, in a court of law it's called blackmail... *Hey Guido, bring in The Gimp!*

[IMG 0081] *Pulp Fiction's* sadistic, psychopathic "The Gimp", *or is it rather America just being in character?*

*HK: Given my experience and the information I have, I believe the USA can considerably help launch the peace process. When I was in Washington one year ago to negotiate the terms of a peace process with the US, **I realized the Americans were speaking on behalf of the Taliban**... The USA has the ability, through Pakistan and directly as well, to bring peace and stability to Afghanistan* (author's emphasis).

While America tells the world the Taliban and other Western perceived terrorist groups are Diablo incarnate, Obama & Co. are in bed with them, just as they are in Syria, Libya, Pakistan, Yemen, Somalia, Iraq, Mali, Niger and all the other US/NATO military colonies (did I leave any out? – To be safe, just throw in the entire Muslim world).

[IMG 0082] *Marsellus Wallace and Butch Coolidge, or America's view of the Muslim world?*

Why? It keeps the Wehrmacht money machine primed and pumping profits. The Gods of FIRE (Finance, Insurance and Real Estate) of course don't want peace. There is no profit in a peace dividend. It's all about the Fortune 500's CEO stock dividends and the pharaonic lucre of war. Just for Iraq and Afghanistan alone, $4,000,000,000,000-$6,000,000,000,000 - trillions, with a titanic T have been squandered.[1] That's enough zeroes to keep Georg Cantor busy for a lifetime, the Russian-German mathematician who elucidated the concept of *infinity*.[2]

[IMG 0083] *Ka-ching baby - banko big time - up, up and away! Note China's military spending compared to the rest of the world.*

President Karzai goes on to complete his tableau of bald faced shame,

HK: …*the BSA, as much as it serves the interests of the USA and NATO, must also serve the interests of the Afghan people. At the Loya Jirga, the Afghan people told the USA: we want a good relationship with you, but you must change your behaviour, you need to behave in a way that doesn't harm or weaken Afghanistan. We have given you assurances of our friendship, you must now behave like an ally, not like an adversary.*

America, Afghanistan's *adversary*? Surely he jests! Why Uncle Sam calls the United States Afghanistan's *indispensable ally*. But let's allow Mr. Karzai to hit the realpolitik nail on the head, with a bunker busting nuclear barb,

HK:*Attacking Afghan homes is an act of aggression. Launching a psychological war on Afghan people is an act of aggression… A psychological war is a war against our economy, a war that encourages companies to leave Afghanistan, that encourages money to leave Afghanistan, that frightens Afghans of the consequences of an American departure, is all this not psychological war?*

Absolutely, this is the outcome of American state propaganda. Without a doubt. If I were not sure of all these things, I would not have been so adamant in my demands… when and where the USA has behaved against our interests - and in spite of our repeated warnings - it's my job to speak out, to tell the truth.

Then he cuts to the quick. President Karzai talks about the value of American lives vs. non-American people, in the eyes of the United States, **HK:** *Why should the Afghan people pay the price of a war on terrorism? Why would you attack an Afghan home, in the pursuit of a so-called Taleb, of which there are many thousands in Afghanistan, and bring death and suffering to children and women? Would the USA launch drone attacks against homes in America in pursuit of a killer, a terrorist? No. Why should the Americans do it in Afghanistan? Do they feel an Afghan life is worth less than an American life? I expect the USA to have an equal respect for an Afghan child as for an American child. We are not less worthy.*

[IMG 0084] President Karzai

President Karzai doesn't come out and use the word, but what he is talking about is racism.

Ouch. Now for a Dracula's dagger to the Conradian Heart of Darkness,

Le Monde (LM): Some American officials have warned that if the BSA is not signed before the end of this year, there will be no BSA at all. And that means no American military presence beyond 2014. That would have huge security and financial consequences for Afghanistan. Do you think these warnings are serious or are they just a bluff?

HK: *Even if they are real, even it's not a bluff, we are not to be pressured into signing the BSA without our conditions being met. Even if they are serious, the Americans can't push us into a corner. If the USA wants to be our ally, they have to be a respectful ally. They can't exploit us. What I hear these days, and what I've heard before, sounds like classic colonial exploitation. The Afghans don't bow down, they have defeated in the past colonial powers. They'll accept a respectful relationship, they are an honorable people and will treat friends honorably.*

LM: Do you think the USA is behaving like a colonial power?

HK: Absolutely. They threaten us by saying "We will no longer pay your salaries, we will drive you into a civil war". These are threats. If you want to be our partner, we must be friends. Respect Afghan homes, don't kill their children and be a partner. So bluff or no bluff, we want respect for our commitment to the safety of Afghan lives and to peace in Afghanistan.

LM: So you don't believe there would be dire consequences if the BSA is not signed?

HK: We will not cease to be a nation if that were to happen. It will be harsher for us, it will be more difficult, but we will continue to live our lives, we will continue to be a nation and a state. If the USA is here, if NATO is here, with us, with their resources, hopefully properly spent and not wasted, or looted, if our homes are respected, if peace is maintained, the American presence is good for Afghanistan, and we value it. But if their presence comes at the price of destroying Afghan homes, at the price of the security and the dignity of Afghans, if their presence here means continued war, and bombs and killings, then it's not worth it.

When Karzai talks about how *The Afghans don't bow down, they have defeated in the past colonial powers*, he knows his country's history. Alexander the Great kicked off the first known invasion in 330BC; Muslims in the 7th-9th centuries; Genghis Khan followed in the 13th century; then Tamerlane in the 14th; Babur of the Mughal had his hand in there briefly in the 16th century; then the British Empire bled its treasury and blood in the cruelly inhospitable Afghan mountains for 85 years, 1839-1919; as did the Soviet Union 1979-89, in what many consider to be the beginning of the end of the British (along with the 1880-1902 South African Boer War) and USSR world empires, respectively. And now in real time, the United States and NATO are replicating the financial and historical folly of the British and the Soviets. (Even if the Soviets did have perfectly logical self-defense reasons and had been invited by the nation's legitimate leftwing government, already harassed and threatened by the reactionary rural insurgency supported by the CIA. Fact is, contrary to the US/NATO narrative, the Soviets did not go into Afghanistan to conquer and plunder that nation, as all other empires had done previously).

What is so telling about all these attempts to tame the fiercely proud Afghans is how ephemeral or feckless they were and are. The only invasion that truly had a lasting impact on this mountain kingdom was the Muslims', causing the adoption of Islam as its national religion. The current American/NATO colonization only has nominal control over the capital, Kabul, Kandahar and the Helmud area. Vast tracks of this sparsely populated, harsh country are exactly that, No-Western-Man's Land.

[IMG 0085] *American soldier helping use Alexander the Great's castle in Qalat City, Afghanistan. A lot of good that will do him. (#86 Image by* <u>Military News Network</u>*)*

We are witnessing Americans' hard earned tax dollars at work, to the tune of about $16,667 of debt (~$5tn war cost ÷ 300m Americans) for every sentient citizen who can fog a mirror. Mind you, much of the total $53,378 per capita American total debt has been borrowed from China.[3] Talk about win-win for Baba Beijing: we are going to help you bankrupt yourself America, while admiring with the greatest of glee and schadenfreude, your 21st century swan dive into societal and economic collapse.

Like in Argentina, Haiti, Greece and so many other countries throughout the last five centuries, where the 99% is keeping the 1% nice and comfy, the Princes of Power will get their pound, I mean, Mount Everest of flesh out of the world's poor and working classes, and hope to do the same to Afghans. Sometimes it does not work, like 1917 Russia, 1949 China and 2013 Iceland, which defaulted on all of its debt, leaving Western banksters in the lurch.[4] Of course we know how swimmingly Germany got out of their national debt after World War I. Segue right into the Big One.

[IMG 0086] *Thank you Baba Beijing, for financing the downfall of the Eurmerican Empire.*

In this interview, Karzai also talks at length about the Taliban office being opened up in Doha, Qatar, crammed down Afghanistan's throat by Washington, and dying an immediate death, as well as how the West's presence in his country acts like napalm on their longstanding history of corruption. I can promise you one thing. Baba Beijing has read it and has distributed it all over kingdom come among their leadership, just watching and waiting for the 21st century to fall into place, Sinoland style.

[IMG 0087] Baba Beijing compound *Baba Beijing's just hanging and waiting for the 21st century to fall into their lap. The Chinese central leadership's compound, Zhongnanhai, with the two lakes formed like an exclamation point, to the left of the Forbidden City (the rectangle on the right). In the lower right hand corner, is Tiananmen Gate.*

1- http://usnews.com/news/articles/2013/03/28/the-total-iraq-and-afghanistan-pricetag-over-4-trillion
2- http://northcoastjournal.com/humboldt/infinity-and-beyond/Content?oid=2276888. *Barry Evans' column is a Renaissance person's delight for intellectual curiosity.*
3- https://en.wikipedia.org/wiki/Invasions_of_Afghanistan
4- http://weeklystandard.com/blogs/us-person-debt-now-35-percent-higher-greece_660409.html
5- http://gather.com/viewArticle.action?articleId=281474979212583.
6- *Iceland's amazingly refreshing riposte in the face of unprecedented pressure from the Lords of Loot in London and elsewhere.*

China's Lunar Rover, Jade Rabbit. Is Sour Grapes for the US

The Great Leap Forward and the Cultural Revolution are like looking through the front end of binoculars – so very, very far away

A Chinese version of Grimm's Fairy Tales is that the beautiful woman Chang'e (嫦娥= Eternal Good), swallowed a magic pill (visions of *Alice in Wonderland?*). As a result, she was transported to the Moon, to live in eternity, becoming the Moon Goddess. She was carrying a pet rabbit, named Jade Rabbit (Yutu= 玉兔).[1] Like in the West, the Chinese see the form of a rabbit on the earthside face of the Moon.

[0088] Rabbits figure prominently in lunar folklore around the world, thanks to the appearance of the moon's earthside seas and craters.

On December 15th, the Chinese National Space Agency (CNSA) landed a lunar rover in the Bay of Rainbows, officially called the Sinus Iridium. Fitting to the legend, this 260km in diameter cul-de-sac plain sits right on top of the above pictured rabbit's shoulder, awaiting the rover's ride of a lifetime.[2] To complete the legendary synthesis, the lunar module that landed on the Moon is called Chang'e-3 and the lunar rover it was carrying, which will explore this Bay of Rainbows for the next three months, is called Jade Rabbit. China is now only the third country in the history of humankind to make a soft landing on the Moon, after the United States and the Soviet Union last did it in 1972 and 1976, respectively.

Most of the world's media was very congratulatory about China's technological achievement, including space race competitors India and Russia. Around the world, many internet news sites gave Chang'e *top-of-the-fold* placement. These reports were complete with photographs and videos of bear hugging, teary-eyed scientists at the CNSA mission control center, celebrating, along with footage of the Jade Rabbit making its successful exit onto the lunar surface for its maiden joy ride.

America's mainstream media is so utterly predictable

In the United States? Not so much. A quick look at the headlines of the *Los Angeles Times* and *Washington Post*, nada. The *New York Times*, *America's newspaper* where *all the news that's fit to print*, didn't even have it on their front page – anywhere.[3] OK, maybe Syrians fleeing to Bulgaria deserved to get top billing that day, but nary a word about the Goddess of the Moon? Even in the NY Times' World News section, Jade Rabbit and a near collision between American and Chinese naval ships came in #13 and #15 down the list of headlines.[4] When it comes to the *official narrative*, what the Princes of Power don't say is much more important than what they put out to the public. The purpose of this book is to fill in all those blanks, from the perspective of looking at the West from the outside, the way the 85% of the world's non-Westerners do.

If dismissiveness was not enough, then mockery will always do the trick, as was seen in an *MSN* news clip.[5] They gloat and smirk that well, harrumph, the Americans did the *same thing* 40 years ago. And then there was just bad, biased journalism, even coming from a well-respected news source like the *Christian Science Monitor*. It's like the author, Elizabeth Barber, got her talking points from Barak Obama and John Kerry.[6] She lambastes China, Russia and India for not signing the European Union's international code of conduct for the use of outer space. In this very selective article, Ms. Barber quotes a space expert,

"We are still waiting to see how China will behave in global commons," says Dr. Krepon. "Will China cooperate to protect the commons, or will it throw its weight around and act in a way that's troubling to other stakeholders?"

"Space exploration is a common benefit for all human kind, but space weapons are a very different story," he says.

But, eeeerrrr, the United States refuses to sign it too.[7,8] Oops!

Uncle Sam, tear down that space weaponization wall!

The United States has been scared of China's aerospace capabilities ever since 2007, when Baba Beijing sent a missile warhead 800km into space and blew up one of their own (defunct) weather satellites. Provocative, true, but was Baba the first to do so? Hardly. Previous US presidents strove to keep weaponization of space off the books, even for the United States.[9] But that all changed in 1983, when Ronald Reagan's administration came out guns a blazing with the Strategic Defense Initiative, or Star Wars.[10] According to the eminently well-informed Paul Craig Roberts, one of Reagan's principal objectives was to bring the Soviets to the negotiating table and end the cold war, and Reagan succeeded. One of the strategies to do so was to outspend the Russians militarily, thereby putting their budgets under heavy strain (something the West had been doing for the entire postwar period, cynically betting that if not in a shooting war they could always force Moscow to spend itself into ruin by keeping up with the US-led arms race, while also keeping the Soviets from delivering the goods to their citizens in the consumer area After all, for every dollar spent by the Americans on weaponry, the Russians had to cough up 3 times as much given the relative difference in their economies.). But in the case of preserving outer space as a peace zone, that ideal went out the window, not only for the United States, but for any other country with the technological prowess to do so. Enter China stage East.

You've come a long way from near oblivion, Moon Goddess

What is so impressive about China joining the United States and Russia as *lunar landing powers*, is to put in proper perspective the timeline in which it has happened. Two generations ago, millions of Chinese were starving to death, in the wake of the drought plagued 1958-61 Great Leap Forward. One generation ago, (at that time) one-fourth of the world's people were consuming themselves during the now regretted, long decade of schizo-sociopolitical madness - the Cultural Revolution, 1966-76. From the ashes of two of humanity's greatest political follies, the Chinese people suffered nationwide post-traumatic stress disorder (PTSD) and miraculously came back to not only survive, but thrive.

A mere 35 years later, China, with its expanding Chinese Dream, is poised to soon become history's greatest economic power, surpassing the United States.

[IMG 0089] 1958 Nighttime photo of Chinese cadres using backyard furnaces *to melt down farm equipment and tools to make steel. The byline says,* 107 *million tons of steel were made, but steel doesn't digest so well on an empty stomach. The above photo byline in Chinese ends with a poetic, enigmatic, Daytime, a Person, Nighttime a Fire.*

[IMG 0090] *The Soviet Union and the US were duking it out during the 50s-70s, in space, on the Moon and in third world countries around the planet. This, while China was sometimes making things difficult for itself in the sociocultural department. Here is a 1969 Cultural Revolution poster, extolling the virtues of struggle sessions. Initiated by Mao, who feared the restoration of capitalism in China, the Great Cultural Revolution was a difficult, often painful process, in which many people suffered, and whose complex context is seldom correctly explained. The topic continues to divide even people on the left.*

Thus, Baba Beijing and the Chinese people have every right to be proud of their latest technological achievement, the near non-recognition from America, its temporal derision and bad journalism notwithstanding. When you are moving as fast as China is in the 21st century, *better late than never* will do just nicely, thank you. Better late than never? Better watch out.

[IMG 0091]

Wave to the Americans, Jade Rabbit. (Image by guancha.cn)

1- https://en.wikipedia.org/wiki/Chang%27e
2- http://factbites.com/topics/Sinus-Iridium
3- http://44days.net/cpl_author/uploads/slider/1388059604NYT%20has%20no%20China%20Moon%20rover%20&%20near%20collision%20news%20on%20main%20page%202013.12.15.pdf
4- http://44days.net/cpl_author/uploads/slider/1388119503NYT%20has%20China%20Moon%20rover%20&%20near%20collision%20in%20world%20news%20at%20n13%20&%20n15%202013.12.15.pdf
5- http://video.ca.msn.com/watch/video/china-s-jade-rabbit-lands-on-the-moon/2tqeber58?from=
6- http://csmonitor.com/Science/2013/1216/China-s-Jade-Rabbit-lands-on-the-moon-but-will-it-play-nice-there-video
7- http://nationaldefensemagazine.org/blog/Lists/Posts/Post.aspx?ID=637
8- http://cfr.org/space/code-conduct-outer-space/p26556
9- http://tamupress.com/product/US-Presidents-and-the-Militarization-of-Space-194,6994.aspx
10- http://atomicarchive.com/History/coldwar/page20.shtml

Uncle Sam Is Baba Beijing's Bank Bitch

[0092] *That Napoleon is such an important person in human history is reflected in his image being presented on the U.S. Supreme Court Building - along with Islam's Mohammed and Babylonia's King Hammurabi, as important law makers. They don't call it Napoleonic Law for nothing. Here, Napoleon is pondering his life, while in exile on the island of St. Helena.*

China has $2.6 trillion in direct government debt (this works out to less than $2/capita) and $3.69 trillion in foreign exchange reserves. In other words, Baba Beijing could cover every government debt in the whole country: local, state and national, by calling in all the loans they have made to finance America's multi-trillion dollar wars in Afghanistan, Iraq, Libya, Niger, Pakistan, Somalia, Syria, Yemen - and Palestine by Israeli proxy - sorry - not enough room to list all the countries. Sad to say, but China is financing much of this international and domestic terror, lock stock and bloody smoking barrel. How does Baba Beijing's balance sheet look, after paying off every *fen and mao* of Chinese government debt? Baba would still be able to start over with $1,000,000,000,000 in the black, after all is said and done. That's one trillion George Washingtons, with a T.

How does America stand up to China's fiscal situation? The US government owes around $18,500,000,000,000 as of mid-2015. This is more than America's entire gross domestic product (GDP) for one year and works out to about $57,000 of debt for every bipedal American who can fog a mirror. Let's be honest. Do you think this debt will ever be paid back in whole? How do you think Baba Beijing feels holding IOUs of US treasury debt, to the tune of $1,300,000,000,000, more than any other country on the planet? Probably pretty good, actually, since like all good vulture capitalists in the same situation, they'll be buying up American public property for ten cents on the dollar, just like Western banks do, using their loan sharking system of the IMF and World Bank. Greece is a perfect example of how this resource extraction model destroys countries. China's collection of its Western debt will be equally very messy. The upheaval to human race in order to collect on it is going to be catastrophic indeed.

From Uncle Sam's perspective, there is only one solution. America's mints are already busily cranking up the printing presses in high gear, to the tune of $80 *billion monthly* in Monopoly money. It in turn is being handed to the world's *too big to fail* banks, at effectively zero percent interest rates, just to keep their true horror show balance sheets afloat, under the Orwellian guise of *quantitative easing*. And as we can see how swimmingly it's going for the 99%, the 1% is using these one trillion dollars a year to buy stocks on Wall Street, creating another fake market bubble. But it will take many more fiat greenbacks when the world's creditors call in their American debts. It won't be unlike the Weimar Republic was forced to do, after World War I, in order to pay back Germany's impossible to reimburse, Western extracted war debts. The Germans had to print trainloads of Deutsch marks, causing massive devaluation and hyperinflation. This of course was the cause of the massive economic upheaval in post WWI Germany that allowing Adolph Hitler to fill the people's growingly desperate sociopolitical needs. Anybody who says it's out of the question that the United States could become the 21st century's 20th century German equivalent has not read their history. America is already a functional neofascist non-democracy. The official step over to the Dark Side is now just a matter of the breadth of your definition. For many, the United States is already there. As difficult as this may seem to accept, studying Dr. Lawrence Britt's research on The 14 Defining Characteristics of Fascism, makes it undeniable:

1. Powerful and Continuing Nationalism
2. Disdain for the Recognition of Human Rights
3. Identification of Enemies/Scapegoats as a Unifying Cause
4. Supremacy of the Military
5. Rampant Sexism
6. Controlled Mass Media
7. Obsession with National Security
8. Religion and Government Are Intertwined
9. Corporate Power Is Protected
10. Labor Power Is Suppressed
11. Disdain for Intellectuals and the Arts

12. Obsession with Crime and Punishment
13. Rampant Cronyism and Corruption
14. Fraudulent Elections

Calling all fellow Americans. Does the above ring a bell back home?

Under the circumstances, which country is going to sit at the head of the world's table of leaders in the 21st century, China or the United States? Remove the scales from your eyes and the answer is obviously sad but true. Time to wake up and smell the 2nd place red ribbon. Repeat after me: Baba Beijing owns Uncle Sam. Or to paraphrase my daughters' generation, America is China's bank B-I-T-C-H, meaning the creditor owns the debtor. Second place may be a rosy scenario for Uncle Sam when all is said and done. After all, the European Union already has a bigger GDP than the United States, and Russia, India and Brazil are not exactly standing still. [All the preceding, of course, assuming the US does not renege on its debt under fabricated war conditions or some other trumped up rationale. For, would China risk a nuclear war to collect?)

In the movie, *Meet the Fockers*, the all accepting, indulgent father, Bernie Focker, played by Dustin Hoffman, was proud of his underachieving son's "Wall of Gaylord", with its mauve, yellow and orange 9th, 11th and 13th place ribbons. Later this century, it might be called the Wall of America.

[0093] Meet the Fockers *Dustin Hoffman channeling 21st century America, in the movie,* Meet the Fockers.

Napoleon Bonaparte was a very perceptive and eloquent leader, albeit, a little too geographically greedy for his country's and the world's good. That said, a great deal of his bad image is probably the result of Anglo-American propaganda initiated by Britain, which in the 19th century saw Napoleon and France as carrying the Republican virus of the French Revolution. For much of that epoch, for the main royal dynasties of Europe—England, Russia, Austro-Hungary— France was seen as major capitalist powers saw the rise of Communist Russia in the 20th century. As a result they decided to snuff out the threat of Revolution and restore the Monarchy, which forced a number of wars on France, including Napoleon's war on Russia, which a number of historians have classified *as a pre-emptive war* by France on a key hostile power. In any case, he knew first hand a thing or two about the crushing cruelty of sovereign debt,

When a government is dependent upon bankers for money, they and not the leaders of the government control the situation [United States owing billions to China], *since the hand that gives is above the hand that takes... Money has no motherland; financiers are without patriotism and without decency; their sole object is gain.* —Napoleon Bonaparte

Amen *Frère Napoleon*, Amen.

[IMG 0094] Major Foreign Holders of US Treasury Securities (Chart)

Makes you proud to be an American, doesn't it? China at bottom, in blue, is the world's biggest owner of American sovereign debt, ahead of Japan, in orange.

This trend in the decline of American Empire is vividly described in Joseph Tainter's *Collapse of Complex Societies* (1990, Cambridge University Press). America and the West are banally right on schedule towards oblivion, thank you; we are living history in action and there is nothing anybody can do to stop the decline, any more than the Mayans or the Babylonians.

A great cultural metaphor for humanity without American Empire is Sam Cooke's gospel inflected worldwide, 1963 smash hit, *A Change Is Gonna Come* – which was inspired by Bob Dylan's great anti-establishment ballad, *Blowin' in the Wind*. In the 21st century, Mr. Cooke's musical inspiration is definitely a case of art imitating life.

[VID 021] Sam Cooke, RIP: Life imitating art.

I've got the popcorn. Who's got the brewskies? Nothing like a political thriller to keep one's imagination fertile and febrile. It's the show of a lifetime, boys and girls, an almost out of body experience sitting here in the belly of the New Century Beast, the Sinoland Special, watching Western civilization collapse in real time, frame by frame, with the 1%'s usurpation of the American Dream via laws, contracts, presidential signing statements and wars. And let's not forget all those trillions of dollars of public sovereign debt for the private bankers' own enrichment, - that'll all be paid back by the 99% of course. Pull up a chair and watch the show: 10, 9, 8, 7...

My Oh My, a Month for the Record Books

[IMG 0095] *Xi Jinping and Vladimir Putin are patient, strategic matadors, playing the West like a hemorrhaging, raging bull.*

Baba Beijing steps up to the Big Kahuna, geopolitical mondo-plate

It was extraordinary. Xi Jinping, China's president, picked up the phone and called Barak "Hegemon Bull in a China Shop" Obama and Angela "Western Collapse - What Western Collapse?" Merkel, to talk about Ukraine. Given the supersonic speed of events which have developed there, starting in 2014, Baba Beijing bellying up to the so-called Great Industrial Powers' colonial, planetary chess game is very noteworthy.

Deng on

Would Jiang Zemin or Hu Jintao, the two previous *modern* Chinese presidents, have called their homologous leaders in the West, about a cataclysmic event taking place in Europe's back yard? As Aerosmith likes to harmonize in concert, *Dream On.* Deng Xiaoping, China's late 70s-early 80s paramount leader cum *non-president*, survived more internecine political backstabbing than a Sinocat with nine lives. Thus he was speaking with these experiential survival instincts, when he famously said,

Keep a low profile and never take the lead [in world affairs].

But times have changed and the balance of power on the world's stage is tilting East, as in towards China and Russia, faster than a history sweeping tsunami.

[IMG 0096] *Aerosmith couldn't sing it any better, thinking about Baba Beijing calling up Western leaders to weigh in on world events outside China's sphere of influence: Dream On.*

Baba knows 21st century history will ultimately be written in Palestine

No sooner did Xi Jinping assume the presidency that he got the nominal leader of the Palestinians, Mahmoud Abbas and the neo-fascist ruler of Israel, Bibi Netanyahu, together for a handshake in Sinoland. It was as futile as any attempt to scotch over one of the 20th century's most heinous colonial land grabs and its accompanying genocide of the Palestinian people, but still, it is indicative of China's newfound sense of having a constructive role to play, to counterbalance the swaggering, drunken, geo-economic suzerainty of the Eurmerican Axis of Evil, which still seems to think the world's still the Belgian Congo during the Gilded Age. Baba Beijing knows that Palestine is the hub on which turns the world's great historical conflicts: East vs. West, South vs. North, 99% vs. 1%, Black vs. White, Poor vs. Rich. The gates of Jerusalem have changed hands 44 times in its heralded, 5,000-year history, and they surely will again. When they do, it often has and continues to carry international implications. That Xi-Abbas-Netanyahu meeting last year was a message to the West that China will play a part when it all comes undone.

The Fall of Western Empire will give us two big birds with one stone

When the plug is finally and mercifully pulled on Eurmerican imperialism, we can all sigh in civilization-saving relief. Then we can hold out for hope that maybe, just maybe,

Homo sapiens' place on Earth can be sustained into the 21st century. With the Western model of unlimited resource exploitation now hopefully off the world stage, and its ongoing ecosystemic destruction, our existence will have to somehow get in equilibrium with Gaia. Fingers crossed. The second great benefit of the Fall of Western Empire will be the deconstruction of the wholly artificial colonial apartheid state of Israel. It only exists as a vassal appendage to the West's waning rule over the Pale Blue Dot's natural and human resources. From the West's perspective, it's been a wondrous 500 year run of Orwellian Perpetual War, genocide, resource extraction, human exploitation, economic and political tyranny and top heavy consumption for the 1%. To coin the more optimistic version of this idiom, all evil things must come to an end – eventually. Or so the holy books say.

[IMG 0097] *American Imperialism goes back, way back, to the 19th century Spanish-American War. Many would say we can go back to the genocide of 15 million Native Americans.*

China, Russia and the West tally their chit sheets in Ukraine and Crimea

On March 16th, 2014, the United Nations' Security Council voted to condemn Crimea's referendum of self-determination. It was mildly disappointing that Baba Beijing did not veto alongside its ever closer political and economic chum, Russia, against the farcical vote, abstaining instead. An obvious predicament for China is the fact that since 1949, the United States, through its CIA, NSA and NGOs has been and continues to finance, train and inflame extremist elements inside and outside of Tibet and Xinjiang, to try to separate these two provinces and their resources from the People's Republic of China. A veto vote with Russia would have given the West endless cannon fodder to

sledgehammer China about "hypocrisy", even though the historical and current situation in the Crimea is very different than Tibet and Xinjiang. But the West and its servile mainstream media would never make the distinction, in their endless pursuit to demonize Communist China.

However, the Chinese foreign minister gave a mild rebuke to the West, which of course was ignored in the Empire's lock step media. Nobody in their right mind would ever dream that Baba Beijing would vote along with the Western Empire and its bought and paid for satraps, against another Hans Solo fighting against history's *democratic* Darth Vaders. In retrospect, China's abstention vote speaks volumes, harking back to that wily, patient, survival meme that Deng so famously talked about.

Baba Beijing's realpolitik vision of the 21st century

Baba Beijing is looking out over the world's terrain these days and sees nothing but real time death and destruction, all perpetrated by

Western imperialism: Iraq, Palestine, Syria, Yemen, Somalia, Mali, Ukraine, Afghanistan, Egypt and Pakistan. Sometimes it gets personal. China has outworked and outbid the West, thus being the big winner in Sudan's oil exploration and extraction. The West's colonial institutions are not used to having to compete for business on the world stage, on a level playing field. When the West can't compete, it does what it does best: divide and conquer. Thus, the completely imperially driven plot to split South Sudan, Christian and oil rich, from Northern Sudan, Muslim and poor, in July, 2011. Yet the West is just dismayed that China doesn't accept with open arms, all of the West's colonial machinations and military presence across the planet.

US military presence overseas

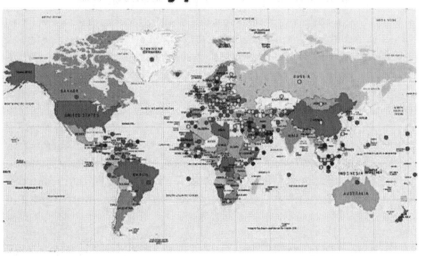

● Country with US Military Base   ● Country with Access Arrangement   ○ Country with other Forms of Military Cooperation

[IMG 0098] *The backbone of the West's colonial empire is America's and by extension, NATO's military presence across planet Earth.*

The hubristic hegemons in the West never learn, like the fascist debacle in Ukraine that has blown up in the faces of Brussels' and Washington's conniving elite. We could also review countless other textbook cases, going back through the annals of Western colonialism: Iran and much of the Muslim World, Latin America and across Asia, which has accelerated since the end of World War II. Thus, Venezuela and Ecuador are now getting the West's ersatz NED-NGO "democratization" program, which the rest of the world knows all too painfully as 1) paid- for destabilization, 2) to achieve favorable-to-the-West regime change, and 3) the IMF/1% are brought in to pick the human and natural resource carcass clean.

This is what Baba Beijing, and Russia for that matter, perceive in history and current events.

[IMG 0099] US bases in the Middle East (Antiwar.com)
[IMG 0100] Who threatens whom? US bases surrounding Iran.
[IMG 0101] *Color revolutions as phony as a $3 bill, all paid for by America's 99%.*

Chinese and worldwide *schadenfreude* for the West

Baba Beijing, along with most of the world's leaders and peoples are all secretly smiling with Cheshire cat schadenfreude at the West's spectacular humiliation in Ukraine. Why? They know by name the clowns who are pulling the strings in this Dantesque, real life, geopolitical *Inferno*. US Assistant Secretary of Hegemony, Victoria *Fuck the EU* Nuland's real name is Russian Jewish Nudelman. She is married to Robert Kagan, co-founder of the neo-fascist Project for the New American Century (PNAC). PNAC is made up of ultra-right wing elitists, often dual nationality Israeli-American Zionists, who have been pacing up and down the halls of power in Washington, going back to the 1970s, only to take control of the reins of power in the 1980s and 1990s, giving us 9/11, Afghanistan, Iraq and on and on, up to most recently, Yemen, with all the millions killed, maimed and starved in the interim.

PNAC is the road map which the West is using to destroy the world. Myrmidons for the cause include such luminaries as Madeline Albright, Susan E. Rice and Samantha Power. Where do they find these soulless, warrior women for the UN? – heaven help humanity – they are all stiletto heeled jackboots for the Princes of Power. Then there are Tony "Bloodlust" Blair and the UK's shill incumbent, David "America's Poodle"

Cameron; France's Nicolas "I Wanna Be a Yankee" Sarkozy bombing Libya and his "socialist" successor, François "I Dibs Mali" Hollande, Japan's wannabe imperialist, Shinzo "Tora Tora" Abe, and too many others to list here. Then there are entire countries, like Israel and Saudi Arabia, which, at the behest of Washington, are spending billions to destabilize and destroy the Middle East, and as far away as Libya and Nigeria – anyway, you get the same picture as Baba Beijing and Russia – they see one big warmongering Cosa Nostra of Western fanatics.

Then to top it off, Nudelman brazenly told the National Press Club, on December 13th, 2013, that Uncle Sam has spent more than five billion greenbacks in Ukraine, *in the development of democratic institutions and skills in promoting civil society and a good form of government*. This of course takes us back to the NGO color revolution cum IMF/World Bank slave state template and being drained dry by the West's 1%, under the direction of a pliant, prostituted puppet government. All the world's *sacrificed* countries have a red phone direct to the White House and Brussels. The red color is a fitting metaphor for all the blood lost in the overthrow of the original, popularly elected, but less compliant governments.

The fall of the West - it can't get here fast enough

After the eventual fall of Western Empire, the 15th-21st history books will be rewritten by BRICS and the rest of the suffering souls, the world's 85% Moral Majority not from the West. These dark skinned peoples, *The Dreaded Other*, will write a new narrative. They will dispense with all the West's self-serving *shining temple on a hill* and *indispensable people* Newspeak shibboleths, which have shamefully glossed over the West's hardcore genocide and resource theft, during a half a millennium of human history.

I have two ardent wishes before I die. First, making contact with an alien civilization. But given how our species is rapidly destroying its only home, Mother Earth, it would appear that Fermi's paradox is probably true. Nobel Prize winning, Italian-American physicist Enrico Fermi postulated that we have not been contacted by aliens, because (like us) they cannot control their technological infancy, thus destroying themselves.

This would explain why none of them have survived technological advancement long enough to contact us.

So that leaves me with wish number two: to read The Dreaded Other's *New World Encyclopedias Britannica*. Unlike wish number one, the latter has a lot more going for it.

First, the Western Empire is printing Monopoly funny money <u>faster than emptying an Apache helicopter's M230 chain gun full of 30mm, depleted uranium shells</u>. The BRICS have a financial neutron bomb in their hands, if they ever decided to use it: just stop buying US and Euro treasury bonds. These bonds are what are financing the West's colonial, worldwide Wehrmacht house of cards. I am confident this will happen sooner than later, at least during my actuarially predicted lifespan.

[IMG 0102] Overall national debt by major nations. The West and its vassal states, like South Korea and Japan, have a much more explosive debt *bomb to deal with, compared to BRICS, which is represented by four countries (Russia, China, India, Brazil).*

If not, we have very savvy world leaders like Xi Jinping and Vladimir Putin to give us temporal hope. We all also owe them a huge debt of thanks. They have Zen like patience and the nerves of deep history in their strategic DNA. While we citizens of Earth often see them as dithering and passive, this is why they continue to let the West hang itself with its own rope of glory and greed. It truly is a calculated, painstaking, geopolitical chess match, where moves must be thought through many steps ahead, years, and decades in advance. This, in spite of the West's seeming rash, short term outlook. Baba Beijing and Russia understand that the tides of world events are changing in their favor. Segue to Syria and Ukraine: these two recent plays are the first overshoots committed by rapacious, Western fanaticism.

[IMG 0103] *US Military and/or CIA interventions around the world. This list is already obsolete, dating to only 2011. But it is continually updated in the minds of world leaders, like Putin and Xi. They can add the Ukraine for Russia and Xinjiang, for China.*

Does anybody in Washington and Brussels read the Chinese newspapers?

Few Westerners paid any attention to the editorial in the Chinese *People's Daily* newspaper, about Crimea. Just like the *Washington Post* and *New York Times* in the US, the *People's Daily* is a government mouthpiece, so whatever they say, you can take it to the bank that it is channeling Baba Beijing, just like a good Pentecostal speaking the word of God in tongues. Western mainstream media has been gloating over Baba Beijing's Security Council abstention vote, since they didn't join Russia with an outright veto. For Westerners, it was seen as a tacit affirmation of China agreeing with the West's shameless regime change in Ukraine. However, in this scathing editorial, another shot was sent across Empire's bow.

The truth, the whole truth and nothing but the truth

The Chinese loves numerology, such as the Four Modernizations, Let 100 Flowers Bloom, Three Principles, Eight Attentions and on and on. Baba Beijing has now published this editorial, *Four Lessons to Be Learned from the Ukraine Crisis*. The topics in this editorial discuss the tragedy of big power politics. They also use the name "major powers" and they both mean the same thing: Western Empire. The paper talks about how the horrific happenings in the Ukraine give the West an incentive to meddle in this genocidal state of affairs, and how Western countries try to promote regime change there. It can't get more in your face than that.

It just gets better. Oftentimes, Chinese section titles say more than the body of the editorial, and can appear as non-sequiturs, leading you to read between and among the printed tea leaves. This is very much the fascinating nature of the Chinese language,

from which this English version was translated, where the layered meanings of so many characters can take you off in myriad interpretive directions.

Thus, in this same editorial, we read, *a geostrategic conflict leads to tragedy in big-power politics, Western countries' failure to grasp the lessons of history results in conflict* and *The double standards of western countries demonstrate their hypocrisy.* These are drop dead understatements that say it all. They then go on to talk about *Neo-imperialism* in Iraq and Afghanistan, which expands the focus out to a global level.

Everything you wanted to know about China's Security Council vote, but were afraid to ask

As a permanent member of the United Nations Security Council, China has a veto vote, if it chooses to use it. The US orchestrated a Security Council vote to condemn Russia for the Crimeans voting to be rejoined with the Russian Federation. Instead of vetoing it, along with Russia, China abstained. Given the level of delusion among the likes of Obama/Kerry (talk about a Janus version of Mr. Hyde), Merkel, Cameron and Hollande, it was a diplomatic, deft dagger to their inflated self-aggrandizement. This, while the Western media touted Baba's non-veto as a victory for their side. Baba understood this would happen and played it to perfection. Xi called Putin *a full five days before he called Obama and Merkel*, undoubtedly to explain China's grand strategy. As this week's official Chinese editorial on the Crimea shows, Putin knows where China's real feelings lie, and the feelings are mutual. Russia was the first country Xi visited after becoming president and proudly stood with Putin on the dais at the very successful, Western-sour-grapes Sochi Winter and Special Olympics.

The Eastern matador and the Western bull

That is why the side-meeting arranged between Obama and Xi, while they are both touring Europe, so that Obama can try to stiff arm Xi into helping isolate Russia on the world stage is such a farce, just as farcical as the Potemkin *peace process* charades between Israel and the world's largest open air gulags, the surrounding lands of Palestine. This, with the President of the United States (POTUS), whose military is sending 60% of its behemoth maritime naval fleet to cruise up and down China's beaches, as it prepares to invade the Mainland.

So, Mr. O (Obama) is in Europe to whip his NATO client states into an anti-Russian, ergo anti-East/China frenzy of paranoia. Meanwhile Mr. X

(Xi) will be signing myriad friendship building deals worth billions upon billions of euros and RMB, cultural, scientific and educational exchanges, and on and on. Xi is the master matador and Obama is the hemorrhaging, raging bull on the world and European stage.

[IMG 0104] *Obama, Nobel Peace Prize winning war criminal and imperial White House fascist, sad to say, the West's Dr. Drone.*

Do I snicker now, or when I read the official Ministry of Truth articles in the Western media about how Obama, finessed with President Xi the basic terms of... yeah-blah-yeah? What the heck, I'm feeling my Sino-oats here in Beijing. I'll chuckle now and then guffaw at tomorrow's Doublespeak headlines.

Are the Filipinos selling their proud souls to counter Baba Beijing in the Spratlys?

O nly three countries have managed to shake off the militaristic yoke of American imperialism in modern times, at least short of having a revolution to do so: the Philippines, Spain and Greece. Of course, a regular scan of the headlines shows that they and most other countries around the world are still under the boot of US dollar/IMF/World Bank financial slavery, but it is still remarkable that they were actually able to force Imperial America to close down big military bases in-country. And, as we shall see, it's never clean cut. Like the amputated tentacles of an octopus, there is still life in them, long after they have been severed.

After the death of Spain's military dictator, Francisco "El Caudillo" Franco, in 1975, Spaniards were anxious to shake off their country's nightmare fascist past. Its elected government was able to kick out the Americans from two huge US military bases, Torrejon (evicted by 1991) and Zaragoza (1992). Two more Spanish installations, Rota Naval Base and Morón Air Base, were kept, ostensibly under "Spanish" command, but totally paid for by Uncle Sam and "co-shared" by the two countries. The Spanish flag goes up the mast every morning and "Old Glory" is nowhere to be seen - except one day a year – July 4th. Yee-haw goobers, break out the Budweiser and bratwursts.

At the Rota Naval Base, the Americans number 4,000 and control 21km^2 out of its total 24km^2, so it's a transparent fig leaf that this place is American in practice. Rota is used by the Americans to help maintain their military meddling in Africa via AFRICOM, Europe (EUCOM) and the resource rich Muslim World (CENTCOM). Each year, there is a large local march outside Rota to protest America's military colonization of Spain, but to no avail. Rota is located about as far from Madrid as you can get, in Cadiz, the southwest corner of the country, below Portugal (as is Morón Air Base), the Spanish are falling prey to the all too human weakness of "out of sight, out of mind".

Morón Air Base, to the north of Rota, is a similar situation, but had a near nuclear disaster caused by American negligence, to keep modern Spanish military history exciting. In 1966, two US B-52s collided in midair and lost two ruptured hydrogen bombs, dispersing radioactive material on Spanish farms and villages below. Better living through chemistry in the nuclear age, I say. Was an epidemiological study ever done of increased illnesses, cancers and birth defects in the affected areas? I doubt it. In the fever of a largely trumped up Cold War Soviet threat, I suspect the nuclear fallout was flushed down the West's Orwellian Memory Hole. A third bomb plunged into the ground outside Palomares and lucky for the human race, it did not detonate. A fourth H-bomb was lost at sea, 12km off the coast. Oh joy. 12,000 jarheads searched three months for the live nuclear bomb with what was then the world's most sophisticated equipment, yet still drew a blank. Enter a Hemingway-esque *Old Man and the Sea* local fisherman, who led the world's mightiest military machine, to show the generals where the bomb was. As in too many near nuclear disasters to count, thanks to America's military presence in Spain, humanity came a whisker's span from a species-destroying nuclear winter.

Still, these same Spaniards saw the wisdom to vote to join NATO in 1982. Joining NATO is like electing to become another one of Uncle Sam's inflatable sex dolls, in America's bloodlust quest to dominate the four corners of Mother Earth.

Thus, Morón was heavily used by the Americans to destroy Iraq during the 1990-91 Gulf "War"; then in 1999 to bomb Kosovo for 79 straight days, during 38,000 "combat" missions, with depleted uranium and civilian slaughtering cluster bombs. The Chinese remember this rogue, internationally unauthorized act of war aggression quite vividly: their embassy in Belgrade was "accidentally" destroyed by CIA guided Tomahawk missiles, with 23 Chinese casualties. Then Morón helped in the destruction and occupation of Afghanistan, still ongoing and then again to further dismember what little was left of Iraq in 2003; and later, to bomb Libya back to the dark ages in 2011, to bring Disaster Capitalism to one of Africa's and the Arab World's most prosperous and socially modern peoples. Spaniards surely stand tall and puff up their chests at providing so much logistical support for the total destruction of four of their regional neighbors, along with the psychopathic slaughter of millions of innocent women, children and elderly, all in satrap support for American Imperialism. *Muchas Gracias.*

Greece, like Spain, was materially aided and clandestinely abetted by America to keep popular left wing political parties from assuming governance of these countries, and if an opponent of the Western establishment did make into office, the CIA, MI6 and their secret Gladio army would do everything in their power to remove them or frustrate their ambition, Greece became an obsession for the Western Empire, when the people voted for communist governments, 1947-1950.

This spy cabal helped keep in power known fascist leaders like Spain's Franco and Greece's military junta in the 1960s-70s. Like Spain, after Greece finally threw off the shackles of dictatorship, it promised to close down the US military bases in-country and to leave NATO. Like Spain, it only came partly true. The United States still has a large naval/ air force base in Souda Bay, on the island of Crete. The area is also used as target practice for Patriot and Hawk missile launches, which must make the local Greeks beam with pride. From 1974-1980, Greece pulled its military from NATO's command. This was due to the 1974 Turkish invasion of Cyprus. However, Greece never left NATO, since joining in 1952 and any government leader or party who tried to pull out, would probably invite their assassination or political ruin, through psyops and black ops.

And then there is the proud country of the Philippines, which managed to do what no other country in postwar history has done: completely evict the American military machine from its territory. And deservedly so. The Philippines were America's Spanish American-War Asian trophy colony, along with Cuba and Puerto Rico, closer to home. After 300 years of colonization by the Spaniards, the Filipinos finally beat their European occupiers militarily. During this time <u>Washington and Madrid were in Paris, to discuss how much America would pay for the archipelago's 7,107 islands, Guam, as well as the aforementioned island prizes in the Caribbean. They settled on a price tag of $20 million</u>. Helping the Americans sink the Spanish fleet in Manila Bay, Filipino freedom fighters thought the Yanks would give them their independence, as they were promised. Apparently, these islanders never read Native American history, with the thousands of broken white-man promises, torn up treaties and oceans of lies, which were used to exterminate 15,000,000 Indians. This figure may be conservative. US historian and professor David Stannard, wrote in *American Holocaust* (Oxford Press, 1992), that "over 100 million Native Americans were killed" and that "[Christopher] Columbus personally murdered half a million Natives." You of course will never see the light of day about this truth behind the Great Western Firewall, but these numbers were fully confirmed in another scholarly research, by Russell Thornton, entitled *American Indian Holocaust and Survival: A Population History Since 1492* (1990).

While not as devastating as what happened to Native Americans, <u>1,500,000 out of a total population of six million Filipinos were killed from 1898-1913, in their struggle against American ownership, including many American perpetrated massacres and other war crimes committed against the local people</u>. ("Waterboarding", an ancient form of torture, was widely used by the Marines in the Philippines to pacify the restive natives.) Thereafter, Uncle Sam, like all good imperial puppeteers, carefully controlled the Philippines' Potemkin, US-inspired "three branches of local government", while Filipinos continued to fight in the fields for their freedom, whereupon they were finally "given" their postwar independence in 1946 by the United States. But the price of this nominal freedom was keeping a huge American military footprint on Filipino soil<u>: Subic Bay Naval Base</u>, which was installed in 1895 by the Spanish, and <u>Clark (Air) Field</u>, which was also taken over by the Americans after the Spanish-American War.

Unfortunately for the Philippines, these two bases were the backbone to launch the Southeast Asian (Vietnam) War, 1956-1975, during which time American forces slaughtered 3.6 million Vietnamese, Laotians and

Cambodians, about twice as many as Pol Pot managed to kill during his postwar reign of terror. This, according to distinguished democide expert, Dr. R.J. Rummel, at the University of Hawaii. Nothing for the Filipinos to brag about, for sure. Both of these megabases were two of the largest military installations in the world, until the Filipino people had the moxy and courage to completely evict Uncle Sam from them, something unimaginable in today's world of pan-global American imperialism.

Since their closures in 1991-92, the American military machine has not stopped campaigning to get back on Filipino territory, in spite of America's shameful violence and genocide perpetrated on the archipelago's proud people, over the course of a half a century, not to mention helping keep Uncle Sam's brutal and avaricious tin pot dictator, Ferdinand Marcos in power, for 21 years, 1965-1986. My Filipino friends say the people used to call Marcos "Mr. Ten Percent" for the $10 billion he skimmed off of every deal in-country. An American puppet through and through, the US's military and corporate contractors were more than happy to fatten Marcos' pharaonic, offshore bank accounts.

And so it is with the utmost perplexity to read that the Filipino government is negotiating to let America's imperial war machine back onto its long fought-for and suffering lands – again – apparently as a riposte against Baba Beijing, in their tiff over the Spratly Islands. Filipinos have a right to be angry with their government for not doing more to fight for its claim of Sabah, on the island of Borneo, whose people voted

in 1963 to join Malaysia. But still, after all they have been through to seek independence from Spain, then the United States, and they are now letting Uncle Sam's mercenaries back into their proud and hard fought country? Is this a price worth paying to "stand up" to big, bad Baba Beijing? [NOTE: As of this writing, new president R. Duterte is apparently re-orienting Filipino foreign policy away from Washington and closer to Beijing. Duterte has many enemies, as can be expected from a nationalist reformer, and his change of course away from Washington's clutches may be easily corrected if he is eliminated via assassination, coup or rigged elections, all tools in which the Western empire excels.]

The pretext is the United States will rotate troops for "military cooperation" and "humanitarian and disaster assistance". Funny, these are the same phrases America has used in countless other countries to gain a military foothold, to then begin the clandestine destabilization and internal manipulations, for evermore justification to increase its military presence in said-country. If there are no natural disasters to attend to, Uncle Sam will be happy to create any number of false flags to justify their ever growing presence. This pretext is almost word for word what Eisenhower and Kennedy used to go into Vietnam.

Let's hope that the Filipinos, a justifiably proud and defiant people, wake up to smell the napalm, depleted uranium, cluster bombs and Obama's assassin drones. They can't be far off if this Faustian agreement goes through. Sabah is old history and can't be undone. And the tiny, uninhabited Spratlys are just not worth selling their national soul to the Filipinos' former and brutal American colonial masters. About the only way the Chinese are going to give up their claim on the Spratlys would be to lose a war against the United States and being two nuclear powers, the chances for humanity's extinction would go up exponentially. Let the International Tribunal for the Law of the Sea do it due diligence, to make a final determination and not jumping to superpowers making their own decisions.

Editor's note: the Filipino government ended up rhalf-enouncing its people's sovereignty, by allowing 1,000 US marines to stay stationed in-country. The situation remains fluid, however.

[IMG 0105] *President William McKinley displays his real attitude about the Filipinos. The answer to the above question is a resounding "Yes". Racism, and the dehumanization of the Dreaded Other is the bedrock of all imperialism, ancient and modern.*

Baba Beijing was at the Geneva Ukraine crisis talks!

Russian Foreign Minister Sergei Lavrov shaking hands with Chinese President Xi Jinping, in Beijing, just hours before Lavrov met his Western adversaries in Geneva, for the Ukraine crisis talks. ([IMG 0107] Image by english.people.com.cn)

What happened was not reported by any media outlet that I can find, outside of the Chinese press, yet it is of Richter scale magnitude in its significance. I can't even find it on *RT.com*, nor *Voice of Russia*.

The supposed "four-way" Ukraine crisis talks in Geneva, with Russia, the United States, the EU and the West's paid for and conspired, coup-appointed Ukraine junta, began on April 17th, 2014. Guess what? China was there too.

The day before these talks, according to the People's Daily, <u>Russia's foreign minister, Sergei Lavrov, flew from Europe all the way across the Asian continent, to meet with China's foreign minister, Wang Yi, as well as with President Xi Jinping, for private consultations *on Ukraine*</u>. Lavrov then flew straight back to Geneva in time to begin Ukraine crisis talks with his three opponents. OK, he may have stopped over in Moscow to refuel and have some fresh *pelmeni* and *shuba* (nationally popular Russian dishes), to succor his Slavic soul and to ready for the fight. After all, who likes to negotiate with the enemy on an empty stomach?

Think about this: Russia's highest level international representative gets on his private jet in Moscow, flies 5,806 km to Beijing, meets with Baba Beijing on April 16th (probably slept on his jet the night of the 15th-16th), to discuss Ukraine. He then gets back on his plane and zooms 8,222km to Geneva to arrive in time to discuss Ukraine, with Russia's Western adversaries on the 17th.

Lavrov did not go China's capital to eat Beijing duck, nor knock back a few shots of Maotai to build up his courage. Clearly, Russia and China are working very closely on Ukraine – I think it's safe to say hand in hand. In fact, it's safe to assume it's not just the Ukraine. The byline of the People's Daily article explaining Lavrov's visit to Beijing says it all:

Xi calls for stronger China-Russia coordination in global affairs

The Chinese press made it a point to show Lavrov and Xi in this article shaking hands after their Ukraine consultations. On the 18th, would you care to speculate who Lavrov called first, after debriefing Vladimir Putin? I'll give you three guesses and the first two don't count.

What the West and NATO are up against in our new, multipolar world

The following chapter is an analysis of <u>an interview that Russian Foreign Minister Sergei Lavrov gave on *Rossiya 24 TV channel*, March 29th, 2014.</u> It is specifically about Russia's and China's close working relationship, not just on Ukraine, but on the whole panoply of current events and world affairs. Putin and Xi are clearly trying to incorporate the vision of BRICS in the 21st century. Starting with the West's huge poke in the eye in Syria, they are increasingly frustrating America's imperial ambitions around our Pale Blue Dot.

[IMG 0108] *The Chinese and Russian presidents, Xi Jinping and Vladimir Putin, sign their historical natural gas contracts.*
Below are extracts from this Rossiya 24 TV Channel and Sergei Lavrov interview, with comments and analysis:

Rossiya 24 TV channel: *Three weeks ago, on our program, Russian Ambassador to the UN Vitaly Churkin said that Russia expects to see moral support from China. China abstained from voting on the [Crimea] resolution. After that President Obama and President of China Xi Jinping held a meeting, during which, as my Western colleagues told me, the Americans were trying to persuade China to scrap gas supply contracts with Russia. And then you met with Xi Jinping. So what is China to Russia?*

Sergei Lavrov: *China is a very close partner of Russia. In our joint documents our relations are defined as a Comprehensive Strategic Partnership of Cooperation (CSPC). All of China's actions reaffirm its commitment to the principles we agreed on. If, as you say, the Americans did try to convince China to review its economic agreements with Russia on the highest level, it's an off-the-scale naïve or brazen attitude. I would even say that not understanding the essence of Chinese politics and mentality is just inexcusable for the officials in charge of such negotiations.*

At the very beginning China said that it takes into consideration the combination of historical and political factors. China strongly opposed using non-diplomatic measures and threats of sanctions to resolve this problem. Our contacts with our Chinese partners show that they not only understand Russia's rightful interests in this case, but are also hand-in-hand with us in the understanding of the initial causes of the current crisis in Ukraine. There is no doubt about it. President Putin and President Xi Jinping spoke on the phone. On March 24, I met with President Xi Jinping on the sidelines of the Nuclear Security Summit in The Hague. BRICS foreign ministers held talks as well.

What could the Assassin-in-Chief Obama possibly have offered Baba Beijing in reciprocity for such an audacious betrayal? More American fiat printed debt? If the Chinese don't stop buying American treasury bonds, as a means of soaking up the billions of dollars it receives every year for all its exports, they are going to have to start storing them in all the empty, cavernous halls inside the Forbidden City. I think Mao's mausoleum is already a pretty tight fit, but maybe they could stuff a few bundles in his crypt's heavenly pillow.

And then there is the revealing line Lavrov said about the origins of the Ukraine crisis,

Sergei Lavrov: *Our contacts with our Chinese partners show that they not only understand Russia's rightful interests in this case, but are also hand-in-hand with us in the understanding of the initial causes of the current crisis in Ukraine.*

In other words, Baba Beijing knows that for hundreds of years, Ukraine was an integral part of Russia and was foolishly hived off, for reasons only known to them, by Lenin (the Western part) and Khrushchev (the Eastern part), just in the last century. Baba also

knows very well that the United States has poured more than $5 billion dollars of CIA/NGO money into Ukraine, starting in the early 90s, including the bogus, American concocted Orange Revolution, 2004-2005. Ample research proves this to be true, including Department of State bigwig Victoria "Nuland" Nudelman even publically bragging about this massive sum of money being spent for the Americans to buy the

<u>Ukrainian government of their choice</u>, although you will never see light of day of these facts, in the Western mainstream media. [NOTE: USD$5 billion is a far more colossal sum in Eastern Europe than in the US or the Western developed nations, and especially in Ukraine, a largely broken nation with millions living under penurious conditions.]

Obama, Cameron, Hollande, NATO and the West in general are in serious denial about how much and how fast the world's dynamics are changing. But then again, all psychopaths are in denial. The definition of a psychopath is someone who can knowingly afflict pain, suffering or death, either by their own hands or by proxy, and feel no emotions or remorse for their acts. One has to assume that throughout recorded history, all leaders at the national level must be psychopathic, by definition. That's how they can relentlessly keep going, in spite of the misery, bloodshed and destruction they cause in other people's lives. I have just the right adjective for the West and its predatory ambitions: *insensate*.

The rub for all of us is that this pan global Western psychopathy, if continued, will probably bring us World War III. It will be the Angloland (US, Canada, UK, Australia and New Zealand), France, Israel, Saudi Arabia and NATO, vs. China, Russia, the other BRICS countries, SCO, CSTO, EAEU and most of the rest of the world. It goes without saying that lapdog, satrap states like Japan and South Korea are American client states anyway. They are occupied with 50,000 and 28,500 US troops, respectively, living in dozens of military bases. All of Uncle Sam's Asian-based troops, missiles, jets, bombers, nuclear submarines and navy are facing China and Russia. Of course, North Korea is a fig leaf to justify all this.

It is safe to say that Japan, Asia's brutal 20th century master, along with its historical colony, (South) Korea, will go down in flames for the Dark Empire. Along with Japan's late 19th and early 20th century Meiji Restoration push into the Industrial Revolution, the country's government took itself to be Asia's superior race, especially with China being at the nadir of its century of humiliation. This justified colonizing and terrorizing much of Asia, including the Rape of Nanjing. Adolf Hitler even called the Japanese *honorary Aryans*. We know how well that worked out. You would think the fiercely proud and oft oppressed Koreans, whose country was colonized by Japan, 1910-1945 and whose women were forced into sexual slavery for the Japanese Imperial Army, would know better.

It's sad really. Great Goddess forbid, if the Western Empire does win WWIII, weak sepoys like Korea and the former East Bloc countries will become Angloland's economic and military colonies. They already are, financially, anyway, with the IMF, World Bank and NATO, keeping them as pliant servants to the Princes of Power.

But, we'll be back to glory days of hardcore, pornographic, *Burmese Days*, Eurmerican Colonial Empire. Ahhh, just think of it: quaint memories of 1% racist floggings, genocide, slavery, child labor, debtors' prisons, megalopolis ghettos-inside Balkanized environmental dead zones, institutionalized barbarism, the vampire extraction of any and all natural and manufacturing resources that these whore states can offer as tribute - all under the caring, watchful guard of armed-to-the-teeth, militarized, police state garrisons. Native Americans understand this all too well and call these just mentioned installations, *forts*. Much of the world is already experiencing all of this to one degree or another. But in the updated, hip World-of-Twitter-&-Facebook version, think *The Hunger Games* on a global scale, with the District of Columbia, London, Paris and Frankfurt as the international *Panem Capitols*.

Shudder this fascist thought on steroids, *Reflections in Sinoland* fans, and wish China and Russia well. They are the only bulwark we have against this all too possible, Hollywoodesque, nightmare way-of-life for the 99%.

This is why the West is treating our two sovereign saviors, Russia and China, like pissant colonies; no different than Iraq, Iran, Libya and Afghanistan. In these latter countries and places like Syria, Yemen, Pakistan, Venezuela and Ukraine, we can see the future as clear as Waterford crystal. It's not a pretty sight and potentially fatal to Homo sapiens.

Our only hope is that non-Anglophone, European countries such as Germany and Italy wake up, smell the Sweet Rose of Self-Preservation, caress the Sage Lion of Deep History's mane, to say,

"STOP!"

And bring down what has ended up as a metastasized, post-Industrial Age malignancy devouring the human race: NATO, the now anachronistically named North Atlantic Treaty Organization; along with its financial henchmen, the IMF and World Bank.

Do we have any brave government leaders out there, who will get the ball rolling?

The Skinny on Hong Kong's Occupy Central Movement

Is it really democracy Hongkongers want? Or is it a level playing field? The banner screams, "Down with Capitalism– Occupy Central". **[IMG 0109]**

I have been watching the Occupy Central Movement with some detachment (some are also calling it the Umbrella Movement, since the protesters carry umbrellas to protect themselves from tear gas canisters and pepper spray). The rubber stamp, Ministry of Truth-Western mainstream media is kowtowing to the Washington-London-Paris consensus, declaring that Occupy Central is hungering for Western style "democracy". It all sounds so predictably déjà vu. The fact that free-wheeling Hong Kong is gladly letting the CIA fronted NGO *National Endowment for Democracy* operate on its soil, is all we need to know. The main "non" governmental organizations (NGOs) that do the CIA's bidding around the world are:

- American Center for International Labor Solidarity
- Center for International Private Enterprise (CIPE)

- Ford Foundation
- Freedom House (FH)
- International Republican Institute (IRI)
- National Democratic Institute (NDI)
- National Democratic Institute for International Affairs
- National Endowment for Democracy (NED)
- U.S. Agency for International Development (USAID)

While some do decent work, like the American Center for International Labor Solidarity fighting human trafficking, the Ford Foundation has some excellent programs, or USAID doing helpful infrastructure projects, they have many other darker, deep state activities that answer to a higher, nefarious power. Often, what they will do is create, finance and train a local NGO. These NGOs invariably have lofty sounding, idealistic names, but then they will work to destabilize the local political structure, with the goal of overturning the government in a coup d'état or "color" revolution, and if that doesn't work, a manufactured war. This revolution will try to install a pliant Western stooge leader to do Eurangloland's bidding. All the color/named revolutions since 1990 – China, Georgia, Yugoslavia, Lebanon, Kyrgyzstan, the Arab Spring and currently in Ukraine, where it has not gone as planned, and Russia and Venezuela, where the same modus operandi is simply not working, are financed directly by the CIA or through their panoply of NGOs and local NGOs.

To understand just how pervasive and cancerous the CIA's bogus NGOs can become in a country, here is a long list of CIA financed NGOs that were in Russia in 2009. Its length is shocking – well over 60. Destroying Russia is a long sought after American goal, so the stakes are high. Since then, the Russian parliament has cracked down on them. Other countries are also starting to catch on and being more vigilant. But given the chance, the United States and EU will flood a country with millions, and in at least the case of Ukraine, billions of dollars, to overthrow national governments, in order to put in puppet leaders who, now bought and sold, will greedily turn their country into a IMF/World Bank resource and asset prostitute.

One of the classic NGO case studies is Otpor in Yugoslavia. Its template has laid the foundation for many of the CIA ginned revolutions and rebellions for the last 25 years. Otpor is heavily CIA financed and infiltrated with local CIA agents, as are all the other CIA NGO assets around the world.

And in other cases, the United States, through its CIA front NGOs, just tries to buy overseas elections. This is the case in Brazil There, Uncle Sam financed a yes-woman named Marina Silva. Ironically, she was the presidential candidate of the "Socialist Party". If she had been elected, she would bark and do tricks for the CIA, the White House and let Wall Street, the IMF and the World Bank come in and plunder one of the world's richest countries, as well as divorce Brazil from BRICS. She would also live out her life with millions in US bribes.

In 1949, when Mao Zedong and the communists kicked out of China the fascist mafia KMT, the Japanese military machine as well as all the Western colonialists, including the USA, the US government, from the White House, the State Department, and Congress to the CIA, all officially bemoaned the fact that the United States had "lost" China. You can't lose something if you do not "own" it in the first place. Thus, the US and Europe believed, in all their colonial delusions, that they owned China and lost it. Even before 1949, the CIA was trying to destabilize and balkanize the People's Republic in China via Tibet, sending spy planes, arms, rebels, and hundreds of agents from Taiwan.

Most recently, the CIA's latest gambit is to finance the transportation and training of hundreds of Muslim Ouighers from Xinjiang to travel to the Middle East, ostensibly for *religious studies*. There, they are trained in the arts of terrorism by America's bought and paid for jihadist groups, Al-Qaeda, Al-Nusra, ISIL/Islamic State and on and on, only to be sent back home to blow up bombs and go on public stabbing massacres, in hopes of destabilizing Baba Beijing's rule in Northwest China, as well as around the country. Again the goal is for the West to install a puppet leader and government to exploit Xinjiang's trillion dollar natural resources and turn it into an IMF/World Bank debt slave. Ditto Tibet.

And so the CIA sees a chink in China's armor in Hong Kong. Like in the Ukraine's conflated Maidan, Hong Kong's citizens have legitimate grievances about their government. It is only natural to want a greater voice in one's affairs, especially when one's economic, educational and professional lives have degraded so much in the last generation, be it in the West or in Hong Kong. In Kiev, the CIA made sure the protesters stayed on Maidan Square for weeks on end, 24/7, while bringing in hard core local operatives, which in Ukraine's case were and are Nazis and fascists, paying them a daily per diem of €20-30 to raise hell, commit destruction and eventually death and assassinations. This was part of America's $5 billion-dollar investment to install a stooge Ukrainian government, which the US Department of State's Victoria Nudelman/ Nuland bragged about publicly.

Hong Kong is no different. The middle class and poor are being decimated by the Princes of Power's draconian, libertarian capitalist policies of pushing the Territory's profits to the 1%, at the expense of the 99%. Students are graduating from college and finding it difficult to get good paying jobs or affordable places to live. This, in one of the most expensive real estate markets in the world. Hong Kong only just passed a minimum wage law in 2010 and it is a paltry US$3.20/hour, less than half of America's slave minimum wage. Standards of living for the 99% are cratering. Like in the US, Hongkongers are having to work 2-3 jobs and much more than 40 hours a week, just to pay the bills, never mind prosper. As fully explained by Hongkonger Ming Chun Tang, his co-citizens have limited collective bargaining rights, no unemployment benefits and meager, almost non-existent government pensions, all of which their fellow Chinese workers have north of the border.

Also, like in all other capitalist "democratic" countries, a handful powerful billionaires owns the real estate, the local businesses, banks, utilities, stock and metals markets and of course, the political process. In Hong Kong, these very undemocratic, dynastic ruling families are named: Li, Lee, Cheng, Pao, Kadoorie, Woo, Kwok, among others. The irony is that many, if not most of these "Dallas" style families are historically of Mainland China origin. What goes around comes around.

No matter where or for what you spend your money in Hong Kong, these monopolistic oligarchs are likely getting rich off your purchase. Tiny Hong Kong, which counts as a second tier city on the Mainland, is like a company town, except there are about ten or so families, who divvy up the public and private spoils. Just as Hongkongers make believe or believe in the fiction that their council elected parliamentarians are in charge, Baba Beijing pays camera time lip service to the rigged "democratic" political process. But it is Hong Kong's one percent master owners, with whom it does the real business of running the lives and affairs of the citizens. Free markets, open competition and Western democracy are bogus illusions, just like in Eurangloland. The carefully cultivated propaganda myth that Hong Kong is the world's "freest market" is a sick joke on the territory's people.

So, while the CIA is fully exploiting Hongkongers' discontent at their status quo, it has much less to do with pangs of democracy, than it does that they, like you, me and everybody else around the planet, are being economically sodomized by the one percent's jungle, libertarian capitalism - the world's permanent reality, except maybe in Cuba, Venezuela, Bolivia, Ecuador, and Eritrea, among a few other Quixotic peoples, who battle for dignity, social justice and a more level playing field.

In truth, the ball is in Baba Beijing's court. They have the power and the ability to read the riot act to Hong Kong's elite billionaires and their corrupt, toady politicians. All Baba Beijing needs to do is say,

OK boys, it's time for a haircut. Your current inverted pyramid of wealth accumulation doesn't need to be re-inverted, but it sure needs to be flattened out enough to keep the peace. Make that apex angle more obtuse, much more obtuse, and take care of Hong Kong's 99%.

I have always said that as soon as China's 99% begin to agitate against their billionaire class, and it is inevitable that they will one day, Baba Beijing will not hesitate to very publicly, not only give their fat cats a full-fledged sheep shearing, but take a chunk out of their backsides too, in order to maintain the Heavenly Mandate and social stability.

It's a little dicier though, in Hong Kong. China signed a UN witnessed treaty that after Hong Kong reverted to the Mainland in 1997, it would not change the Territory's way of life for the next 50 years – until 2047. Thus, Baba Beijing has committed themselves to not overtly interfering in Hong Kong's local affairs. However, according to the same treaty, Baba Beijing does vet and select who will run for chief executive. The same treaty says it is possible, but not guaranteed, that chief executive candidates could (not *will*) be chosen by citizens, instead of the current Electoral Commission, which is ironically, the same indirect system the United States uses to pick the president, via the electoral college. The same treaty, the Basic Law, signed by Margaret Thatcher and Deng Xiaoping, states unequivocally that starting in 1997, Hong Kong is sovereign Chinese territory and China's National People's Congress and Central Committee have the final say on any interpretation of Hong Kong's laws, in perpetuity. Thus in fact, Hong Kong's American led color revolution is not respecting the letter of the 1997 Basic Law. Baba Beijing is respecting it and it is laughable that China would allow the possibility of a fifth column turncoat to end up on the chief executive ballot and once elected, allow the West to do to Hong Kong, what it has done in Ukraine, Serbia, Venezuela and countless countries around the world. Would the United States allow China to pick its candidates for president?

While Baba would find it next to impossible to influence Hong Kong's billionaire class' investments in the Territory, all of them have billions in investments on the Mainland. If Occupy Central drags on, and it undoubtedly will, with the CIA's NGOs continuing to put money into Hong Kong's color revolution. It might take Baba Beijing giving a financial haircut from north of the border, in order to get Hong Kong's Princes of Power to share more of the Territory's wealth, passing laws to funnel money to the working and poor classes.

Otherwise, the United States and its CIA, which would give anything to shatter the People's Republic into a bunch of balkanized, subservient smaller countries, just might take this chink in Baba Beijing's armor, and rend it into a full-fledged, hemorrhaging gash. At the very least, if the CIA can get Baba Beijing to overplay its hand, by say, sending in PLA troops or declaring martial law, which would be a massive propaganda coup for the West, just as the CIA's support and financing of the Tiananmen Square demonstrations and bogus "massacre" charges are continuing to wound China on an annual basis.

OK, Baba Beijing, game on? It's the Heavenly Mandate or CIA Chaos.

U.S. Secretary of Defense Robert McNamara was the creator of America's long-run, strategic policy to contain China.

President Lyndon B. Johnson kept stating that the goal of the Vietnam War was to secure an "independent, non-Communist South Vietnam". However, a January 1965 memorandum by McNamara explained that the real U.S. goal was "not to help friend, but to contain China."

On November 3, 1965, McNamara sent a memorandum to Johnson, in which he explained the "major policy decisions with respect to our course of action in Vietnam". The memorandum begins by disclosing the rationale behind the bombing of North Vietnam in February 1965:

The February decision to bomb North Vietnam and the July approval of Phase I deployments make sense only if they are in support of a long-run United States policy to contain China.

McNamara accused China of harboring imperial aspirations, just like Nazi Germany and Imperial Japan. According to McNamara, the Chinese were conspiring to menacingly "organize all of Asia" against the United States.

China—like Germany in 1917, like Germany in the West and Japan in the East in the late 30's, and like the USSR in 1947—looms as a major power threatening to undercut our importance and effectiveness in the world and, more remotely but more menacingly, to organize all of Asia against us.

In order to encircle the Chinese, the United States aimed to establish "three fronts" as part of a "long-run effort to contain China", there are three fronts to a long-run effort to contain China (realizing that the USSR "contains" China on the north and northwest):

(a) the Japan-Korea front;

(b) the India-Pakistan front; and

(c) the Southeast Asia front.

McNamara admitted that the containment of China will ultimately sacrifice a significant amount of America's time, money and lives.

I would say that McNamara's China containment goals have not changed at all, only the methods. Yes, it has been and still is costing Uncle Sam much time, money and blood across Asia. So far they have failed miserably and it is up to the Party and Chinese people to make sure that it never happens in the future.

Dr. Jekyll China and Mr. Hyde America

It is of the greatest irony that in 1947, the US "War Department" was re-christened the "Defense Department", just as the CIA was created by Harry S. Truman at the same time. This, while George Orwell was finishing his classic on modern totalitarianism, *1984*. Orwell saw the world as it really was, not as the vast majority of the people perceived it to be. **[IMG 0110]**

The state of current events has only gotten worse since then. Watching and researching China's leadership versus the West's, tells a very transparent story about world affairs. Knowing what Baba Beijing knows, the patience of China's leadership, and the country's people for that matter, is almost unfathomable. In any case, Baba Beijing is preparing for World War III against the West. The *Global Times*, owned by Baba Beijing, has officially published an article that Big Number 3 is a real possibility and China needs to get ready for that eventuality.

First, the United States' hatred of all things Communist China goes back before even the People's Republic's independence, 65 years ago, on October 1st, 1949. As a result, the CIA has been fomenting upheaval and chaos here since the end of WWII, when Uncle Sam could see the writing on the wall, that the fascist Japanese and gangster KMT were going to be defeated by Mao Zedong's People's Liberation Army (PLA). A very well researched article by Tony Cartalucci at Global Research, demonstrates conclusively, that the USA, via the Vietnam War and more recently, funding Muslim extremists in China to commit acts of atrocity, is just another day in the life of the CIA and its China hating soul. Hong Kong's Occupy Central color revolution is just the latest manifestation of America's ceaseless efforts to overthrow Baba Beijing.

While the Occupy Central tactics are a manifestly cookie cutter CIA operation, like Maidan in Kiev, the US is so full of hubris these days as to even admit they are financing the chaos in Hong Kong. Again, hats off to Mr. Cartalucci for his excellent research here and here, exposing America's deep involvement in Hong Kong's civil unrest.

Of course, Xi Jinping, China's President, the top level Politburo Standing Committee, the Central Committee and the National People's Congress members know every detail of what's going on in Tibet, Xinjiang and Hong Kong, via China's very capable spy outfit, the Ministry of State Security (MSS). So do many everyday Chinese citizens on the street, for that matter. In my daily contact with China's everyday people, they are very aware of the role the United States has and continues to play in its desperate attempts to return their country to pre-liberation servitude and slavery. This history lesson and current events news are routinely reported by China's media. These American machinations are undisputable, recorded fact, with much of the evidence coming from Freedom of Information documents and Wikileaks released around the world. Since this is all very incriminating to the Washington-London-Paris consensus, the West's water carrying mainstream media goes out of its way to report none of this conclusive proof. Many more Chinese than Americans had a chance to read and learn about Russian Foreign Minister Sergey Lavrov's interview, where he stated,

I very much hope that the US will finally see the light and realize that they can no longer act as the prosecutor, the judge, and the executioner in every part of the world and that they need to cooperate to resolve issues… Grievances are okay if it's a family issue or an issue between friends. There's no room for petty grievances in politics when one country takes actions to spite the opponent. In doing so, they simply shoot themselves in the foot.

Sitting here in Sinoland, watching the West, it is like a giant, geopolitical storyline of Dr. Jekyll China and Mr. Hyde America. America is bombing the Muslim world into the Middle Ages, while Baba Beijing continues to quietly go about its business of projecting soft power and signing hundreds of billions in cross border commercial and trade deals. Dr. Jekyll China has made allies of most of the Africa's peoples. Mr. Hyde's riposte is to offer Africa a US military command for the continent, AFRICOM, which no respectable

African country will accept on its soil, so it's based in America's gutless military garrison, Germany. The first is offering transportation, communications, infrastructure and education projects to Africa's peoples. It's not all a bowl of cherries and there are some inevitable disagreements among the many billions China is investing in Africa, but Baba Beijing is offering useful projects for the people and is staying out of Africa's internal affairs. Mr. Hyde America? The latter can only offer what it has left in its foreign relations arsenal: arms, covert chaos and war. The American government's answer to the Ebola crisis in Africa: send 3,000 biowar troops (several private US organizations sent doctors and supplies), while Cuba and a number of other countries send doctors, supplies, medicines and equipment, China included. Onward Christian soldiers.

Xi Jinping's recent trip to India and Indian Prime Minister Narendra Modi's visit to the US are instructive. Xi and Modi signed multi-billion trade and investment deals and they were able to put aside and defuse ongoing tensions over their longstanding border disputes. Like Africa, it is not all honey and sweet dreams between these two colossus nations. But the intent of goodwill and cooperation is manifest. They both know they've got Uncle Sam breathing down their necks, just waiting to destabilize them, given half the chance.

And what did Obama offer India's Modi, during his visit to Washington? Why, what else: military contracts. When you are a bloodhirsty hammer like Mr. Hyde America, everything and everybody looks like a nail.

[IMG 0111] *America's foreign policy has been reduced to all it knows: racism, guns, chaos and war*

And of course, Obama and Co. could not resist rolling out America's favorite chestnut: human rights. This from a country that has massacred multitudes, starting with 15 million Natives and on and on across Latin America, colonial Philippines and up to the

present in Iraq, Afghanistan, Pakistan, Yemen and elsewhere. We could go back a couple of hundred years and get into the many tens of millions slaughtered around the planet. In Iraq alone, the US has massacred

3,300,000 Muslims, including 750,000 children. Did Modi have the guts to cite this to Obama? Unlikely, and that's part of our planet's problem: world leaders not speaking plain, in-their-face, truth to the Western Princes of Power.

While Mr. Hyde America tries to dominate the world with guns, violence and chaos, Dr. Jekyll China continues to promote its "win-win" diplomacy, cross-border investment and trade. Not perfect, nor is Baba Beijing a monastery full of angels, but their compass is pointed in the right direction, as is Russia's. Two cases in point. China is going to build a particle accelerator more than twice as big as the Large Hadron Collider in Europe. It will attract thousands of the best and the brightest from around the world, to seek new discoveries about our cosmological origins. As Professor Gao Jie, one of the leaders of the super collider's planners at the Institute of High Energy Physics in Beijing says,

This machine is by and for the world.

Meanwhile, Obama told the United Nations,

This is what America is prepared to do – taking action against immediate threats. The United States will never shy away from defending our interests.

On the one hand, Dr. Jekyll China seems to be seriously reaching out to the world, to help build a more prosperous 21st century. On the other, Mr. Hyde America will invade any country it sees fit, kill anybody it deems unhelpful, bomb and drone any people seen as against Uncle Sam's interests, and economically sanction any nation that does not lick Mr. Hyde's boots. This is the promise of America, Bill Clinton's "and Obama's indispensable nation". Adolph Hitler also considered his German people and homeland, as indispensable. All empires do. It's in their DNA of domination and racism.

Secondly, while Mr. Hyde America is cranking out machines and committing billions of dollars to destabilize many peoples around the world, China is building a better future for its people. Shenzhen, China's powerhouse economic hub in Guangdong Province, north of Hong Kong, it going to build an ecofriendly city of the future.

[IMG 0112] Shenzhen architectural projection. *While Baba Beijing is building dreams for a better future, the West builds a web of death, chaos and unsustainable debt. Pictured, an architect's rendition of Shenzhen's ecofriendly city.*

So, let me ask you. If you were a government, politician or citizen of any country in Africa, Central America, South America or Asia, who would you want to work with? Dr. Jekyll China or Mr. Hyde America?

Chapter 4

China, Baba Beijing, the Old the New, Inside and Out

[IMG 0113]

After thirteen years of living and working in China, learning the language, traveling to 30 of its 34 provinces/regions and meeting thousands of this nation's citizens, from all walks of life, I am a changed person, just as the Chinese people have themselves changed, since I first arrived here in 1990. In both cases, I'd like to think it has been for the better, much better.

This section of the book sometimes looks back on the 1990s as a reference point, to help put today's China in proper perspective. If humanity survives until the 22nd century, and there is no guarantee that it will, volumes will be written about China, since its liberation in 1949. This amazing country and its people continue to stump the pundits, surprise outsiders, frustrate their detractors and true to form, will likely continue to do so for decades to come.

To Every Overseas Move, Turn, Turn, Turn- Or a Time to Look Back and Reassess My Life

When I left China in 1997, the country and its people were, shall we say, still a little rough around the edges. The scars of the Cultural Revolution were raw in the minds of the vast majority of Chinese, so there was a meanness and a strong sense of retribution and vindictiveness in the attitude of the people and their behavior with one another.

Because the Cultural Revolution was also a period of overwhelming paranoia and fear of not only strangers, but even loved ones, colleagues and neighbors, there was also this terrible hangover of no one trusting anybody else for even the most mundane, daily aspects of conducting one's life. Being a foreigner, or "laowai" (老外, old outsider), just added a fascinating, macabre twist to an otherwise intense, small minded, suspicious and accusatory atmosphere to live and work in.

As just touched on, this environment, resulted from one of the most psychotic and disastrous social engineering experiments ever conducted, on a scale never before seen in human history. To make the 1990s scene even more Orwellian (or Bradbury-esque or Burgess-like – take your pick), it was further distorted by the sudden influx of material goods and the ability of just about any Chinese with half a hankering to "get rich quick". And the rules to get rich were either non-existent or just made up along the way! At the time, foreigners had so much more than 98% of the Chinese population. So, we laowais had added to the social cocktail of the day a serious, serious streak of envy, wantonness and vanity to deal with.

Chinese by the millions walked around with price and brand name tags still hanging on the cuff and collar buttons of new clothes, on their new sunglasses, briefcases, and anything else that they were in the process of acquiring (I kid you not). In this surreal world of crass MTV materialism (one can argue that westerners are really only six degrees away from this shallow buffoonery), laowais were looked upon as a ready source of money, goods and material connections. This unfortunately muddied relationships with almost all of the Chinese I worked with, met and tried to befriend. To say that naked cynicism and a strong urge to become a new found misanthrope were hard to suppress, is an understatement! Surely the ghosts of Nietzsche, Kafka, for social psychology, plus Mencken and Twain, for the joy of levity, were smiling!

It is for these reasons I always used to say that living and working in China at the time was like a really bad case of nicotine addiction: five packs a day. Its hooks were way deep in my flesh and I knew it was really, really bad for my health and wellbeing, but I just couldn't get enough of it. And did I have my two spare lighters in my pockets to keep the chain smoking going? When I moved from China to France in 1997 after having been here since 1990, it truly felt like it took me about six months to detoxify myself from this drug-like life that was so intense, thrilling, combative, adversarial, frequently hysterical, outrageous and which I led 24 hours a day, 365 days a year.

Flash to 2010, 13 years later and our return to China. Now it is the urban Chinese who have more than I do. Houses, apartments, cars, clothes, disposable income, travel, vacations, the works. And more importantly, they have evolved as a people and as individuals as much as they have materially. Gone are all the bad vibes of envy, vanity, overt suspicion and lack of trust. I can now buy a kilo of oranges without feeling like I am being ripped off. And the seller can now sell me said kilo of fruit without feeling like they should have gotten more than advertised. And no, I did not have a fight in the process, nor was it a pushing or arguing match with all the Chinese around me to conduct the transaction.

History books will be written on how the Chinese people successfully evolved into the 21st century, after surviving one of the most intense 30 years of revolutionary fervor, on human record.

In short, my bullshit antenna is no more raised now in Beijing than it is in any other major metropolis in Europe, the US, Africa, etc., where a healthy dose of cynicism is a great security blanket for survival. In 1990s China, when I was in large cities like Beijing, Shanghai and Guangzhou, my BS antenna was as big as the Puerto Rican Arecibo Observatory Telescope. And in the boondocks, like *Transformers*, it morphed and swelled into the Very Large Array! In 1990s China, when I was awake, my BS antenna throbbed like a raging pulsar and when I was asleep, I trained it to work on emergency standby.

Now I find the Chinese to be confident and proud, in a natural way of being that was unimaginable in the 90s. Instead of trying to flagellate foreigners with their 14 tortured words of English, those who speak English seem unfazed by their opportunities and for those who don't (99% of them), there is the expectation that I should be the one learning *their* language. And as the language of one-fifth the world's people, I should and am happy to do so. Chinese from all walks of life talk to me about world affairs, history and modern cultural phenomena, in spite of all the filters and prisms the Chinese government puts on the news. They are pleasantly informed about the world around them and genuinely interested in history and current events.

I really do believe that coming to Beijing with next to nothing in the way of personal belongings had a strong and positive influence on this process. The slates were cleaned and my perspective was without a compass to orient me, nor an anchor to hold my position. I was an open book, just waiting to see what was out there. Or as Einstein would describe it, I was a free falling mass in the fabric of space and time. In this case, my geodesic trajectory was stopped in China and the new life it proffered.

It is almost like I entered a time machine between 1997 and 2010. Coming back to a country that I had not seen in years, only to find all the amazing and mostly positive changes that have transpired (especially juxtaposed to the terrible degradation I have seen in the US since I left the first time for the Peace Corps, in 1980) was a perfect mirror for me to reflect on myself, my life, my Western civilization and its roots, where I have been the last decade or so, and where I would like to go in the next one, as I approach the third trimester of my life.

China West vs. China East

There's more to the symbol of Yin-Yang, than meets the eye. Read on.

[IMG 0114]

Travelers to China cheat themselves out of huge rewards and a more satisfying local experience, by not doing just a little bit of reading up before coming here. As a Westerner, I can safely say that most of us have a self-absorbed point of view about humanity's history and the world around us. Western reference books are filled with pages on Mesopotamia, Greece and Rome, but they usually give China, and India for that matter, short shrift, even though their civilizations and stories are just as old and meaningful. It's simply human nature to think this way and given that the Eurmerican Empire has called the shots around our planet for the last 500 years, our provincialism can be somewhat forgiven. We wrote the history books that we read and it's all we know.

But the 21st century is ushering in a fresh perspective to Earth's timeline. In just 35 short years, China has redefined current events and this millennium's history books. The Middle Kingdom has garnered the majority of the Planet's "#1s" among the many (socio-) economic indicators - those which take the pulse of our species' progress, including the largest economy in purchasing power parity terms. The only category that *Baba Beijing* is happy to accord to the United States, is military spending. Unlike Eurmerica, the Middle Kingdom has had many opportunities in history to be a regional and world hegemon, but has chosen not to, due to Baba Beijing's Heavenly Mandate.

Thus, for starters, the Heavenly Mandate must be understood in order to appreciate traveling in China. Basically, the Heavenly Mandate can be summarized from the citizens' standpoint as follows:

OK Baba, you can govern as long as you keep the country together, you know, keep us proud, protect us, make sure we can feed and shelter ourselves - and just don't muck it up too badly while you're at it!

Since at least 221BC, when China was unified for the first time, this is basically how the country has been governed. Minding the business of statecraft at home has taken and will always take precedence over any imperial designs outside the Middle Kingdom. Keep this in mind as you read and watch Western current events, which usually reflect Baba Beijing through Eurmerica's prism of world domination.

Once you have digested the concept of the Heavenly Mandate, three other guiding principles define China, its peoples and their outlook on the world at large. First is *Confucianism*. Confucius lived and changed the world as we know it (at least in Asia), 600 years before Christ. This was around the time of Buddha's entrance onto the world stage, but neither ever heard of the other. In fact, Confucius was not particularly religious (he revered his ancestors), but he had a keen sense of what was needed to maintain a harmonious, peaceful society. His philosophy was elegantly simple: good government takes good care of the people (early foundations of the Heavenly Mandate), the family is loyal to the country's leadership and the individual members of the family are loyal to their domestic unit. This mutual triangular support of stability at all levels of society was guided by Confucius' Golden Rule:

Do not do to others what you do not want done to yourself.

Thus, for Westerners, with their strong sense of individualism, from Aristotle to Jefferson to Thoreau, they can have a devilish time wrapping their heads around the Chinese's amazing tolerance for self-sacrifice, in the name of social stability. Remember this, while navigating through jam-packed Chinese train stations, sidewalks and parks. Baba Beijing and its citizens are re-establishing roots of Confucianism into the 21st century. You can feel it everywhere you travel.

The third Chinese concept that is totally alien to Westerners is *Daoism* (= Taoism), or *The Path*, which is very entwined with China's history and adoption of Buddhism, starting in the first century AD. Buddhism brought with it the Hindu sourced Laws of Manu.

Together with the Dao, Confucianism, and Buddhism, a huge canon of philosophical and spiritual themes rapidly permeated Chinese thought, including injustice, good and bad governance, the cruelty of war, etc.

Like any metaphysical idea, it can be a little squishy to pin down. But in essence, the Chinese path to happiness and long life can be found through simplicity and naturalness, as well as the *Three Treasures*: moderation, humility and compassion. Given the Chinese's over-compensating, post-revolutionary yen for materialism, one can cry foul on their search for The Path. But in Baba Beijing's new national campaign to promote the popular *Chinese Dream*, it is pointedly non-American, as it very much espouses the noble tenets of Taoism/Buddhism/Confucianism. This includes less emphasis on materialism, the shallowness of acquiring things, and getting rich. It espouses a moderately prosperous socialist society that values family, social cohesiveness, stability, shared wealth, with pride in China's own culture, philosophers and origins. In fact, the Chinese Dream is a manifesto combining Confucianism, Buddhism and Daoist tenets on how to live life, with a dash of national pride, which is very metaphysical, indeed.

The fourth Chinese philosophy that needs to be appreciated while traveling here is *Harmony*, also known as *Yin-Yang*. Harmony is the circular, cyclical nature of our existence; balance, equilibrium and the duality in all of life: male-female, light-dark, Sun-Moon, fire-water, sweet-sour, good-evil, love-hate. It is reflected in all aspects of Chinese life: food, society, art, poetry, politics, architecture and on and on.

The West is not circular, nor cyclical, but unidirectional. Westerners' vision is driven towards ceaseless progress and endless growth, with clear winners and losers. Starting in the Renaissance and building up to the Age of Enlightenment, Eurmericans were and still are cocksure of their destiny to rule the world, its peoples and resources, forevermore.

Yes, all kinds of different social experiments and political movements have been tried in the West, utopias, free love, cooperatives, anarchism, communism, socialism, militias, prairie progressivism, new religions, spirituality, but the foundations of a hierarchical, competitive, ownership society has never been allowed to be seriously threatened.

The West's self-assuredness is totally alien to Baba Beijing and its Chinese citizens, with their concepts of the Heavenly Mandate, Confucianism-Daoism-Buddhism and Harmony. Instead, they would invoke a popular Yin-Yang inflected proverb,

What goes up must come down.

And they speak from experience: Chinese civilizations have collapsed at least six times in their 5,000-year long history, as has every world civilization to date, since the very first one in Eridu, Mesopotamia, five millennia ago.

As you sit in an ancient Sichuan tea house, eat in a boisterous Guangdong restaurant, walk in a wooded Beijing park or stroll around a crowded Shanghai square, it will pay huge dividends if you keep in mind just how different and refreshingly un-Western is China's holistic outlook on the human experience. It is a way of life and form of society which is rapidly gaining recognition around the world, as an alternative path to fulfillment, inner contentment - and dare I say, yin-yang and world harmony. *Bon voyage.*

The American Dream, the Chinese Version and Everybody Else

[IMG 0115] *This graphic lays it out clearly: the American Dream as a world model of success is unsustainable, for its massive consumption of resources - and lethal to humanity's prospects for survival.*

I am so thankful that in coming back to the United States for the second time in four years, I am able to re-immerse myself in the lifestyle in which I was born and raised. It's just the perspective I needed, compared to currently living in China's capital, Beijing, with its 21 million souls. The entire state of Oklahoma, including its biggest town, Oklahoma City, only has 3.8 million inhabitants. That is how many people live in my Beijing district. Lots and lots of land for just a few people out here west of the Mississippi. My upbringing was twofold. One was growing up in suburban America and the other spending considerable time on our family farm. What has got my head spinning while back is my suburban childhood and adolescence, is all its iconic *American Dream* glory.

If people like the Chinese gorged on natural resources at the same rate as Americans, the planet's 7,300,000,000 humans would need an additional 4.1 Earths, in order to satisfy their daily demands for water, food, housing, land, energy and other resources. Interestingly, the Chinese were almost at equilibrium in 2012, 1.1 Earths. But the world's most populous country is trying its damnedest to catch up with America's consumer driven gluttony. If they continue to aspire to the US model, current Chinese growth rates will assuredly deplete our planet's very limited resources just that much faster, starting with clean air and water. The end result for the whole planet will be spiraling atmospheric temperatures and fresh water depletion.

[IMG 0116] The world's gluttonous, Hampshire hogs: Americans. If too many Chinese try to live the same lifestyle, we can kiss our ecosystem goodbye, just that much faster.

To its credit, Baba Beijing's vision of their widely touted *Chinese Dream* espouses, in part, a return to the Confucian, Daoist tenets of simplicity, harmony and respect for the natural world. However, after a total of 13 years living in the belly of the New Century Beast, I'm not so sure how many of Baba's citizens are listening. The Chinese's recent public outcries and mobilization against air, water and land pollution are a hopeful sign that they at least see a ray of light. But like the frailty and hypocrisy of all humanity, there is still way too much of,

Don't watch what I do, just listen to what I spout out of my mouth.

Wearing PM2.5 face masks when the air pollution index climbs above 300 is fine and dandy, but like their peerless American avatars of resource gobbling excess, too few Chinese are investing in the difficult, lifestyle changing process *of reducing consumption*. Americans and Westerners in general wouldn't recognize the word *reduce* if it hit them between their Visa and MasterCard. The fact that this wasteful, Western paradigm is to many Chinese's goal to aspire to, is not only genuinely disappointing, but lethal to humanity's ability to survive into the 22nd century.

It is impossible to see the effects and consequences of the American Dream, if one does not live outside it in another milieu, for perspective, as I have had the opportunity to do so, for 25 of the last 34 years. The nine unaccounted years were when my family moved back to the United States, 2001-2010, which as a world traveling interlude, was also very instructive, what with the Clintonbushobama presidency, and its rabid drive towards Orwell's Perpetual War and imperial collapse.

Five years in France was a great perspective on how the Old Continent's lifestyle compares to Uncle Sam's. The fact that France's relatively modest consumption comes in at a *mere* 2.5 Earth equivalents is notable, compared to the USA's 4.1, and the desert Disneyland called United Arab Emirates, with its 5.4 Pale Blue Dots needed. Tongue in cheek, if the French would just cut down on their consumption of 300+ kinds of amazing cheeses and thousands of labels of great wine, they could weigh in with China's 1.1 Earths. But then, it wouldn't be France anymore, would it?

It has been the last year in China which has made all the difference. For most of my international residences, there was always an effort to live well beyond the means of the local people, seeking that much ballyhooed *expat life*. With Beijing's current cycle of ever increasing real estate costs, last summer, my family decided to move into a local Chinese neighborhood, to live like everyday urban locals do, at least in Beijing. Truth be told, having traveled in many of China's megalopolises, apartment living in Beijing is not materially different than any other supercity, be it Chongqing, Shanghai or Chengdu.

For the first time while in a non-Western country, we really did *reduce*, down to a plain 75 square meter (about 750 square feet) apartment, in a Chinese housing community composed of high-rise buildings. Two bedrooms and one bath for my wife and me, as well as our teenage daughter. Working class people in older American cities like New York, Boston, Chicago and San Francisco can relate to these dimensions and density, as well as large cities in Europe. But for 95% of Americans hanging their hopes on *The* Dream, it is difficult to imagine, especially out here in my childhood's suburbs, with their oversized McMansions, on expansive, lawn covered lots.

Unless of course, you are first or second generation immigrants who are willing to compress down even more, in hopes of eventually climbing their way up to working and middle class comfort. Westerners disparage immigrants living 4-6 in a room, like it's just not quite right. But, it's the first rung of the ladder towards upward urban mobility

around the world. I suspect some of my ancestors did no differently when they came to the United States during the Irish Famine Genocide of the mid-1850s.

Seventy-five square meters is solidly middle class in urban China, and in much of Asia for that matter, where more than 50% of the world's people live. The same could be said for Europe's larger and America's older downtown neighborhoods. But there the similarities largely end. Many millions of urban Chinese start out by staying at home well into their twenties, then sharing an apartment with (several) friends or total strangers (viz the aforementioned immigrants), as they work and save their way up to the middle class, which is emblematic of our modest, highrise apartment.

Comparatively speaking, rural Chinese, about half of the nation's people - farmers and villagers - often live in quite spacious country houses. The iconic *siheyuan*, or open courtyard house, allows for a lot of space to move around and live. Since the dawn of the Industrial Revolution in the 18th century, increasing urbanization has been the relentless world trend. China finally became majority urban, only in 2011. But cultural attractions and McDonald's aside, China's 21st century rural citizens live a quite healthy and comfortable existence. For millennia in the Chinese countryside, what used to be a cycle of feast and famine, the waxing and waning of the Heavenly Mandate, has, since the 1980s, settled into a mostly prosperous life.

Sadly, all of the aforementioned, including you and me, live in sumptuous luxury, compared to the more than 3,000,000,000 Earth citizens, who live on less than $2.50 a day. Even worse, more 1,300,000,000 live in extreme poverty, less than $1.25 every 24 hours. There are more than 6,000,000,000 struggling souls, who live on less than $10 per day. That is over 80% of humanity. Try eating, keeping shelter over your head, clothes on your back, not to mention going to school and seeing a doctor on ten George Washingtons a day – day in, day out.

And here's the rub: the only way Americans can consume 410% more than they need and the French 250% in excess, cheese and wine and all, not to mention China's exploding and very acquisitive middle and wealthy classes, is for half the world's peoples to sacrifice their hopes, dreams and ladders to a decent and dignified existence. In any given environment, be it humpback whales or Homo sapiens, there is a finite set of resources for the population, even when measured on a global basis. For humans it has been this way for 8,000 years, since the dawn of settled civilizations, starting in Mesopotamia. The dialectic of the 99% versus the 1%, regardless of the scale: village, city, region, country or planet, has been and continues to be the status quo since time immemorial. On a planetary scale, for the bottom half of humanity, where 1,200 calories of daily intake is an embarrassment of riches, you and I are their 1%. Yet, only a microscopic percentage of us, Chinese,

European or American, even attempts to make life changing, sustained efforts to *reduce* consumption, to live with less Fluff and Stuff, for the commonwealth of all humankind.

So wherever you are, in rural Russia, the mountains of South America, the projects of urban Europe, the wastelands of inner city and small town America, or the packed megalopolises of Asia, count your blessings. Pay your humble respects and thanks to humanity's bottom half, who can only dream of your and my outrageous luxuries.

Mao Zedong: Ow! Or Wow?

Talking about a revolution. Mao Zedong and Deng Xiaoping, discussing Great Leap Forward strategy, in 1959. It was tough three years for China and the CPC. (**[IMG 0117]** *Image by xinhuanet*)

In researching *44 Days*, this book, *China Is Communist Dammit – Dawn of the Red Dynasty* and now, *Red Letters – The Diaries of Xi Jinping*, I keep coming across what psychologists call *cognitive dissonance*, when your mind is grappling with two conflicting ideas simultaneously.

On the one hand is Western media and books, describing Mao Zedong as everything from the devil incarnate to the world's blood thirstiest butcher and on and on. James Corbett, a well-known "liberal", alternative press guru says that,

Mao was a disgusting, horrible, cruel, perverse person – probably the greatest mass murderer in the history of the world.

As Little Richard would sing, *Good Golly Miss Molly*. Corbett's supposed to be an enlightened liberal. Wanna hear what *CNN* and *Fox News* have to say? Maybe best to get a rabies vaccine before you do.

All this venom, versus Xi Jinping's and the Chinese people's undying pride and loyalty to this same said person. Whether you love him or hate him, Mao was truly a giant on history's 20th century stage.

So, I kept asking myself, if Mao was such a depraved, demonic, diabolical fiend, who brought China to its knees and destroyed his nation's people – why do the Chinese love him so much? I've talked to thousands of Chinese over my twelve years here and lots of them vent their spleen at the Communist Party, the corruption, the hypocrisy, just like Westerners mock their political parties and process. I've heard Chinese criticize Deng, Jiang, Hu, China's post Mao leaders for all kinds of reasons, too much of this, too little of that. I can find Chinese today who criticize Xi Jinping, but it is usually for him not doing enough to clean up the Party's corruption. Yes, I've talked to a handful of Chinese who don't like Mao. If they are older, they usually suffered during the Cultural Revolution, or they are children whose parents lived through it.

But through it all, I can safely say that about 98% of the Chinese I've talked to like Mao and what he did for China. His image adorns taxi cabs, like an amulet of St. Christopher, to ward off accidents. He is on walls of privately owned offices, businesses, restaurants – these are private, not government. They are citizens who have decided to show their admiration for the man, on their own. He's everywhere. How can this be in the face of relentless demonization by Western media, educators, historians and politicians?

[IMG 0118] *Mao Zedong is everywhere you look. Here is a Mao amulet hanging in a tuk-tuk. (Image by Jeff J. Brown)*

[IMG 0119] *Posters of Mao can be found everywhere, especially in the countryside. Here is one that greets you in a small hotel in Sichuan. (mage by Jeff J. Brown)*

After doing much research, including sleuthing around museums across Beijing, here is what I found out.

First, you have to understand where China was, when Mao became leader of the new People's Republic of China. In 1949, China was basically a 19th century hellhole. There was widespread rural starvation, which was endemic over many areas of the country. Twenty-five percent of the adult population was addicted to opium, up to 100 million people. Due to generalized misery, prostitution and child trafficking were rampant, because the peopled did not have enough money and food to survive. There was almost no industrial capacity in the hands of the Chinese. It was all owned by Western and Japanese colonialists and occupiers. Electricity was a luxury for the vast majority of the citizens, even in many big cities. Eighty percent of the people could not read or write, a true hallmark of imperial subjugation. Many millions of children died, or were handicapped every year with many diseases, since there was no immunization program. Infrastructure had largely been ignored for 100 years, except for what was useful to the Western and Japanese colonialists to bring in opium and haul off all of China's silver, natural resources and goods. Most tellingly, in 1949, a Chinese citizen could hope to live for an average of only 35 years. Furthermore, for female citizens, women were little more than chattel property and the cruelty of feet binding was still common.

So here was China, which until 1872, was the world's largest economy and historically one of the most technologically advanced. After unwise policy decisions during the Qing Dynasty, and 100 years of brutal colonial exploitation and war, China had been reduced to a social, economic and political, 19th century basket case. That was the China that Mao Zedong inherited on October 1st, 1949.

Under the direction of Mao and in only thirty years, 1949-1978, which I call the Mao Era, the Communist Party of China used its centralized, socialist authority, organizing human and natural resources to develop China's industrial and civilian infrastructure, thereby turning China from a 19th century wasteland into a modern, 20th century developing economy.

Mao and the CPC eradicated opium use and cultivation, prostitution, child slavery, child trafficking **_and feet binding in only two years,_** saving many tens of millions of lives and improving the lives of hundreds of millions more. They also wiped out war lords, organized crime, gangsters, gambling, loan sharking, drugs, gun running and the protection rackets in the same record time. This is unprecedented in such a short period of time, especially with such a vast population. All this alone transformed the lives of the Chinese from misery and exploitation to hope and security.

When Deng Xiaoping took over after Mao's death and started to implement his farsighted economic and social reforms in 1978, decent roads connected most cities and towns on a provincial basis. Using local grids and constructing over 10,000 hydroelectric dams (which I've seen in my travels), over 60% of the people had access to electricity, including remote and low income rural areas. Incredibly, the nation's literacy rate reached two-thirds of all the people and 80% of school aged children, one of the highest levels in developing countries at that time, and this was done in the world's most populous country. It is now virtually 100% literate.

The vast majority of the masses were immunized, including almost all babies at one year of age. Life expectancy skyrocketed from 35 years of age to 65 years of age. It is now 76, on par with Eastern European countries. Although still very patriarchal, women's status was modernized, with many millions becoming doctors, lawyers, engineers, teachers and administrative and political staff. Women also gained free choice over their bodies for the first time and were offered full pre- and post-maternity and child raising services.

While the aforementioned, life changing measures would be any country's national pride, by a huge margin, that is not all. The following statistics really bring into dramatic focus just how successful the Mao Era really was.

Numerically, Mao and the CPC, from 1949-1978,

1. Increased China's GDP 600%, and average of 7% per annum.
2. Increased China's grain production 300%, from 100MMT (million metric tons) to 300MMT.
3. Increased rail lines 266%, from 22,677km to 60,367km.
4. Increased passenger train traffic 750%, from 102,970,000 passengers to 814,910,000.
5. Increased rail freight tonnage 2,000%, from 55,890,000MT hauled to 1,101,190,000MT.
6. Increased the road network 1,000%, from 80,000km to 800,000km.
7. Steel production went from almost zero, which was destroyed during WWII, to 35MMT/year.
8. Postal and telecommunications increased 800%, from 600 million to 48 billion letters, calls, telegrams, etc.
9. Population increased 57% from 542 million to 956,000,000. From 1840-1949, the population only increased from 413 to 542 million, due to all the opium addiction and misery from colonial exploitation.

All of this was done, while being totally shut out from the world economy, technology and commerce, until the mid-seventies, by the brutal US blockade, like what they've done to Cuba (and in a fashion did to Russia and the USSR for most of its revolutionary life.)

How many politicians and their parties would like to run on accomplishments like these? Talk about bringing home the bacon. With a record like that, now you can appreciate why 98% of the Chinese think that Mao metaphorically walks on water. Not to mention the intangibles, that Mao inspires hard work, dedication, patriotism, team work, community and nation building.

So, this is what we Westerners need to understand. Without all this impressive, let's admit it, spectacular social, economic and infrastructural development, Deng's daring reforms would have failed – miserably, when he started in 1978.

Just as importantly, without Mao's inspiration and struggle for the people of China to stand up and be free, after 110 years of Western and Japanese resource extraction and exploitation, Deng's reforms would have been for the benefit of foreign powers, banks, militaries and Wall Street, and not for the people of China. Most countries around the world have been consumed and lost their sovereignty to globalization, Western debt, or had their popular governments overthrown by the West, via assassination, rigged elections, false flags, war or psyops/black ops. Thanks to Mao, the Chinese have been and continue to stand up to Western imperialism, control their destiny and resources, both human and natural. Thus, their opening up to the world is for the benefit of the masses and not Uncle Sam. There are very few non-Western countries that can say this. China is at the top of the list, along with Russia, since Putin was elected in 1999/2000.

People forget that one of Senator Joseph McCarthy's biggest PR weapons was Mao Zedong, back in postwar America. You remember that demagogue, don't you, who destroyed thousands and thousands of people's lives, during his maniacal communist witch hunt and pogrom? McCarthy would raise the specter of Mao to Presidents Harry Truman and Dwight Eisenhower, taunting them with the line, literally beating them over the head with,

How could you lose China, to Mao and the communists? How are you going to get China back?

Think about that for a moment. You can't lose something, unless you think that you already owned it in the first place. And you can't take something back, unless you feel it is something due to you. This was and still is the West's racist attitude about China: to be owned and exploited. To this day, China's economic and political independence is what Washington, London and Paris cannot accept, and why they are so committed to overthrowing the Communist Party of China. Instead of a Mao or Xi Jinping, they want to install a Western puppet, like Russia's Boris Yeltsin, in 1990s Russia, or Poroshenko, in today's Ukraine, willing to let the West come in and rape and plunder the country. Without Mao's legacy, that nightmare scenario would have surely already happened a long time ago, as it has in most non-Western countries around the world.

All of this is why Baba Beijing officially says that Mao was right 70% the time and wrong 30% of the time. Now that we've looked at the 70% good, let's take a look at the 30% bad. Like the 70% good, we again have to look at some background and history.

First, Mao was a committed revolutionary, there is no doubt about that. Here are three quotes by him that confirm this:

Political power grows out of the barrel of a gun.

Revolution is not a dinner party or writing an essay or painting a picture or doing embroidery. It cannot be so refined, so leisurely and gentle, so temperate, kind, courteous, restrained and magnanimous. A revolution is an insurrection, an act of violence, by which one class overthrows the other.

To keep the revolution strong, one person needs to be killed out of every 1,000-2,000 citizens.

For the last quote, in other words, set an example for everybody, by getting rid of someone who is against the cause.

While at first glance this all may seem bloodthirsty and shocking, it is by far not out of the norm. The French Revolution was a blood affair. Very bloody (but guess what, the counter-revolution was much bloodier). The American Revolution was a blood affair. The Russian Revolution was just as bloody, especially since the native privileged class and its domestic saboteurs and counter-revolutionaries were also supported from abroad by most Western powers, including the US and Japan, who actually sent their militaries into Russia in an effort at restoring feudalism and smashing the young Bolshevik state. By necessity, revolution is a mighty battle between the rich and the poor, the haves and the have nots, the bankers and the citizens, the government tyrants against the oppressed masses.

As an example, here are a few quotes from American luminaries,

Americans can exercise their constitutional right of amending it [the government], *or their revolutionary right to dismember it or overthrow it.* – Abraham Lincoln

In other words, if you can't make the government work through normal channels, it must be changed by violence.

We must fight, I repeat it sir, we must fight - an appeal to arms! -- Patrick Henry

Hmm, this sounds just like Mao to me.

I know not what course others may take, but as for me, give me liberty or give me death! – Patrick Henry

Normally, when you die in action, you kill a few people along the way.

What country can preserve its liberties, if its rulers are not warned, from time to time, that this people preserve the spirit of resistance? Let them take arms! The remedy is to set them [the rulers] *right as to the facts, pardon and pacify them.* – Thomas Jefferson

What signifies a few lives lost in a century or two? The tree of liberty must be refreshed from time to time with the blood of patriots and tyrants. It is its natural manure. – Thomas Jefferson

I hold it that a little rebellion [revolution] *now and then is a good thing and is necessary in the political world. It is a medicine necessary for the sound health of government.* – Thomas Jefferson

Again, Mr. Jefferson sounds just like Mao to me, doesn't he?

That historical radical, Thomas Paine said,

We have in our power to begin the world over again [revolution].

The greatest purveyor of violence in the world is my own government. I cannot be silent. – Martin Luther King, Jr.

Of course, pacifist King was killed by his own government, for speaking revolutionary truth to power.

Outside the United States,

A revolution is an idea taken up by bayonets. – Napoléon Bonaparte

Fidel Castro laid it on the line,

A revolution is not a bed of roses. Revolution is a struggle between the future and the past.

Castro meant that the have nots of the future are taking what is rightfully theirs from the past.

So, think about this. In a proper historical context, Mao's vision of violent revolution is not so outrageous and obscene as it seems (to Westerners and especially thoroughly ignorant, disinformed and pacified Americans). In fact, it is very mundane and mainstream. Now that we know Mao was a bread and butter revolutionary, in a long line of proud principled rebels, let's take a look at the two events that tarnished his image at home, and give Western talking heads so much propaganda fodder.

The first one was the Great Leap Forward. From 1958-61, Mao and the CPC tried to do collectivization of farmers and agricultural production, and essentially the collectivization of industry too, especially steel, by building "backyard furnaces".

We'll tackle the latter first, because this was really the big faux pas of the Great Leap Forward. Mao & Co., wanted to catch up with the Soviet Union and the West in industrialization, doing it rapidly and with what they had an abundance of, muscle, pride and determination. Being completely shut out by the Western world's draconian anti-communist economic, trade and technology blockade compounded the problem. With the help of the USSR, the Chinese were building large, modern steel plants, but at the rate they were going, they calculated it would take years to get the capacity they needed to build all the railways, bridges, dams and other large engineering and architectural projects that were one the books.

Because of all the destruction, due to the pre-liberation Chinese Civil Wars, there was a lot of damaged and scrap iron, tools, implements and the like, strewn across the countryside. The leadership apparently talked to the wrong people or the people they talked to were ill-informed, because it was proposed that the masses could build miniature foundries across the land, the now infamous backyard furnaces, that were supposed to transform all those millions of tons of rusty scrap iron into high tensile, shiny steel. This was tried just as one of China's worst droughts of the 20th century kicked in. Huge amounts of resources, firewood, coal, bricks to make the furnaces and untold millions of work hours and toil were all invested into the project.

Looking back, Baba Beijing and its people learned the hard way, that it is not possible to achieve the necessary temperatures and conditions to make good quality steel in a backyard furnace. Here, the CPC's ability to mobilize a lot of people in a short period of time came back to bite them in the butt. Instead of testing it in a province or two, it was rolled out overnight and launched so fast, nationwide, that the damage and lack of positive results had already happened, before they finally called it off.

I am convinced that this experience is one of the major reasons that Baba Beijing now almost always tests new policies and initiatives in two or three provinces, before slowly rolling them out on a national basis.

Thus, it was the backyard steel furnaces that were the big black eye for Mao and Baba Beijing, and truth be told, it was an embarrassing shiner they royally deserved.

The other aspect of the Great Leap Forward that raises a lot of eyebrows in the West, is rural collectivization. This is where large groups of people, usually farmers, are moved from their current, traditional or historic homes, to a new area, to develop these previously underdeveloped or unused lands. It is essentially government organized pioneering and settlement, writ large.

Collectivization does not get a lot of love in the world's history books: Stalin and Mao; Ethiopia and Tanzania did much later. From an individual standpoint, it must be difficult and stressful, being uprooted from one's home and being asked to start a new life in a new area, often with new neighbors.

From a historical standpoint in China, looking back a couple of generations, to the 1950s, the long view gives a different perspective. Many thousands of square kilometers of marginal, scrub, waste or desertified lands were transformed into highly productive farmland. Vast tracts of land in Inner Mongolia and Manchuria are now some of the best corn and soybean production areas in the world, and helped feed a rapidly growing population after liberation in 1949.

I have met families who were collectivized. In retrospect, they have no regrets. Yes, they suffered tremendous hardship, but what pioneers don't? They are proud of what they accomplished, their selfless, patriotic and collective efforts, for the good of their country. I have seen these families wave their arms across the horizon, as corn and soybean disappear into infinity, as well as what has now turned into a prosperous rural town, saying, "We did this, this is what we accomplished".

It is difficult to imagine, being thrown together with not much more than hand tools, some building supplies, in howling, subzero weather. Then, they were pointed to 10,000-100,000 hectares of wasteland, as far as the eye could see, to the horizon and told,

For the love of New China, for the love of the communist revolution, transform this land!

That would have been difficult in the best of scenarios, but as bad luck would have it, much of China was struck with a 100-year drought at the same time. As a result, millions of people starved to death. What China haters do not consider is that even without collectivization, millions of Chinese *would have still died*, because it was one of the worst droughts in the 20th century. Undoubtedly though, the tumult of collectivization at the exact same time probably did aggravate suffering.

Actually, the most important blueprint for these modern collectivizations was US President Andrew Jackson's 1830 Indian Removal Act, which is brushed over in Western history books, since it codified the genocide of 15 million Native Americans. America's collectivized, gulag Indian reservations have been and continue to be a massive failure of ethnic cleansing on a continental scale, for the small percentage who survived Eurmerican extermination.

During the Great Leap Forward, the Chinese say about 16.5 million died. Westerners say somewhere between 18-45 million perished. Let's take the average of these figures, which comes to 26.5 million and round it up to 30 million, so no one can say I'm being biased. In 1958, when the Great Leap Forward started, China's population was 654,000,000, about half of today's 1.37 billion. So, 30 million is 4.6% of China's total population of 654 million. Sounds like a lot, but how does this compare to other tragedies in the not so distant past?

France lost 5% of its population during World War I, a pointless slaughter between greedy, Western colonialists. Ireland lost 15% of its people during the British legislated Great Potato Famine Genocide 1845-1853. French colonialists in Vietnam, in a terrible drought, forced two million to starve to death in 1945, which was 9% of the local population. The United States massacred 7% of the Filipinos, starting in 1898, when it colonized that island country. More recently, the United States killed 3.3 million Iraqis, 1990-2012, including 750,000 children, the total which represents almost 19% of the population. Way to go Uncle Sam, a job well done. You have to hand it to the Americans. When they institute forced collectivization and genocide, they do it right.

I could keep going on all day about massacres and genocide in Palestine, India, Asia, Africa, the Americas, Oceania and Europe, during the last 500 years of Eurmerican colonialism, with whopping percentages of the local population decimated every time. It is hardcore, visceral racism and greed against dark skinned people, pure and simple. The point is, in historical perspective, yes, 5% of the Chinese population lost during the Great Leap Forward is a tragedy, which Baba Beijing officially accepts. But it is by no means unusual, as an event, nor is its magnitude.

The flip side is, after a century of Western colonization, 1939-1949, China's population only grew 0.7% per year, a total of 128 million over 110 years. Then, after communist liberation, China's population grew 57%, 415 million more from 1949-1978. The Great Leap Forward cost China 30 million souls during one generation, but Mao's policies still increased the overall population by 415,000,000. Again, Baba Beijing's 70% right, 30% wrong, is not unreasonable.

The other sociopolitical project that tarnished Mao's reputation was the Cultural Revolution. There is much speculation as to why Mao started it. The common Western refrain is he did it to keep his political rivals off balance and to compensate for the failure of the Great Leap Forward. The Chinese say Mao really did want to rid the country of counterrevolutionary elements, who were sabotaging the country. They were corrupt and needed to go. In fact, there are people who have written books to that effect: millions of peasants in the countryside liked the Cultural Revolution, because it gave them the authority to remove corrupt local Party officials, who were getting too fat and happy and abusing their positions of power. To be honest, taking both explanations together doesn't sound too off the mark.

When Mao did launch the Cultural Revolution, it probably went in directions that he did not think would ever happen. It is safe to say that at times, it got out of control of the leadership, especially the Red Guards. Probably the costliest aspect was the fact that public education, primary, secondary and university, simply shut down from about 1968-1976. Many of the students, with nothing better to do, were formed by Mao into Red Guard gangs, to rid China of "all the olds". This is the famous episode which caused so much of the terror against adults, teachers, civic leaders, as well as extensive damage to Chinese heritage sites, temples, museums, etc. In the West, it is depicted that this went on for years. In fact, this burst of persecution and vandalism only happened during a brief six-week period in the summer of 1968. They did do a lot of damage in such a short period of time and the leadership quickly sent out the People's Liberation Army to stop it. It was one of the big reasons that Mao, soon thereafter, planned on sending youth into the countryside, for rural education. It was a great way to get these overzealous kids out of the cities and take some starch out of them. In fact, it worked like a charm.

The rural education program is still highly valued in China. If you ask Xi Jinping, in spite of the hardships and suffering, the youth rural education program was overall a big success. It helped make him the man he is today and like all my personal sacrifices living like a peasant in the Peace Corps, it was life changing for the better.

It must be said, the Cultural Revolution set China back. GDP growth slowed to an average of 6% per annum, 1966-1976, after torrid economic growth from 1949-1965, with numbers that make the Deng Era look anemic. Countless innocents were unnecessarily persecuted, imprisoned and many died during what the Chinese call their "decade of chaos". You know ideals have lost their compass bearing, when millions of school children spent their days memorizing revolutionary slogans, instead of grammar and math, while repeatedly stabbing straw effigies with bamboo spears, and screaming over and over,

Down with Deng Xiaoping! Down with Liu Shaoqi!

This, being the memories of Chinese friends I know who grew up during this period. And then the ultimate perversity of revolution, China's education system, kindergarten through university, virtually shut down, 1968-1976. Not the best way to advance the cause of New China. All in all, the whole period was a muddled, dispiriting and depressing mess for many Chinese, a violent, terrifying and deadly one for some, and it did not end until Mao's death, on 1976.

Regardless of its origins, Baba Beijing officially admits that the Cultural Revolution was a mistake, and puts up acceptable figures on the number of people wrongfully persecuted, imprisoned and killed, as well as an inventory of the damage done to cultural heritage sites. Baba Beijing has even officially apologized to all the victims. They even instituted a national program to find and return stolen goods to their original owners. The CPC has also apologized for the 1950s Anti-Rightist campaign.

Behind the Great Western Firewall, the mainstream media's coordinated intention is to deliberately focus China's modern history on only three negative events: the Great Leap Forward, the Cultural Revolution and the fictitious Tiananmen "massacre".

But here's the real story:

We know the horrors and misery in pre-liberation, colonial China. The accomplishments, numbers and statistics are bulletproof: Mao and the CPC transformed China into a modern, developing, agricultural and industrial powerhouse, proudly self-reliant and without any help from the West. This is more than incredible. In fact, it is these almost unimaginable socioeconomic gains that the Chinese benefitted from, during the generation of Mao's rule, that are the real Great Leap Forward.

But even more importantly, the fact that the Chinese people are continuing to stand proud, independent and free of Western occupation and balkanization, that makes Mao's 30% wrong totally forgivable. Even if he was pegged 10% right/90% wrong, that alone would be worth the sacrifice. No country can put a price on the freedom of not being a Western whore. Just ask the scores of occupied, exploited countries around the world about working on your knees, under the boot heel of the West's "democracy" and "free markets", just to survive. The Chinese lived this humiliation for 110 years. The Russians were sodomized by the West for a mere ten years. Iraq, Afghanistan, Syria, Libya, Yemen,

Sudan, Nigeria, the Ukraine, Palestine and many other countries are still getting the West's "enslavement program" shoved down their throats. A century or a decade is irrelevant. One day is too long.

Thoughts on Xi Jinping

Xi Jinping is giving a lot of thought to his people's future – and the future of Planet Earth, well into the 21st century. (Image by Tavis Coburn the New Yorker) **[IMG 0120]**

Note: Jeff is currently writing an historical fiction, *Red Letters – The Diaries of Xi Jingping.*

If you are a member of the Western elites, their military and/or the deep state, you should be very, very worried, now that Xi Jinping is in power (ditto Putin in Russia). To better understand Xi, it helps to know about his father, Xi Zhongxun, as Xi is a proverbial chip off the old block.

Xi Zhongxun was a committed revolutionary from an early age. He was sent to prison at the age of 14 for trying to poison a teacher, whom he and his schoolmates considered to be a lackey for the foreign colonialists. He joined the Communist Party of China behind bars, in 1928, at only 15 years of age. Quite an auspicious adolescence.

Xi Zhongxun was also a very successful military leader in the Red Army and had fabulous organizational and managerial skills. Without him setting up operations in Shaanxi Province, where Mao & Co. arrived after the Long March ended in 1935, the Red Army may not have been able to push on to defeat the fascist Japanese and KMT, and kick out the Western colonialists, towards eventual national liberation in 1949.

Xi père and Xi's mother, Qi Xin, were unfailingly committed to the Party and the Chinese communist revolution. Herculean and bitter personal sacrifices were made by Xi's parents for their country and Party. All their lives, they never gave up on the cause of socialism for the Chinese masses, even though they were purged, imprisoned (father) and sent to hard labor on farms (mother), 1962-1976.

Xi's father was also very empathetic, being a successful conciliator and negotiator in Western China, before and after liberation in 1949, with local Tibetans and Muslim Ouighers. Xi's father avoided as much bloodshed as possible and the more violent aspects of revolution. It was Xi's father, who Deng Xiaoping sent to Guangdong Province, across the border from Hong Kong, in 1978, to defuse the volatile discontent among the locals, who were clamoring over the border, into the British colony, seeking work and a better lifestyle. It was Xi's father, not Deng, who came up with the brilliant idea to create little Hong Kongs inside Guangdong, where the masses could work and realize their dreams. Thus, Shenzhen and the other Special Economic Zones (SEZs) were signed off on by the National People's Congress, Central Committee, Politburo and Deng. Deng & Co. didn't have any money, but they had the power of the pen to make Xi's SEZs legal. The rest is history.

Xi's father was also incredibly well read and erudite. Their house was full of dog eared books. Xi Jinping was sent to the countryside in 1969, to work as a peasant for seven years, during the Cultural Revolution. Xi did backbreaking, barefoot labor and learned to live with fleas and lice, while developing his nascent leadership and managerial skills. He arrived with boxes of his father's books to keep him company. He read every one of them, many in the evenings, reading out loud under a kerosene lamp, to his less educated rural neighbors.

To this day, Xi Jinping is probably one of the best read world leaders in office, having and continuing to read hundreds of Russian, Greek, French, German, English, Spanish and American classics (fiction and nonfiction), all the huge canon of Chinese works, as well being extremely well versed in Marxist-Leninist-Maoist writings. Xi even got an additional college degree in Marxist Theory and Law, 1998-2002, while he was governor of Fujian. He never stops reading and learning, claiming that it is his greatest personal passion.

It also needs to be pointed out that Xi Jinping, like his father, is a military man. He has been in the PLA since 1980 and held high level, military command posts everywhere he went throughout his 35-year career, at the local, provincial and finally, national level. His wife, famous revolutionary songster Peng Liyuan (she sings Russian folk songs like a native), is also a lifelong member of China's military. Like Xi's mother and father, he and Peng are proud Chinese soldiers and communists, through and through.

Finally, like his father, who also saw the highs and lows of the human condition, Xi Jinping's broad life experiences and empathy make him an excellent judge of character, which is invaluable as a leadership trait. As president and top military leader of China, he is involved in choosing hundreds of team members, and he has a knack for picking the right people, as well as removing the ones who don't perform.

So, all of this was imbued in Xi Jinping from birth. While a child of privilege, due to his father's legendary standing in China's modern history, his parents emulated and taught Xi Jinping empathy, frugality, simplicity, humility, hard work, sacrifice, fairness, reasonableness, tolerance for other people's differences, a thirst for knowledge and loyalty to country, revolution and Party. If much of this sounds like Buddhism-Daoism-Confucianism, well it is. When Xi was in Fujian Province, 1985-2001, he was in contact with many Taiwanese visitors. While an avowed atheist, Xi became very interested in this ancient foundation of Chinese society, which richly flavors Taiwan's people. Today, Xi is reaching back to this tripartite cornerstone of Chinese civilization, to invoke his "moderately prosperous" Chinese Dream (much as Putin has with Russian Orthodoxy), and to hone his decidedly anti-Western Empire sentiments.

Lastly, unlike his father, who always preferred to work in the background, Xi Jinping is showing himself to be a master of media and public relations. He deftly uses TV and print media to the Party's advantage. His books are being translated into several languages and, *The Governance of China*, has already sold four million copies overseas. *The Chinese Dream of the Great Rejuvenation of the Chinese Nation*, is also available internationally.

All of his books and speeches are now available for free via a phone app in China. Over the Chinese New Year, the Party produced three short animated cartoons that went viral, depicting Xi cleaning up corruption and working for the masses to achieve the Chinese Dream and Great Rejuvenation of the Chinese Nation. His wife, Peng Liyuan, and Premier Li Keqiang, add savvy media support for Baba Beijing at home and around the world too. No other modern Chinese leader, apart Mao, has used the media as masterfully as Xi.

As I have said in a number of radio shows and columns, the West has no answer for Xi Jinping (nor Putin, for that matter). The world is officially in the Xi Era (and you could just as well add, Putin Era). All of this will be fleshed out in fascinating detail, from his birth to the present, in my upcoming 2016 book, *Red Letters – The Diaries of Xi Jinping* (including all those meetings and phone calls between Putin and Xi).

Western Demonization of Xi Jinping - Let the Slime Begin

The West is desperate, really, really at wit's end, in trying to respond to Xi Jinping's incredible success at home and around the world. Time to start throwing dirt. **[IMG 0121]**

The West has no answer for Xi Jinping and Baba Beijing's relentless success across the world, with their many institutions founded (BRICS NDB, AIIB, Belts & Roads, SCO, etc.). When Western Empire is unable to overthrow a government and is not ready to go directly into to a hot war with a formidable foe, when the false flags, psyops and black ops just don't seem to be doing the trick, and sanctions can't exterminate enough local people to bring them to their knees, there is the timeworn playbook special: demonization of the country, its people and especially its leaders.

The newest manifestation of this desperate anti-China move is the MSM slime machine cranking up to destroy President Xi Jinping's reputation. The first line of attack is that he is trying to create a cult around himself, like Mao Zedong and to a lesser extent, Deng Xiaoping. This has been fleshed out by China expert Willy Lam, among others. Sometimes you read articles like his and ask if it was written by the CIA and handed to him to publish in his name.

What it boils down to is a huge platter of sour grapes, because Xi is clearly not going to be a Chinese Yeltsin, as the West was hoping, and more to the point, he is anti-Western to the core. Thus, the Western Empire is still cut out of dividing up the colonial spoils, as they did for 110 years here, 1840-1949. The West has not been able to destabilize China, since 1949, which is a polite way of saying, government overthrow. Nothing is working to balkanize and plunder China, so Xi is the next best punching bag. As frustrations for the West's colonial designs mount and mount, you can track the ever increasing efforts to character assassinate Xi, the CPC and the Chinese people. This is just tired, boilerplate empire. Think Castro, Chavez, Maduro and of course Russia's Putin is the billboard poster child for total Western demonization. Rest assured, Xi is not far behind.

Another favorite line of attack is to discredit Baba Beijing's administration and policies, especially where it comes to reforms. Xi's and Premier Li Keqiang's reforms are being fully implemented and they are significant in their import. But these reforms, which are great for China its people, do not make it possible for the West's banks, Wall Street, speculators and wheeler-dealers to come in, control and rape the economy and its people. Thus, behind the Great Western Firewall, the CPC's current platform cannot be taken seriously and has to be demonized as much as the leaders.

Willie Lam's CIA screed is fairly typical,

Xi is trying to consolidate power out of a Maoist styled, self-aggrandizement, rather than a Deng style commitment to liberalization.

Never mind that China and its people have never given up their foundations of communism and socialism, even during the Deng Era.

Mr. Lam went on to say that,

There is Western corporate skepticism, if not frustration, that it is not easy for Western corporations to break into areas that are monopolized by well-connected Chinese firms.

Well, boo-hoo-hoo. Western capitalists have been so used to having the laws and rules written in their favor, while using gunboat diplomacy and colonialism to steal the world's natural resources and keep enslaved the Dreaded Other, in the mire of poverty and oppression, that they are not used to a fair fight. So much for Adam Smith's invisible hand. It was a lie from the day it was published. It only works when the system is rigged for the 1%.

The next line of attack against Xi is that he is trying to establish a cult of himself. Thinking back through Western history allows us to put this slime ball in proper perspective. What about, "Reagan is God". That was a common refrain in the West, during the 1980s: "Ronald Reagan is God". I heard it all the time. I think it's safe to say that millions of downtrodden poor and middle class Americans thought that Franklin Roosevelt was God too, for what he did to give them hope, dignity and a future. Churchill was worshipped by many Westerners during World War II, and still is. There was definitely a cult around the Kennedys and Camelot. The adulation for Margaret Thatcher, with her, "There is no other way". Charles De Gaulle in France.

Behind the Great Western Firewall, for these leaders, it's charisma, building a following and rallying the people to a noble cause. But when Xi is doing the same thing, he's trying to establish a C-U-L-T.

The other Western slime ball that is getting thrown more and more is that Xi feels entitled to his position of power, that because of his background and station in life, what he has is owed to him.

I would feel exactly the same way if I were Xi Jinping and came from his background. It is again instructive to compare this accusation through the prism of Western hypocrisy.

What about Barak Obama, who was a graduate of Columbia and Harvard, and his wife, Michelle, who also graduated from Harvard? Not only that, but conclusive research shows that he and his family were/are CIA agents or NOCs (non-official covers): his mother, grandmother, stepfather and father were in the thick of it. For 18 months after graduation, Obama worked for a well-known CIA front company - and get a load of this - they paid off all his student debt. How nice of them. Reverend Cornell West was onto something, when he said that,

Obama was selected before he was elected.

Barak and Michelle are together worth $24 million. Taking all this together, you don't think Barak and Michelle feel entitled to their station in life?

And George W. Bush? He was an underperforming Yale graduate, who only got accepted there because of his family legacy. He comes from a wealthy, aristocratic family and has never been allowed to fail in his life. Daddy was CIA, grandpappy headed up the American Liberty League in the 1930s, which tried and failed to organize a fascist coup against FDR. His whole family is Pure-D blueblood one-percenters. W's worth $35 million, living the good life off his family name and fortune. I wonder if he ever felt he wasn't entitled to his position of power?

Then there are Bill and Hillary Clinton, both Yale graduates, well off and very well connected when they came to the White House. Together, they are worth (an estimated) $150 million. Given their behavior, I think it's safe to say they feel very, very privileged and entitled. [Incidentally try to accumulate $150 MM on a president's salary alone. The size of their fortune since their career began is its own indictment.]

In fact, except for Harry Truman, every US president since the 20th century, has come from a combination of wealth, Ivy League schools and/or privilege, when they entered office.

Then there is France's President François Hollande, who is worth €2 million and a graduate of France's Ivy League equivalent: *Les Grandes Ecoles*. I don't think he ever thought he is undeserving.

David Cameron, the Prime Minister of Britain, he's worth $50 million and graduated from Oxford. Hear how he talks about his countrymen and you know he feels his position of power is owed to him.

At least Xi Jinping lived in a cave for seven years and suffered being covered the whole time, with fleas and lice. He did backbreaking work, toiling in fields barefooted, among some of his country's poorest citizens. He then worked his butt off for 30 years in the trenches of government and military administration, slowly climbing the CPC ladder of meritocracy, managing counties, cities and provinces, before becoming president. Like his aforementioned homologues, he went to a high powered university, Qinghua. His father was a Communist Party and PLA hero, so he had good connections. Like most Western leaders, of course Xi feels entitled.

Xi does not have what many Western leaders have: wealth. Western websites that claim he is worth $100 million are totally ignorant of this man. He does not seek wealth. But it is possible that his brother, sisters and in-laws together are worth that much. Like many family members of powerful people (see George W. Bush), they have traded up on Xi's good name.

The bottom line is that power, money, elite education and (family) connections go together like a hotdog, bun and relish on top, be they Eastern or Western.

So, by all means, Xi feels entitled to his position of power. Just like every other political leader you can name. When you read/hear a character assassination piece on China's president, be sure to honestly ask yourself,

How does this accusation compare to high powered Western leaders?

You will invariably find that there is not a whit's worth of difference between them. Ergo, it's propaganda. That's why psyops works so well. Most people don't go beyond what they are told. Be different. Think for yourself.

Behind the Great Western Firewall, the demonization of Xi will continue to increase in frequency and level of desperation and vituperation. Let the slime begin.

Baba Beijing's Edward Snowden, Chelsea Manning, Julian Assange, Glenn Greenwald, WikiLeaks Challenge Has Arrived

[IMG 0122] CHART *Just a handful of the 22,000 Chinese Princes of Power exposed for having overseas tax havens.*

Note: *this chapter is dedicated to Chelsea Manning, Julian Assange, Edward Snowden, Glenn Greenwald and all the other hundreds of courageous whistle blowers, who are surely the first long knives into Western Empire's Conradian Heart of Darkness. Mother Earth's rapidly changing state of affairs would not be possible without their heroic and noble efforts. So, to them and for all the sacrifices they have made in their personal and professional lives, all of humanity owes them a huge debt of gratitude.*

President Xi Jinping and Premier Li Keqiang, China's two top leaders, are putting their national reputations on the line in trying to clean up the rot and graft in the Communist Party of China (CPC) hierarchy. At the very least and most cynically, like all good politicians with their ears to the ground, they are giving the people the impression they are equal to all the hype in the country's media, which they are intentionally ginning up. And therein lies the rub. Which is it: symbolic, superficial low hanging fruit being harvested, or are they really going to go after the upper echelons of Baba Beijing's political elite? Only time will tell. There are encouraging and disparaging signs at the same time.

On the face of it, Baba's Politburo Standing Committee and Central Committee are putting on a stern face of resolve and determination to clean the house in the offices, businesses and the CPC. It's a daily mantra on the airwaves, across headlines, on TV news teleprompters and it's safe to say, being fed into the national dialogue via text messaging (Wechat/Weixin and Sina Weibo) and email, through Baba's tens of thousands anonymous accounts. Like any government in a democracy that knows it needs to be responsive to the citizens' anxieties and frustrations, if it wishes to stay in power, Baba is obsessed with the zeitgeist of the moment, and they follow, poll and track its trends like a supercilious, OCD Lee Atwater or James Carville, two of America's heavyweight, dueling presidential election campaign managers. The anti-graft campaign is being carefully orchestrated down to the lowest levels of government. Our little neighborhood's weekly newsletter, which is left in front of our apartment door, has picked up on the language and is singing in faithful unison, as I'm sure every village rag across the country is.

This obsession with public outrage at official corruption is nothing new. It has been slowly bubbling its way up the list of people's gripes for years, going back to 1989's Tiananmen Square protests, where graft was fueling the protesters' outrage. Outgoing President Hu Jintao said in his last speech to the National People's Congress in 2012, that corruption in the CPC is the one thing that could bring an end to its preeminent position, as the keeper of the Heavenly Mandate, since China's independence in 1949. He was surely chastened knowing that the New York Times exposed the $2.7 billion fortune of Premier Wen Jiabao's immediate family, shortly before that. That's "B" for a billion. As 50s-60s US Senator Everett Dirksen apocryphally said,

A billion here, a billion there, pretty soon, you're talking real money.

This is a staggering amount of filthy lucre. The New York Times had the audacity to include a Chinese version of the article on its website, so it is still blocked in China, safe from curious local eyes. Too bad the NYT doesn't apply the same rules of engagement with the American government, like when they supinely obeyed the White House not to publish their report on George W. Bush's spying operation on US citizens, thus helping assure he won the 2004 presidential election. Craven satrapy to the Princes of Power. They only released it a year later when it got outed by a principled journalist. Integrity by any other name? Not.

Other previous leaders in Baba Beijing's pantheon, such as 2000s President Jiang Zemin, talked the anticorruption talk, but that's mostly what it amounted to, except for brazen, egregious cases which were beyond the pale to ignore - until now. Enter the Xi and Li Show, stage left. President Xi, the son of highly respected Xi Zhongxun, a 20th century icon of the Chinese communist revolution, appears to be consolidating power in China that no other leader has been able to muster since at least Deng Xiaoping, and maybe even Mao Zedong. He is governing with the swagger of a Ronald Reagan or France's president, Nicolas Sarkozy. Luckily for China, Xi and his administration are, if nothing else, competent technocrats who know how to operate the levers of statecraft.

A leader in Xi's position does not take his Paul Bunyan bluebeard axe, to the rot of government and business, without creating a lot of enemies in the process. Long knives are surely being surreptitiously sharpened in anticipation that Xi & Company may slip and fall one day. Compared to previous leaders and administrations, this campaign looks encouraging. China likes to talk about *tigers* and *flies*, just as Anglophones say *big fish* and *little fish*. No sooner did Xi's administration take over, that Bo Xilai, the powerful, charismatic provincial governor of up and coming Chongqing and a Politburo Standing Committee member as well, was put in jail and disappeared for corruption and malfeasance. A true tiger indeed, with big fangs to boot. His wife, Gu Kailai, was convicted for murdering by poisoning British businessman and suspected MI6 stringer, Neil Heywood, escaping by the hair of her chinney-chin-chin, with a suspended death sentence. She's a nice piece of work.

Soon thereafter, Liu Zhijun, a former minister of railways was given the death sentence for embezzling over ¥64 million (roughly €/$10 million). Yes, egregious corruption is punishable in China, with an AK-47 lead slug in the back of the head. General Gu Junshang, deputy head of the PLA General Logistics Department has gone down in flames for taking a 6% kickback on a ¥2 billion (about €/$285 million) military land deal in Shanghai. That's a cool €/$16 million in pocket money. Not bad for a day's worth of handshakes. China's revered People's Liberation Army (PLA), up to its commercial yarbles (gonads) to the tune of billions of RMB, has always been deferred to, when it comes to all their shady business dealings around the country. This is not the first high level military corruption scandal exposed this last year. Thus, the PLA's historical invulnerability may be showing some cracks in its political phaser shields.

While pontificating Westerners denigrate China's one-party electoral process, the following case suggests there is room for intrigue. Why just go after one head, when Baba can take down a whole football field full of crooks? Recently in Hunan, Mao Zedong's home fief and an historical crucible in the founding of the CPC, <u>56 provincial lawmakers offered bribes to 518 municipal lawmakers and 68 staff members, totaling more than ¥110 million (around €/$16 million)</u>, in order to buy votes in a municipal legislative election. So, what's Baba Beijing to do? Why, get rid of every last one of them! Talk about a Hunan house cleaning hat trick. Too bad America doesn't do the same thing to its equally corrupt and venal legislatures, from Washington, DC, to all 50 state capitals.

Sixteen million euzies/bucks in duffle bags begs the question: where did all that money come from in the first place, and what is so profitable about being a provincial legislature that makes that level of investment so compelling? Cold hard cash is what China's crooks like the best. A just released poll shows that 63% of all official corruption is good old fashioned bribes. Every legal crook loves the briefcases full of fungible bills, green Stateside and red in China. In the West, it is quaintly called *sunshine bribery*.

Before President Xi Jinping's and Premier Li Keqiang's Anti-Corruption Campaign, publically exposed corruption scandals like these were about as rare as real 100-year old eggs and authentic Ming Dynasty vases. The rot was and is there, but as is around the world, most of it we never see. Building an ever increasing head of steam, we, the local masses, are now disappointed if a head is not on a pike or chains are not clinking on some ne're-do-well's corpulent ankles, every day, as we wake up to scan the headlines. We've raised the bar. It's getting to be like a Roman Circus.

Is favoritism going on here? Of course. Are Xi's and Li's perceived or known rivalries and their sycophants getting the short end of the stick, or better yet, the fat end of a Louisville Slugger baseball bat? Undoubtedly. Politics is riot and rumble the world over. It goes something like this,

Xi: Why Comrade Li, this must be more fun than those Canadians bashing the brains out of little baby seals!

Li: Or American police pummeling helpless citizens to death with steel toed SWAT jack boots… Oh joy!

Baba Beijing has done a brilliant job of keeping the NYT's Wen Jiabao family fortune from becoming Wechat/email fodder. Curiously, it was published when Wen was still China's premier, albeit in the final 3-4 months of his tenure. If it had of spread virally on the one billion mobile phone screens in-country, it would have been as explosive as Chelsea "Bradley" Manning's disclosures about Iraq and Afghanistan, and which were released by Julian Assange and WikiLeaks.

Like Edward Snowden's damning revelations, Baba Beijing is dealing with an even more explosive journalistic exposé, which dwarfs the NYT scoop. In January, it was splashed across the globe that the International Consortium of Investigative Journalists (ICIJ) had a list of nearly 22,000 elite Chinese with offshore tax havens, including relatives of President Xi. Talk about some big fish-eating tigers of the highest order. Hidden billions in secret bank accounts on the British Virgin Islands and Cook Islands would not just be political dynamite on the streets of China, but on the scale of a neutron bomb. You don't open secret accounts in these tax havens for passbook savings. Millions barely cut it. We're in the "B" for billions stratosphere here.

If you are in China, the ICIJ website, and now the *Guardian* and *CBC* are only available here via a VPN, since they are all carrying the story.

It would have taken great courage, but Wen Jiabao could have taken down his children and all the other maggoty parasites who have made billions in ill-gotten gains from his name and high level position. He could have gone on national TV and held a press conference to announce the whole lot of them were being marched to prison. Tigers on steroids. But he didn't.

Former Premier Wen and President Hu Jintao were never considered very concerned about corruption, the one big criticism that really sticks to their ten-year reign at the top of the Heavenly Mandate. But President Xi Jinping and Premier Li Keqiang have staked their administration and reputations on rooting out not just flies, but the tigers as well. Xi's brother-in-law, Deng Jiagui, who is prominently featured in the ICIJ exposé, would be a great place to start, to really show Baba Beijing's resolve, to rooting out Party corruption at the highest levels.

Others related to former Premier Wen Jiabao, former President Hu Jintao, former Premier Li Peng, paramount leader Deng Xiaoping and many others are also exposed in the ICIJ report. It's like the who's who of the Chinese Party pantheon. The Xi and Li anti-corruption drive looks superficially good on paper. But not until some of these *Red Nobility* take a hard fall and do some hard time, will I be able to take all the chest

beating and theatrics genuinely seriously. Mind you, it would not happen in almost any other country, the West included. But Baba Beijing is different. China's leaders govern with the Heavenly Mandate and if they want to do something, this powerful historical notion gives them the right to do so. In this case, as difficult and painful as it may be, they should – really, really should.

[IMG 0123] Image satirizing Chinese official corruption. Ouch.

The Way It Was Supposed to Be in 21st-Century America vs. the Way It Really Is Across the Big Pond

Musing on Corruption and Alternative Forms of Governance

Many people who voted for Obama in 2008, including myself, were expecting him to channel an amalgam of Upton Sinclair, Franklin D. Roosevelt, and George Orwell. He sure talked the talk during the campaign, didn't he? Instead, we got a tetra-headed, deleterious mutation of Ulysses S. Grant, J. Edgar Hoover, Thomas Friedman, and The *Manchurian Candidate's* dictatorial Senator Iselin. Fool me once. My, how time flies. Just imagine an America today where the pre-election promising Obama is president and if we channel recent current events, the following satire would have happened:

Prez-O Sets the Tone

The crusading federal Attorney General (AG), Perry Mason, brings down the mayor of Houston, with a damning open-and-shut case of corruption, kickbacks, and bribery, forcing a hasty resignation. President Obama senses a building up of anger on Main Street and his pollsters concur. During a routine press conference, he stuns everybody by telling the world he thinks the AG is doing a great job and should be encouraged to carry on with this and numerous other private-sector/government-collusion cases on the books. To drive the point home, Obama goes on national TV to talk to the American public about corruption among the big oil companies and to express his commitment to root it out and make sure that the perpetrators of all this white-collar crime are put behind bars. The corruption is so bad that there is suddenly viral chatter of breaking up Big Oil, into smaller, more-manageable corporate units, because they are currently *too big to fail*. Several of Petroworld's senior management have already stepped down pending investigation. Harking back to the journalistic glory days of My Lai and Watergate and seemingly emboldened by the government's mien, the New York Times

(NYT) and the Washington Post reported a pipeline of alumni from Texas University's petroleum engineering school, into these high-level executive posts, where so much corruption is being found.

[IMG 0124] For those of us who voted for him, this is the fantasy speech we hoped he would give.

Meanwhile, the state AG in Florida, Erin Brockovich, indicts two retired US military officers for trying to collude with a foreign enemy to sell influence. The message emanating from the White House on down is clear: it is all systems go to exorcise the rot from America's corrupt halls of private and public power.

Wall Street on the Ropes

On Wall Street, the feds are up the backsides of the leading investment banks, investigating massive corruption in the fixed-income markets. Lloyd Blankfein's mug, CEO of Goldman Sachs, is all over the mainstream media, being derisively called the *Bond King*, while the whole sector is swarming with SEC investigators on a mission to root out insider trading, collusion, and graft. After all, a fed up public demands no less.

In Illinois, six state police were handed sentences to prison terms of four to 14 years, for torturing and accidentally killing a detainee suspected of real estate fraud. They confessed they were irate at not being cut in on the deal.

The Secretaries of Treasury and Commerce this week come out with major policy speeches, discussing the need for deep reform in the dysfunctional housing and real estate sectors and with the White House's blessings, will be pushing hard to bring this critical sector back into the real economy, with regulations to stimulate rational market development. America's insider newspaper, the *New York Times*, kowtowing as usual to the White House's current spin, comes out with a major editorial calling for meaningful reform in America's broken-down housing and real estate industries. The federal government also announced plans to thoroughly look at the rules and regulations on the books, so as not to liberalize *free* markets, but in order to help root out corruption at all levels of the regulatory process, both state and federal.

[**IMG 0125**] *Goldman-Sachs' Blankfein, The Bond King, wowing the Chinese elite before his imaginary downfall.*

Media Yes Men

For those who scrutinize the West's MSM, they know that the *Washington Post (Wapo)* is just as prone to Pennsylvania Avenue pressure as the *NYT*. But *Wapo* does its journalistic job of *Comforting the Afflicted and Afflicting the Comfortable*, by coming out with an investigative piece about rampant corruption in the skimming of money from state welfare coffers.[1] While local and state officials are enriching themselves at the taxpayers' expense, by colluding with corrupt private-sector vendors, the most vulnerable of society - the poor, children, and the elderly - are suffering the consequences. This report is based on leaked documents from the Department of Justice, which is conducting a massive nationwide investigation, for once not to snare the whistleblower, but into the perpetrators who use of federally mandated, state welfare funds.

Meanwhile, a high-level member of the National Science Foundation was sentenced to 13 years of hard time for embezzling $20 million in federally granted research funds. The word is out: crooks in all sectors, private and public, will not be tolerated and you could be next, if you've got your hand in the cookie jar of corruption.

In the food sector, another huge concern among the nation's consumers, one executive was sentenced to life in prison and more than a dozen more for up to 15 years, for knowingly selling tainted cooking oil, violating numerous food safety laws, and endangering the lives of thousands of consumers.[2]

[**0125**] *The mainstream media delivering the exact message the Princes of Power want you to see and hear.*

Fearless Foreign Press' Journo-Cojones

The British *Guardian*, one of the last Western newspapers with any journo-cojones (Spanish for *gonads*), has a big exposé on a high-ranking, retired CIA chief, who is still one of the most powerful members of America's internal-security apparatus, and who is widely believed to be under top-level investigation for graft and corruption. Having kept a low profile for months, the fact that he showed up at a big Stanford University petroleum engineering school alumni celebration did not escape the notice of this UK newspaper, which is unafraid to report what America's lapdog media obediently avoids. Is this alumni bash a signal that this all-powerful state security titan has pulled the necessary strings to call off the dogs? Yet another foreign newspaper fearlessly ready to step on the toes of America's power elite, Brazil's *O Globo* reports on the same scandal, that a former American vice-president is linked to this CIA mogul, and is in cahoots with a shady, private-sector dealmaker in numerous, highly profitable land-development schemes. Will America's mainstream media pick up the story? Probably not, unless Obama really get up and bangs on his bully pulpit, taking the cause to the people to get them to put pressure on Congress.

One US newspaper, the *San Francisco Chronicle*, seems to be inspired by the foreign press' courage to speak truth to power. One of their reporters, Suzy B. True, has just been detained by the Department of Homeland Security (DHS) for a scathing report about gross acts of corruption and graft among the many private-sector contractors, who are apparently skimming off contracts with their colluding DHS paymasters. Even though the paper was issued a gag order by America's highest authorities, the *Chronicle* bravely and brazenly ran a huge four-inch front-page headline that screamed, "**RELEASE HER.**" Only time will tell of the outcome and the safe return of their courageous reporter.

Obama's Legacy

Reports continue about frustrations in setting up a national database on property held by government officials, especially in the banking, energy, and transportation sectors, due to rampant tax evasion and graft. Knowing this wave of frustration could easily turn into a tsunami of popular 99% revolt, Obama comes out with a major policy speech and appeals to America's people to help him rid the military-industrial complex of brazen corruption and graft. He announces that General "Buck" Turgidson is being indicted for multiple white-collar crimes and that this is just the beginning of a long campaign to clean up one of America's most secretive and rotten sectors.

To round up a busy month of crusading in America for clean government and transparent, ethical business practices, the #2 director of California's state investigation bureau, Jack Friday is all over the media, photo'd in prison fatigues and manacles, after receiving a well-publicized life sentence for corruption and bribe taking. Again, Obama is sensing the frustration and well-grounded anger of America's citizens, against a country in dire need of reform at all levels: business, government, and military. Obama decides to make his upcoming State of Union speech the rallying cry to fight sleaze across America. He now knows that the legitimacy of his administration and his tenure

as president will be judged by his tireless fight to make the United States a better place for all people - poor, working, and middle-class alike, and not just the power elite 1%, and that he will be conducting the rest of presidential tenure with the long view of American history looking over his shoulder.

[IMG 0126] *The real criminals of society finally get the justice they deserve. Dream on.*

Pipe Dreams

A pipe dream, a far-fetched fantasy? It is if your passport is blue and has the American seal embossed on the front. But not if your passport is bright red and sports a seal with four small stars arching over a larger one - the national symbol on China's flag. Everything detailed above is happening in the People's Republic of China. For a foreigner like me living in China and used to bemoaning the corrupt, completely dysfunctional US economy and the sorry spectacle of so-called governance across the Big Pond, these are exciting and breathtaking times.

Western pundits like to say that a one-party state such as the Communist Party of China (CPC), cannot maintain any legitimacy, because the people cannot go to the polls to make their voices heard, to keep their representatives honest and accountable. Throughout China's 5,000 years of continuous civilization, there has never been the notion of pluralistic democracy. Never. Not even one time. Yet let's face it, Baba Beijing and its billion-plus citizens are doing just fine, thank you: the soon to be world's biggest economy is already the world's largest trading country and by 10,000 *li* (miles), is the biggest creditor in human history. With each passing year, the Sino-superlatives just keep piling up, even as this country is continuing to deal with rampant corporate and political corruption, and one of the most polluted environments on Earth.

Polling Pols

So how do they do it? Guess which entities are the biggest and most numerous clients of China's hundreds of polling companies? Why Baba Beijing and the CPC of course, starting at the macro-federal level down to the smallest villages. China's leaders are avidly keen to know what their citizens think - about corruption, about inflation, medical care, etc., down to the neighborhood level of garbage collection, traffic congestion, pollution and water cutoffs. And they don't just put the results in a file cabinet and ignore them. They want to stay in power, maintain their legitimacy in the eyes of the people, and join the annals of China's long line of rulers, as having done an admirable job of fulfilling their Heavenly Mandate. Thus, they act on these results. Corruption has been an ongoing concern for more and more middle-class and poor Chinese, paralleling the country's explosive economic growth and rapid social evolution. President Xi Jinping, Premier Li Keqiang, and the 300-member Central Committee and 1,500 members of the National People's Congress are not only listening, but responding to these public concerns of the 99%.

[0127] *The biggest polling company customer in China is Baba Beijing. Pictured here is a pollster taking the sociopolitical pulse of a Chinese citizen.*

SMS and Street Protests

There are other avenues for the "voting" public to vent their discontent. China has over one billion mobile phones and the world's largest 3G and 4G networks. Millions of SMS can cascade virally across this continent sized country in a matter of hours, over an incident of injustice, police brutality or corruption. Baba Beijing has established tens of thousands of text-messaging accounts, so they can keep track of the lightning-fast zeitgeist changing by the hour on the streets, as well as to respond to this electronic fury and to help massage the message. This wireless release valve is not enough though, as there are an estimated 300-500 public protests *a day* across China, usually to redress local concerns about greedy businessmen and bureaucrats, slimy land deals with citizens getting screwed out of their property, unwanted building permits for polluting industrial projects that the town folk are against, police brutality and the like.

Westerners Just Don't Get It

Western pundits love to round on Baba that these tens of thousands of protests around the country each year are a sign of weakness in China's centralized, authoritarian system of state-regulated economy. But they miss the point entirely. All these protests are assiduously compiled in Beijing to add to Baba's arsenal of information and statistics from the polls and SMS messages, in order to better respond to the public's grievances in a targeted fashion. This powerful expression of redress is not just Kabuki Theater. The government frequently responds to this constant tide of public protests with solutions. The people often win their cases. For a Chinese protest to be put down with force, the crowd usually has to get violent first, unlike Occupy Wall Street (OWS), where protesting Chicago teachers and so many other scorned public protests are brutally repressed by America's militarized local and state police forces. Instead of setting up a national system of response and redress, the Obama regime used the FBI, Homeland Security, universities and banks to coordinate crushing the OWS movement and killing it in its tracks.[4]

[IMG 0128]

Democracy expressed on the streets of China, 300-500 times a day.

Corruption Comes in Many Flavors

Is corruption a big problem in China? Yes. But it is also a malignant cancer in corporate America, on Wall Street, all through the military and medical-industrial complexes and a plethora of other sectors. What Baba Beijing is showing to its people and the world is that leadership is not counted in performing miracles and realizing overly ambitious expectations (Mao tried that during the Great Leap Forward), but is measured in the public's eye that they are doing something about any perceived problem and are making ongoing progress. Honest effort, not cynical sideshows, is a necessity and counts for much. The Chinese understand all too well the challenges Baba Beijing faces. A common refrain when I meet people on the street is, *China has such a huge population, is so big, has so many competing regions and peoples, that it makes it difficult to manage.*

What this means is the Chinese understand the daunting task that Baba Beijing has to govern such a colossal country and they are willing to give them the benefit of the doubt. The bottom line expectation is that they want their leaders to at least be making an honest and sincere effort to do the right thing. That in essence is the Heavenly Mandate.

[IMG 0129] *Yes, this kind of corruption is a problem in China, but it is also true in many countries touting themselves as pluralistic democracies.*

Baba Beijing Is an Expert at This Stuff

This recent barrage of anticorruption activity in China has waxed and waned over the years, depending on the zeitgeist on the street, but progress has still been remarkably steady. This improvement can be quantified. Since it first started its Corruption Perception Index (CPI) in 1995, Transparency International (TI) has been tracking China's progress and the results are impressive. They are a strong indication of China's undulating but steady improvement in fighting corruption in the halls of government, and, by extension, in offices and boardrooms of the corporate sector, that collude with bureaucrats for filthy lucre.

Comparison of Transparency International's Perceived Corruption Index, 1995 and 2012

1995 TI Corruption Index

Change overla[...]

Rank	Country	Score out of 100	2012 Rank	2012 Score	1995-2012 Change
1	New Zealand	96	1	90	-6
2	Denmark	93	1	90	-3
3	Singapore	93	5	87	-6
4	Finland	91	1	90	-1
5	Canada	89	9	84	-5
6	Sweden	89	4	88	-1
7	Australia	88	7	85	-3
8	Switzerland	88	6	86	-2
9	Netherlands	87	9	84	-3
10	Norway	86	7	85	-1
(1999)	Iceland	92	11	82	**-10**
11	Ireland	86		69	**-17**

(1997)	Luxembourg	86		12	80	-6
12	United Kingdom	86			74	-12
13	Germany	81		13	79	-2
14	Chile	79			72	-7
15	USA	78			73	-5
16	Austria	71			69	-2
17	Hong Kong	71		14	77	6
18	France	70			71	1
(2009)	Barbados	69		15	76	7
19	Belgium/ Luxembourg	69			75	7
20	Japan	67			74	7
21	South Africa	56			43	-13
22	Portugal	56			63	7
23	Malaysia	53			49	-4
24	Argentina	51			35	-16
25	Taiwan	44			61	18
26	Spain	43			65	22
27	South Korea	41			56	15
28	Hungary	41			55	14
29	Turkey	40			49	9
30	Greece	40			36	-4
31	Colombia	34			36	2
32	Mexico	32			34	2
33	Italy	30			42	12
34	Thailand	28			37	9
35	India	28			36	8
36	Philippines	28			34	6
37	Brazil	27			43	16

38	Venezuela	27		19	-8
(1996)	Russia	26		28	2
(1996)	India	26		36	10
39	Pakistan	23		27	5
40	China	22		39	17
41	Indonesia	19		32	13

© Transparency International and the University of Gottingen, 1995

Food for Thought

The above table tells many stories. In the last 17 years, while taking their economy into Star Trek warp drive, Baba Beijing has improved the country's public-sector corruption index by a full 17 points, second only to Spain and Taiwan in gain. Several countries that have imbibed deeply from the waters of deregulation, Argentina, Iceland, Ireland, South Africa, and the United Kingdom all dropped precipitously by double digits. The United States and Canada, two more champions of chest-beating libertarian policies, have also gotten worse, not better, since 1995, dropping five points each. Two countries with the world's longest history of democracy, Italy and Greece, both members of the European Union, are China's neighbors on the 2012 roster: Greece's 36 ranks below China's 39 and Italy's 42 is just above. India, "the world's largest democracy", has improved eight points, but still lags behind China, with a score of only 36 and tied with Greece. In fact, looking at the full list on TI's website, over half the countries ranked *below* China in 2012 tout themselves as pluralistic democracies. So much for pluralistic voting keeping governments legitimate, accountable, and honest. The correlation is weak at best.

Those Darn Socialists and Damned Statistics

The other telling observation on the list is the preponderance of Western European countries at the top. According to this ranking, Scandinavians, with what American conservatives like to describe as their cradle-to-grave, nanny-state socialism, sure seem to run a tight fiscal ship. Neocon, Ayn Rand worshipers would say,

You'd better watch the public treasury, what with all those undeserving blue-collar parasites and white-collar middle-class leeches sucking on the hind tit of Big Bad Gubment. I'm telling you, there oughta be a law. Even those vile Western European NATO vassals, unrepentant Canadians, misguided Asians, like Singapore and Hong Kong, not to mention the lunatic Kiwis and Roos Down Under and what, who's that - coconut crazy Barbados, all have - heaven forbid - universal health care and other pinko-commie social programs for the 99%.

Yet, all these aforementioned countries rank in TI's top *fifteen*. I don't know about you, but as an armchair ruminator of all things weighty and portentous, and having taken several courses in statistics during my time in the ivory towers of undergraduate and graduate academia, I'm seeing what those high-falootin' analysts and soothsayers call a *trend* here. What I see here is what those pesky number-crunchers and bean counters like to bandy about – a *correlation*, meaning when one thing has an attribute, like social programs for the 99%, there is a strong tendency to also have clean government and less corruption.

Looking Forward on the Arrow of Time

This bodes well for China, since it is phasing in countrywide social security and a national health-care system, while at the same time working hard to rid itself of corporate and political corruption. So statistically speaking, China has only one way to go on Transparency International's CPI, and that is in the direction of the uber-clean Fab Fifteen.

What is just as impressive is how the more things change, the more they stay the same. Since 1995, the year the first TI Corruption Index came out, there has been a remarkable consistency in the Top 10 countries. Clearly, economies with humane social programs are doing something right, which is what statistic studs call *persistence*.

Corruption by Any Other Name

Mind you, TI's index only considers public or bureaucratic corruption: bribes, graft, kickbacks, and the like. But who needs these tawdry tools of the 1%'s errand boys, when you can just spread millions of dollars into the pockets of henchmen in the hallowed halls of statecraft, write your own laws to be passed in the middle of the night and signed with Mont Blanc 18-carat gold, diamond-studded fountain pens? Oops, I forgot, that's not really corruption, in what passes for democracy these days in the United States. It's all legal and codified, right? There is a name for it: sunshine bribery. Much of what the West considers "business as usual", is deemed colonialism by the world's dark skinned peoples. Where would America be ranked on a comprehensive business-corruption index, with its Gilded Age economic model of government-in-service-to-the-Princes-of-Power? Below China? Interesting to ponder.

What's Good for the Chinese Goose Would Sure Be Great for the American Gander

Too bad Americans can't put handcuffs on all the members of Congress and the Senate in Washington, DC. They are just as corrupt, using laws they pass and Supreme Court decisions to make it all nice and "legal". Same difference, different culture. Baba Beijing knows it has a serious corruption problem and is making a serious effort to cut it down to size. In Hunan Province, 570 legislators were told to pack their bags and were sent home, for blatant corruption.

Both Chinese and Western pundits can say, "Yeah, but what about all the other city and provincial officials who are just as corrupt?" They have a point, but where I grew up, we have a great philosophical take on situations such as this,

How do you eat an elephant?

One bite at a time…

At least corrupt and venal corporate crooks in China can spend hard time behind bars, or even more dramatically, pay a last visit to the gallows. Corruption is a way of life in the American business world these days, not to mention all those with whom they collude in the hypocritical, pocket stuffing halls of state and federal government. Yet, very few of them have paid a price, other than wrist-slapping token fines, while never having to admit guilt. About the only scapegoat I can think of is Bernie Madoff. Any self-preserving white collar criminal would much rather plunder public and private purses in the United States than in China. Much, much better odds for staying in business. Sic'em Baba Beijing, sic'em, boy! *Grrrr…*

[IMG 0130] *The most destructive corruption to humanity happens with the strokes of 18-carat, diamond-studded pens: laws, regulations, directives & contracts, regardless of the country where it happens – East or West.*

A New World Paradigm, or Hell or High Water?

All of this is not lost on the Moral Majority around the world. The hubristic Western mantra that the only avenue to leadership legitimacy and popular success is pluralistic democracy and a deregulated economy (i.e., markets rigged for the 1%) has lost its luster. Clearly, if the West wishes to remain relevant into the 22nd century, some serious soul searching needs to happen, while radical changes in the current libertarian model of faux "free markets" must transpire, hell or high water. More and more countries are looking at other models of governance, with China's authoritarian, state-economy model at the top of the list. The way things are trending around our Pale Blue Dot, for better in China and for worse in the "democratic" West, the profile of the United Nation's 193 national political systems will surely be different in the decades to come.

The 21st century is shaping up geopolitically to get very intense indeed. So, buckle up boys and girls for the realpolitik ride of a lifetime. Living here in Sinoland, I've got a Mohammed Ali, Angelo Dundee cornerman, boxing ring seat, baby. And from my vantage point, I'm wagering five to one that Baba Beijing is ready to **RUUUUMBLE**.

Note: a big thanks to _sinocism.com_, China's best English/Chinese news aggregator, for providing the press articles and references listed in the first half of this article.

1- This is actually the motto of the venerable political journal, the Oklahoma Observer. (#131 Image by _okobserver.net_)
2- For a sobering and gripping real life look at comparing how China and the United States handle serious consumer safety cases, read the excellent essay by Ron Unz at the American Conservative: _ronunz.org/2012/04/18/ chinese-melamine-and-american-vioxx/_ .
3- _http://inquisitr.com/460605/fbi-homeland-security-coordinated-with- banks-and-universities-to-crush-occupy-wall-street/_

The Real Truth about China's Plenums

Why, it's really quite elementary, Dr. Watson

It has been amusing to peruse all the Western mainstream media blather about Baba Beijing (the Chinese leadership) and its much ballyhooed *Third Plenum* meeting.

Chinese plenums are when Baba gets together for a big Sino-powwow to discuss and reach consensus on the strategic vision they want to take their country and its citizens - 20% of the human race, over the next five years. These masters of the 21st century's future are led by the Politburo Standing Committee (PSC). The current PSC is the 18th since 1927.[1] It is composed of Baba's most powerful decision makers, typically a group of 7-9 leaders. It is something akin to a Western leader's cabinet. The PSC oversees these plenums, which include the Central Committee (CC). The CC is composed of 300 or so elite members of the Communist Party.[2] This two tiered model of governance is what pulls the levers of Sinoland statecraft, and steers the country and its people towards the future.

[IMG 0131] China's plenums. *The leaders of China's PSC will determine our Western standings of living and lifestyles in the decades to come.*

A sexist glass ceiling as thick as a nuclear blast shield

There has never been a woman member in the all-powerful PSC. Not surprising in such an uber-patriarchal, Confucian infused society. The great philosopher-teacher instructed women to obey their fathers and husbands, remain chaste before marriage, remain chaste until death if their spouse dies before them, always remain silent in the presence of men - and sew. Doris Lessing and Emma Goldman would not approve. While China's communist and socialist revolutions greatly improved the status and lives of women, compared to pre-liberation times, like everywhere across the planet, to quote James Brown, it's a man's world.

Like most communist revolutions, Mao's vendetta against *old thoughts* (in this case, very sexist Confucianism) opened up many avenues professionally for women (doctors, engineers, business owners, managers, etc.), after independence in 1949. Since 1980, when China hopped into the economic cockpit for warp speed take-off, work opportunities for the silent, sewing sex have exploded exponentially. But in the political mosh pit of power and persuasion, a glass ceiling as thick as a bank teller's window on the wrong side of town is still very much in place. These days, there is a score or two of women in the CC, but it all still feels very much like tokenism, considering China's history, modern and ancient.

[IMG 0132] Confucius is at least as influential on human society today, as Jesus or Mohammed.

Symbols and Oblique Phrases

The Chinese people scrutinize all the symbolism divined in their leaders. This includes perceived omens, signals and oblique phrases, with arguments over which Chinese character was used and why a different synonym was not used instead. As rich and nuanced as Chinese is, debates over this character or that one can take on monumental proportions. Linguistic symbols coming out of the mouths of China's leaders is important, but how they look also counts. Like Ronald Reagan, Chinese leaders all dye their hair pitch black and invariably wear spiffy, Western, coal black suits, with China-flag-red silk ties.

Western pundits snivel with acid sarcasm about what they see in this as Orwellian Newspeak. What they forget is that Barak "I'm really good at killing people" Obama has to wear a flag pin on his Whitehouse pajamas, in order to not be called a traitor.[3] Reagan dyed his hair for a reason. Remember "It's Morning in America"? That nifty piece of propaganda wouldn't fit as well with a white haired saying it.

For Baba Beijing, it's simple symbolism: unity, harmony and concord. Speaking of Ronnie, the thought of a grade B actor, no matter how much "The Great Communicator", leading a country worthy of the name, is beyond the pale in Sinoland. These men have spent their entire lives working up through the ranks, managing billions of yuan and governing millions of their citizens, at the local, regional and national level. They are often highly educated, trained engineers, city planners, business managers of huge state owned enterprises and the like, technocrats all, who understand processes and systems.

Sorry to say, but yahoos like George W. Bush, Barak Obama, François Hollande and David Cameron would last about a Nanjing nanosecond over here, with their family jewels left twitching on the slaughterhouse floor. Bill Clinton might last an hour, max, just because he's such a brilliant bullshitter. If he got his much ballyhooed, inside the Beltway triangulation tango going, he might make it a day or two, then the stiletto across the neck would come from behind: ffffffffffffffffftt.

[IMG 0133] *Serious business: the uber-macho 18th Central Committee in 3rd Plenum session. (Image by Guizhou Minzu University)*

Plenums Past and Present

Each new leadership team gets five years to run this greatest show on Earth - 21st century China - renewable one time. When they meet, they are called plenums. Third ones have a bit of an aura about them and are considered fortuitous. This is because of the 1978 Third Plenum, when Deng Xiaoping was brought back from political oblivion, after being purged by the Gang of Four in 1976, following the death of Mao. It was at this plenum that Deng took control of China's levers of power, became the (unofficial) paramount leader of the country and pushed through what were then radical rural and policy reforms, the ones that helped launch China into economic hyper drive starting in the 80s. A meeting like 1978 is a hard act to follow. Baba Beijing is obsessed with historical precedents on the timeline of previous leaders and lose sleep fretting over their legacy in the pantheon of the Heavenly Mandate.

China's President Xi Jinping and Premier Li Keqiang have boldly promised major reforms in this 3rd Plenum and continue to be on a full national PR campaign with their citizens, pitching support for their platform. It is said in Chinese politics that it's when you get elected, that the real campaigning starts, within the Party and among the masses. It's all over the media and continues to be so. Many other past plenums have promised much, but the follow through on some initiatives have sometimes petered out. Since Xi and Li are much attuned to historical references and their Heavenly Mandate, they have a lot riding on what happens during their tenure.

[IMG 0134] *Deng Xiaoping's 1978 plenum changed world history. Long before, he was a take-no-prisoner, guerrilla war fighter, with a lot of revolutionary blood on his hands. His diminutive size would disarm people. Deng is pictured here in the glory days of killing Japanese and Western colonialists and fascist KMT thugs by the truckload, 1930s-40s.*

Analyzing a chess match using the rules of gin rummy

Watching the Western media, which Paul Craig Roberts deliciously calls *presstitutes*, trying to fathom all of this through their monochromatic prism of economic reforms and pluralistic democracy, is something akin to a bunch of people watching a grandmaster chess match and the only game they know is gin rummy. Or a roomful of Steinbeckian Lenny Smalls listening to a discourse by Socrates.[4] They don't follow much of it. The Chinese have 5,000 years of continuous history *sans* one iota of democracy, except now, China's one million villages vote for their local governments. Given the decline of Western corporate-democracy-for-the-1% that we are witnessing around the world (endless and rigged, boom-bust market bubbles, false flags à la mode, an unsustainable worldwide Wehrmacht, unpayable government and private debt, corrupt Bretton Woods financial institutions), I don't think Baba Beijing is losing any sleep over it, or feels terribly left out. No, they are in fact offering the world's other 191 countries a decidedly different way to run a country and govern its people. It is like nothing that Caucasian people have going on these days, with their pointless, Potemkin elections between MBA Tweedle Dee and CEO Tweedle Dum, both Pinocchio-nosed puppets of the Corporate Party. This model, my Western friends, is getting to be a harder and harder sell these days, to any leaders with a conscience, looking to amend or start anew with their countries' constitutions.

In Sinoland, it's all about building consensus - *from the top down*

As the sum of this book's research and synthesis amply demonstrates, the West's *Washington-London-Paris consensus,* continues to bully, bludgeon and bomb the world's dark skinned peoples, especially of the Muslim stripe. These 500 years of colonial pain and persecution has been and continues to be foisted on *The Dreaded Other.* It is painful and gut wrenching for Westerners to face the truth about their genocidal, racist past and present in Africa, the Americas and Asia, all glorified and romanticized in our sanitized history books. It is one of the hardest changes in my mindset that I've ever overcome, so I know how difficult it is to accept.

[IMG 0135] *The White Man's burden: racist, Western, colonial masters dispensing their civilizing mission, showing The Dreaded Other their definition of respect. It's ongoing today, albeit more sophisticated. (mage by Greanvillepost. com)*

[IMG 0136] The Chinese understand the racist perfidy of Western Empire, just as much as all the other non-white peoples around the world. Pictured above, the metaphorical rape of China by the English, Germans, French, Russians and Japanese, planning their colonial gang bang. Chine means China in French.

[IMG 0137] *This is the dream China that Western empire still lusts for to this day: weak, powerless and ready for colonial rape, pillage and plunder. (Image by The Greanville Post)*

Then there is the *Beijing* consensus, which is a different wok full of geopolitical stir fry altogether, compared to the West. It is not to project external power, intimidation and domination. It is to project persuasion internally, among the country's decision makers and on down to the most distant peasants in the hinterlands. It is unabashedly un-pluralistic from Westerners' paradigm, and this drives them to political psychosis. It especially smarts, since Baba has been succeeding on the economic, financial and diplomatic fronts for the last 30 years, with no topside in sight.

In China, the tiny but powerful nine-person Politburo Standing Committee spend months consulting with the 25 person Standing Committee, the 300-member Central Committee and the 1,500 legislators in the National People's Congress. This coalesces into the PSC setting the vision, almost a mission statement for where they see the country going and the goals that can be realized with it over the next five years. All of this is hammered out at the different levels of consultation. Once the course has been decided, these powerhouse politicians, in spite of often different approaches and philosophies, dye their hair black and put on identical tailored, coal black suits, sporting red silk ties.

All of them, the PSC, the SC and the CC, work and massage the message down through the Party ranks, laws are written for passage in the NPC, all the while drumming up support among their 1,300,000,000 citizens. Is there horse trading, bare knuckled bullying, à la LBJ (Lyndon Baines Johnson) and corruption coursing through China's corporate and political system? Of course. But one only has to look at America's own corporate Congress, Senate and Whitehouse these days to see that the

West's mythical, idealized pluralistic democracy is in reality just that: mythical - and no better or worse than China. While it is still somewhat better in Europe, their democracies are also slowly being crushed and brought under the iron fist of the 1%. At the end of the day, choosing a form of government anywhere on Earth is always going to be a Faustian tradeoff.

A half a pie is better than no dessert at all

Western talking heads love to chortle with their Caucasian air of superiority at this political process. Especially since, as Baba's vision is promoted down to lower and wider levels, the directives are oftentimes ignored and not fully implemented; mainstream media pundits chest thump that this is prima facie evidence of a failed system, which is unresponsive to the people's needs. This is a Lennie Small, gin rummy interpretation of an ancient system that the West just does not fathom, nor wants to even begin trying to understand. For the West, if the plenum's mission statement is not pegged as being too tepid and lacking punch, then occidental spin meisters go to the other extreme by pronouncing the platform as overly ambitious or unrealistic. But from Baba Beijing's perspective, they use the old W. Clement Stone adage,

Aim for the moon. If you miss, you may hit a star.

They understand in a continent sized country with over a billion souls, across regions of peoples who are just as antagonistic to each other as Northerners and Southerners in other countries, that a half a pie is better than no dessert at all, and tomorrow is a great day to get back in the hell's kitchen of cage fighting politics, to concoct and promote the next dish. Only one other country is probably as hard to govern as China: India. Westerners, especially Americans have serious attention deficit disorder when it comes to the weighty issues of the day. It's more about the 24-hour news cycle, today's bond prices and upcoming corporate quarterly reports. Over here in Sinoland, the internal dialogue of Baba Beijing goes something like this,

So, only half of our dreams got realized this go around? No matter, we've got the rest of the 21st century to keep moving forward, sometimes a step

backward or no gain at all, but keep on keeping on, as our Heavenly Mandate dictates.

That's what the West is up against: triathlete technocrats, who are patient politicians, with a strong compass fixated on deep history, and who dream of the future in decade-long timescales. Sitting here in Sinoland, gazing East at the degrading debacle across the Pacific, and westward to the tip of the Eurasian continent, with Europe trying so hard to imitate Uncle Sam, my vision is no optimistic. I see pervasive house-of-cards financial debt, governments unresponsive to their citizens, due to being coopted by corporations and the 1% and institutionalized corruption, what is euphemistically called *sunshine bribery*, which passes for business as usual.

It really seems like an unfair fight. Maybe Baba Beijing should fight with one arm tied behind the back, you know, just to make it more entertaining.

[IMG 0138] *Premier Li Keqiang (front) and President Xi Jinping, on a mission of consensus - working a crowd, Beijing style. (#139 Image by Renminwang)*

1- http://en.wikipedia.org/wiki/List_of_historical_makeup_of_the_Politburo_Standing_Committee_of_the_Communist_Party_of_China.
2- https://en.wikipedia.org/wiki/Central_Committee_of_the_Communist_Party_of_China.
3- https://www.youtube.com/watch?v=YUW1-oilDlc
4- http://shmoop.com/of-mice-and-men/lennie-small.html *Lennie Small was the physically powerful, mentally retarded character in John Steinbeck's dramatic masterpiece,* Of Mice and Men *(1937).*

How Baba Beijing Moves the Body Politic from the Bottom Up

Western and Chinese democracy are like Yin and Yang

China's leadership governs much differently than the Western ideal. The Western ideal is pluralistic democracy, that the power of the vote will keep the people's governments at all levels honest and accountable. As any who can fog a mirror can attest, over the last generation, this ideal has and is becoming more and more of a myth than reality, especially in the United States, but with Western Europe, France and the United Kingdom in particular, trying very hard to catch up with America's decline. Thus, we have the democratic and republican wings of the 1% Corporate Party in the US, the Tory, Labor and Lib-Dem wings in the UK and the socialist and conservative versions in France. They are all cultural variants of One-Percent Tweedle Dee and Tweedle Dum, Alice in Wonderland's irritating, self-mimicking twins. Stick to the script and do exactly as the board of directors dictates.

[IMG 0139] *Tweedle-Dee and Tweedle-Dum: Democrats and Republicans, Labor, Lib-Dems and Tories, they all work for the 1%.*

Baba Beijing to the West: *Frankly my dear, we don't give a damn!*

China makes no pretenses about pluralistic democracy. For 5,000 years, Baba Beijing has been governing China, with the onerous weight of the Heavenly Mandate on their collective shoulders, in a patriarchal and authoritarian fashion – very un-Western, indeed. Since 1949, China has not had the 1% Corporate Party, but the Communist Party of China (CPC) to concern itself. My argument is that the latter system is actually more responsive today to the dreams and needs of its citizens, than the former.

The Western press loves to cluck that Baba Beijing, deep down, in its heart of hearts, knows that it needs Western style, pluralistic democracy at all levels of government. Nothing could be further from the truth.

China's one million villages have had secret ballot elections for years, for their local governments and like America's president, all other levels of administration are elected by indirect voting. Since liberation, China's people's democratic dictatorship has been functioning at least as well as the West, although no one behind the Great Western Firewall will admit it.

Just like Western candidates with any serious chance of winning, China's politicians are carefully sifted and gleaned, like wetland rice, to make sure that one size fits all. In the West, the winnable candidates are beholden to the capitalist Democratic and Republican Parties, and in China, it's the CPC. That is why when the people don't follow the script and a gate crasher makes a serious run for the office at hand, invariably the Princes of Power do whatever it takes to make sure this deviation from the usual Kabuki theater election ritual gets sidetracked.

The fate of Louisiana's Huey "Kingfish" Long is instructive. When his uber-socialist, revolutionary *Share Our Wealth* platform began to seriously threaten Franklin's bid to be the 1936 democratic presidential candidate, the deep state does what it does best: they shot Huey Long dead. The reaction of the powers that be can be very extreme indeed. Yet, very sincere and intelligent people look past the *raison d'être* for the assassinations of John and Robert Kennedy, as well as prophets like Martin Luther King, Jr. The American one percent don't screw around and they can rest assured collective denial and amnesia will let them run roughshod over their pliant 99%.

Yes, Scarlett, Europe and the United States are still different in many ways

A contrasting example can be found in France. The rightwing Front National (FN) came in second place ahead of the Socialists in the first round of the 2002 presidential elections. Thus, the much loathed and fear generating FN got to face off against the establishment conservative candidate, Jacques Chirac, and as a result, the French body politic blew a collective gasket heard across Europe. For the French, so rightfully proud of their illustrious revolutionary past and the world changing Declaration of the Rights of Man and Citizen, the FN's Jean-Marie Le Pen was very lucky that the French 1% don't eliminate real threats to their grip on power, Yankee style. In this case, they didn't have to. Everybody and their dead dog who could get to the urns, communists on down, showed up, many retching and holding their noses, as they dropped their ballots in the boxes, and Le Pen lost 18% to 82% in the deciding round, which almost qualifies for sham election results in a banana republic. Like the Reds and Greens and Socialists, I dutifully lined up and voted for Chirac. Not a bad guy actually. He told W. and Blair to stick Iraq up their neocon oil well.

No, the Chinese don't bother with all these arcane democratic amusements. Baba Beijing governs from the top down. But Baba also adroitly moves the body politic from the bottom up, as usual, with very distinctive Sinoland characteristics, the kind that drive Westerners, foaming at the mouth to red-faced distraction. Living in a sea of local Chinese in the suburbs of Beijing, I am living Chinese reality TV.

Working the Chinese body politic, block by block, house by house

Our brand new housing addition resembles a big, Western city projects, with dozens of 10-15-story apartment blocks, but there the similarities end. Western projects are warehouses for the Corporate Party's human overstock, the unwanted, the offal of society. Not here in Sinoland. The thousands upon thousands of high-rise apartment complexes that cover the landscape of China's mind boggling megacities, are frequently occupied by citizens who have lost their historical or ancestral homes to development projects, and their new apartments are Baba's way of making *fair* compensation for their loss. Fair compensation is a sociopolitical minefield here in Sinoland and with hundreds of millions of people concerned, there are plenty of cases where unscrupulous, local CPC officials connive with venal contractors for filthy lucre.

Western pundits focus on these cases as prima facie evidence that a one-party state must ineluctably be a failure, compared to the perfection and nobility of the all-knowing market economy, where everybody can be a millionaire if they just work a little harder, in an Ayn Randian jungle of naked capitalism. The fact of the matter is, for the overwhelming majority of Chinese concerned, this system of real estate compensation works just fine, including our neighborhood, which is owned by former village farmers who saw their cropland bow to the exigencies of modernization. Compared to the many millions of foreclosures, ruined lives and tens of thousands of destroyed cities and boarded up communities that dot the American landscape, like fractured glass, lumber and brick confetti, Baba's system looks relatively benign, warts and all. This is especially true when one knows that China admits it has 90 million citizens living in poverty and they are spending billions to pull them out of it. I can also attest that my thousands of neighbors are living the good life and are obviously prosperous, most of whom are former farmers.

The US and the West have been slowly cannibalizing themselves, starting in Vietnam

The Western consensus always chortles with superiority that the Chinese tried to commit socioeconomic suicide during two chaotic spasms in the 20th century: the 1958-61 Great Leap Forward and the 1966-76 Cultural Revolution, and lived to tell the story. But the rest of the world knows another story just as gripping and devastating. This tale is happening in the West, especially in America, and the vast majority of their citizens are in complete denial of its truth: Americans have been slowly cannibalizing themselves, at the behest of the Princes of Power, starting with the Vietnam War, 50 years and counting: decoupling the dollar from the gold standard, Iraq, Afghanistan, endless militarization around the planet, dysfunctional representative and executive government and a financial and economic house of clay. It will be my survivor neighbors who will be reading America's political and economic obituary on the world's 21st century stage - you can just sense it.

Apartment fires have local residents' attention, and thus Baba Beijing's too

Beijing has recently had a series of residential fires in apartment towers just like the ones we live in. Thanks to the 2008 Beijing Olympics, millions of homes here have been equipped with piped in natural gas for heating and stoves. Millions more have replaced dirty coal with bottled kitchen butane. Remembering that many of these new rural immigrants grew up using coal to heat their farm homes and cook on potbellied stoves, a number of these fires have been started by these hardy farmers not using their gas stoves properly. Given Baba's recent response to the problem, it is clear they were and are worried about the citizens getting outraged, by what they perceive as their government not responding to valid concerns about fire safety. Time for Baba to move into action - from the bottom up. This is an example of how Chinese democracy works, and while not earth shattering, it does show how the system functions here, in the daily lives of the citizens. Chinese democracy is totally alien to Westerners – heck – the national constitution calls it the *people's democratic dictatorship*. This burns the ears of most Westerners, but the following story displays how it works.

Beijing is a screen set for Ridley Scott's sci-fi masterpiece, *Blade Runner*

One of the habits of these country folk turned city slickers is to use their high-rise stairwells like grain silos, food larders, parking lots and construction material warehouses, with predictable results. If an apartment gets lit up, it can easily spread into their floor lobby. Like in our building, they have piled high dried grains, vegetables, lumber, Vespa scooters with huge, flammable lithium and acid batteries; throw in piles of cardboard and newspapers to eventually sell to the recycling lady downstairs - *someday* - along with laundry hung up everywhere to dry, making for perfect wicks blowing in midair; all this detritus of humanity sitting in the chimney effect of the air drawing up through 15 stories and, well you get the picture. For exercise, I walk up and down the ten flights of stairs our apartment block, and I always flash back to that great scene in *Blade Runner,* where Harrison Ford's Rick Deckard is in the incredibly, eclectically cluttered apartment of the character J. F. Sebastian, portrayed by William Sanderson. Our apartments and surroundings are just as full of junk. Looking out the big windows in my stairwell and gazing out over too many days with stratospheric, thick-as-mist urban smog, it's not hard to feel like I'm walking through the computerized screen set of Ridley Scott's sci-fi masterpiece. Some days I can see the mountains stretching along the horizon, 50km away, the ones that trap Beijing on three sides in its coastal plain. Then there are other days when visibility is only a few hundred meters, as it dissolves into creamy white opacity.

[IMG 0140] No other place on Earth reminds me more of Blade Runner *than Beijing.*

Thus, one recent morning I'm going to work and downstairs at our entrance, and on every one of the other scores of tower entrances in our neighborhood, is an official proclamation from our social committee, something akin to a residents' association in the US, but the Sinoland version is a bottom of the pyramid extension of Baba Beijing and the CPC, not a private one. It is telling us that by such and such a date, all the piles of self-storage must be removed from the stairwells and that there will be fire marshals coming to make floor by floor inspections. I flash back to the beginning of October, during the weeklong National Day celebration, and there were eerily cheerful proclamations posted everywhere, appealing to our higher selves, asking us all nicey-nicey to do the same clean up. The soft touch was a total flop and the edicts were roundly ignored, disdained even: most of them were ripped down by my neighbors after 1-2 days. And nobody came to do any inspections either. Maybe scared to. But that first attempt was only signed and stamped by the local social committee and this late November salvo came from our town hall government, backed up by the Beijing fire department. I suspect that Baba Beijing was already signaling to the residential level organs to do something back in October, to help prevent fires. Like any good leadership, Baba Beijing takes their trials and errors with empirical earnestness and when they fail, they take another tack. From their perspective, it's either adapt or start losing their grip on the Heavenly Mandate. So, for this round two, they had to up the authority ante to make their point clear.

Time to unfurl a bunch of *dazibao*, campaign banners every which way you turn

But that's not all in China. Town crier tracts being posted on entrances would never be enough. Baba Beijing has been honing their campaigning skills for five millennia and is always ready to move into election style mode. As soon as I go outside these days, our neighborhood is flooded with red, horizontal banners everywhere you turn, on both sides of the street, at intersections and on buildings. They are called *dazibao*, which means *big letter report*. Each one is about one-meter tall and five meters long, with big, bold white Chinese characters. As I ride my bike to work, I can't help but think about Chrissie Hynde's Pretenders song, Ohio, and George Carlin's great number, _Americans Are Dumb_, with both of them lamenting that the United States has been overrun with malls and parking lots. Undoubtedly so, and Beijing has its fair share of places to shop, but they get lost in white noise of living with 20 million fellow citizens. In this teeming sea of humanity, it's the little things that get noticed. Over here in Sinoland, it's not so much malls and parking lots that infest the place, it's _dazibao_ - they are everywhere in any case, but when Baba Beijing gets a bug up its butt, their prevalence is taken to a fever pitch. If a couple of Chinese doppelgangers of Chrissie and George ever manifest themselves and catch the local zeitgeist here, they will have a field day being bombarded by red _dazibao_ every which way they turn.

[IMG 0141] _Mr. Carlin and Ms. Hynde would have a field day in China writing material about the culture here. The Pretenders song Ohio easily pops into your head riding around Beijing._

Some dazibao have strong revolutionary roots embedded into the past

Most of my neighborhood _dazibao_ are direct and to the point, much like Smokey the Bear. Good common sense reminders about fire safety, doing the right thing and taking sensible precautions. Unlike American public service announcements, the Chinese ones all have a patriotic, strident sense of urgency about them, akin to WWI and WWII propaganda in Europe and the US. Several of them take it up a notch and are remarkable for their atavistic roots deeply embedded in the fiery language of the communist revolution. For example, one banner blazes,

ALL THE PEOPLE MOBILIZE - EVERYBODY PARTICIPATES - STRIKE HARD TO SOLVE LAWLESSNESS - BUILD UP A STORMING OF THE FORTIFICATIONS

Wow - what a great, packs-a-punch retro-_dazibao_. I give a faint smile of satisfaction every morning and evening, as I pass by it on my bike to work, like I have just savored a morsel of something exceptionally delicious.

Out of the dozens plastered all over my neck of the woods these days, there are a couple more of these similar cultural chestnuts, historical throwbacks just waiting to be savored. All this to simply prevent fires. Funny, I haven't seen folksy old Smokey ever talk in that kind of martial, revolutionary language before. But this is how Baba Beijing mobilizes the masses of people on the streets, when they want to move the body politic - from the ground up. In this continent sized country with 20% of the human race within its borders, there are tens of thousands of similar *dazibao* campaigns going on across the land, for whatever Baba Beijing senses or polls is a potential local hot button issue, to be mitigated and massaged, *before* it blows up in their faces. And you know what: it often works. Our stairwell is spick and span. Well, nearly so. There are still a few gunny sacks full of eared corn waiting to be taken into the owners' apartments. The fire marshals, whom I saw making the inspection rounds, apparently determined that stacks of wilted cabbage and *bok choy* do not represent a flammable hazard, so I still have to navigate around those. And there are a couple of dust covered, rusty bicycles still stranded in the stairwell above. Their tires are flattened and they are forlornly pining for a spin outside, to take a look at the latest *dazibao* campaign. One of these days.

[IMG 0142] *Here, there everywhere: four dazibao on the left and three on the right, as I leave my apartment block.*

Baba Beijing Abolishes Much Hated Labor Camps

[IMG 0143] *Detainees in a Chinese labor camp.*

The much hated Chinese labor camp system is being abolished by Baba Beijing, China's leadership. They were a relic from the early days after independence and an estimated 650,000 citizens are now free. Not sure why Baba Beijing chose to do this now, after two generations, but it's a good sign. Like America's packed-to-the-rafters prisons, most of these detainees were in for non-violent offenses. The sentences, up to four years, were very arbitrary and skewed against the have-nots, just like many of America's Blacks, Native Americans, Latinos, and the ever growing, ever swelling pool of working poor and poorly educated.

Before this new Chinese law, the US had *six times* as many people in prison as China, as a percent of the population.[1] Yet, my family and I are much safer here than in the US. Ironic. There's something criminally wrong with this graph and it's all very much a part of the neocons' 1%'s economic model, which really began to bear bitter fruit for the 99%, starting in early 1980s:

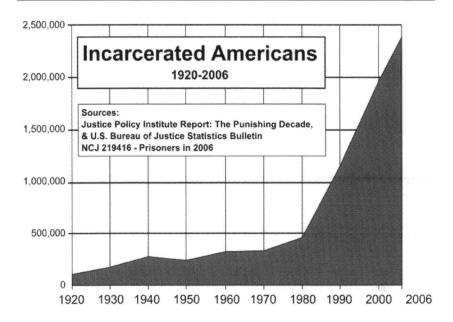

When they get out, they can work at McDonald's part time or sweep floors as an orderly. The exponential spike, starting with Reagan's neocon takeover of power, is no coincidence. [IMG 0144]

America's prison population in a supposedly democratic country is increasing exponentially; in autocratic China, it's going down. Another geopolitical irony.

What Goes Up Sometimes Comes Down, with Backhoes (Excavators) and Bulldozers

In our local community of Kangying Jiayuan (康营家园), a weekly community newspaper is distributed to all the residents. Our neighborhood, which is a suburban Beijing community in the village of Sunhe (孙河).

We used to get local community newspapers when we lived in France and the United States and the content was quite predictable: ribbon cuttings, new construction, new parks, new parking, tree plantings, road, sewer or electrical lines repaired or added and the like. Our local rag is called the *Sunhe Weekly*. It is strange that it has this English name, being a Chinese publication. Only one other word in the paper is in English: *E-mail*, which of course has a Chinese equivalent. Not sure what's going on with that, except maybe they are trying to burnish their cosmopolitan credentials. As I unfold the paper to scan the front page, I can read right away its priorities are quite a change from the Western norm.

The headline blazes,

Speeding Up Community Implementation of the Budget to Meet Council Requirements
Sunhe Village Expands Intensity of Illegal Construction Demolition

Yowzer, now that is an eye grabbing headline. Can't say our local Chinese government representatives don't know a thing or two about effective PR. This is already getting interesting. Below it are two large photographs showing hard hatted police officers standing ever vigilant, as big backhoes (excavators) reduce buildings to piles of rubble.

The white hard hats have blazed on each side in big Chinese characters, *City Management Law Enforcement*. Hi-Ho Silver and who cares about Spiderman! A third photo shows a worker shimmying up a concrete electrical power pole, disconnecting the high power lines coming into said illegal construction site. shimmying up a concrete electrical power pole,

[IMG 0146] *Time to demolish? Who 'ya gonna call? Not the Lone Ranger. Gimme a mob of white hatted, do-goodin' Chinese city cops instead! Or Spiderman? Who needs 'im! Send in the white hard hats!*

The article goes on to extol the heroic efforts of our local government and workers for enforcing the law, wrapping up with the total demolition of not one, two, or three named neighborhoods, but four, with an *etc.* after this string of called out culprits, suggesting there are other neighborhoods that have been affected. The Chinese, being scientifically minded people, love to put numbers to their efforts and the following statistics are vaunted,

- 3,100 people were devoted to the demolition.
- 170 vehicles/machines were used.
- 80,000 square meters of construction were demolished.
- 3,800 citizens had their illegally lost property restituted back to them.

Our town council held a meeting to pass the demolition resolution and thus, *it was all over but the shouting*, as we say where I grew up, meaning it was as good as done. The machines and their white helmeted operators were on the move. Just in case any other ner' do well land developers have ongoing schemes in mind in our neck of the Beijing woods, the article closes out saying these demolition efforts are going to be increased in the future. Over to you, Tonto.

Why is it a good thing to tear down all these illegal apartments? Given that they are a shining example of corruption in the building system, that is reason enough. But they are usually also very shoddily built, and thus a public safety concern for the citizens who move in. Most of the people who move in know these places are illegal, but the rent is appreciably lower than in legal, safety certified projects

Mind you, 80,000 square meters is a full eight hectares of buildings, which is a lot of bricks and mortar. Obviously, it begs the question, how could 11 football fields of construction go unnoticed in the first place? The key is the last statistic touted above,

about *restitution*. One possibility is the projects were approved by the Sunhe government and were so shoddily built that they had to come down. The Chinese cynically call these out of code structures *tofu dregs* (*doufuzha*= 豆腐渣), which is the watery, curd-like residue leftover from fermenting soybeans. The citizens who were buying these apartments, or receiving them as compensation for their land being developed elsewhere, may have protested loud enough and long enough that our local government felt compelled to act. Baba Beijing acknowledges there are an estimated *300-500 public protests a day* in China, an effective form of democracy in action that should not be alien to Western perceptions.

Furthermore, Chinese citizens have become masters of using social media applications on their mobile phones to create *text message tsunamis*, where in a matter of hours or days, an injustice or public outrage can spread to thousands, even millions of readers. Baba Beijing tracks these text tsunamis assiduously and if they see a flashpoint developing, will not hesitate to take action via appeasement, restitution and policy changes. This can easily happen in our community. The Sunhe government's email is proudly posted on the front page of our community newspaper and mobile phone numbers are *de rigueur* on any Chinese business card, including local officials. If the citizens have cause, their email and text message inboxes can easily be overwhelmed with a flood of angry protests.

Building permit and construction corruption is legendary around the world, including in the West. I saw it first hand when I was working on a turnpike construction project while at Oklahoma State University back in the 70s. Talk to anybody living in a big American city. If they are building or remodeling, they have plenty of stories to share about corrupt building inspectors. Bribing building and construction inspectors is a time honored ritual that probably goes back to early urban civilization. Twenty to thirty years ago, the Chinese were just happy to receive a new house, damn the quality. But times have changed and expectations have grown alongside the evolution of the people here.

Given the ever growing quality expectations of Chinese citizens, it's not surprising to see that governments at all levels in China feel the need to show their demolition do-gooding. Reports are easily found on the Chinese web, showing with pride the dismantling of various projects around country.

[IMG 0147] Police looking on as an illegal construction project is being demolished, this one in Xining, the capital of Qinghai.

ABOVE: [IMG 0148] In Wulingyuan, the province of Hunan, hard-hat wearing police are actually rolling up their sleeves to dismantle illegal construction themselves.

NOTE: THIS SECTION CONTAINS OTHER IMPORTANT PHOTOS ABOUT THIS PHENOMENON OF ILLEGAL SUBSTANDARD CONSTRUCTION IN MODERN CHINA, AND SUBSEQUENT DEMOLITION, AND WE ENCOURAGE READERS OF OUR PRINT EDITION TO INSPECT THE ONLINE FILE FOR FURTHER GRAPHIC DETAILS.

The Sinosky Is Falling? *Really?*

Just so you can talk like an expert when world affairs get brought up at happy hour or around the water cooler.

A Chicken Little article just came out about China's debt. I'm not an economist, but I can compare numbers. Bloomberg is screaming that China's total private and public debt was 215% of GDP in 2012 and thus, its economy is going to implode at any minute. Really?

Let's do what stat geeks call a quick comparative study. Here is the debt of the world's mature economies:

[IMG 0149]

OK, lemme see, according to the chart the United Kingdom and Japan have total debt levels of 500% of GDP, the United States and a slug of other traditional Industrial Age colonial powers are weighing in at the 275-350% range. And then we compare all this to China, which has the world's second biggest and fastest growing economy, is the planet's manufacturing powerhouse and which has the world's largest foreign exchange reserves, drags in at 215%, well below any country presented on the chart, including supposedly "bankrupt" Greece.

Perception is everything and the Washington-London-Paris consensus controls the official Western narrative with an iron fist. Furthermore, the author of the aforementioned Bloomberg article, Patrick Chovanec, is the manager of a hedge fund, so I am very leery of his ulterior motives as a high flying investor. Since the economy in the United States is a mirage for the 99%, you gotta try and keep your 400 kilo Sino-sparring partner unsteady on their feet as much as possible. All I know is China is building infrastructure for the masses and goods for the West, while continuing to buy billions of dollars of US government debt and as much gold as Baba Beijing can get its hands on, preparing for the day when the whole ball of Western wax enters meltdown phase.

Four-time Super Bowl champion, superstar quarterback, Terry Bradshaw, once said self-deprecatingly, *I may be dumb, but I'm not stupid*, in reference to the popular notion that he was not the greatest mental genius walking around. For all of us having to do the necessary research to find out the real truth behind the mainstream media, I know how Mr. Bradshaw feels.

[IMG 0150] *Terry knows how much the gold in his Super Bowl rings is worth. Too bad most bought and paid for mainstream economists and pundits don't.*

Grotesque Priorities

Sitting here in Sinoland, it is really interesting to see articles and photos of Dennis Rodman, the retired NBA superstar, bringing his posse to play basketball with North Korean b-ballers, while hamming it up with the country's leader, Kim Jong-un. Known as *The Worm*, five-time NBA champion Dennis Rodman is well known for his theatrical antics, wild make up, pierced jewelry and rainbow colored hair. To say that he is a one-of-a- kind character is a gross understatement. There is no middle ground with Mr. Rodman. You either love him or hate him, admire him or despise him. Thus, it is not at all bizarre that this multimillionaire, attention craving athlete is freely splashing his cash and outsized ego wherever he damn well pleases. After all, he has F.U. money out the yazoo, the sole criterion for success in the Land of the Once Free.

What is so surreal is to know that if the once green-haired Worm flew to Cuba to so much as even shake Fidel Castro's hand, he would be vilified by the press, persecuted by the Feds and likely attacked in court for "Trading with the Enemy", all part of the absurd set of laws and embargoes that Uncle Sam has had against the island state of Cuba and its people, since the country's independence from American colonial satrapy in 1959.

North Korea and Cuba have a lot in common. Both fought for independence from Western empire, albeit, North Korea lost millions in its war against the US, whereas Cuba' liberation did not have nearly as many casualties. Both are fraternal, communist countries. Both spent decades in Africa, helping peoples there throw off the yoke of White colonialism. As a result, both countries have been targeted by the West, particularly the United States, for destruction and overthrow. This includes crippling and costly economic, financial and technological sanctions and blockades, on the part of the West.

The propaganda in the West against North Korea is so over the top, so sensational, that it's hard to parse the truth. We all know that the West portrays North Korea as a real life *Hunger Games*, calling it the

Hermit Kingdom and giving everyone the impression that its citizens are chronically starving to death.

The West works tirelessly to portray North Korea as a real life example of The Hunger Games _storyline._

North Korea's literacy rate is 100% and its life expectancy is 70.11 years, the first being world class and the second below the world average. Another indicator, infant mortality rate, ranks it #74 in the world, about average. This suggests that endemic hunger is a Western myth. The _Washington Post_ did a life expectancy analysis between the US city of Baltimore and North Korea. Fourteen Baltimore neighborhoods have a life expectancy less than that of North Korea, as would hundreds of poor areas across America, especially its Native American reservations.

The North practices its home grown philosophy of "juche", or "self-reliance". All the Western sanctions and blockades probably helped inspire Pyongyang to eschew outside help. and that would include China. Northerners are obviously a very proud and independent people, and they prefer to figure it out for themselves. Andre Vltchek has visited North Korea several times and writes that Western propaganda is just that. North Korea has inspired at least one other country. Eritrea, in Africa, has an almost identical national program, as North Korea's _juche_.

Baba Beijing has a long common border, the Yalu River, and a bloody history with the Korean War. As a fraternal communist country and neighboring ally, China will do everything needed to maintain the status quo. Any kind of hot war on the peninsula or upheaval in North Korea would cause chaos in China. The Yalu River is so shallow you can wade across, and Baba Beijing wants to avoid any possibility of having North

Koreans pouring over the border, creating a humanitarian nightmare, as much as the West would love to see it happen.

The last thing China wants is divisions of US soldiers building huge military bases on the south side of the Yalu, in a futuristic, unified and occupied South- now All-Korea. North Korea provides China with a huge buffer zone against imperial NATO. Too bad Russians can't have the same buffer in Eastern Europe, where NATO forces are routinely practicing pointless military drills only 200 meters from Russia's border.

Hey, I have a great idea. Maybe The Worm ought to be cast as a *Hunger Games* tribute who slowly dies from starvation, exposure and untreated health issues, in its fifth film installment of *Hunger Games - Mockingjay Part III*. Now that would be channeling an unforgettable experience. They can shoot the movie in Baltimore.

[IMG 0151] Dennis Rodman / *Double dare you Dennis, baby, to survive on the mean streets of Baltimore, homeless, out of a job and in desperate need of medical care.*

The beauty and elegance of Chinese characters put to fiendishly good use

In the Beijing subway. **[IMG 0152]**

As part of its public relations and contribution to society, J.C. Decaux, the huge French billboard company, puts up public announcements in Beijing, frequently cooperating with "green" or conservation oriented groups, such as the IFAW (International Fund for Animal Welfare), pictured above. This one in the Beijing subway quickly caught my eye. It brilliantly uses the beauty and elegance of Chinese characters to make the impact of the message doubly meaningful.

The first character on the left is "elephant". Blood splatters replace certain pen strokes in this character, particularly the ones that are associated with the tusks:

Below, the sentence says, "Elephants without tusks"? Of course, banned ivory comes from elephant tusks.

The second character is "tiger". The blood splatters are in the interior of the character and the sentence continues down below, "Tigers without bones"? This is because tiger bones are thought to be a miracle cure when ingested as a Chinese remedy, principally for arthritis, weakness and stiffness:

The third character is "bear". Again, part of the character is missing strokes, and in this case, the sentence continues, "Bears without gallbladders"? Like tiger bones, in traditional Chinese folk medicine, bear gallbladder is supposed to cure fever, liver disease, convulsions, diabetes, and heart disease. Go figure.

And then we get to the fourth one, the last one on the right. This is the character for "person" or "human" and it is missing one of its legs. Below, it simply says, "Humans? Humane"?

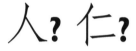

They make this last phrase even more impactful, since both of these words in Chinese, *people/humans* and *humane/benevolent*, are pronounced exactly the same. They are perfect homophones. In pinyin, they are written as *rén*.

The bottom sentence sums up this superbly nuanced message by entreating the public to not buy illegal animal products and to just say, "No!"

And then, there is one final, subtle and sublime touch. The four characters are not just written on a white background. They are each written inside a Chinese character template box, which is what children use, in order to learn to write each character in a centered and balanced fashion. It is a square that has dotted lines running across it, north, south, east, west and then from corner to corner, so it looks like an eight-piece square pizza. But this template grid also looks like something very apropos to the sign's entreaties: they each look like the crosshairs of a rifle scope. Thus, each animal, *including the human,* is being hunted! Touché!

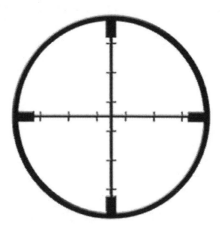

[IMG 0153] Hunting rifle crosshairs inside a scope. (Image by regionalextensioncenter)

Somebody put a lot of thought and creativity into this public service announcement. Hats off to J.C. Decaux. Bravissimo!

Try catching a taxi in Beijing when it's raining or snowing: a lesson in local culture

One of the counterintuitive conundrums of living in Beijing is when the weather gets bad, when you need one the most, trying to find a taxi is Mission Impossible. Rain, snow and ice are surefire predictors that you are going to be standing on the street for a while, waving your arm in vain. They will fly like bats out of hell in heavy traffic, weaving, speeding and tailgating ever onward (although truth be told, most of the taxi drivers here are pretty decent), but at the first hint of precipitation, the streets clear. Drivers tell me they are very worried about safety and having accidents. This could be due to a general superstition. More likely, it's just that the Chinese only started driving in huge numbers in the last 10 years, so it's a question of experience. When we came to Beijing in 1990, there were 25,000-50,000 vehicles on the streets and about 10,000,000 bicycles. Today, there are 5,500,000 vehicles and maybe a few hundred thousand bikes.

Not only that, but Beijingers have options: China's capital has the largest metro system in the world, ahead of Seoul's, plus, Beijing has an excellent, comprehensive metro bus network of over 1,000 lines, which extend far out into Beijing's peripheral suburban and even rural townships, for citizens coming into the city to work each day.

While it's getting better, the "call a cab" system leaves a lot to be desired. All of Beijing's taxis have service phone numbers plastered on their back windshields. However, if you call, it is totally elective if a driver wants to come pick you up, even though they get paid an extra ¥13.00 (€1.65/$2.15) for making the detour. The problem lies when confirming whether someone is coming to pick you up or not. The dispatcher

often does not call back and there ensues a cat and mouse game of redialing and trying to find if they got a driver to agree to come or not. Negotiations and pleadings can come into the cultural mix.

It used to be worse, much worse. Beijing's big taxi companies are very well politically connected and for years, kept their drivers in a state of near penury, sucking ¥3,000/taxi/month (€375/$500) in licensing fees. Not having had a rate adjustment since 2006 and seeing gasoline creep up over ¥7/liter (€0.90/$1.15), things came to a head last year. The city's 66,000 taxis went on a coordinated slowdown. You could stand on the street and wave to one sullen taxi driver's face after another's stone faced blank stare, as they would drive past you, empty. Beijing's citizens, using their favorite method of protest, email and SMS, expressed their displeasure, and the drivers got their raise. While more expensive than the steal it used to be, taxi prices here are still dirt cheap compared to the US or Europe. I think the only way they can still make it work is to amortize each taxi 24/7. Most of them have two drivers who run 12-hour shifts, so that the taxi never leaves the road.

Bicycling in the Beijing snow is a blast. I went out today for 2.5 hours and swerved, slipped and slid with my fellow citizens. Since the streets clear of most cars, it's really nice cruising through huge, deserted intersections, which are typically cram packed with ensnarled, chaotic traffic – normally, it's like surviving mine fields. While slipping along, I saw hundreds of idle taxis parked on the sides, in some cases, whole parking lots full of them.

This was our first snow for the entire winter and a light one at that. This is one of the driest winters on record. Fresh water is a constant concern in Beijing. After all, we are only a couple of hundred kilometers south of the Gobi Desert in Inner Mongolia. Most of our water comes from dammed, holding reservoirs in the mountains surrounding Beijing, especially Lake Miyun, about 50km northwest of town. It's so late in the season, one can't be optimistic for much more precipitation until the late spring and summer. It is during this short, intense period, May-August, when we get about 85% of our annual total.

If we go into a dry spring, we can expect Baba Beijing to roll out a public service campaign to conserve water, replete with billboards and thousands of dazibao everywhere we turn.

Lei Feng was an electrician? Only in America – errrr... China

ei Feng, Mao Zedong's alter ego super hero of the Chinese communist revolution, is omnipresent in China, exhorting the people to feats of sacrifice, common good and Herculean effort. Here is just one of many Lei Feng billboards found riding around Beijing, or China for that matter. I saw him everywhere I turned during my *44 Days* journey. Each Lei Feng billboard or *dazibao* is invariably different. This one says,

Study Lei Feng

Contribute to others

Lift yourself up

Not exactly a public service announcement that comes to mind in New York, London or Paris. But in China, this is vintage political wine. Grand Cru. Mind you, Lei Feng lived through the Great Leap Forward (1958-61), but died in 1962, at the tender age of 22, only to miss the grand finale in revolutionary fervor, the Cultural Revolution, 1966-76. His brief existence though, has not stopped Baba Beijing from taking his love of the communist revolution and apotheosizing his life and image into something along lines of Superman crossed with a Greek god. Like George Washington and Abraham Lincoln in the United States, or Marianne in France he is emblematic of everything righteous and noble about the Chinese ethic, taking on mythic proportions. Lei Feng is truly an icon, an avatar of China's hard fought communist revolution.

Thus, I was more than a little surprised to see several billboards on the Beijing-Tianjin expressway using the Lei Feng motif to sell services from the Zhonglian Electrical Service Association.

It can be taken two ways: as an abomination of modern national history or that Lei Feng has finally arrived. It's like they say, if an artist's music is being played in elevators or department stores as background tunes, then that means they've sold a ton of records. I've heard Beatles songs rendered via syrupy orchestra strings in China, for crying out loud. I have the utmost respect for the Chinese people and the incredible, almost miraculous sociocultural evolution they have managed in just one generation.

Many other peoples would be hard pressed to survive what 20% of the world's people suffered here through almost 30 years of brutal, harrowing, relentless and cannibalistic revolution, 1949-1976. They have come far, so, so far.

But, as they are continuing to try to find themselves, they also forge their own unique identity, socialism with Chinese characteristics, which Western pundits derisively pan. As is the case for human frailty, it's often two steps forward and one step back. Their big step back is the Chinese have a knack for adopting many of the worst aspects of American culture, especially when it comes to money, making money and spending it. Which is to say, ummm... the essence of the United States, pure and simple. I mean let's be honest, it's pretty one-dimensional in the 50 States. Always has been. Money talks and shit walks. Bling, McMansions, supersized portions big enough to make Roman epicureans retch, and SUVs mammoth scaled to serve as shoreline ship tugs. And it's never enough. Why rent a jet ski when you can buy two - on credit?

Too many Chinese are not savvy or experienced enough to understand the vacuity and meaninglessness of consumerism on steroids. They are just aping what they consider to be the defining apex of success: working harder and longer to buy and pile up more and more inane Stuff and Fluff – shop till you drop, as they say, in malls across America.

There are street peddlers in every culture and country, but none more so than the United States. Alexis de Tocqueville made these same observations during his travels, which generated his foundational 1835 masterpiece of social studies, Democracy in America, a must read for anybody who claims to know a thing or two about the good old U.S. of A. Nothing's changed in 400 years: money's been talking and shit's been walking in North America, since Jamestown in 1607.

American businesses, especially local ones in dire need of some marketing inspiration, will drag out hoary chestnuts, like George Washington and Benjamin Franklin, to sell everything from stereo equipment to plumbing services.

The Zhonglian Electrical Services highway billboard. Apparently, somebody at Zhonglian Electrical Services Association has lived in the United States. (#162 Image by Jeff J. Brown)

[IMG 0154- 0157] Examples of marketing using national heroes.

The Good, the Bad and the Ugly on China's Environmental Pollution

Western hypocrisy I can see for kilometers and kilometers

Is Beijing's PM2.5 Air Quality Index, (AQI) hovering at nearly 400? Check. Is the atmosphere outside as dead calm as a mouse fart? Check. Is there a patina of smoky residue coating the environment, from all the fireworks during Chinese New Year, and 15 days later, Lantern Festival? Check. Baba Beijing has just issued its first 3-day smog alert, which has crept from Code Yellow to Orange. Roger that.

Will it climb to Red over the weekend, shutting down all the factories, schools, as well as many businesses, until it clears? The suspense is palpable. Envelope please.

This is what the rest of the world is waiting for: bad news about environmental pollution in China. Why? Because it sells for the hubristic West's mainstream media. More generally, it's another arrow in its 500-year old quiver of Caucasian sociocultural and economic superiority. The West loves to point out all of China's problems and insufficiencies, while there are usually several critical factors that are omitted.

Looking through the other end of history's looking glass

First, a little bit of transoceanic history. People forget that the word *smog*, smoke plus fog, comes from London, England, where during the 19th and well into the 20th centuries, much of urban United Kingdom was a Petri dish of cancer, emphysema and toxically induced heart disease. In the 1830s, 98% of the peppered moths in London were white and 2% were black. By the 1880s, those numbers were reversed. Why? Thanks to the brilliant process of evolution and natural selection, the mutated black variety was suddenly better suited to the now grimy, gritty, grey environment, due to all the millions of tons of poisonous coal soot and air pollution being vomited into the air. Tree bark color went from light to charcoal black, as years of aerial filth coated everything in sight, including people's lungs, sinuses, eyes and skin, all being rapidly absorbed by every living thing. People didn't live very long back then, nor very healthily. For those lucky mutated black peppered moths, their sudden survival advantage made them perfectly camouflaged on the now tar black tree trunks and limbs, and England's soot-soaked birds feasted with relish on the now highly visible, white variety.

[IMG 0158] *No, not Tiananmen Square, it's an English bobby asphyxiating on putrid British air – in 1952.*

For 500 years, Europe, Japan and the United States fouled and raped their own countries. When they had no more land to sodomize or indigenous populations to exterminate, they went overseas in search of territories inhabited by dark skinned peoples around the world, enslaving and killing billions of these historical landowners, via war, occupation and colonialism, extracting their stolen resources for a song. Back home for too long, Western and Japanese urban and rural areas were all too happy to live and die, mired in industrial filth and effluent, eating, drinking and breathing toxic food, water and air, respectively.

The Industrial Revolution was not a pretty, nor clean and healthy sight

For centuries, Industrial Revolution zones around the world were urban cesspools of vermin infested tenements, ghettos, squalor, pestilence, disease, parasites, misery and frequent malnutrition, even starvation. The 1% kept the toiling masses alive just enough to work 80-100 hours per week. Institutionalized religion helped these wretched souls hold out for a glimmer of hope, a brighter future during their stunted, shortened lives. Rural communities and agrarians lived no better, subservient to their political and landlord owners, hanging on from one harvest, one drought and one economic bubble and bust to the next. The likes of Charles Dickens, Victor Hugo, Bertolt Brecht, Leo Tolstoy, Ernest Hemingway, Juan Gelman, and many others, had a literary field day. There was a lot of experiential material to be incensed and indignant over, much to write about.

This canvas of *economic progress* (sic), writ large as humanity itself, changed relatively little for centuries. It was the worldwide Great Depression that helped bring populist sentiments to critical mass around the world, combined with the hope of communism for the 99%, and its sanitized Western version, socialism. Industrial Revolution's poor, working and middle classes overwhelmed the Princes of Power, albeit, it only lasted for a couple of generations. In America, it was called Roosevelt's New Deal. During this ephemeral halcyon, the world's Lords of the Loot had to share a tiny sliver more of their ownership of the world's resources. Going back to the origins of the New Deal and until the 1980s, it was the only 50 years in the five-century history of Western capitalism where all the lofty, Orwellian propaganda actually translated, ever so slightly, into the real lives of the 99% (incomes rising with climbing productivity, strong unions, high taxes on millionaire incomes and corporations, a plethora of government programs for the poor and middle classes). But enough was enough. As we have all seen and lived since the 1980s, with the rapid destruction of the working (now poor), middle and poverty classes in OECD countries around the planet, it was five decades too long for Earth's owners, to be so extravagantly generous, thank you. It was time to stack the deck, tilt the gaming table and load the dice of human civilization back to their natural, rigged order.

[IMG 0159] *The 1%'s sweet smell of success. Typical 19th century industrial revolution urban nightmare. Early industrialism was neither pretty nor gentle. Its nature has not changed.*

Look no further than China's next door neighbors, Taiwan and South Korea

Postwar Taiwan and South Korea are darlings of the Western version of market liberalism, pinup, centerfold countries and shining beacons on the capitalistic hill. My how our inflated egos are so selective in their storage of information. Both of these countries, along with many more were, not so long ago, brutal, fascist dictatorships. These IMF/World Bank prima donnas killed untold numbers of their compatriots, in the name of fighting communism, socialism, liberalism and leftist tendencies. As is true of countless examples, ongoing today, these two countries, peninsular South Korea and island Taiwan were horror show monsters of environmental insanity, libertarian capitalism run amok, the land, air, water and food be damned. It was not until they reached a modicum of broad prosperity, more than a generation later, that their rulers were forced to hew to the demands of their citizens for a greater voice in their daily lives, and their refusal to live in a toxic toilet environment. Other countries have been or are going through the same arc of political-environmental development: Malaysia, South Africa, Ecuador and Thailand, to name a few.

And now it's China's turn. The irony is that the pasty grey sky outside my 10th floor window is composed of much of all the accoutrements, the Stuff and Fluff that the materialistic West has deemed necessary for superficial happiness: Chinese manufactured and exported cell phones, clothing, shoes, handbags, backpacks, computers, household goods, trinkets, consumer junk, toys, televisions, MP3 players - manufactured plastic, synthetic, woven, carved, molded and cut everything, not to mention trillions of Chinese components and subparts which you cannot see, but are used to assemble our acquisitive lives around the world– try finding something, *anything* in your daily lives that does not have China imprinted on it – and it's getting harder and harder by the day - all of that is what I and 1,300,000,000 million fellow

Chinese living here are breathing, eating and drinking – the OECD's consumerist "success story" in a globalized economy, along with the same vacuous Stuff and Fluff being bought by China's ever richer, more prosperous people.

[IMG 0160] Chinese manufacturing human/environmental costs. *The West's materialist Fluff and Stuff brought to you by China's manufacturers.*

You had to be here to believe it

When I lived in China in the 1990s, the pollution was worse, much worse. Like the early cowed citizens of South Korea and Taiwan, the Chinese were mostly ignorant of their condition, and even as they became more aware, through travel, education and news from around the world, they kept their mouths shut, as they worked to make a better life for themselves. In any case, in fascist Taiwan and South Korea, you could be imprisoned, tortured or worse for speaking out.

Back in 1990s China, we had to dust the furniture in the house *daily*, because the coal soot was so thick. We used a big feather duster to clean off the car windshield at least a couple of times a day. Otherwise, you couldn't see past the dashboard of your car by lunchtime. The air was heavy with particulate matter from thousands of primitive factories that were thick across the landscape, urban and rural. The skies, waters and land were *Charlie and the Chocolate Factory* iridescent and surreal, from plumes of noxious, rainbow colored chimneys, belching purple, green, yellow and red Goddess-knows-what, into the skies and onto the land of cities and rural villages all over the country. Having a sinus infection, bronchitis and smoker's cough, even for non-smokers, was a day in the life. We would go for weeks, barely able to see tall buildings across the street, as we sucked in and absorbed the opaque, consommé thick sky into our bodies. A blue sky day or two was celebrated like the Saturnalia, as we waited for the winds to die down again, the ones which had blown it all away in the first place, only to start another long period of atmospheric oblivion. And it wasn't just the air. Cities, towns and villages all over China, including Beijing, Shanghai and Guangzhou, were dumping millions of tons of raw sewage and garbage into their rivers, creeks, seas and lands, and it smelled like it too.

[IMG 0161] *90s China skies were all the colors of* Charlie and the Chocolate Factory.

The thought of an air quality index, which we could access with the touch of a smartphone was like a *Jetsons* cartoon, something laughable to even envision. Based on my daily observations of using the AQI now, I can safely say we had many long weeks of the index, stubbornly vaulted above 500 in the 1990s, which is the highest it's technically supposed to go. Like the mock hard rock musical group *Spinal Tap* turning the volume of their amplifiers up to 11, on a dial that only goes up to 10, China has had recent reports from around the country of the AQI shattering the 1,000 level. I have experienced a couple of times in Beijing a few hours of 700-800 and when it happened, I kept flashing back to my go-go 90s life in China. When we moved to France in 1997, I can still remember the last time I coughed up black gook out of my lungs, six, months after leaving Sinoland.

Public perception, unstoppable social evolution and information transparency have also changed

Moving back here in 2010, those seven years seem so far away. Yes, the pollution can still be bad by international, and now Chinese standards, but those days of murky haze are fewer and further between and last much less long. Clear, azure skies are no longer cause for a Dionysian frenzy of celebration. There are so many now that friendly chatter with my Chinese neighbors and colleagues is now fixated on those less prevalent days when it is not so clear outside. Smog shrouded days are more and more the exception to the rule.

Another difference is perception, both in-country and around the world. The Chinese people are on their path of development where the South Koreans and Taiwanese were back in the 80s-90s. Let's not forget that Taiwan didn't even bother with legislative elections until 2005, and held its first presidential ones in 2008, more than 50 years after it started out as a murdering, fascist dictatorship. Ditto South Korea, with its phony show voting, which was just as derisory as anything Hitler could concoct, until the first free presidential elections in 1987. When I visited South Korea in the early 80s, it was a polluted filthy landscape, and an Orwellian police state.

Mind you, this is not a new problem Baba Beijing and its citizens are suddenly having to deal with. It has been simmering in the Chinese zeitgeist for years. Even back in the 90s, Baba was addressing environmental issues, albeit policy implementation was not always as grandiose as the hoped for inspiration. Now the environment is front and center in their policy making decisions and implementation is coming with more and sharper administrative teeth. Can you imagine another country that would dare to even imagine shutting down their capital for two or three days, costing the economy billions in gross city product, like the smog alert system Baba Beijing has set up? I can't either.

[IMG 0162] South Korea and Taiwan were fascist police states for their first 40-50 years after WWII.

Sorry historical Greece, but democracy has Eastern versions of its very own

Baba Beijing has its own version of authoritarian, Confucian democracy, which is much more responsive to their citizens' needs than the West will deign to admit. Straddled between a pathetically gutless Europe, which refuses to shake off its slavish satrapy to America, especially the United Kingdom and France, and planet Earth's out of control, fascist-police state hegemon, the United States, I can say with a high degree of confidence that China's version of 21st century participatory democracy is much more beholden to its masses than the West's Potemkin corporatocracy.

I see it here in my neighborhood, with phone numbers and public announcements being pasted all over the place for citizens to call and complain about private and public services, up to the texting tsunamis and Wechat waves that can sweep towns, cities, regions and even the entire nation, forcing Baba Beijing to respond and redress. **Try writing your bought and paid for corporate whore congressperson or senator, or filing a complaint in corrupt Brussels. It's shameless Kabuki Theater, all vacuous show and ritual, a *Matrix* unreality.**

Don't believe me? Unbiased, Western polling companies, like Gallup and Pew, prove that around 80% of China's people are happy with their lives and leaders. This, versus the capitals of the West, where politicians are routinely polling in the teens and sometimes even in single digits.

China's democracy above the village level is not by popular vote, which in the West has now been reduced to choosing between Clique A or Clique B of the Corporate Party. But in their own inimitable way, the Chinese often get what they want from Baba Beijing by speaking out publicly and addressing obvious problems about an injustice or crime. Being obsessed by their place in China's Heavenly Mandate, Baba Beijing listens to these public outbursts, which happen hundreds of times a day around the country, and will quickly respond if they feel their credibility is on the line. Of course it is not a perpetual motion machine and it frequently breaks down. This is a manifestation of human pathos, not that China's way of conducting politics is inherently faulty. People are vain, greedy and foolish, regardless of race, religion, nationality or political affiliation.

But comparing what has happened in the West over the last generation versus what has and is transpiring in China, the contrast is frighteningly and shockingly revealing. Since 1980, just ask the World Bank and the IMF: China has created the world's largest middle class in the world, over 300 million, while adding to this tally, 10,000 per day. Baba Beijing has done this in the shortest amount of time in human history, and continues to do so. Yes, China is also creating a lot of wealth at the highest levels of society, but so far, not at the expense of the urban and rural classes.

Conversely, the United States is destroying what used to be the world's largest middle class, in record time, to the tune of 1-2 million personal bankruptcies per year, since 1990. That's 2,700-5,400 a day, and that's a whole heap of misery. Talk about a lesson in contrasts. And Europe is trying so hard to imitate and follow in the America's tragic trajectory. Sitting here in Sinoland, I don't know which is more disgusting, looking west across the Asian continent to the tip of Eurasia, or east across the Pacific. It's pathetic, really.

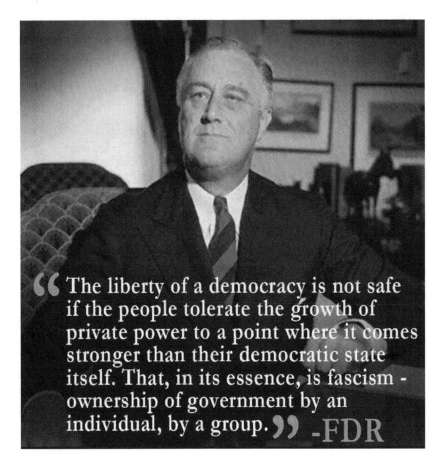

[IMG 0163] *It all seems so quaint now, doesn't it, Western democracy? By the way, FDR forgot to say "class". (Image by gettingaround.org)*

I know how many kilometers I can see now

It also explains how come China's environmental problems are front page news across the globe: access to information. Until the internet, until mobile phones, SMS and emails, it was next to impossible to quantify the quality of our air, water, food and soil, much less trying to disseminate the information to a larger audience. That is no longer an issue. If anything, there is too much information now, forcing us to separate the wheat from the chaff. Now we get two or three polluted days in Beijing and I keep seeing the same stock photos plastered all over the international media for weeks on end, while our skies have long since turned a gossamer turquoise, or by world standards, at least an acceptable pale blue. Reading media headlines outside of China, you would think we live in a Dante's *Inferno* of endless, airborne tumors floating in the atmosphere, landing on and in us like the virus in Danny Boyle's sci-fi thriller movie, *28 Days Later*. If I were writing this book in the 1990's China, a case could have been made to write a theme along those lines, as well as postwar South Korea and Taiwan, or prewar United States and Europe. But not 21st century Sinoland.

In the meantime, enjoy and use all the Made in China consumerist Fluff and Stuff of your daily lives, with which the dank air outside today was used to provide for you. The weather report indicates a windy cold front blowing through Beijing the day after tomorrow. T-Bone Walker's *Call It Stormy Monday* will be re-written for me: *Call It Azure Monday*. I can't wait.

The Oriental Dragon, oops, I mean Chinese Lion roars

Chinese President Xi Jinping is in France, a classy, historic stage indeed. It is this country's tumultuous revolution, more than any other, that inspired Mao Zedong and likes of Deng Xiaoping, Chen Yi and Xiang Jingyu, who studied in France back in the 1920s. Ah, Paris, with its Bastille Prison break, Louis XVI's head on the bloody end of a proletarian guillotine, along with his wife's, Marie "Let Them Eat Cake" Antoinette. All this while Xi and the Chinese First Lady, Peng Liyuan were visiting Versailles. This just so happens to have been the royal House of Bourbon's grandiose digs, where all those high falootin' Louis and previous kings lorded it over France's peasantry for a thousand years. And not just any visit. The Sino-First Couple got an exclusive tour, with French President François Hollande acting as a personal guide. We'll have to demur on whether Xi and Peng bought a snow globe of this august chateau, one of the world's most sumptuous examples of aristocratic, architectural excess. Maybe they just settled for Eiffel Tower key chains, but splurged and got the ones that double as an alarm whistle. They can come in handy in Paris' rough and tumble, dark skinned, immigrant *banlieues*, suburbs like St. Denis and Clichy-sous-Bois. Bet Xi and the Missus didn't request a visit out in *that* neck of the woods.

[IMG 0164] *Louis XVI's ignominious end, being watched by Marie Antoinette, waiting for her just-as-grisly fate.*

Baba Beijing just loves symbols, and lions definitely evoke popular, romantic images. Not only is it considered in folklore to be the biggest, baddest quadruped of the jungle, the lion represents royalty, bravery and strength. And wouldn't you know it, Xi just so happened to talk about lions in his keynote speech, given during his presidential state visit. Hmm, the French Revolution, Versailles and lions. I'm seeing a trend here.

And the trend really starts clicking, very fast. During Xi's speech, he recalled an oft quoted remark that another titanic world leader was supposed to have said, Napoleon Bonaparte. Napoleon, who lost it all in Russia (is the White House Fool listening?) opined that,

China is a sleeping lion. Let her sleep, for when she wakes, she will shake the world.

Xi then counterpunched with a great one-two across the bow of Western Empire,

Today the lion has woken up. But it is peaceful, pleasant and civilized.

Of course China watching pundits had a field day with this one: since when are lions peaceful, pleasant and civilized? I dunno, I mean Mufasa was a class act, as were those cute, darling love cubs, Simba and Kiara, in the Disney movie, *Hamlet* inspired, *Lion King*. But that Scar was a nasty bit of business, wasn't he? So which one is it, Baba Beijing? I'm not much of a betting man, but I'll put my geopolitical *Reflections in Sinoland* token on the sage and regal Mufasa. But like the big, bad, red Russian Bear, the Empire of the West has to bet the house on that evil, demented Scar, in order to keep its worldwide Wehrmacht in perpetual motion - at least until China and Russia quit buying US treasury bonds. Between these two allies, they own around $4.15 trillion in American government debt. When they either stop buying American bonds or start selling them off on the international market, the Federal Reserve's armada of color Xerox machines turns into Cinderella's midnight, hyperinflation pumpkin. We can only hope that William Dudley, President of the Federal Reserve Bank of New York and his boss, Chairwoman Janet Yellen turn into mice. But in the meantime Barak & Co. have got a throbbing war hard on.

Which brings us to the next fascinating facet of this ongoing Shakespearean-Beijing Opera thriller. US Secretary of War, Chuck Hagel invited all the head honchos of Asia's militaries to meet together, North Korea excepted of course, for a little Hawaiian luau and generalissimo powwow. Thereafter, he visited the lion's den in Sinoland, his first time in the People's Republic of Mao. His declared mission in Baba Beijing's back yard is to reduce possible miscalculations and misjudgments off the coast of China (and Russia's Eastern flank), where Hagel's blue water boys are parking 60% of their total earthly fleet.

Well, Chuck E. Cheese, if you want to avoid possible military incidences right off China's shoreline, then don't park the planet's most lethal naval killing machine 22.2km (the distance from shore to international waters) plus a meter away from Shanghai, Tianjin, Fuzhou and Guangzhou. The last time I checked, there weren't any Chinese military ships cruising off Padre Island in Texas, ogling all the drunk, horny, in-debt-for-life, college students overrunning the beaches. Nor have there been any reports of them cruising outside the Golden Gate Bridge in San Francisco, waving to Chinatown's finest. Like Uncle Sam, they could legally do this. But Baba Beijing doesn't have to, because China is not hell-bent on pan-planetary hegemony and military domination.

America's Air-Sea Battle plan to invade China is of course on every hard drive that matters in the People's Liberation Army (PLA), plus all the terabytes of top secret hacked information PLA Unit 61398 has absconded with. The PLA knows that Hagel knows that they know what's going down in the Yellow Sea. But Chuck E.'s hosts don't have to say a thing. They sized him up and carefully interpreted every last grunt and facial tick he showed behind closed doors, while sharpening their Shaolin Kung Fu swords in the back room for a later, more meaningful engagement. Baba Beijing, I have one humble, civilian suggestion: make sure the blades are 22.2km long, plus *two* meters, just to be safe.

So, it's official. Baba Beijing is sending a clear message of strength and engagement to the White House Caesar and his spineless, European centurions. It's bye-bye Dragon. Now the 21st century is all up to the Russian Bear, the Chinese Lion and a crazed, rabid Western Empire Hyena. Bring out the long knives, boys. Even the orneriest, nastiest, razor fanged, mega fauna hyena will have its bloody paws occupied, being sideswiped simultaneously by the Bear and the Lion. Come to think of it, this century is starting to shape up like a new generation *Narnia* battle royal. Game on.

[IMG 0165] *I'm going to miss you, Imperial Dragon. Enter the Lion.*

It's official: Baba Beijing says no to Western democracy

Well, it's official. Since Mao Zedong's death in 1976, a Chinese leader has finally spoken the real intentions of Baba Beijing about the future of *Western* democracy in China. Since perpetual revolutionary Mao ended up in his mausoleum for all of eternity on Tiananmen Square, China's leaders have mostly paid mealy mouthed lip service and empty rhetoric to the West about the need to seek greater political freedom in the People's Republic. Feisty, elfin Deng Xiaoping, never had an official government post, but as China's post-Mao paramount leader, he brought this sleeping giant back from the revolutionary brink. Back in those humble days of national post-Cultural Revolution detox, Deng had the sense of humor and the political heft to take a stab at the West, saying,

The United States brags about its political system, but the President says one thing during the election, something else when he takes office, something else at midterm and something else when he leaves. (1983)

How timeless and astute. Actually, I think he stole this line from film actor/stage entertainer/journalist/author Will Rogers, America's genius savant back in the 1920s-30s, who relished twisting a verbal knife into the faces of the Princes of Powers, with a chuckle on his face, as he carved them up. Rogers was so popular that his weekly radio show had *50% household penetration* across America, along with a Q Score that went off the charts. The Q Score is that media mumbo jumbo test they use to measure how commercially popular are actors, reporters, weather forecasters, etc. Jimmy Kimmel, David Letterman and Jay Leno, you guys are third rate pikers compared to ol' Will. He was that adored and followed. So was Deng Xiaoping, even though he was the one who made the call and pulled the plug on the Tiananmen protests, sending in the People's Liberation Army to save the Communist Party of China's Heavenly Mandate. Enter the West's idealized avatar, Tank Man.

This happened, on June 4th, 1989. Hard to believe it was a generation ago. Deng and Rogers had a similar sense of humor, and they both had powers of observation over the tragedies and triumphs of humanity's travails that few people possess. Rogers was deadly with the pregnant pause. After almost six weeks of deadlock, the CIA backed organizers came out with Kalashnikovs and Molotov cocktails. Deng knew when he had to give his PLA soldiers guns and tanks, as they had been unarmed the whole time before.

As the United States implodes economically, socially and politically, Americans will live hundreds of Tiananmen Squares across the country, fighting highly militarized local, county and state police goons, as well as Homeland Security armed forces soldiers sent in to mow down the citizenry. Thanks to the Orwellian Doublespeak Patriot Act, the totalitarian National Defense Authorization Act (NDAA) and ongoing presidential directives, Posse Comitatus' enshrinement in American constitutional law has been eviscerated for years now. Think of the movie, *V for Vendetta*. That's where it's heading Stateside – fast.

[IMG 0166] **V for Vendetta.** *What Baba Beijing sees across the Pacific and throughout the western tip of Eurasia.*

The symbolism of a post-Tiananmen world, coupled with <u>the recent zombie like knife massacre at Kunming's train station, perpetrated by Xinjiang separatists</u>, plus <u>raucous street protests down in Guangdong Province (Canton), in the cities of Maoming and Shenzhen, to protest a chemical refinery plant construction project</u>, has got the tension on the streets ratcheted up higher than usual. Baba Beijing has slowed down the country's internet speed to frozen molasses pace, in order to frustrate overall wireless communication across the East Asian continent. I think it's a good time to practice, *patience is a virtue.*

At Tiananmen Square, the magnificent China National Museum is exhibiting the visiting Pablo Picasso *Suite Vollard* of copper engraved etchings. I could just feel the electricity and frayed nerves of the uniformed and plain clothes police officers on the sidewalks. Walkie-talkies were clacking and crackling away, while officers' voices were uncharacteristically raised to the screaming threshold. This, as millions of tourists crawled over ground central of the Heavenly Mandate.

The civility of the Chinese people in public situations, which I describe as *eyeballs to elbows*, in *44 Days*, was really put to the test at Tiananmen, and they continue to come through with flying colors. If Americans were thrust into similar social-public situations, there would be a mass murder on an hourly basis. I honestly don't know how the Chinese do it. I just kept grinning as I waded through walls and waves of pedestrian flesh.

And no doubt about it: Picasso was a creative genius - egocentric and narcissistic to be sure - but a giant of an artist, and more than worthy of the all his fame, public adoration and professional admiration for his avant-garde work. I was pleasantly surprised at the museum crowd. I never knew so many Chinese cared about Western art.

[IMG 0167] *Thousands of Chinese have turned out to see up close and personal the raging genius of Picasso.*

And then there was <u>Xi Jinping's speech about democracy, which he gave at the College of Europe in Bruges, Belgium</u>. The Chinese have a great idiom, *paimapi* (拍马屁), which literally means, *slap a horse to make it fart*, and is the equivalent in English of *to flatter, to kiss ass*, etc. In Xi's new and resurgent 21st century China, making horses fart is definitely old school. He laid it on the line about even envisioning the thought of China considering Western style democracy, saying,

China cannot copy the political system or development model of other countries, because it would not fit us and it might even lead to catastrophic consequences... The fruit may look the same, but the taste is quite different,

He said, using a wonderful Chinese metaphor.

<u>He went on to spell it out in no uncertain terms</u>,

...the uniqueness of China's cultural tradition, history and circumstances determines that China needs to follow a development path that suits its own reality... In fact, we have found such a path and achieved success along this path.

Starting in early 20th century,

The Chinese people then started exploring long and hard for a path that would suit China's national conditions. They experimented with constitutional monarchy, imperial restoration, parliamentarism, multi-party system and presidential government, yet nothing really worked, he added... Finally, China took on the path of socialism. Admittedly, in the process of building socialism, we have had successful experience and also made mistakes,

He said, adding that,

We have even suffered serious setbacks.

[IMG 0168] *President Xi Jinping says no more* paimapi *from Baba Beijing for the hypocritical West. (#182 Image by stnews.cn.com)*

So there you have it. I can recall <u>when El Presidente Billy Jeff Clinton insulted the Chinese back in 1998, by haughtily chastising them,</u>

For being on the wrong side of history.

Really? This coming from a country that is barely two centuries old and whose so-called greatness is founded on the filthy lucre of 300 years of slavery, the holocaust of 15 million Native Americans, and starting in 1846 in Mexico, its imperial terrorism in scores of countries across Mother Earth. China is no beneficent angel of history, having lost tens upon tens of millions of hapless citizens in the pursuit of political power plays and wars, going back for millennia. But they at least had the decency to liquidate their own peoples. For 500 years, the West has been and continues to exterminate many times more of its *Dreaded Others*. These days, that would be mainly Muslims or any peoples with precious natural resources.

A good Russian friend of mine says that his compatriots and neighboring Chinese should learn a lesson from the West and Israel. When we racist Judeo-Christian Eurmericans commit genocide, we always make sure to slaughter other races and ethnicities, not our own kind. When Russians and Chinese do it, they cannibalize their own countrymen. A very astute observation indeed.

After seeing the China National Museum's visiting Picasso exhibit, I spent the rest of my day ambling from one gargantuan display room to another, to check out Bill Clinton's perceptions of Chinese history. I gazed on thousands of priceless relics and works of art from the world's longest continuing, extant civilization, over 5,000 years and counting. Display after display of jade and bronze going back to 3,000BC, money going back to the Neolithic period, 8,000BC, and sublime Buddhist art and statues going back 200 years before Jesus Christ was born. Mind you, back in those days, most Europeans were living not much better than wild animals, shitting and peeing under trees and living in crude lean-tos. This while the Chinese had a written language, full spectrum culture and a plethora of inventions out the yazoo.

It's something to remember the next time you hear a gonadless, gormless, jingoistic Western fool pontificate on the moral and cultural superiority of Euramerica. And Bill Clinton? Can't really recall what he did for the good of humanity. Don't think the history books will either.

Tall Tiananmen Tales and the Little Red Pill

[IMG 0169] *Neo taking the red pill of truth in* The Matrix. *Count me in.*
(Image by matrix.wikia.com)

June 4ᵗʰ is the anniversary of the Tiananmen protests in China, 1989. Then teaching children in my international school in China, even for 6ᵗʰ graders, *liusi*, (六四 = Six Four) is a shibboleth that gets bandied about quite a bit, towards the culminating date. It may seem surprising that 12 year olds know about June 4ᵗʰ. While many of my students are full or half Chinese by parentage, this is not a local neighborhood school. The students come from families with money: professionals and business people from the upper middle to upper class. Most of them have already traveled around China and they take holiday and summer vacations in places I can't afford. This is a pretty sophisticated bunch and we can discuss Chinese politics much more openly that would be allowed in Chinese public school.

In all fairness to China, as someone who taught in public schools in the United States, there is just as much self-censorship and possible professional retribution for teachers who broach topics that do not fit the mythical, conventional version of the American way. **The official consensus, be it in China, America or Bangladesh, is overpowering and stifling.**

As June 4th approaches, the most mundane refrain is that the internet slows down to an Arctic molasses pace. Then there is a general increase in the presence of security forces on the streets. They seem to grow exponentially as you travel to the nexus of the Middle Kingdom's universe, the Forbidden City, and its accompanying Tiananmen Square. In keeping with all the myriad, mind boggling, socioeconomic superlatives that China has and is accruing on the world stage, Tiananmen is the planet's fourth largest public square, weighing in at 440,000m² (880m by 500m). China still grabs the _We're Number One_ medal in any case, as Xinghai Square, in Dalian, stretches out an expansive 1,100,000m². Bring your compass or GPS.

As usual, a few bright sparks in my class, those young minds who love to read through our class' subscription to the print edition of The _China Daily_ newspaper and peruse articles on the educational current events website, _The Day_, dutifully asked me,

Mr. Brown, so how many people were killed during the Tiananmen massacre?

Before returning to China in 2010, I would have undoubtedly spouted the pedantic, Western mainstream media mantra,

Oh, I understand the Chinese army massacred many thousands.

Back in the day, even grade school kids always seemed to bring up the iconic, Western media image of _Tank Man_. We would all dutifully extol the virtues of this allegorical saint of resistance to tyranny and oppression, like some political superhero version of *The Epic of Gilgamesh.* This year, when Tank Man was proffered, I reflexively held tight.

At least this year, I had enough of a fledging knowledge to say,

I have read estimates from the low hundreds to a few thousand. My guess would be maybe a thousand.

This year's classroom discussion was even more poignant. One student told us that his father had a friend who was killed during the protests and it was after all, the 25th anniversary, a quarter of a century since that fateful night. The Chinese take numerology very seriously.

Why am I questioning what is taken as absolute fact, that thousands of innocent, idealistic Chinese students were gunned down like dogs, by a soulless, bloodthirsty People's Liberation Army (PLA), in and around Tiananmen Square, on June 4th, 1989?

This is simply because the arc of my understanding about world history and current events has changed radically, since moving back to China in 2010, traveling around the country, writing *44 Days* and this book, with all the incumbent thousands of hours of research involved. My horizons have expanded exponentially and I now have the courage to question and refute the official [Western] narrative.

All this research gave me a much different perspective.

I learned that Baba Beijing and ordinary Chinese also have their version of the story to tell: the Tiananmen protests were ended with very little bloodshed, given the

huge numbers of people involved, up to one million in and around the square. That out of a total of 300 deaths, a number of these were unarmed PLA soldiers, who were first sent into this teeming mass of humanity to stand sentry, almost six weeks before the denouement. Well organized, well-armed protesters, with materiel that could have only been provided by outside agents, upped the ante of violence with automatic weapons and Molotov cocktails, and Baba Beijing responded by sending in armed soldiers to suppress these violent groups. The rest of the protesters slowly left the square and the surrounding streets were emptied. The photos are eloquent.

[IMG 0170]

Unarmed PLA soldiers hung or tied up then torched with Molotov cocktails by Tiananmen's protesters. The bottom photo's soldier was even disemboweled with some bus trim. Nice. Once the West's "peaceful" protesters turned bloodthirsty, Baba Beijing gave the soldiers arms to clear out the square (mages by Voltaire.net)

If Baba Beijing was such a heartless bunch of leaders, why was the protest allowed to completely disrupt the country for over a month (there were protests in numerous other cities as well), and during all the time, the security agents and PLA soldiers were unarmed? It was only when a few bands of protesters suddenly had automatic weapons, that the PLA came in to stop them.

ABOVE: *AK-47s thanks to the CIA and the US Embassy's diplomatic pouch, June 3rd, 1989. The PLA soldiers on duty in Tiananmen Square were still unarmed, until the protesters started shooting them. (Image by Jeff Widner, Associated Press). Also PLA soldier lynched by the crowd and set on fire.*

[IMG 0171]
BELOW: *If Baba Beijing was such a heartless bunch of bastards and the PLA just a gang of psychopathic killers, why did they not run over Tank Man? (Image by petapixel.com)*

Not only that, but every Western journalist worth their salt, eventually came out and recanted all the lurid reporting of massive bloodshed around Tiananmen Square. Nicholas Kristof of the *New York Times* actually reported the truth of a non-massacre, but it was buried to make room for all the Western, anti-communist China propaganda. Wikileaks documents smoked out BBC journalist James Miles, that he had "conveyed the wrong impression" and that there was no one killed in Tiananmen Square in 1989. In 1998, in the Columbia Journalism Review, Jay Matthews, who was the Washington Post's Beijing bureau chief, wrote a piece entitled, *Reporting the Myth of Tiananmen and the Price of a Passive Press*. Mr. Matthews recounts in depressing detail, how the mainstream media propaganda megaphone fabricated the myth of a student massacre. Numerous other Western reporters later testified that they were under tremendous pressure to exaggerate the casualties. Even uber-establishment *Daily Telegraph* had to write that it was all a lie. Human Rights Watch decided not to publish in 1989 their own 52-page eye witnesses' report that confirmed the Chinese side of the story, undoubtedly due to intense official pressure to maintain The Big Lie. This same organization still keeps the Big Lie going on every June 4th anniversary, because by continuing the anti-Chinese propaganda, they can garner a spike in donations every year.

One of the most devastating, iron clad pieces of evidence was film footage from a Spanish TV crew, who got lost in the confusion that night. It conclusively showed that no massacre took place, there were no PLA machine gun nests atop buildings, spraying the square with lead, nor were there soldiers gunning down innocents with sadistic abandon. As soon as the footage became known, it was just as quickly buried by the powers that be, since it did not fit the iron fisted Western narrative of an evil, Chinese Communist Party, hell bent on massacring its citizens.

There is also irrefutable evidence that the CIA was aiding, abetting and organizing the protests, providing money to pay for everything needed to keep the protests going: money on the streets to buy food and necessities, faxes, mimeograph machines, phone lines, strategy and training manuals, expensive Coleman gas stoves and unlimited supplies of very costly cooking fuel, ample supplies of gasoline to make Molotov cocktails at a time when cars were rare and fuel was rationed, and when the disappointment of over a month of overthrow effort was ending in failure, Kalashnikovs (AK-47s) smuggled into the country via diplomatic pouch were finally provided on June 3rd, in one last desperate attempt to overthrow the communist government.

That night of June 3rd, when reports came in to the Central and Politburo Standing Committees that unarmed PLA soldiers were being gunned down in cold blood, Deng Xiaoping called an emergency meeting and gave a speech. In it, he said they all knew that outside forces were instigating this insurrection and that these outside agents were hell bent on destroying the CPC. None of them blamed the students. They knew these kids were being manipulated by the CIA and its local subversives. These protesters had legitimate grievances and they were being corrupted by the West.

Heck, after Baba Beijing spent days talking to the students, the CPC even invited protest leaders on national TV, as a means of dialogue. Imagine that, protest leaders being on national television, to meet with Premier Li Peng, the third most powerful leader in the land, after paramount leader Deng and President Yang Shangkun. And what did these protest leaders do? They insulted Premier Peng and spurned his efforts and insulted him and the other leaders on TV. Rebuking elders in public is beyond the pale in Chinese culture and it was a massive loss of face for the CPC.

Enough was enough. At that point, Baba Beijing knew that the protest leaders were nothing more than Western stooges. Deng told his colleagues that was either the CPC or the West that was going to control their country and they could not allow China to relive another century of colonial, imperial humiliation. The time to act was now. Declare martial law and send in the PLA with arms, to protect the thousands of unarmed soldiers already in harm's way, and end the protests peacefully.

Hats off to the CIA. It got that close to turning China's proud people into Western lackeys, just like 1839-1949. The near success of the orchestrated Tiananmen protests became the blueprint for the many "color revolutions" that the West started cooking up a year later, with the fall of the Berlin Wall,

and which are still ongoing in places like the Ukraine and Hong Kong. The Tienanmen Square "Massacre" is without a doubt one of the most successful Fake News operation in history.

The Chinese government came flat out on the 10th anniversary, saying that Tiananmen was orchestrated and implemented by the United States.

The Unites States played an inglorious role by directly masterminding schemes and giving money and goods to support those making the disturbance.

Every year since, on June 4th, the Chinese press repeats the same observation, as a reminder to the masses. This is not partisan speculation. Thoughtful research demonstrates that it is historical fact.

The way Tiananmen was portrayed behind the Great Western Firewall was not random happenstance. There was a deliberate, concerted, willful effort by mainstream Western journalists to destroy Baba Beijing's and the Chinese Communist Party's reputation, and ultimately, to overthrow the government. The fact that many of these people came out 10, 15, 20 years later and confessed to their perjury is nice. But, it's like someone who waits to fess up about a lie that put someone on death row, only to see them lose their life in the electric chair – and only then recant after the fact.

In this case, the bludgeoning of the truth has resulted in the execution of China's and Baba Beijing's dignity and reputation, year after year after year. For the Western slime machine, it is the gift that just keeps on giving, as every anniversary, Western TV, radio and print media ceaselessly vomit all over the world, the "Tiananmen Square Massacre" and "democracy protests".

The original protests had nothing to do with "Western democracy". They were sparked, due to the death of popular CPC General Secretary, Hu Yaobang. They were protesting three things: rampant inflation, which for the previous 18 months, had skyrocketed to 25-30% per annum. Number two, all of the reforms that were removing China's Mao Era socialist programs were beginning to hurt the masses' pocketbooks and quality of life. So in fact, Tiananmen was in support of communism and a rejection of newly adopted capitalist policies. Finally and again, due to all the market deregulation, business and government corruption were becoming rampant, and this stuck in the craw of the people, who were suffering from inflation and disappearing socialist benefits. These were the real reasons for the protests. It was not until the CIA and other Western spy agencies infiltrated the square with their hired and trained traitors, that the alien concept of "Western democracy" became a fabricated "issue".

This reminds me of the great lecture that Michael Parenti gave about Julius Caesar, how the powers-that-be can so brilliantly turn reality completely inside out. Today, Caesar is portrayed as a despotic tyrant, who crushed Rome's hapless citizens like bugs. Not true. He was a liberal who was doing many good things for the masses, redistributing wealth from the millionaire senators downward. *That's* why he was assassinated. Western propaganda about Tiananmen is just as bogus and insidious.

Australian journalist, Wei Ling Chua, wrote an excellent book, *Tiananmen Square "Massacre"? The Power of Words vs. Silent Evidence* (2014), which pulls much of this information into a cohesive whole.

As my students and I were talking together, I couldn't help but ask myself,

How would Uncle Sam respond if a few hundred thousand protesters were packed into Washington DC's National Mall, and well organized, well-armed groups began assaulting and killing the authorities' security forces with automatic machine guns and Molotov cocktails?

I kept coming to the same conclusion: it would get really ugly, really fast.

A serendipitous juxtaposition also happened right before this year's *liusi*: I had just finished reading *Killing Hope (2004, Common Courage Press), by William Blum*. It is a factual, scathing exposé of the American Central Intelligence Agency's and National Security Administration's long, long rap sheet of covert and violent regime change in dozens of countries around the world, since World War II, including China. My eyebrows raised more than just a stretch while reading about all the ceaseless American efforts to destabilize and overthrow the communist government here, starting even before October 1st, 1949. It included hiring the Dalai Lama's older brother, as America's lead Tibetan saboteur. For years, the CIA and Thubten Jigme Norbu planned to invade the Land of Snow, using hundreds of exiles trained in Colorado and on America's Saipan Island, and flying numerous weapon drops onto the Tibetan Plateau to arm the overthrow. Elsewhere in China, scores of American and Taiwanese agents were sent to infiltrate, sabotage and foment antigovernment revolution in-country. This has been documented in detail to have gone on well into the 70s.

[IMG 0172] US Military & CIA Interventions since World War II —*In reality, we can add the United States to the map, for the Kennedy assassinations, 9/11, internal psyops, propaganda and violent interventions. (Image by killinghope.com)*

Now I know why Baba Beijing will have nothing to do with the Dalai Lama. In the Chinese familial hierarchy, if your gege (哥哥 = older brother) is rotten and corrupt, then all the younger siblings are equally so, by filial association. The fact that *Radio Free Asia*, a CIA propaganda megaphone, used someone with a voice sounding exactly like the Dalai Lama, to egg Tibetans to violent insurrection the day before the March 14th, 2008 riots in Lhasa, riots which were obviously well planned and coordinated in advance, it is easy to see that the United States continues to try to undermine China's sovereignty unabated.

Thus, one has to ask, is the recent string of so called Xinjiang Muslim terrorist acts getting outside support of the Red, White and Blue variety? Based on all I have learned, I am convinced they are. F. William Engdahl and Tony Cartalucci have done extensive research on the involvement of the CIA and its proxy NGOs in Xinjiang, and the evidence is overwhelming. All this goaded me to do more research on Tiananmen, and I came away from the experience enthralled and ashamed.

Enthralled that we Westerners are so convinced of our moral superiority, thus this Great Con is so ruthlessly effective and pervasive, all over the world. Indeed, as previously stated this is manifested in one of the United States' greatest post-WWII media propaganda coups: the Tiananmen Square "Massacre". We all dutifully regurgitate the annual international flogging that Baba Beijing, and by extension, China's 1.3 billion citizens have been and will be subjected to, by Western Empire's state-corporate mass media. This worldwide juggernaut, a system that makes Orwell's Oceania blush with envy, will go on in perpetuity every June 4th, for an ersatz massacre that never was. It's a hoax that just keeps on giving. The fact that Tiananmen was financed, planned, aided and abetted by the CIA, makes the whole affair especially galling and diabolical.

I'm equally ashamed that I have been an unwitting dupe to fall for this blatant, state-corporate brainwashing most of my life. Not anymore. Like Neo in *The Matrix*, since returning to China six years ago, I am renouncing the blue pill and opting for the red one. Thanks to my experiences here, I can now forgo the Matrix's fabricated reality and stop living in its *illusion of ignorance*. Living and working here in Sinoland, inside the belly of the 21st Century Beast, has taught me to escape from the Matrix, to be fully sentient in the real world, embracing Morpheus' *truth of reality*.

What could be more profound and liberating than that? And who would have guessed this new found freedom would be found in the West's big, bad, *communist* China? My research continues into the truth of reality and honestly, not only Tiananmen Square, but all over the world. It is difficult to bear just how evil are the American and European governments. At the same time, it is easy to see why the vast, vast majority of humanity prefers to swallow the blue pill, living inside that comforting, soothing illusion of ignorance, in an amniotic womb of infotainment and soulless Stuff. I am learning that real freedom is not free. The truth of reality is hard, humbling and sobering work.

But as Morpheus told Neo, there is no turning back now. I read *NATO's Secret Armies – Operation Gladio and Terrorism in Western Europe*, by Daniele Ganser (Routledge, 2005). Inevitably, the West's deep, dark, colonial state metastasized and continues to terrorize and kill its own citizens, per the needs of the Princes of Power, on both sides of the Atlantic, as well as around the world. *JFK and the Unspeakable*, by James W. Douglass (Touchstone, 2010), gets at the deep, dark heart of America's very own, homegrown, violent regime change. Amazingly, polls show the majority of Americans have known since that fateful day that they have been lied to.

With one more week of school to go, I already apologized to this year's class for my earlier analysis of what happened on June 4th, 1989. Next year, when *liusi* rolls around, I will be a much better teacher to my students, from the get go. I didn't swallow the red pill until I was in my fifties. Better late than never. I hope from now on that I can teach my students, regardless of their age or nationality, to embrace the truth of reality, no matter how much it goes against the official consensus. Better earlier than later. It's the only hope humanity has for its future salvation, starting *now*.

Below is some suggested reading. Like me, if you do your research, you will know you have been lied to:

http://voltairenet.org/article177063.html
http://voltairenet.org/article177116.html
http://weidb.com/t3849
http://highbeam.com/doc/1P2-596462.html
http://globalresearch.ca/tiananmen-square-massacre-is-a-myth-all-were-remembering-are-british-lies/5386080
http://globalresearch.ca/what-really-happened-in-tiananmen-square-25-years-ago/5385528
http://american-buddha.com/cia.secret.war.htm
https://blog.hiddenharmonies.org/2012/05/30/lets-talk-about-tiananmen-square-1989/
http://cjr.org/behind_the_news/the_myth_of_tiananmen.php

Baba Beijing sez: we don't need no stinkin' Western democrassy!

President Xi Jinping is robustly and authoritatively pointing the way to China's future, and the future of rest of the world as well. (mage by scmp.com)
[IMG 0173]

In a series of carefully prepared, meticulously worded speeches, Xi Jinping, the President of China, has all but declared any ambition, any notion of adopting Western style "democracy" as misguided and dangerous. The son of a well-respected communist revolutionary, Xi is taking the mantle of Mao Zedong and Deng Xiaoping, and acting very presidential indeed. He is a force to be reckoned with, not only in China, but for adversarial US/NATO too. Thirty-five years ago, when China was still broke and broken after a long generation of ceaseless, internecine revolution, Deng Xiaoping said,

Keep a cool head and maintain a low profile. Never take the lead - but aim to do something big.

Baba Beijing has resoundingly rejected one-third of Deng's aphorism – the middle one. The other two are living large in the minds of Baba Beijing, as it faces off with Eurangloland, not just in China's backyard, but on every landmass and ocean in existence.

Like any good conservative, Baba Beijing is finding an alternative pathway by seeking answers and guidance from China's millennia of existence, and its multitude of philosophers, historians, authors and teachers.

Xi has recently been pulling quotes and axioms from China's ancient texts going back 2,500 years ago. Confucius is hip again and citizens of all socioeconomic strata are seeking out his wisdom and sage advice. Westerners are all in a snit that China is formulating its own identity and system of governance on its own terms, while moving and shaking across the planet. How dare them!

Xi is staking out China's own version of authoritarian, collective democracy, while working to integrate the concept of *rule of law*. This is causing China watchers fits, as they try to make sense of it all, parsing and divining every Chinese character uttered or printed.

Nor is Baba Beijing reticent about invoking Mao Zedong's more visionary ponderings on socialism and communism. Baba is also talking about and defending the *people's democratic dictatorship*, which is straight out of China's constitution. What exactly is China's people's democratic dictatorship? It means that the people have invested in the state and Communist Party to represent them and act in their best interests. At the same time, Baba Beijing reserves the right to use dictatorial power to combat outside or fifth column forces bent on destabilizing or overthrowing the established order. While people's democratic dictatorship sounds jarring to Westerners' programmed ears, it is simply an updated, revolutionary synonym for the Heavenly Mandate, i.e., maintaining stability, unity and sacrificing individual needs for the common good of all the citizens.

Xi is also taking his message of a *new pathway* to the four corners of the Earth, along with Premier Li Keqiang. Both have been traveling and meeting fellow leaders on every inhabited continent, talking about the Asian Century, several Eurasian Silk Roads, and Strings of Pearls, while signing hundreds of billions in trade and commerce deals. The intent is clear: after 500 years of Eurmerican colonialism and exploitation of, the 21st century will be very different, and China will help lead to make our coexistence more peaceful, more equal and more multipolar.

Baba Beijing's people's democratic dictatorship has been most recently and thoroughly tested in Hong Kong, with the US financed, instigated and managed Occupy Central color (Umbrella) revolution. As has been pointed out to everyone, but ignored in the West, China has assiduously adhered to every tenet of the 1990 Basic Law, signed in agreement with Britain, and simply wants to follow the letter of the law for the upcoming 2017 elections. In effect, America's CIA puppet protesters are demanding that China violate an international treaty. That is something that Baba Beijing is simply not going to let happen, America's corporate, crass and corrupt "democracy" be damned.

Baba Beijing is not isolated. Xi Jinping and Russia's Vladimir Putin have met face to face no less than twelve times since Xi became China's president. They've got each other's back in Ukraine and are against all of the CIA's many color revolutions and government destabilization efforts around the world. India and Pakistan are set to join the Shanghai Cooperation Organization (SCO), which with Russia and China, stands as a serious counterweight to US/NATO's colonial ambitions in Asia. It's breathtaking, when one thinks Bretton Woods was only signed 70 years ago, a blink of a Sino-eye.

[IMG 0174] India's PM Modi *Xi Jinping applauds Prime Minister Narendra Modi, during his recent trip to India. Like Russia, India sees the light in turning East towards China. Problem is, Modi, a hardcore chauvinist right-winger quickly proved to be an unreliable partner. By mid-2016, India was joining Obama for his infamous "Pivot to Asia".*

Baba Beijing and the Chinese think in terms of decades and centuries. Americans can't think past the 24-hour propaganda spin and quarterly stock reports. As the American Dream rapidly fades from unequal reality to universal deception, Xi Jinping's Chinese Dream is tapping roots across the People's Republic, and into the 21st century, not just for China, but for all the people of the world.

[IMG 0175] *The Chinese Dream stresses stability, social harmony and sacrifice for the common good. The billboard says, You and I work together. The American Dream vaunts individual accumulation of wealth and endless resource extraction. For now, too many Chinese are binging on the American version.*

Another week in Sinoland, ho-hum

[IMG 0176] *The new Asia Infrastructure Investment Bank (AIIB) is just one of many manifestations of how China is radically changing the world's economic and political landscape, all at the expense of Eurangloland.*

While Eurangloland is trying its darnedest to destroy the world, at home and abroad, Baba Beijing is just going about its business of governing China's 1,300,000,000 citizens, while changing the world's political and economic landscape faster than you can say *chop suey*.

Here is a not so atypical two-week news cycle in *Sinoland*:

While gangsters, loan sharks and assorted psychopaths roam the halls of Wall Street, stealing and destroying lives with impunity, Baba Beijing is trying to clean up sleaze and go after the bad guys here in China. In the halls of government, the Communist Party has gone after 84,000 miscreants in just the first half of 2014. This, while sunshine bribery and legislated, "legal" corruption grease the wheels of "progress" in Washington, London, Paris, Brussels and Tokyo. Baba Beijing just shut down many classic ghost employees scams around the country, to the tune of 100,000 phantom salaries. Baba is also scouring the planet for crooks who have fled the Motherland with millions, sometimes billions of RMB in dirty lucre, 730 perps since 2008 and the pace is picking up fast. It is affectionately called *Operation Fox Hunt*. Meanwhile in the US, economic fugitives are renouncing their American citizenship. Heaven forbid if these cardboard patriots had to pay their fair share of taxes.

Elsewhere, China knows it is sitting on a mountain of worthless American treasury bonds – $1,300,000,000,000 - that will never be paid back, unless Uncle Sam cranks up the printing presses, Zimbabwe dollar style. So, they are making headlines dumping off this worthless paper to buy assets overseas. This is true for mergers and acquisitions (M&A) and outright investment purchases.

Another audacious way to jettison China's junk American bonds is to create your own bank and make the capitalization in US dollars, not

RMB. That's exactly what China has done with the establishment of the new Asian Infrastructure Investment Bank (AIIB). The United States has been fighting it tooth and nail, as it would reduce Uncle Sam's iron fisted financial hegemony via the World Bank, as well as the Asian Development Bank, which is Japan's little fiefdom. Uncle Sam was able to browbeat South Korea, Japan and Australia from becoming founding members, but 20 other countries stood up to the American bully and joined the newest international Chinese club. The one gaping non-entrant was Russia, but it has since joined as a founding member. Obama and Company are sitting on the sidelines, licking their wounds, while the AIIB cranks up with 50 billion George Washingtons in starting capital. That's now much America spends every 20 days to colonize Planet Earth, with its worldwide Wehrmacht and to maintain its police state back home. It's a question of priorities.

On the home front, Beijing is now being called the New Silicon Valley. Haidian, a large neighborhood in the Chinese capital, due west of where I live, is now a very happening technological hot house of creativity and innovation. It is not only IT, but industrial innovation is also improving dramatically, from just being a copycat of Western technology. One of the great myths that was perpetrated on the Western 99% is that by destroying national industries in North America and Europe, no one had to worry about having a great, high paying job, since all that research and development (R&D) would stay in-country. Do your due diligence in studying history and it is clear that R&D always follows manufacturing and industry. I remember growing up in the 1950s-60s, with all the jokes on TV about Japan and Taiwan only being able to make and export cheap junk. We can see what happened since then. Ditto South Korea, which came along a generation later. Now it is China's turn to draw international R&D. Samsung, Motorola, Microsoft and other companies brought their R&D to China previously, often pressured by Baba Beijing as a quid pro quo for entrance into the world's biggest market, and now Chinese IT is expanding worldwide, thanks to all that previous R&D.

It is not only in the law enforcement and economic realms, but Baba Beijing is taking its cue from the West, about how powerful and effective its think tanks are, to maintain the Washington-London-Paris consensus. Outfits like the Hoover, Foreign Policy Research, American Enterprise and Cato Institutes, Freedom House, Heritage Foundation and others are incredibly influential in determining the West's continued slide towards extreme neo-conservatism, some would say fascism. Thus, Baba Beijing is <u>creating its own stable of think tanks, which will look at the world from a Chinese perspective</u>. If you can't beat 'em, better 'em!

As long as you are running yin-yang circles around the world's self-declared King Kong on the Mountain, you might as well go astronomical. China did something no other country has done in 40 years: <u>send a lunar module to orbit around the Moon and safely return back to earth</u>. China's *Xiaofei* (小飞 = Little Flier) lunar orbiter utilized the challenging *skip reentry method* to make it safely back home. As if to rub salt in the astro-wound, the US lost a very valuable payload on takeoff the same week, and the Russians, who like the Chinese are endlessly attacked by the United States via color revolutions and CIA operations on every front, showed graciousness and diplomacy, by immediately sending up their own rocket to the International Space Station (ISS), to replenish badly needed supplies. Talk about brotherly love! It must be said that the US, Europe, Russia and China have all had their aerospace foibles. It's a hugely risky venture. But still, the timing could not have been more ill-fated.

The fact that Uncle Sam spends billions trying to destabilize and eventually overthrow countries like Russia, China, Venezuela, Cuba, Iran – well, the list is long, very long – has been thoroughly exposed and researched. <u>Those poor, idealistic suckers in Hong Kong, Kiev, Caracas and elsewhere think they are righteously fighting the good fight, whereas in reality, they are stooges for American Empire</u>. It's sad really. You don't even have to be America's enemies. <u>The United States overthrew the elected government of Australia via a palace coup, historical fact, thanks to Wikileaks bright beacon on official documents</u>. Starting in 1971, Australia's principled, anti-colonial, anti-Western Empire Prime Minister, Gough Whitlam, had the temerity to try to rid the CIA from his country's intelligence services, while removing Aussie troops from Vietnam, traveling to communist China – a month before Nixon did, as well as establishing diplomatic relations with North Vietnam and North Korea. All this and much, much more was beyond the pale for Uncle Sam's deep state. Working with the UK's MI6, Mr. Whitlam was deposed in 1975. Luckily for him, he was not assassinated, like JFK. So much for spreading so called Western *democracy* and *civil society*.

If your country is not a shoe shine boy for Uncle Sam, especially if your land has valuable natural resources, watch your back. In fact, Uncle Sam is probably already there, right under your noses. Mother Jones has shown that the United States has embedded secret armies in 134 countries around the world. That's 70% of all the 192 member countries in the United Nations. [NOTE: For all the good that Mother Jones has done, it has recently joined with alacrity the Democrat/CIA putschist and anti-Russian mob trying to pull a color revolution in the United States. Once again, proof that liberals can never be trusted.)

Wanna bet they are not in yours? And if you are an American? Make that a total of 135 countries.

Why China's centrally planned, communist economy runs circles around capitalism

[IMG 0177] China's New Silk Road map.

For millennia, China connected Asia to Europe and the Middle East, via the celebrated Silk Roads. Baba Beijing is now taking this ancient concept of continental connectivity to 21st century heights, and it would all be impossible without China's centrally planned, communist economy to make it happen. Capitalism could never pull off the Belts and Roads Initiative (both inside and outside the country), because of too many selfish, individual, competing, short-term profit interests, and all the corruption and greed that go with it. The above map shows the status of China's ambitious and visionary Belts and Roads Initiative, as of 2015, including Africa, but not the Americas. China has already started building the Grand Nicaragua Canal and plans to build a rail line from the Pacific to the Atlantic, across the Andes Mountains and Brazil. Western empire and capitalism have absolutely no answer to this towering Chinese mission statement, except to keep on doing what it does best: racist and resource inspired wars, genocide, sanctions, false flags, government overthrows, assassinations, color revolutions and plunder. Hats off to Merics for such an outstanding map.

To see an enlarged version, check it out here: http://www.merics.org/fileadmin/ processed_/csm_ChinaMapping-Silk-Road-Nov2015-DE_e9ebe044d8.jpg (Or visit image [IMG 0177]

Seventy-nine percent of the world's people live in countries and economies that are under various forms of capitalism, from cutthroat libertarianism, like in what is left of the Ukraine, to Western Europe's rapidly disintegrating socialism-capitalism. Comparatively speaking, China, being a communist country, is responsible for 19 percent of humanity.

That leaves two percent of the human race. One-half is composed of non-capitalist countries, and like its capitalist counterpart, there is a range of different approaches. North Korea, Cuba and Eritrea are communist, like China. Iran is not communist, but very anti-capitalist, with its organic Islamic Revolution. Starting in 1999-2000, Russia saw one of history's most impressive sociopolitical renaissances, with key sectors of the economy nationalized and socialist welfare programs brought back for its citizens. Then there are countries like the ALBA group, in Latin America, which have also nationalized key sectors of the economy, governing with a strong commitment to socialism, and are decidedly anti-capitalist. ALBA's most well-known members are Nicaragua, Ecuador, Bolivia and Venezuela.

The one unifying characteristic of all these countries is their visceral hatred of Western imperialism and colonialism. They have all been and continue to be attacked by the West, with the hopes of overthrowing their governments and ideologies, in order to replace them with satrap stooges. This says a lot about empire's zero tolerance for any expression of independence and liberty, that is outside its complete subjugation and exploitation.

Let's see… Seventy-nine percent for capitalism, plus nineteen for China, plus one percent for other anti-West countries, that leaves one percent of humanity. Who are they? They are the billionaire one percent, who were made into a household name, thanks to the now-crushed Occupy Wall Street movement. They harvest the 79% of humanity and their resources, those in all the capitalist countries. But, the true owners of the 79% only number about 400 people (mostly Western Caucasians), what I like to call the *trillionaires*, because they in fact dwarf even the billionaire class, in terms of wealth concentration.

The rest of this top level one percent are merely millionaires, and are their superiors' centurions and praetorian guards – the assassins, factotums, lawyers, judges, politicians, generals and business people who prostitute themselves and profit handsomely from their dirty work. These are the ones who make sure the transfer of the 99%'s declining wealth and income continues to flow up to the trillionaires, while in the process, pillaging what they can, or are allowed to rake off, by their infinitely more powerful trillionaire handlers. It's all part of the capitalist plan for 79% of humanity. The 20% of the human race in the anti-West countries can count their blessings.

Among all the anti-capitalist countries in the world, China stands shoulders above the rest, simply due to its size, population, the fact that the Communist Party of China (CPC) is in the dawn of its Red Dynasty, and the Party's and Chinese people's incredible success story, since liberation from Japanese fascism and Western colonialism, in 1949. One of the biggest and most important Western propaganda myths to brainwash most of the world concerns China's economy during the Mao Zedong Era, 1949-1978. China's GDP during this 29 years of pure communism grew at a rate of 7% per annum, this, in spite of Mao's penchant for continuous revolution and numerous political campaigns, which set the economy back during several of those years. Not to mention that Uncle Sam enforced one of the longest running and cruelest blockades in modern history, shutting off New China from financial, commercial and economic relations with the Western Bloc, similar to the brutal and totally illegal blockade that the United States has been and continues to use to shut off Cuba from normal relations with the rest of the world.

So, you might ask, what was the average American GDP growth rate, during this same time period, 1949-1978? Eight percent per year, *only one percent more than China.* Yet, postwar America was sitting on the pinnacle of planetary economic power, garnering 50% of global GDP, being the world's largest manufacturer, exporter and creditor, and possessing the only international reserve and trade currency accepted then, the US dollar. Another telling sign, which country is now the world's largest manufacturer, exporter and creditor? Communist China and it's not even close.

And let's not forget that this all happened with China shut out from the outside world, thanks to Uncle Sam's cruel and vindictive blockade. It is estimated that the blockade on Cuba, since its inception in 1960, has cost this small island country $1.1 trillion - that's with a "t", not a "b". China has 125 times more people than Cuba, so do you care to wager how much it cost its people? The number is probably incalculable. But, in spite of it all, communist China's economy still ran neck and neck with the world's capitalist Leviathan. And since 1978, during the Deng Xiaoping and Xi Jinping Eras? Communist China has been humming at a 10% annual GDP growth, to declining America's six percent. Thus, from 1949-2016, Red China has significantly outperformed the US and the capitalist West. Proof? From 1980-2015, Chinese wages have increased by 7% per annum, net of inflation. There isn't a capitalist country in the world that can say the same. In fact, it's the exact opposite, as wages and standards of living have been steadily declining during the same time period.

Thus, from 1949-2015, Red China has significantly outperformed the US and the capitalist West.

Now you know why the West's owners brainwash their citizens, to immunize them against this fact-based truth. How could a largely agrarian, communist country, totally shut off from Western markets, goods, technology and financing, be so incredibly successful, socially and economically? The West's owners surely wouldn't want their people to start asking intelligent questions or looking for different ideas and alternative possibilities. Heaven forbid, they might even revolt and start an income redistributing revolution. Can't let that happen. Won't let it happen.

Well then, you might ask, how did China do it, and why are they succeeding so triumphantly now? The CPC governs China, using a system with three broad platforms, which you can look upon as a three-legged stool of governance.

First, the Chinese *have taken control of the means of production.* What this signifies is that all of the land in China has been nationalized, every square meter of the place. Thus, there is no private real estate in China, only private personal property. "Buying" a house, business or land here is, in actuality, a long term lease (up to 70 years), whose landlord is ultimately the citizens of China. North Korea has the same system, and I believe Cuba and Eritrea, as well.

Other anti-West countries, like Russia, Iran and the ALBA group, don't control all the real estate, but own the means of production (or a majority) of key industrial sectors in their economies. These often includes hydrocarbons, nuclear energy, aviation, armaments, utilities, media and the like. China is no different. State owned enterprises (SOEs) dominate or totally control key sectors, such as finance, banking and insurance, telecommunications, steel, aviation, energy, mining, rail, the media, and on and on.

The second support of China's three-legged stool of governance is *democratic centralism*. This idea came from Russia's Vladimir Lenin. It means that all proposals, policies and laws can and should be discussed and debated, in order to make the best decision, for the needs of the people. However, once the final decision is made, everybody - citizens and leaders alike, must wholeheartedly support the plan, for the common good, and sublimate individual and group desires to go against the collective grain. This faith in the commonwealth must continue, until at which time the law or policy is changed.

While individualistic Westerners may find this concept superficially alien, it is in fact, part and parcel of capitalism too. Government officials are expected to tow the policy line, regardless of their personal inclinations. Employees and managers of businesses are expected to do so as well. Vocal, rebellious workers tend to get the axe. Any grievances should be shared with their superiors in private, or at the appropriate meeting time. Loyalty is demanded until the rule, policy or strategy changes in the process. Isn't capitalism's *teamwork* just another word for democratic centralism, after all?

Another successful brainwashing of Westerners, at the hands of mainstream media and government propaganda, is the myth that China is governed by tyrannical, one-man rule. This was and is utter nonsense. Even during Mao Zedong's heyday, he was constantly having to negotiate, accommodate and compromise on his vision. The CPC has a long and illustrious history of fierce debating, frank criticism and finally compromise, under the mantle of democratic centralism.

The only difference is it is almost always done in meetings, away from public view. Is this really any different than the West? Not really. Outside all the buffoonery and grandstanding that takes place in the public eye, and which the Chinese find beneath the dignity and solemn duty of governance, let's face it: the vast majority of decisions that affect the lives and livelihood of the citizenry are done behind closed doors.

The other very successful brainwashing of Westerners, is that China's National People's Congress (NPC, the legislature) and the China People's Political Consultative Conference (CPPCC, all the major lobbies) are nothing but hollow shills, mindless Myrmidons and toothless, powerless rubber stampers. Orwellian hogwash! Again, the debating, arm wrestling, jockeying and waxing and waning of supporters for a given law or proposal is fast and ferocious. But it is done in halls and meeting rooms, away from the cynical public eye.

Thus, when the NPC and CPPCC meet every year, in March (it just concluded this week), there has been a year of nonstop, hard-nosed debating, arguing and decision making that took place. The real voting, and they do vote, is done during all the negotiating and debating, before these bodies convene publicly. What we see on the television is democratic centralism in action: putting into effect laws and policies that have been honed, perfected and voted on, long before the signatures and public ritual in front of the cameras.

The final and third leg of Baba Beijing's governing stool is the *democratic dictatorship of the people*, or *people's democratic dictatorship*. While it admittedly has a jarring ring to Western ears, it makes perfect sense when properly explained. The concept has its roots in 19th century communism and was early on adopted by Vladimir Lenin, as *people's democracy*, in the USSR and later in Eastern Europe.

What it means is that the citizens confer their trust in the country's leaders to govern effectively, for the livelihoods, safety and betterment of the people, and if threatened from outside forces or internal sabotage, then the leaders promise to protect the country's borders and way of life.

This is not a new fashioned, modern political theory. The Chinese were way ahead of Karl Marx, Friedrich Engels and Vladimir Lenin, like about 2,300 years, to be exact. The democratic dictatorship of the people is essentially the political philosophy of Confucius. That's right, the people's democratic dictatorship *is Confucianism*, writ large. Add to it the even older concept of the Heavenly Mandate, and you have China's system of governance, going back thousands of years. The Heavenly Mandate simply states that if the country's leaders do not maintain the democratic dictatorship, then the people have the right to replace this failing government with a new one. This is Confucianism, hook, line and sinker.

All three of these platforms of governance, controlling the means of production, democratic centralism and the democratic dictatorship of the people, are enshrined in China's national constitution. Since 1949, it has been and continues to work more than just fine, thank you, Western capitalists. As a result of this three-legged stool, Baba Beijing is able to effectively guide the country, its economy and development. As the map at the start of this article demonstrates, it is working wonders for China's diplomacy and international cooperation, long term, as well as for its partners overseas.

Capitalism could *never* pull off the Belts and Roads Initiative, because of too many selfish, individual, competing, short-term profit interests. This is a truism that the 79% need to come to grips with. They need to think long and hard about the socioeconomic dilemma of their static or degrading standards of living.

New China adopted the Soviet Union's Five-Year Plan, again, a Leninist concept. Since 1984, China has actually made their goal setting into a rolling ten-year plan, looking at the current five-year plan, as statistics and results come in, thus, tweaking it each March, then penciling in projections for the following five years thereafter.

The 13th Five-Year Plan, which was just endorsed and passed into law this last week, by the NPC, with mothering input from all the lobby groups in the CPPCC, is instructive. Below is a summary and chart, showing what Baba Beijing is going to do for its people and their future, 2016-2020, *in infrastructure only*. This does not include reams of laws, regulations and policies legislated for social programs, housing, health care, poverty elimination, education, research & development, military, energy, conservation, taxation and the thousands of other clauses and line items that go into any national policy and budget. For readers in capitalist countries studying this information, ask yourselves,

How much is my government doing to improve our country's infrastructure and economic development for the common folk?

I know the answer in the United States, almost none. American infrastructure is falling apart at the seams, entropy, the Second Law of Thermodynamics in fast motion.

Infrastructure Projects set in the 13th Five-Year Plan

1. **3,000km of urban rail lines will be built and made operational. Think trams and trolley cars. The goal is to reduce the time city folk spend, going to and from work, bus to subway to bus, etc.**
2. **Transportation hubs will be improved and streamlined in China's many metro systems. This is a big complaint among the citizenry (including my wife!), the long transfers between subway stations.**
3. **The nation's high speed train (HST) network will be expanded to 30,000km. Currently, it is 19,000km and by several magnitudes, is the world's largest system (Spain's is the next biggest, at 3,000km). Baba Beijing is going to expand China's HST network another 58% in the next five years and in the process, serve 80% of the country's bigger cities.**
4. **30,000km of expressways will be added to the existing network of 123,000km. These are highways like the US Interstate system and autobahns in Europe. This shouldn't be a problem, since *China added 11,050km of expressway in 2015 alone.* A stated goal is so people can get out of the cities and travel in their region, on the weekends. How thoughtful. Hey, it's a quality of life issue.**
5. **China is going to integrate its road systems in what it calls megalopolises, massive urban conglomerations around cities like Beijing, Shanghai and Guangzhou.**

The reasoning? So that citizens living on the outskirts of these supercities can commute to work in under 1-2 hours. Another quality of life concern.

6. 50 civilian airports will be built in third tier cities, so that less populated areas can travel around the country, like their big metropolis brethren. The new **Beijing Airport**, on the southern edge of town, will be finished, to take badly needed pressure off the current **Beijing Capital Airport**, on its northeast fringe. Seven other big city airports will get a major expansion and facelift.

7. Roads with shuttle bus systems will be built and installed, to connect China's one million villages. How? By building 152,000km of paved roads to connect them, more than all the current expressways put together. It shouldn't be difficult to go visit grandpa, grannie and take care of business in one's neighboring bigger town. Another quality of life issue for hundreds of millions of farming families.

8. Another big complaint among the rural citizenry is that too many villages do not have post offices and courier services, so country folk have to travel to a nearby bigger town, in order to send and receive mail. That is going to change during this 2016-2020 Five-Year Plan.

Compare this ambitious action plan to improve the lives of the vast majority of China's citizens, to the malaise and degradation of infrastructure in many Western and other capitalist countries. The last thing the West's owners want is for their subjects behind the Great Western Firewall, to wake up, smell the soy sauce and steamed dumplings, asking,

Hey, how come those evil, commie reds in China can create so much prosperity and a better life for their people? What the hell is going on here? I'd like to know more about the Chinese Dream!

2st Century Dazibao

This article has been incorporated into Chinese study syllabuses in the United States. I have updated it for clarity and detail. Enjoy.

*D*azibao in Chinese have a celebrated and sometimes infamous history in the annals of a civilization that goes back for thousands of years. In fact, dazibao only made it into China's lexicon during the communist Revolution and especially during the Cultural Revolution from 1966-1976. Dazibao's (大字报) three characters from left to right literally mean "big (Chinese) character poster", and they have always had a very political connotation.

Here is sample of dazibao from the Cultural Revolution: *(Image by [shm.com.cn](shm.com.cn))* **[IMG 0178]** (More samples online).

It reads,

Criticize Lin, Criticize Confucius - it's the most important matter for the whole party, the whole army and the people of the whole country

This poster is from 1974 and painted by Zhang Yan (张延). You can just see the anger seething on the faces portrayed and that vengeful energy was vented on the entire Chinese people during the Cultural Revolution, in a frenzy of social upheaval. The Chinese calligraphy pen posing as a knife or spear, being heaved like a javelin, is a deft touch. This was a character assassination of Lin Biao. Lin Biao was designated by Mao Zedong to be his heir apparent. He was the person who collected and edited the smash hit book, *Quotations of Chairman Mao*. Lin seemed all set for an illustrious career in the annals of post-liberation China. What happened next is shrouded in mystery. Based on a number of sources, Lin apparently became very distraught at how the Cultural Revolution spun out of control, with the concomitant destruction of cultural sites, public education being suspended and brazen, young Red Guards terrorizing the people. Lin apparently was too nice, and instead of murdering Mao, tried to lock him up in a kind of house arrest, so that he could assume power.

That idea backfired, Lin was smoked out and he apparently tried to flee to Mongolia, by piloting an airplane. The plane mysteriously crashed in September, 1971 in Mongolian airspace. Either he was very unlucky or was shot down by the Chinese Air Force. Take your pick. To this day, Lin Biao is still a scapegoat in Chinese modern history. Sort of the Benedict Arnold of China, or more in parallel with his story, the Aaron Burr of modern China.

Mass Movements

Dazibao became a way for actors to make pronouncements and instigate mass movements. Dazibao functioned like a local internet site of its day, with news spreading like wildfire, with each one going up for the public's perusal. At a time of great social and political chaos, dazibao were powerful, sometimes useful and frequently destructive tools. They were used to inform and move the people in desired directions. One thing is for sure: you did NOT want your name posted on one of these walls! Back in the darker days of the Cultural Revolution, which was something akin to a vicious society-wide Spanish Inquisition turned sociopolitical feeding frenzy, your name up on one of these walls could mean being beaten, harassed, standing accused in a public humiliation kangaroo court, being sent to the countryside for a few years to ponder your perceived indiscretions, or on rarer occasions, even public execution.

Vitriolic, witch hunting Cultural Revolution dazibao. If your name went up, you were going down. (Images by shm.com.cn)

Liu Shaoqi was China's president and expelled from the CPC in 1968 by Mao, only to be rehabilitated by Deng in 1980, and is now canonized as one of the four great founders of China. However, as seen below, Mr. Liu went through hell and back before getting canonized in the China's communist pantheon. This dazibao reads,

Resolutely overthrow the great turncoat-hidden traitor-big strikebreaker Liu Shaoqi

The persecutors are saluting in unison holding Mao Zedong's *Little Red Book* in their right hands. *(Image by shm.com.cn)*

If it wasn't personal, then graven images were a favorite target of revolutionary *dazibao*. Dazipaos could be seen even on a statue of Buddha in a temple, which was plastered with them. The big one up top says, **Number one big bastard (or asshole)**

Nothing was sacred, everything was profane.

NOTE: More about Dazipaos and this chapter in China's history on this book's online concordance edition.

My, oh my, how times have changed! Today's 21st century dazibao have become public service announcements extolling the virtues of good citizenship and doing the right thing. They are everywhere we go: on factories, bridges, buildings, fences, walls, billboards and hung across roadways. Now it is not about inquisitional persecution, but all about being good citizens, good neighbors, making good choices and being upright and honest. The overriding theme, the key word is *civilized* and *civilization*. It is like an iconic mantra everywhere you go in China and lately it is sharing wall space with the hopeful theme of the recently touted *Chinese Dream*, a not so subtle adoption of the *American Dream*.

Westerners can scoff at these ubiquitous *dazibao* seeking civilization, but for those of us who lived here 15 years ago, we can attest to the almost miraculous evolution of Chinese society and the ever-increasing sophistication of the hundreds of millions of Chinese who are joining the ranks of the middle class.

When we were here 1990-1997, 99% of the people, even those in the big cities, with their diplomas and good jobs, still acted and lived a vindictive, dog-eat-dog mentality. After all, it had only been a little over ten years before, that these same people were being convulsed, beaten, harassed, humiliated and driven to the countryside for re-education, their families broken up, their lives shattered.

It really is a testament to the resilience and resourcefulness of the Chinese people that in only one generation, they have gone from a broken society and crippled economy to a world power and financial behemoth. Those with a knowledge and understanding of

China's 5,000-year history know it could have so easily slid in the other direction. Westerners don't want to admit it, but it is the steadfast presence of the CPC that has held it all together, and continues to do so.

And China's leaders, who have just as many political warts as all the others, are doing everything they can to make sure the incline stays towards progress and to avoid the tides of history tilting back towards cycles of internecine warlords, invasions, famine and abject misery.

If these modern day dazibao are an essential ingredient to the Chinese people's *civilization*" and their rapid 21st century climb to global superpower status, it is hard for me to be cynical about their use. Anyway, they are a non-stop Chinese language lesson during every taxi ride, stroll and bike outing. Below are three brand new dazibao right on the main street outside the Riviera Country Club where we live [Note: we have since moved into a much more modest local, Chinese community].

On the other side of our road is the village called Maquanying (It means *Horse Springs Camp*), this sign says,

Improving the living environment upgrades the city's civilization

Note the old, rusted out sign below that the new dazibao replaced. It will quickly be relegated to the recycling heap, I'm sure. On the other side of Maquanying's entrance, this one says:

Pushing for civilized suburbs builds a beautiful homeland

Symbolic celestial lion statues guard the community.

Not to be outdone, Maquanying's next door village, Sunhe (where our metro station is), put up this sign that says,

[IMG 0180]

With one heart and one mind, let's pool our resources and make a concerted effort to establish a civilized suburb and to build together a harmonious Sunhe. [Signed by] The Sunhe Village People's Government". Sunhe means *(Paternal) Grandson's River*, or *Sun Family River*.

Amazingly, during the summer of 2013, this Sunhe dazibao was replaced by none other than that Great Leap Forward, Red Army Maoist do-gooder turned mythical society saving superhero, Lei Feng, who is sort of an American Uncle Sam and French Marianne all wrapped up in a revolutionary whole. During my *44 Days* journey, I find Lei Feng everywhere, Mao's idealized id, exhorting the people to common nobility and collective greatness.

Chapter 5

China in the Wild East, Buckaroo, Deng Xiaoping 1990s

These end-of-year *letters offer a rare glimpse into the life of expats living and working in the China in the early 1990s. This is a very personal section of the book. Family, friends, expat life, chatty. They amply show just how high energy, frenetic and exciting a lifestyle we enjoyed back in the day. I finished rereading these letters and kept scratching my head saying, "We did* all *that in* just one *year"? A few observations: China's population has slowly increased in the last twenty years, but the rural/urban demographic has dramatically changed. Just in the last year, China has more city dwellers now than rural residents. That's why Shanghai and Beijing now both have populations around 20 million, which means they have increased in size by about 75%. Yet China's national population has only increased from 1.1 billion to 1.3 billion over the same time period, or a growth of 30% in 20 years. Like so many other Chinese superlatives, this mass movement of human population from farm to town will go down in history as one of the most dramatic of the 20th/21st century.*

Looking back over these letters, I also have to hand it to the Chinese. In spite of this huge influx of humanity flooding into all the cities, big and small alike, they really are trying to do something about the air, water and land pollution problems here. Is it pristine? Far from it. Clear azure sky days in Beijing used to be as rare as transits of Venus across the Sun. Now, we have more of them than we do muggy, smoggy ones. And the polluted days are much less severe than they were 20 years ago.

The other aspect that really shocks me now is how much the government security services were a part of our daily lives back then. I don't remember that so much now. I guess I was too busy working hard and having fun to be bothered. Today of course, China's PSB and America's 16 spy agencies *don't have to follow us in big black Red Flag saloon cars and open our mail, to know our every move and note who we are in contact with. They just have to get online. Now they just use thousands of drones and satellites to track our every move, and locally, watch us with the millions of traffic cameras that have been installed on the planet.* That *is truly Orwellian. We never even see it happening now with their invisible, omnipresent eyes and ears. At least in the bad old days, we could look them in the face and jokingly wave to them, smiling from our car, which we often did with good humor. I think the goons enjoyed those humanist piercings of the veil, as much as we did. They were just doing their jobs.*

It is manifestly clear that I, as well as my wife, were burned out on China and it was time to "get outta Dodge City", to coin old cowboy, western movies, which we did in 1997. I was still bathed in the aura of the West's moral and cultural superiority, and it sadly shows in these letters, somewhat embarrassingly. 1990s China was a very intense, misanthropic, psychologically draining way of life. Very addictive, but equally very harmful to the soul. The Chinese people were going through one of the greatest socioeconomic upheavals in human history, from egalitarian communism to soulless, Sodom and Gomorrah, Western consumerism. It exposed so many human weaknesses, in me and in them. It truly was dog-eat-dog. My, oh my, how time changes things.

Thereafter, we lived in France for five years and the United States for nine years, and I began to realize that the differences between East and West, in reality are six degrees of nothing. This long interlude has been incredibly instructive for our return to China, since 2010. I personally have changed dramatically during that time, philosophically, spiritually and intellectually, and my personal growth continues unabated. At the same time, China and its people have changed phenomenally for the better, much better, and continue to do so. Those years in Europe and the US highlighted the fact that no place on Earth is a paradise and wherever you choose to live, it has its good points and its bad points, nice people and jerks, saints and crooks. Pick your pleasure and your poison, so to speak. The last five years in China have been some of the best times of my life and now, ironically looking back on these amazing glimpses into the past, I don't want to leave. Such is this incredible tragicomic journey we are all on, called the human existence.

1991 End of Year Letter

15 November, 1991

10,000m above the International Date Line. It is a suitable setting, on a return flight to China from the U.S., that I begin my 1991 update. In fact, it is almost a year ago to the day, 17 November that we got off the airplane in Beijing and touched Chinese soil for the first time. And what a strange journey it has been.

Preconceived ideas have garnered us both pleasant and unpleasant surprises. We have both invested a lot of time in learning to speak, read and write Chinese. Progress in any other language would be much faster, but this is a particularly user-unfriendly language, even for the Chinese. It has been an adjustment in work and play to suddenly not speak the local languages fluently. Despite this, we're enjoying the challenge and see steady improvement. We have surely taken advantage of our time in China, going to more spots in one year than most people probably would in five.

We have traveled to a number of the provinces and their major urban areas south of the Yellow river: the province of Guangdong, a.k.a. Canton with its capital Guangzhou - the Pearl River, fabulous varieties of food, tropical night life, teeming street scenes as you might imagine all of China, the museum of the Tomb of Chao Mei, and outside of Guangzhou the Temple of Ancestors in Foshan;

Shanghai, a city-province of only 14-15 million citizens at the crossroads of China's north-south dichotomy, the economic engine driving the Yangtze river valley, the symbol of 19th-20th century Western colonialism on Chinese soil, with one of the world's premiere museums, Buddhist temples, glitz and decadence the central government would like to wash away down the Yangtze and a civic pride that rubs the rest of the regions in China the wrong way;

Nanjing, the capital of Jiangsu province, on and off as the national capital of various Chinese emperors through the millennia, the site of the famous *Rape of Nanking* by the Japanese in 1937, the tombs of Sun Yat-Sen and the Ming Ancestors, the Cliffs of 1,000 Buddhas, several beautiful temples and parks and many streets eternally shaded by huge sycamores planted by the French;

Qingdao in Shandong province, once a German colonial concession, so of course it claims China's oldest and most famous brewery and it even looks European in architecture and design, except it is on the Yellow Sea, with sandy beaches, seafood and the beautiful coastal mountain national park area called *Laoshan* which amazingly resembles the southern coast of France;

Xian in Shaanxi province, a major Silk Road city piled high with 3,000 years of history, glory and tragedy, the Temple of Confucius, the huge fortified wall still encircling the town, the tomb of the first emperor of China, the celebrated Museum and Tomb of the Terracotta Soldiers;

Suzhou, about half-way between Shanghai and Nanjing, the *City of Silk* and canals (now, like most waters in China polluted to the point of being open sewers), great street scenes, generations of urban architecture, with some very beautiful gardens which were in fact once residences of the elite, with names like Master of Nets, Simple Politics, Lion Forest, Liu and Tiger Mountain;

Hangzhou, the capital of Zhejiang province with a human-made lake of awesome proportions, called *Xihu* (West Lake), nested in beautiful rolling hills, in which are ensconced some majestic temples, pagodas and quaint rural villages;

Tianjin, another city-province, a former British colonial stronghold. As one of the great deep water port cities of China, which is closest to Beijing, its strategic importance has not been lost on rulers and conquerors through the centuries;

And although still British by law until 1997, Hong Kong, with one of the world's great skylines, dim sum for breakfast and taking the Star Ferry for $0.15 across the harbor, with the sun setting over the South China Sea.

Most of these visits gave us the opportunity to get out into the rural areas where 80% of China's 1,300,000,000 citizens live. That's the real China, the one most visitors never see, where one of every six citizens of this planet lives, Chinese peasants all. For annual leave this year we chose to stay in China and with visiting British friends Alan and Janette, we traveled to far off Xinjiang province in the northwest near the Soviet border, seeing Tianchi (Heavenly Lake), Nanshan (the Southern Pastures) and Urumuqi, the capital. It all looks much like the Rocky Mountains in New Mexico except with two-humped dromedaries roaming the desert and Muslim citizens who speak Turkish and hate the Chinese.

The four of us also went to Datong, exploring the sights around this city in neighboring Shanxi province: the ceramic Wall of Nine Dragons, the mind boggling Grottoes of Yungang, the Suspended Temple and the massive wooden pagoda of Yingxian. The *prime time TV-esque* escapades of getting in and out of Datong, although all too common a *travel tribulation in China* experience (quite frankly the system and the people make travel here an on-going pain in the keester), will provide us with many years' worth of war stories and laughs. For those in the know, we christened our travels with Alan and Janette the *AHP Middle Kingdom Tour 1991*. It was a most suitable sequel to our wild and woolly trek together across the Tassili Plateau in Algeria in January, 1990. Although we would have preferred the other members of this select travel team to have joined us, we made sure we lived up to its reputation and maintained its honor with great enthusiasm.

With my mother also visiting during my annual leave we took a great five-day road trip to Chengde, the capital of Hebei province. Although the eight famous temples show the cruel scars and twisted insanity of Mao's "Cultural" Revolution, the drive up there and back is spectacular, winding in valleys, on top of mountains and through the villages of rural northern China. The manual harvesting of the corn and rice made picture taking a cultural and natural joy.

Although it took some prodding by Florence (my wife), we did buy a car soon after getting here, a 1986 Peugeot 309 for a tidy sum of $13,600 - that is how bullish the used car market is here (let's hope it's still bullish when we resell it). Nonetheless, it has enabled us to explore the surrounding areas of Beijing on the weekends. We have found some great spots to explore: mountains, gorges, lakes, swimming in natural springs (in national parks, the only place in China where the water is clean), temples, isolated sections of the Great Wall, beautifully manicured agricultural land and bucolic rural villages.

Beijing itself is a real mixed bag. By Chinese standards it is the best: huge 4-6 lane wide boulevards and good streets are everywhere. There are lots of international trappings in the way of restaurants and stores (we can dine at Chez Maxim's or shop in supermarkets à l'Américaine. We can go to numerous famous temples, parks and other cultural sites, fly kites at Tiananmen Square and eat great Chinese food at one of a million local eateries. For entertainment, we go to dances on the weekend with surprisingly good live bands (the local music scene is unbelievably vibrant, equally populated by Chinese and foreigners, often times playing together), listen to jazz or classical groups in appropriate settings. On top of all this, we belong to a health club, replete with indoor lap pool.

Our apartment is small but nothing you would not expect in the U.S. or Europe. Public utilities and communications are excellent. There is a comprehensive (but often crowded) bus system and a limited-in-scope but very modern subway. And finally, unlike in Algeria, the level of enthusiastic socializing between the different western communities is incredible. We have lots of contact with Europeans, North Africans, Africans and Americans. Sounds too good to be true doesn't it? The down side is that Beijing is a city of 12 million souls (10 million officially) and even though it is spread out on a vast scale, for us westerners, it is crowded.

As the spiritual center and bastion of the communist party in China, it is impossible not to feel and chafe under the ubiquitous and omnipresent Big Brother. Beijing has an international reputation of having some of the worst air pollution in the world and deservedly so. The creeks and canals look and smell like turd soup.

But most of all it is the stench of Big Brother in our apartment, office and everywhere we go. The security apparatus is an Orwellian nightmare and all foreigners are looked upon as a potentially destabilizing element. Are our Chinese friends really *friends* or are they reporting back to Public Security Bureau (China's KGB) on what we said or what they saw in our apartment? Who knows? For my Chinese employees it is common knowledge they can be told to go to PSB any Saturday afternoon and report to their leaders what they heard and saw. PSB cars and agents are everywhere, hanging out in front of our apartment complex. They open our mail. Everyone we talked to last year said our holiday message arrived obviously opened. Hence, we'll look for a way to mail this year's on the outside. Phones are tapped. Some people have proof their apartments are bugged and we have to assume ours could be too.

Surly police are regularly spaced on the highways and if we want to drive outside of Hebei and Tianjin provinces, we have to sneak by them, pay bribes or get turned back. Abject pervasive corruption and intrigue are a way of life here and we sometimes get caught up in it living and traveling in China. Truly frightening isn't it? For free spirited, fun loving westerners like us, this element of living in China is very difficult to adapt to and weighs heavily against all that is good here. Imagine what it is like for the Chinese, knowing that even their family members could be compromised by the machinations of the system and possibly betray them? They can only trust themselves. In silence.

I am reading a book on Chinese history. Except for the fact that the Party here has replaced the dynastic emperors as the usually despotic dictator and there are some modern trappings of the 20th century, virtually nothing has changed here in the way the country is run, its people are treated and the way the elite class manipulates power and the purse strings, nothing for the last 4,000 years. Anyway, on to more pleasant thoughts.

China is incredibly photogenic and the people in general are very happy to have portrait shots taken of them. So, it goes without saying we have amassed quite a collection of pictures and slides for nostalgia's sake. Only foreigners use diapers. Chinese children wear split britches, rain snow or shine. They are seen everywhere squatting or being held splay legged by a doting adult, shitting and pissing to their hearts' content on the sidewalk, under trees, over trash cans and yes even indoors in airports, stores and restaurants. Sometimes the adult participant cleans the mess up. Usually they don't.

Our card this year also is to celebrate Florence's pregnancy. We expect to be parents about 28 March, 1992. I look forward to cutting the umbilical cord in Paris. Thereafter we plan on returning to Beijing till we take home leave to the U.S. for Christmas 1992, at which time we will show off the new pride of our loins to my family, we suspect the world's first *Langlois Brown*. After all the traveling Florence has done since getting pregnant in June, I suspect she must have amniotic carbuncles the size of grapefruit holding the baby in place. We weren't surprised when the doctor told us the 4.5-month sonogram showed a very active moving fetus. It started learning to travel from conception.

It is now mid-December and we just had our last visitors of the year, Howard and Tom from New York, who stayed the week of Thanksgiving. They unfortunately caught the brunt of Beijing's budding winter weather, but the sights in and around Beijing, including a return to Chengde and two adventures to the Great Wall continue to amaze us. One thing is for sure. Deserving or not, China's reputation precedes itself. We've had more visitors in one year than we had in Algeria in five. How ironic that we couldn't hardly drag people to come to Algeria, because its reputation also preceded itself. It is completely different visiting a country as a tourist and being hosted by friends and that is no truer than in rip-off revolutionary countries like China and Algeria.

I don't know, but I feel the few who did come to the Barbary Coast and its interior left with a deeper sense of satisfaction than those who have come to visit us in the Middle Kingdom. As I reflect on my ten years before China, am I nostalgic for Africa and the Mediterranean coast? Yes. It is hard to put a value on freedom and the tentacles of the PSB here are hard to shake off. Then again, as residents, maybe we were able to shield our guests from some of the more egregious aspects of Big Brother here.

Baby on the way notwithstanding, we look forward to taking advantage of our Asian situation to visit other interesting places in China: Guilin, Nanning, Yunnan, Fujian, Sichuan, Tibet (PSB permission needed), the

Khyber Pass and some of the surrounding countries in the region. Only problem is the distances are incredibly vast. The flight to Tokyo is over 4.5 hours, like flying from DC to LA. This year's staff conference took us to Tokyo for a week and next year's is scheduled for Penang, Malaysia, which Florence will just miss unfortunately, as she goes to Paris end of February. We especially want to go to Thailand, hit the beaches and tropical mountains and let our hair hang down so to speak. Hopefully I'll be able to recount some stories along those lines in next year's update.

Africa one year and Asia the next. They say once you live overseas more than ten years it becomes increasingly difficult to go back home, which in our case is the U.S. or France. I'd give anything to live in Europe for a few years, but with my experience, a job there would probably entail extensive travel time in the region and little time at home. The great thing about North Africa and China is my travel time was/is only about 1/4 of the time and in both cases, Florence was/is able to travel with me for not a lot more money. Nonetheless, with a baby in the oven, I am keeping my ear to the ground for opportunities in other parts of the world. Until next year. Pax Vobiscum,

1992 End of Year Letter

We're really late for the New Year as you know it and now even late for the Chinese version of the same, the Year of the Cock, which took place 8 days ago. So we celebrated New Year's TWICE this month. For the oriental do, we saw from our 29th floor apartment the amazing spectacle of 12 million Beijingers lighting millions upon millions of dollars' worth of fireworks simultaneously at midnight. This ancient New Year ritual has its roots in trying to scare away evil dragons that lurk in the ethereal turf of our universe.

We made a big party out of it with friends, using a fishing pole to let fly out and then up and down the length of the tower chains of 1000 big firecrackers. Each chain only costs $1.75. Close to a case of champagne later, well, it was a blast. Hmmm. It would appear that my chronology this year is going in reverse, and why not? We spent the rest of the world's New Year traveling to New York, as close to Times Square as the teeming masses of mostly drunken revelers would allow us. I used some of my airline miles to fly up my dad and his wife (mom couldn't make it). The major attraction was to visit the co-godfathers of our daughter, Howard Helmer and Tom Arsenault; more on her later. While in Fat City, we saw the Henri Matisse collection that is touring a few cities. The more than 400 works of art were humbling and it was really a once-in-lifetime opportunity in the culture department.

New York was at the tail end of our home leave, which spanned a week in Hawaii with friends Patrick and Monique Singley, of Algerian lore, then Thanksgiving and X-mas in Oklahoma with my family. It was the first time my side of the family had a chance to see the newest edition to the clan, Maia Carina Langlois Brown, the biggest story to tell this year. More on her later. Or is it earlier? Anyway, through the course of the year we had a chance to see new areas of this huge country that we had not seen before and visited a couple of old haunts in between. New Chinese turf seen was Sichuan (means *Four Rivers*) province, the land of spicy hot foods. In the bucolic department, I rank it as one of the most scenic places we have seen here. The immaculate, verdant rice paddies with quaint country homes dotting the landscape, many of them looking Tudor and others looking *southern France* was all a big surprise.

While traveling the environs of Chengdu, the provincial capital, we drove to Leshan (*Happy Mountain*), where a medieval Buddha and hundreds of other icons are carved into the faces of cliffs running along the banks of the local river. This is no ordinary Buddha, mind you. As he sits into the cliff face with his toes nearly in the water, he measures over 75 meters high. The cuisine is intriguing. They serve a boiling fondue in the middle of your table called a *hot pot* using a meat broth. With chop sticks you dip raw veggies, noodles, shrimp and shaved meat into the large, angel-food-cake, pan-shaped pot to cook them. Once done, each person has in front of them 5-6 small bowls of different fresh sauces to choose from, all of them spicy in one form or another. Copious quantities of surprisingly good beer, quaffed out of 640ml bottles between mouthfuls, kept the spices at bay. Charcoal sits underneath the ringed pot and over its opening is a towering brass dunce-cap looking flue to carry the smoke above your head on its way to vents in the ceiling. Nobody succumbed to carbon monoxide poisoning and it was great eating. At more formal banquets, they served us alternately spicy dishes and sweet ones. The logic behind the sweet dishes is to give your palate a reprieve between the pepper hot dishes.

We also explored Guilin and Yanshuo, in Guangxi province, with its mythical, internationally renowned sugar loaf mountains, replete with a river cruise in a small local boat, snaking through the towering spires and rustic villages. Florence was not able to accompany me on a trip to the northeast part of China, once known as Manchuria. It is a fixture in Chinese history: the invasion in the Middle Ages from this region's people, called Manchus who took power from the *real* Chinese, the Hans in the south and surviving till 1912, to the Japanese occupation of this region. Inland there is little of interest from a tourist standpoint.

However, I'd like to go back to Dalian, the impressive coastal city at the tip of the Liaoning peninsula. Western in architecture, due to years of European and Japanese colonialism, it is perched at the foot of some gorgeous coastal pine and hardwood covered mountains, looking a lot like a drive along Highway One in northern California. We went back more than once to Guangdong province, a.k.a. Canton, as well as Hong Kong and Nanjing, and while Florence had to return to Paris to wait out her waxing 3rd trimester, I traveled to Singapore and Kuala Lumpur and Penang in Malaysia.

Canton is absolute sensory overload from the moment you get off the plane. Touted as the newest member of the *Asian Tigers*, its economy growing at more than 20%/annum, it is an experience of immersing yourself in the gold-rush-boom-town chaos of greed and speculation. Officially still a part of China, it is now so far out of the sphere of Beijing's influence, it will be interesting to see where it ends up during the next 20-30 years. A blessing and a bane to the Communist Party's leaders here in the capital, they have no choice but to hold up Canton as the avatar of their *stay in power at any cost socialism with capitalistic characteristics*. In any case, going there must be something akin to living during the explosive first years of the industrial revolution during the 1880's in the U.S. and Europe; impressive and exciting but also casting a long and depressing shadow.

With making money as the only fashion and raison d'être, the less fortunate people are being exploited in the grossest Dickensian sense and the land and the environment are being buried under an avalanche of pollution, erosion and exploitation; before it all began the word *zoning* was thrown into the sewer of lakes, rivers, ocean coastline and chemical and industrial land dumps they've created. So, what else is new in 3/4 of the world? Along with Shanghai, Canton is the most exciting urban environment to visit in the PRC, panting and humping like an obsessed animal in economic heat during the day and pulsating with night life from dusk until practically dawn.

As the Party crassly casts its revolutionary roots to the dogs of prosperity through greed and graft, not just in Canton but nationwide, many old demons in China's ancient closet are being let out in the process. Virtual indentured labor is the only existence for a growing number of people. Rampant prostitution and a reinvigorated drug industry are running at full speed again. With Hong Kong coming under the *protection* of China in 1997, the Triads and other assorted Chinese mafia types are just licking their chops.

Even more frightening is the renaissance of real time human slavery rearing its ugly head across China. Didn't I say in my letter last year that when scratched below the surface, nothing has changed here in five millennia? Mao and his gang did abate or actually stop some of this for a few years after 1949 and the odd emperor put a dent in some of it for a time, but I am even more convinced after my second year here about the above statement.

Anyway, it is an amazing place to experience and work in, both the good and the bad in the most dialectical sense of the word. In fact, so interesting that Florence and I have decided to extend my contract one more year beyond the current one. That means that unless some other position comes up to lure us away from here, which is always possible, we will be leaving China in September, 1996. This decision was made rather easier, upon our return from home leave, by getting our hands on a villa here in Beijing. Mediterranean in layout with a walled in garden, upstairs terrace and LOTS of room, it is a little déjà vu from our *House on the Hill* days in Algiers. We are very excited. The only glitch is that I will no longer be able to walk to work in 3-4 minutes; it is about 5km from the China World Trade Center (CWTC).

The one great cultural advantage is that we are really being forced to dive head first into the Chinese language. Both of our Chinese have improved dramatically, since we have had to do everything from negotiate the contract ourselves to buying lots of goods on the local market to get the villa presentable. We have christened our new home *Villa Orion*.

So finally we get to The Divine Ms. M, that fabulous pride of my loins, who I saw birth into the world on the 22nd of March in the City of Lights. Almost all the inconvenient things I heard about being a parent, I find myself living out and I love it. Who knows about the future, but up to now it is obvious to me that all the hype I got before Maia was born just doesn't matter when it concerns my daughter.

Although there are plenty of good arguments (and great results) to prove/do otherwise, I now realize that I would not want to be any younger as a parent. Even a few years back I would have felt a little like a youngster raising a baby. I think a few of the changes one makes becoming a daddy would have bothered me five or ten years ago. Having had more time to sate and indulge myself on various pursuits and intellectual passions makes me much less selfish of my time.

She looks even prettier from the front. Sorry, this is one of those true instances where you can't have the best of both worlds in two dimensions. So, I guess I am saving the best for last. We'll make an effort to catch the other side on glossy paper in a flattering pose for next year's card. Can't wait for the year 2000 to roll around. What an amazing journey it has been for the last 38 years.

Pax Vobiscum from the land of a billion plus earthlings, the country that will be pregnant with influence on the rest of us, as we approach the gates of the 21st century. Barring a sweeter offer, that's why it is worth hanging around here for the next three years. CIAO.

1995 End of Year Letter

Prologue - and Don't Even Think Twice About Holding Your Breath.

Dateline Monday, 6 May, 1996: Yikes. Twenty-two pages. I don't know whether to be embarrassed or proud. Like some creature who is compelled by natural function, I have planted this seed to be passed on to the next generation, having fulfilled my atavistic duty, without little trepidation and much relish.

Reading this letter will be an eye opening and hilarious experience, promise. It can be read in one sitting, in about ¾ hour.

Hey Maxy, give dis gal duh prize of duh day. She did it, I tell ya.

Or maybe your subscription to *Guns and Ammo* or *The New England Journal of Neurocranial Microsurgery Procedures in the Dark* or *Popular Bulldozing and Road Grading* ran out and you're waiting for the renewal to start back up. So, for a month's worth of morning constitutionals, keep it handy by the crapper, you know, a page a day. I dunno, maybe this novelette will make you laugh so much, it's bound to keep you regular. Just think, no All-Bran or Metamucil for a month.

Then again, maybe your doctor wants to hold off on renewing your prescription for Halcion for a couple of weeks to make sure you are not addi-di-di-di-di-dic-ted. A couple of pages each night at bedtime should soothe those heat flashes, pangs of insomnia and gnawed finger tips.

Disclaimer: Names were NOT changed to protect posterity and my style is scatological at times. Rated R.

What the Hell Happened to You, Jeff?

Dateline: Sunday, 21 January, 1996: The last time I tried to write an *annual* letter was in March '94. At least that's the date in the computer file, where it has been cyber-preserved in some virtual drive, clinging to existence by the byte of its sector FAT. The last one to actually be sent out was in February '93. We even made personalized cards for New Year's '94 and they never went out either.

The whole exercise of writing an annual letter has taken on a life of its own, become an ongoing family joke, supplying us with endless hours of in-house laughs. It's like a famous line from a sitcom well into its third season, and it still hits the funny button every time. We've even gone back and printed a new greeting on those cards, hell they cost a small fortune, to play out a postal version of *old wine in a new bottle*. Please indulge us. It has been a long and amazing journey.

But through it all, the inertia to get this letter out has clung to my heart and soul, like a little wedge of dog shit stuck between my shoe sole and the inside of my heel. You know the kind I'm talking about, it never quite dries out. Months later, you take a stick, dig below the surface and there's a corner, a thin layer still as fresh and redolent as the day you stepped in it. You've already dug it out before, but there's always still some there.

Part of the problem is that my annual letter had begun to take on a life of its own. Friends would write back specially to tell me how much they enjoyed it: it was funny, interesting, informative, provocative and to **please** make sure and send them the next year's. Friends who received them locally or with whom I would see during the year would volunteer their praises. Naturally, I would beam with pride, but the pressure was on and a level of performance was expected. By the way, a common complaint was font size and a lack of paragraphs, so the customer is always right.

The China Syndrome, Part I

The crucible of all my annual letters has always been a joyful mixture of family, friends, travel, work and the excitement and fascination of the place where we happen to be living and its people. And as I review that inchoate letter of March '94, really quick jottings of people and places experienced, mostly logged as two and three letter abbreviations, I was indeed able to cascade back over numerous milestones since February

'93. However, I have long known the most important catalyst that has always driven my imagination has been sadly missing these last three years: my lack of excitement and fascination with the place we now live: China.

And that has been the nexus of the problem. It transcends a mere lack of interest. Who wants to write an annual letter that you know will be full of decidedly un-holiday spirit, sometimes agonizing experiences and an overall tone of disillusionment and resignation? How to put a positive spin on an overseas experience that has rendered not **one** true local friend in five years of daily contact, when in every other country I lived and worked, I felt a real emotional, fraternal involvement with many local friends and associates. Where to start when I know that my last day in China will illicit absolutely zero feeling and a zero sense of loss vis-à-vis the local people and their country?

This brings up another problem with a *China* annual letter. Its very nature is going to be frank and opinionated about this country and its people, a lot of it not terribly positive, and I know that some of my friends who read this epistolary are going to be affronted and maybe hurt in some way. China seems to leave no one lukewarm about the subject and I do know a few persons who are ape shit about living and working here. They are in the minority, but feel just as strongly as I and the majority do at the opposite end of the poles.

But for the most part, I am not alone. China and the Chinese do this to the majority of foreigners who come here to live and work, not just come for a two-week vacation, usually conducted by well-orchestrated tours escorted by carefully groomed politically correct government trained agents. Just yesterday a German friend opined that when he came to China in '94, his usual Christmas letter was full of optimism and hope and after another year here, he has still not written his letter for '95 because it broke his heart to write a *depressing, negative* letter. I of course could not help but smile at the uncanny familiarity of his unsolicited story.

It is so difficult to convey my sense of disappointment and disillusionment with China, its people and culture, especially in the face of so much great PR promulgated by the Chinese government, legions of overseas Chinese, visiting tourists, and with the advent of economic reforms, the many business people here among the money-making hoards, who thrive in a jungle of Jurassic capitalism. It's a gold rush here, a place for dreamers, schemers, wheeler dealer Fast Eddies, carpetbaggers, pimps 'n' whores and ordinary shmucks like me who can be somebody. We're all in China for mainly two reasons: career opportunities and, sing it Jerry Lee and Lyle: m-o-n-e-y. And sadly, these are the only distilled *raisons d'être* that fuel our continued presence here.

The disappointment has come that much harder, since we came to China with so much enthusiasm and excitement. I cannot tell a lie: yes, after 10 years in the Arab world I was getting burned out. As much as I love the people and the land and their unfailing sense of history, purpose, passion and romanticism, my linguistic skills had peaked: Arabs hearing me and thinking I was an Arab had lost its cachet, plus the surge of 20th century style fanaticism among a very effective minority began to take its toll. The pervasive hostility towards all things female was also getting old fast. It truly was time for a change. Ironically and fortuitously, we left just 3-4 months before all hell broke loose in Algeria. All said, would you be surprised to know that we of course now pine for those days and our many friends and contacts in the Arab world?

Catching Up on the Lost Years, or a Great Title for Simon and Garfunkel's Reunion Album

So, arriving bright-eyed and bushy tailed to the Middle Kingdom, we lived the first two years in relative ease. That's because we were ensconced in a *world within a world* in Beijing, a place called the *China World Trade Center* (CWTC). And there, we were effectively insulated from the *real China*. We used to call it *The Bubble*. An ultra-modern island-complex of western expectation, it was a security blanket of great comfort and minimal hassle. We lived in one super modern tower, I worked in another super modern tower and if we chose, except for medical problems, one could never leave there and still find most all that is needed from a non-Chinese consumer's point of view. After foraying into the real China for a weekend or a business trip, we knew we would be returning to our miniature city-mama, with her arms wide open, ready to take us back in.

But for a couple of culture freaks like Florence and myself, it started getting old very fast. We knew it really was a cocoon-like existence of ersatz contrivances. We knew we were never going to learn the language in those conditions and we felt some atavistic desire to not just scratch below the surface for a weekend at a time, but to get religion so to speak, baptism by fire. We knew from our limited experiences that it was not going to be a cake walk (and to this day we would not do it any other way) but hell, we each had enough hair raising tales to account for from years of collective ex-pat living, we felt shall we say, up to the task.

Also, from a personal standpoint, we had a new member in the family and being cloistered in an apartment tower was starting to feel unhealthy. Florence and I both grew up in big free-standing houses, with lots of outdoors to roam and play in. The thought of raising Maia where the only escape was a long elevator ride down to the confines of The Bubble was becoming unpalatable. While I in no way want to denigrate wonderful upbringings in big city apartments around the world, we are all the product of our childhoods and our roots were hankering for a yard, cooking on the Weber BBQ and a door that opens on the ground floor.

Where We Left off and the Decision that Would Change Our Lives Forever

And that brings us up to the last letter, written in February '93. Within one week after licking the stamps for that letter, we were leaving the safe womb of CWTC and moving to a house on the outskirts of Beijing at the Luyuan Guesthouse. In spite of the fact that it is situated in a bit of an environmental disaster zone (at least a degree or two worse than the average of the whole country; China will keep Greenpeace and every other environmental concern busy till the Age of Aquarius), for overseas residents in Beijing it was a *dream home*: large, private walled-in garden, two stories, high ceilings, well over 350 m² (3,800 ft²), bedrooms and bathrooms out the yazoo, secure parking AND for a market-relative, phenomenally low price. It was a bit of a reminder of our wonderful

House on the Hill when we lived and worked in Algiers, 1985-1990 and we were excited as hell.

There was also the added benefit of already having some good friends who lived there, so we did not have to do the pioneer shtick (even today, it has maxed out with seven ex-pat families in the whole complex).

Contract, What Contract?

We signed a contract for three years for the new house, hired a contractor and began doing all the interior work (it had to be gutted and done over from scratch: it looked and smelled like a cattle yard inside). Then, 36 hours before we were supposed to move, the Year of the Rooster, 1993, was turned on its head. After canceling the lease at our CWTC apartment, arranging for a moving company to haul off our effects, starting major renovations on our new house and proudly announcing to world our change of address, quite simply, the landlord called us to meet and proceeded to tear up our contract, saying we could not move in. No reason was given, that's just the way it was, and by the way, we're really sorry, but tough shit.

I've been through a lot during my 16 years of overseas living but this was the first time I had ever been literally **homeless**. There was no way to take back the China World apartment. By the time we vacated our apartment the *boom* was on and within hours of submitting our lease cancellation it was renting at twice the price to new tenants (real estate in China? That 130 m² apartment was rented at a *bargain basement* price of $2,450 per month in '90; by the time we left it was up to $4,500 and today people are standing in line and paying bribes to get in for a mere $12,000 per month.). Where to go with a family and what to do with all our household effects boxed and the moving company downstairs with the truck preparing to haul it to our *new home*? And 36 hours to come up with something?

Clearly, trying to get another apartment on such short notice was out of the question as there were huge lines of foreigners flooding into Beijing to make their fortunes, glutting an already demand-saturated real estate market. And anyway, getting another apartment would defeat the entire purpose of us moving in the first place. While CWTC was and still is at the top of the *ex-pat island community* shit heap, there were and are a growing number of them. But that's not what we wanted.

The Long March to Victory or Slow Descent into Hell?

Our friend who already lived at Luyuan suggested that in spite of their unconscionable decision to renege on our contract, some Keystone Cop School of Business Administration maneuver (nothing new here.) probably happened among the compound's bosses and if we still wanted to get the house, we should use the very powerful tool in Chinese culture called *guilt*, put the monkey on their backs and <u>continue</u> to make them part of the predicament they got us into instead of us leaving the scene so they could wash their hands of us.

Since there is in reality no sense of legal recourse or body of law in the Chinese tradition, many misdeeds, misunderstandings in agreements, contractual shenanigans, and petty to mid-level illegalities to this day are resolved between the two parties on their own terms. There is an incredibly entrenched mentality of *peícháng* in Chinese culture, or *compensation*, usually on the spot. Primitive and usually messy, but if you are clearly in the camp of *to be compensated* and the other party has clearly fucked up, which was our case, then you can use guilt/ *peícháng* like a blunt cudgel.

So, the beginning of a uniquely Chinese experience notwithstanding, we *still* wanted the house. We took the advice of our friend, went to the Luyuan office and would not leave. With little Maia in our arms and Florence acting domestically distressed (not a hard role to play under the circumstances) we laid the guilt trip on thick.

As a result of us refusing to go elsewhere and sticking to our guns that we wanted to live in our house contracted at Luyuan, little did we know that we would be untied from our residential moors for another **seven** months and be *homeless* in the interim.

But we didn't know that yet. We just knew we only had a few hours to get ourselves extricated from our apartment in CWTC. The moving truck was packed up and ready to leave CWTC, to head to Luyuan. Of course the biggest headache was where to store an entire household of effects in a country that has no real market or system of retail storage. And with a child in hand, where could we find a roof over our heads until this mess was resolved? On the streets?

Alea Jacta Est, or Chinese Bungee Jumping with only One Foot Laced Up

These two problems were thus dumped in the lap of the landlord. And the guilt trip worked well *to start off with*. They agreed to use one of their poorly utilized store rooms to put all of our effects in and they agreed to let us stay at their *hotel* in the same compound as the houses. We demanded and got one of their *suites*, which gave us a little more wiggle room. Mind you, this hotel would fit in very nicely in a backwater city in Algeria or Russia in terms of service, hygiene, decor and management, but we got into where we wanted to be: in their faces and in their hair every day to remind them of what had happened and what they had done to us. And we could keep a close eye on our effects, which were now stored in the same compound.

We wasted no time throwing around the weight of our guilt/*peìcháng* cudgel. We demanded and they bought off the redecoration company that we had hired and who had already done quite a bit of work on the house. We soon got another hotel room next door, so that daughter Maia could have a *place of her own* and it gave us more breathing room to sort out some badly needed things we dug out of some boxes in the storage room. We demanded and got a key to the storage room so we could manage our very small floor space in the hotel. We made it clear we were there for the long haul by going out immediately and buying a small refrigerator, electric plates, unit heaters, fans, and soon thereafter bottled gas and a little two burner stove to cook. We made a *de facto* kitchen. They were pissed off as hell, but we kept up the assault with our blunt instrument and it kept them off guard. So far, the strategy was working.

Franz, Say Hello to Fyodor

However, our cudgel was getting us nowhere in terms of getting our house back. In fact, within a matter of days, the whole affair began to take on a truly Dostoyevskian, ulcerating life of its own, as we tried to get to the bottom of what had happened and tried in a nation without laws to resolve a clearly big fuck-up by our landlord. In spite of repeated attempts to get an interpretation of the events that led to our contract being signed and then torn up, we hit brick wall after brick wall of silence or lame and vacuous verbal meanderings.

We began to turn up the heat some more. We wrote a letter to the landlord, who was really just a hired *manager* of the hotel. Nothing happened. We tried earnestly to get behind this hired manager and learn who the boss/es were above him. False lead after stonewall after false lead. We asked to see his boss/es. *They,* whomever they were refused. We wrote and contacted the U.S. ambassador and to his great credit got the DCM to follow up on it. The embassy could not find out who was behind the Luyuan, so we were still stuck at the stooge manager's level. When the embassy agreed to go to Luyuan to talk to them, they told the embassy representative that,

If Mr. Brown does not like the situation, then he can sue us,

And then they were not so politely told to get the hell out, we knew that whoever they were, the mysterious bosses of Luyuan were obviously well connected and/or powerful folks.

We then followed through on our threats to the manager and as a last straw, by contacting foreign correspondents. We even got written up in a full article in Hong Kong's largest daily paper, *The South China Morning Post.* Quite a coup, but the machinations of our real life Kafkaesque *Der Proces* continued.

As the weeks turned into months, we kept chipping away at this mysterious monolith. Everybody and their dead dog had a theory, an angle. The possible scenarios presented to us, the who's and why's were myriad. Some sounded entirely believable, a few were blown into plots that went way above our level and the Luyuan manager's level. Some were down right paranoid, but sadly plausible under the circumstances. We were truly pawns in some sort of Byzantine Chinese chess game and could not figure out who was pulling the strings of the marionette players.

Finally, we got a clue that provided us with our first credible account of the events. One of the other renters at Luyuan used to be the military attaché for East Germany and we had heard that after the Wall came down in Europe in '92, it was his military connections that got him in as the first foreign resident of Luyuan. While we did not know him very well at the time, we pleaded with him to use his contacts to try to get some answers and hopefully our house. We got answers, but at the same time found out we were not going to get our house.

And the Dirty Bastards Are...

Our new friend told us the Luyuan compound was jointed owned by the People's Liberation Army Chiefs of Staff and the Beijing State Council. We were stupefied. The PLA Chiefs of Staff and the Beijing State Council? Gee-zuz Key-ryest. We were dueling with the equivalent of U.S. Joint Chiefs of Staff and the Executive Cabinet of the President. No wonder they could thumb their nose at the DCM and the U.S. Embassy. No wonder they told the embassy that I could go sue them if I didn't like it. Where, in their jury-rigged courts? No wonder they refused to see us. We were a small gnat in the morass of two of China's most powerful entities.

And as far as what happened, it was explained to us that the State Council faction approved the lease of our house without telling the Army Chiefs of Staff faction. And when the generals found about it, they were pissed off galore. That's because the role of the Luyuan villas was originally envisioned to be rest houses for visiting generals, colonels and state government level leaders coming to Beijing. By the time we were going to rent our house, the other four were already being leased. And ours was twice the size of the other houses. It was the last big enchilada and it was still being used by the high falootin' army boys as a safe house to fuck prostitutes, house mistresses, have drinking parties, etc. It was the biggest, the best, it was isolated, it was the last one and they were not going to give it up.

In other words, we could kiss our dream home good-bye.

We had truly reached the nadir of our *get-into-the-Chinese-culture* nightmare. All our planning and scheming was lifted from our hearts, so that some star-lapelled jar heads could have a place to dick their little queenies.

Lies, Filth and a Guardian Angelette of the Southern Persuasion

Dateline: Sunday, 04 February, 1996: Having fun? At that point in our lives, we weren't. We resigned ourselves to moving back into an apartment, as there were really no other options. We started shopping and it was uniformly grim. At the same time, we knew that one of the other houses at Luyuan was not being rented by a foreign family, but by some unknown, unnamed Chinese company. We asked the Luyuan manager to contact them to see if they would be interested in talking to us about buying out their lease.

Weeks passed and we narrowed our apartment search to one in the diplomatic compounds. In fact, we considered ourselves lucky to even find one; we were not even asked to pay a bribe. We were not entirely satisfied; even many of our friends who live in these compounds jokingly refer to them as the *diplomatic ghettos*. The apartments are big and spacious, but they were built back in the days when foreigners really were devils, which was not that long ago now. The grounds and apartment buildings have a real *Soviet Bloc* feel about them and are depressingly run down. But we were kissing that ground and making the best of a bewildering and frustrating retreat.

At the same time, the Luyuan gang kept telling us that the Chinese company that was renting the last house was not interested in talking to us. Had Luyuan called the top boss?

Oh, yes, of course,

The manager said and their boss is definitely not interested. Florence suggested that we go over and see for ourselves. We were in the process of reviewing the contract for the diplomatic apartment, so what did we have to lose?

To our disappointment, we learned from the head of this company group living there, that Luyuan had never even contacted them. Those lying sons of bitches at Luyuan. And what a strange company it was. The stench of urine, vomit, alcohol, tobacco and filth permeated every surface of the place. It was occupied by about 6-8 kids from Guangzhou (Canton) and the whole place looked and smelled like a squatter camp. Garbage was strewn everywhere and unoccupied rooms were full of refuse that had not been moved or cleaned in years. These guys made my college apartment on a bad day after a wild night of debauchery look like the Vatican.

There were cases of mineral water out in the garden that were rain soaked and the cardboard boxes were rotting off the plastic bottles. Strange business indeed. Casting value judgments aside, these kids told me they came from a *trading company* and besides mineral water, they had lots of stuff to sell. Trading companies in China these days are as ubiquitous as *land men* were in the oil patch during the petro-boom of the early 80s. I feigned interest in looking at some catalogs and inquired about their plans in Beijing. They bragged that business was going so well that their company was building a new office tower here and they would be moving in 2-3 months. **Bingo.** I took the dive, gave them my sob story and made my sales pitch.

To my grateful surprise, they nonchalantly said they didn't see any big problem in moving out early, why they could go live in the basement of their new tower until it opened. So far so good, but they couldn't make the decision. I got the name of the big boss in Guangzhou, a woman named Madame Zhang.

Deus Ex Machina Orientalis

I had to go on a business trip the next day to Shanghai (with my old job at the Feed Grains Council I was still traveling about 1/3 of time). I called Madame Zhang in Shanghai and was truly expecting to be on the ugliest receiving end of Sun's *The Art of War* and Machiavelli's *The Prince*. I remember sitting on the hotel bed and talking to this woman, just knowing I would have to grovel, go to Guangzhou, kiss her ass, wine and dine her, suck up to her inferior complexed ego and humiliate myself to get a favorable response. I already had my agenda out on the bed to pick a time to fly down there and start kowtowing into the crack of her powerful ass.

I found out she was the top dog on the Chinese side of a big joint venture in Guangzhou with General Motors, making an endless variety of car parts for distribution overseas. A real swinging dick of the female persuasion, to say the least. It made the ambiance at the *company office* at Luyuan all the more curious. The kids were probably scions of the business and the *trading company* was a convenient way to get them out of her hair. I also learned Luyuan had never bothered to call her about our situation - those lying sumbitches. So, I sat there talking into the mouthpiece to this total stranger, giving her the same sob story about my wife, my daughter, being homeless for months, knowing that this was the defining moment of our life in China. And praise be the benevolence of the female race, she said she was sorry to hear about our predicament, said there was no problem and she would ask the boys to move out of Luyuan within one week, to the basement of their new office tower. She promised to call Luyuan and make all the arrangements.

And I proceeded to just about fall off that bed. You mean no strings attached? No groveling, no ass kissing? I couldn't believe it. To this day, I believe what saved us were her maternal instincts. I think it would have been a whole new chapter if it were Mr. Zhang instead of Madame Zhang.

Profuse thanks and appreciation were extended to this unknown, unseen charitable woman and her actions remain to this day one of the few selfless, magnanimous acts I can chalk up after five years in China.

Holding my breath and hanging on to the barest thread of hope (betrayal and reneged promises are the word of the day here), I went back to Beijing and talked to the boobs at Luyuan. Praise be the Goddess. She really did call and they really were moving out within a few days. Luyuan's lie had been exposed. We began the negotiations with the buffoons at Luyuan. But we were taking no chances this time. We arranged with the kids in the house when they would be leaving, got the keys from them and within five minutes of their departure, we made the symbolic act of taking some of our effects from the Luyuan hotel and *moving* into the new house, urine, vomit, filth and all. It was *peícháng* payback time baby, and we were not going to lose this one this time.

Culturally in China it is very difficult to just kick someone out on the street and once you occupy a place, possession is to a great extent 9/10 of the law. Once burned twice shy, so, by going over to the house and staking a claim, it gave us a powerful psychological advantage in negotiating for the lease. And while the negotiations were going on over the next few days, we more or less surreptitiously began moving our effects from the hotel rooms to *our new home*.

The Three Comeback Kids and a Seedy Swedish Sauna

For the first time in four months we felt like we were in an ascendant position and it was now or never. We gave back the unsigned lease for the diplo apartment and turned our sights on the bozos at Luyuan and to hell with those big mysterious guns in the army and the executive cabinet above them.

We knew now that there was no way we were not going to get our new house, it was just a question of using the guilt trip for all the misery they had caused us to get the best deal we could out of this new house's lease. The victory was getting a two-year lease instead of one, so we could for the time being feel secure about our lodgings. That we got. The sticky wicket was a so-called Swedish sauna that was attached on the back end of one of the two guest bedrooms, which connect off the back of the house by a long corridor. It is the kind of small, wood sauna that sits 4-6 people and has a heater inside, with rocks piled on top, to get the inside temperature up to a toasty 160°-180°C. These two bedrooms were designed for the drivers/guards of the visiting army and government officials and now would make a superb *guest wing* off the back of the house for our visitors.

This sauna was ostensibly to be used by the visiting hacks who came to stay and whore at *our* big house we had originally sought. And try as we might, there was no way they were going to move the sauna at that time, so there was no way we were going to get the two back bedrooms. The only solution was to block off the end of the corridor with storage cabinets and hope one day we could negotiate to get the sauna removed and add the back bedrooms to our floor plan. We were promised that, *they would only use the sauna a few times per year and not late at night*. More on that promise later, remembering what I said about Chinese promises.

So, what we got was a smaller version of the big house. We got our two story home, private walled in garden (about 250 m²) and even without the guest wing, there were three bedrooms, two full baths, two half baths and by Chinese standards, a huge kitchen, all totaling 220 m². But remember, the place was a disaster zone, an assault on every one of our bodies' senses.

The Three Stooges of Interior Design

The next big step was to gut the place and redecorate it from top to bottom. But where to stay while this was being done? There was no way were ever going to move out temporarily during renovation for fear of another heart crushing *déjà vu* experience. The two back bedrooms were still not sealed off and they had a separate door leading into our garden. Again, possession is 9/10 of the law, so we moved into the two back bedrooms, pretty much as we had done in the hotel. There was a full bath between the two bedrooms (off of which was attached the infamous sauna), so we could eke it out in the confines of these two small bedrooms until the renovation and decoration were completed.

The contracted *3-week* job ended up being a 3-month long ordeal; enter the 2nd phase of our nightmare Chinese move. It is difficult to describe the sheer incompetence and buffoonery of most of the work done here, unless the workers have been trained patiently for months by good hearted foreigners. Paradigms such as *pretty, clean, neat, straight, consistent, smooth, even, level, plumb, well-built* and *solid* are in a Chinese anti-universe to the existence of foreigners, and westerners in particular.

It was the middle of summer, it was hot as hell, it was raining almost every day and the mosquitoes and flies were thick like an animal barn party on the edge of a swamp. On the back side of Luyuan is a creek of sorts, in reality a trickling inferno of industrial effluent and flotillas of human excrement. We fondly call it *Shit River*. <u>Great</u> place for a picnic on a Sunday afternoon. It is unfortunately a terrific spawning grounds for six-legged flying creatures, so our two bedrooms were a war zone of insect extermination.

Since the rest of the house was wide open all the time to haul out mountains of garbage, piss- and vomit-soaked carpet, buckets of scraped paints, etc., we were sitting ducks for flies by day and skeeters by night.

Besides constantly burning mosquito coils, we lamely hung up a sheet across the corridor opening to keep out the bugs and dust. About ten workers lived and worked in the rest of house, filthy mattresses strewn about on the floors, dingy, hand washed laundry hanging everywhere and the refuse of daily cooking on little gas stoves and eating bedside. To save money, all the construction companies in the big cities here hire uneducated, uncouth, unclean adolescents from the armpits of China's interior, so the whole scene had a kind of oriental *Deliverance* flavor about it, as we were ensconced day after day, night after night in the back of the house, a diaphanous bed sheet hanging in the corridor marking the line of demarcation.

Florence Gives 'Em Hell - All Over.

Coming from the rectal regions of rural China, most of these workers can barely speak Mandarin. The foreman is cut from the same cloth, but maybe made it through junior high school so could speak enough Mandarin to communicate with us. At that time our Mandarin was still not very good so as the three weeks stretched into three months, it became a war of nerves and attrition. Fuck up after fix up, comical construction idea after absurd engineering design, and I have to hand it to Florence, she never gave up.

While I had to work every day, Florence became the *bête noire étrangère* of their worst nightmares. It was part principle, part pride, part vengeance for everything they stood for and all we had suffered for the last several months and she drove those dirt balls crazy. No mistake was sloughed off, no *chābùduō* (half-assed) job was accepted, no spot of paint on the floor was allowed, not one piece of trim was to be uneven or unlevel, and no finger prints on varnish were missed. We had crawled across broken glass to get this place and it was going to be created in her image.

The clown of a construction company manager was relentlessly hounded and harassed, numerous jobs were done over twice, thrice, multiple times and she stood her ground until they got it as right as they were ever going to get it. They must have painted the walls and ceilings 15 times and varnished the newly laid wood slat floors a half a dozen times. She would call me at work, vent her spleen and after work and on the weekends I would take off my gloves to join in the battle, playing mock white hat to her take-no-survivors black hat, but she gets the credit for turning this pig's ear into a real silk purse, this pig sty into a palace. It was torture after being beaten to a pulp, but it was sweet torture and I do not think she has any regrets.

The Victory Lap with Fists Defiantly Raised towards the Firmament

Finally, in October '93, the construction gang of hooligans were finally out of this place, broken and humbled. And it really was turned into a beautiful house. I am very proud of Florence. I am not just bragging when I say I think we have one of the most beautiful interiors of all the houses I have seen in Beijing.

Finally. It was a long-fought down and dirty Year of the Rooster, seven months of daily struggle but we had won. As I look back, whether it can be attributed to hard headedness, pride, a sense of right and wrong or what, I don't know how many other families could've done what we did and stuck it out to the end. And through it all, it made us a tougher, closer family. Through all the adversity and humiliation, it brought us together. It was a crucible I would not want to wish on anybody, but we came out of it with tensiled domestic alloy.

The End-Around Alley-Oop Chinese Style

But it never stops in China. The onslaught to your dignity, morals and principles is endemic, pathological. Every act of faith is shat on by a people who have lost their principles, their pride and their dignity.

Within 48 hours of finally, officially moving in to our long sought house, Luyuan put four men in the two guest bedrooms in the back of the house and they weren't there for a quick sauna either. It was apparent that they were moving in for an extended stay. They were grease balls from the hinterland, staying up all night drinking and playing *majiang*, standing in **OUR** garden for hours in their underwear and undershirts, drinking and smoking cigarettes. Even the mosquitoes didn't seem to want them. Their appearance was disgusting and comical at the same time. Here we were at the dinner table, looking out the window and these scum bags were standing there in the garden, in dingy A-shirts and with their jockey underwear so stretched out the crotches hung down to their knees, sucking on cigarettes and watching us dine. In was an incredible affront to our sense of home and privacy. But those kinds of cherished institutions are of no concern in this country.

Luyuan's manager answered our invectives that *those rooms are ours to rent as we see fit*. Entreaties about *home*, *family* and *privacy* might as well have been a language spoken by extraterrestrials, concepts from another world. So, let the battle begin. A call to arms. A line had been drawn in the sand, a *promise* shat on and only one side was going to win this one.

Florence had shown her mettle with the renovators, now it was my turn to show my stuff. Years of criminal quality pranks and shenanigans in junior high and high school gave me a wealth of experience in the *revenge* department. You remember the days, right, when being an asocial asshole was a campus badge of honor. And it's like riding a bike: if you have to, you never forget how.

You Picked the Wrong Asshole, Mofo's, or Our Battle of the Marne, Part I

I began by running speaker wires the length of the corridor and installing my two mega-big and mega-heavy duty *Kicker* brand boom boxes, that used to play a crucial role as the rear speakers in my Nissan, good ol' Bessie, Goddess love her 500-watt-RMS-per-channel Linear brand amp. My home stereo only has 240 watts per channel, but can still do serious aural damage.

I then played at high volume all night long over and over again choice CD selections like The Jesus and Mary Chain's *Barbed Wire Kisses* (two Scottish brothers who sing songs from experience like *Psycho Candy* and *Psilocybin*), *Acid Visions: The Best of Texan Punk and Psychedelia* (you get the picture) and Sonic Youth's *Daydream Nation*, a 70-minute screed of feedback, fuzz and fingernails-on-the-chalkboard guitar noises and grungy vocals. They are all fun once and awhile, but non-stop bed time music?

I'd set the player on *repeat* and they would play over and over and over and over till we'd wake up in the morning. To keep them on their toes, I'd also put them in the multi-CD magazine and set the player for *repeat* <u>and</u> random. Oh, what fun. We'd shut our bedroom doors upstairs and with the air filter running, couldn't hear a thing. That went on for several nights. But these were tough old gizzards and a cannon had been shot across their bow, so the war of nerves and attrition was on. They weren't going to give up that easily. I had to stick the knife in a little further.

And there was also a slight sense of urgency on security grounds too. Luyuan had forgotten we had the key to their door, so on the second or third day, while they were out, I went in to see what was up. These guys were the cream of society: there were brief cases with chains and wrist locks, lethal-length knives in sheaths and a hand gun in a holster. Probably bag men for the Mafia/government boys who control Luyuan. It was now not just a question of principle, a line drawn in the sand. I wanted these slime ball motherfuckers out and fast.

The Art of War, Okie Style, or Our Second Battle of the Marne

I decided the *in your face* method of midnight music merry-go-round was a good battle field softener, but I had to come up with something blameless, yet effective. Eureka. My weapon was the fuse box that controls all the electricity in the house, <u>including</u> the back bedrooms. We figured out which fuses controlled their electricity and luckily, being a wing off the back of the house, theirs were not connected to ours.

First, like a roadie after a Rolling Stones concert, I rolled up my wires and put the Kickers back in their boxes. Then, I just turned off all their fuses. No lights, no air conditioning, no fans, no nothing. Just blackness and dead still air in the heat of the night, the drone of millions of mosquitoes in the background. Of course in a New York City minute the Luyuan guy would come over and ask to turn on the fuses. Instead of making a statement that I had done it, I played dumb. Gosh, I guess with two groups of people in one house, the circuit must be overloaded. Here, let me help.

Then as soon as the Luyuan guy got back to the hotel, I'd go back to the breaker box and shut 'em down again. Fortunately, the breaker box is situated in our house so the goons in the garden and the boob from the hotel could not see me in action. I could hear the goons in the back telephone the hotel and back he'd come. Gosh, really strange. Must be a problem with the wires are something. <u>What are they using back there, the sauna to dry their hair</u>?

One whole night of this and the next morning, undoubtedly eaten alive with mosquitoes, those mangy dogs packed their bags and weapons and were out of here.

Luyuan knew I was tripping the breakers but as long as I maintained my innocence, there was not a whole lot they could do. The message was clear: you break your promise and your guests had better bring camping gear. Another notch in our gun. It never happened again.

Suckers for Punishment, Stupidity or What? We then Take a Vacation - in China.

Our first house guest was Florence's mother, Françoise. We'd been talking about it since coming in '90, doing a cruise through the Three Gorges area on the Yangtze River and after all we'd been through, we really did deserve a break, you know, a relaxing boat cruise, but why did we have to choose China?

It was the classic bait and switch scam, except the difference in China is that the government sets the example and does it the best. Organized through the state run CITS, our bus pulls up to the wharf in Wuhan and, should we be surprised? Our reserved 3-star boat is not there, but there is another *3-star* boat. You've got the mother-in-law, the wife and the baby sitting there in the bus, they are unloading your baggage and what are you going to do? We reluctantly went, cussing all the way up the boat ramp.

From 3-Star Luxury to a Double Booked Boatful of Hundreds, or a Relaxing Cruise under Chinese Leadership

It did not take long to figure out what CITS had done and apparently does quite routinely: they keep one boat at the dock and put all of a second boat's *customers* onto the already nearly fully booked boat. A nightmare of fighting, pushing, fisticuffs, screaming and spleen ensued as two boat loads of people were reduced to Darwinian survival instincts to get a berth to sleep in. Finally, after several hours of chaos and body bruises, we got one second class room with two beds for all four of us, instead of the one first class room for my mother-in-law, Françoise and our baby daughter, Maia and one second class room for us.

As it turned out, almost all the western tourists got doubled up in rooms and the 75-100 overseas Chinese? They were given blankets and got to sleep on the floor together, assholes to elbows in the dining room after we all ate. Can you believe it. And this was going to go on for five long days and nights.

Chinese Lesson #1: Never, Ever Fuck with an Okie Who Believes in Right from Wrong

All the foreign tour operators we talked to that first day said it was *business as usual, been this way for years* and any talk of a refund was out of the question. For established tour operators, CITS may give a couple of hundred dollars' credit for the next group of 15-20 suckers. But just our one first class room was $782. Not to mention the misery of four persons crammed into a room for two and the ambiance and relaxation of a *pleasure cruise* ruined from the word go. This was a major state-sanctioned multi-million-dollar scam and I was not going to take it sitting down.

During the chaos of registering I had seen on the ship manifest that we had in fact been registered for our two correct rooms. That first night, I hung around the reception area and as soon as the attendant left briefly, I reached over the counter, lifted up the desk glass and stole the manifest. I had the evidence I needed. It showed how they had marked up the manifest, cramming two boat loads into one sardine can.

I then told the head purser I had seen the manifest and knew we had been shorted one first class room. I started making threats about complaining to higher authorities. Surprised I could speak and read Chinese and knowing I was not going to be leaving China in two weeks, but would be staying around to create potential problems, she offered to telex back to her head office in Wuhan to confirm the room arrangement and offered us her purser's room, saying she would sleep below deck. A generous offer to say the least, but I think it was more out of a sense of *peícháng*, hoping I would drop it. Yeah, sure.

The telex response the next day confirmed my claim. I badgered her into giving it to me as evidence to try to get compensated upon my return. Scared, she agreed. And never mind that her purser's room looked and smelled like it had not been cleaned in years, it at least took the pressure of the ladies in my life upstairs, AND it afforded me the opportunity to gather more evidence for my case.

I found in her room boxfuls of previous boat manifests, just like ours, many all marked up, doubling up boats and rooms. I took a few of these ranging over '93. I suspect no one had ever had so much rock solid evidence on such a huge scam.

Okie Justice in the Land of Cheats and Swindlers

Upon our return to Beijing, I made copies of all the original evidence and went to CITS for a chat. I came in with guns blazing. I had gotten the address of the *Jiang Zemin Anti-Corruption Commission*, the President's vehicle to gather evidence on the pathological corruption that eats at the very marrow of this country. I also got a book which lists all the newspapers in China. Wasting no time, I said in a voice loud enough for the dozen or so factotums in the room to hear that if my case was not resolved, I was going to send copies of all the evidence to the anti-corruption commission <u>and</u> to all the newspapers listed in this book. Now, people just don't do this kind of shit in China. It was so quiet in that room you could've heard a mouse pass gas under the floor boards. I left the copies there and told them I would be back in a few days.

First trip back they tried to buy me off with candy. Un-huh. Then they tried to give me gift coupons for $10-20 at, you guessed it, a CITS store. They were as stupid as they thought I was. My starting point was a refund for the whole boat trip, costing about $1,200. After several trips and continued references to going public on a big scale, I agreed to settle for full reimbursement for the first class room, or $782, and no, not in RMB or FEC, but cold hard greenbacks. Not bad for one customer who believes in right from wrong.

I was very proud of my efforts. If only those tour operators and their hapless customers knew. I suspect no one ever has ever stuck them for such a big refund. Too bad, but I am sure the same scam is still going on.

Our Expat Bubble of Immunity Bursts and the Final Wagon Gets Put in Our Laager

A couple of months later, one of our expat friends at the Luyuan compound was robbed and our little village of tranquility was jostled out of its sleep. Police state China was changing with the reforms and foreigners were no longer immune from the widespread criminal activity that has always taken place in the local neighborhoods. None of us were even locking our windows. After several other attempts we all got alarm systems of one form or another. Luyuan hired a couple of Chaplinesque *armed guards* to patrol the perimeter, we got Luyuan to build the outer wall higher and after that little burst of felony, nothing has happened since. Before it was all resolved, the thief got as far as removing one of our window screens, but luckily, we were never broken into.

The thief was a funny guy. After climbing over the wall, he'd go and get a beer out of our friend's frig kept in the garden outside, smoke a cigarette in their jeep and leave the bottle and stub there before going to work. He was supposedly caught once by the ferocious hotel armed guards, asked to go take a piss and used the opportunity to flee. By now, he's probably either dead or is China's up and coming Rupert Murdoch.

This felonious digression almost brings closure on our house situation. With a burglar in the neighborhood, we were able to get the Luyuan for security reasons, to put a gate on the garden doorway arch, where visitors going to the sauna would pass. So, as soon as we got a lock on it, Luyuan had to ask us to open the garden gate to get to the sauna. Over the next two years, they asked a few times and every time we would say we had lost the key, but that they were welcome to come through our house, go out our living room door into the garden and then to the sauna. Never once would they accept. It was just too embarrassing, a loss of face for everybody concerned. Another notch in the old gun.

The War of Attrition Ends - At Least for Now

Then when we renewed the contract in '95, Luyuan realized that they had lost control of the two back bedrooms and the sauna. We finally worked out a deal where they took out the sauna and with our good friends next door, they took one bedroom and we the other. We remodeled it (another mini-battle running into over two months.) and turned the shell of the sauna into an attached storage room, which always comes in handy. Finally, after 2 ½ years, we could finally say we had a house of our own, **all** ours.

The China Syndrome, Part II

If we are forced at every hour to watch or listen to horrible events, this constant stream of ghastly impressions will deprive even the most delicate among us of all respect for humanity. Cicero, 106-43 BC

Cicero traveled to Asia and based on this quote, I suspect he must have passed through China for inspiration. This is the first country where I have lived and/or worked where the resulting change in my being is a negative. I am different here and much for the worse. No matter how hard I try, the lowest common denominator is the vast rule, not the exception, so I get sucked down to the same gutter level. Everywhere else I feel like the experiences and contact with the people made me a better person, a broader minded, caring citizen of Earth. I do not know where this country's people lost its moral compass, but the needle of conscious and self-respect fell off a long time ago. Acts of humanity are considered a tactical error to be exploited. Machiavelli's *The Prince* was required reading when I grew up, but I didn't know anyone who tried to adopt it as a *modus vivendi*. Here, *The Art of War* is required reading and nearly everyone seems to follow its principles in their daily lives. Being an inhumane asshole is a sign of social evolution and respect. This creates an atmosphere of distrust and cynicism and since everybody is sure that the person they are dealing with is also an asshole, the level of self-loathing I feel among the people transcends any other in my 16 years of international experiences.

The biggest difference I have noted in China to the many other places I've been is the incredibly high level of isolation this country has suffered over the millennia. This in-bred history has also tangentially created the predictable level of xenophobia and racism one would expect and 40 years of paranoid communism on top of that makes shamelessly fleecing foreigners a glorified act of patriotism. While it is true much contact between cultures across the ages has resulted in one usurping or annihilating the other, very often the victor would knowingly adopt or passively absorb those aspects of the vanquished's society, culture, technology or political structure superior to theirs. China has largely been deprived of this valuable interplay for thousands of years and when exposure was finally forced upon them during a very weak period in their history 150 years ago, China was too big to vanquish and the Chinese, who were convinced that their nation was literally the center of the universe, their emperor God and their people chosen, were not receptive to any assimilation. Now that China has finally, after 5,000 years of insular arrogance decided to look outward to adopt and absorb on their own terms, they are starting in a very deep social and cultural hole of their own making. And boy does it show.

It wasn't until Maia came into our lives, but now I can describe what it is like living here: we are residing in a nation of children. The people for the most part are impetuous, dishonest, self-centered and egotistical. Sounds just like a 3-year-old doesn't it? This realization has made staying here much more entertaining, in a perverse sort of way.

Another problem is that while it is very fashionable these days to poo-poo the role government plays in our lives in America, the fact is a government's behavior sets the moral tone and social mandate of the people. If the government is benign and compassionate, these traits tend to be reflected among the masses. Quick, juxtapose Americans' sense of purpose during the Eisenhower and Raygun administrations. If the government is paranoid and corrupt, these traits are equally reflected across the land. Which is why adjectives like *Darwinistic, Jurassic, dog eat dog* and *cynical* roll of my tongue in the same breath I speak of China.

And What Do You See for Their Future, Oh Dearest Seer Natasha?

In spite of all the environmental and spiritual stench surrounding us, it is out of allegiance to Frank Kuchuris (my boss at East Balt Bakery), the job that I have and the money we can continue to sink into investments, that we have committed to staying here with EBB till February '99. But we are under no illusions. One thing is for sure. We are NOT extending and we WILL go someplace where the people do not savagely treat each other like the devolutionized children in the penultimate chapter of William Golding's *Lord of the Flies*. February '99 will have meant nine years in this moral concentration camp and that is enough.

Still, I am confident that I can de-program upon departure to more civil climes and begin again to share my sense of right and wrong, my humanity, trust and compassion with strangers, casual acquaintances and friends. Bursts of misanthropy even towards close friends continue to vex me. Through it all, China has focused my passions and feelings inwardly towards my family, which has strengthened bonds that will last me a lifetime. Thank you Cicero for the heads up. I promise you I will maintain my self-pride, my self-worth and my dignity, no matter how many kicks to the groin, slaps in the face and shit thrown at me that China can muster.

Chapter 6

Interviews with Author Jeff J. Brown

International Reporter and Katherine Fisk's Interview with 44 Days Radio Sinoland's Jeff J. Brown

1. Jeff, could you briefly describe what a "color revolution" is, as best you understand it?

Katherine, that's a great question. Color revolutions are just the latest mutation in the West's ongoing, worldwide psyops-black ops-false flag wars, on what it considers to be countries, leaders and governments that are not supine satraps to its economic, political and military empire. Not coincidently, the targets are frequently countries with valuable natural and human resources, for extraction and exploitation. For humanity's 85% non-white, non-Western population - whom I call the Moral Majority or from Empire's perspective, the Dreaded Other - these criteria include almost all of them.

Color revolutions used to be done directly by the West's spy agencies, principally America's CIA and its 15 other "intelligence" groups, the UK's MI6 and France's DGSE. However, with revelations that Europe is still running a secret Gladio army network and Edward Snowden's exposure of Angloland's Five Eyes, which pull in Canada, Australia and New Zealand, and now Nine Eyes, with Denmark, Norway, France and the Netherlands added, we can safely say that all of Western *spydom* is tightly managed and coordinated across the planet.

There are too many pre-color revolution psyops-black ops-false flags to discuss, but early ones include the overthrow of the Iranian, Guatemalan and Congolese governments, in order to install whore leaders willing to open their countries to Western pillage and plunder. If they are not compliant and will not get out of the way, the West just kills them. It is documented that the DGSE has assassinated at least 23 African leaders and that is just the tip of the iceberg, for the West as a whole. We can fast forward to Chile in 1973, thousands of murders, rigged elections, phony revolutions, fascist juntas, oligarchic states, through to the 2009 palace coup in Honduras, the 2012 "express coup" in Paraguay and the Syrian and Ukrainian genocides today. These Western spydom operations are ongoing around the world. Just ask Venezuela, Ecuador, Kyrgyzstan, Iran, Nigeria, Eritrea, to name just a few.

Western spy agencies do not do this in a vacuum. There are always willing, fifth column compradors in-country, often capitalists and/ or wealthy, aristocratic families, who want to maintain the historic 1%-99% society and economy, much to their highly favored pillage and enslavement of the masses. What the West provides every time is organization, management, human and signal intelligence and bags full of money to buy off the hesitant ones, as well as to pay to keep the streets filled with "angry" protesters.

Western spydom also routinely subverts its own so called "pluralistic democracy", using this same poisonous playbook of terrorism and violence. Conclusively proven assassinations include John F. Kennedy, Robert Kennedy, Martin Luther King, Jr. and Italy's Prime Minister, Aldo Moro. Factually proven false flags include 9/11, the Boston Marathon "Bombing", Sandy Hook and Charlie Hebdo. For coups d'états, Western spydom overthrew Australia's visionary, tour-de-force prime minister, Gough Whitlam, in 1975 and in Britain, MI5/MI6 have a long history of sabotaging the political fortunes of its leftwing leaders.

Color revolutions are exactly the same modus operandi. They are just done openly and "legally" by adding a layer of deniability between Western spydom and the overthrows on the ground, via supposedly "non-governmental" organizations (NGOs). But they are *not* non-governmental. The US Congress finances them to the tune of hundreds of millions of dollars a year. So does Brussels in Europe. The State Department and EU foreign ministries spend many more hundreds of millions, working with the NGOs to cultivate, train and corrupt fifth column compradors inside and outside each targeted country. Add the tens of billions that the West's spy agencies lawfully receive from their sheeple (sheep people) taxpayers, as well as the many billions more spent off budget, from managing the global drug trade in Latin America and Southcentral Asia (cocaine and heroin, respectively), the West's worldwide dictatorship essentially has an unlimited budget to outspend and outlast even the most tenacious freedom fighters, such as Cuba, Eritrea, Ecuador, Venezuela, Donbass Ukraine and on and on around the globe.

Color revolutions offer two other powerful advantages to Western worldwide dictatorship. Who can be against "NGOs" that promote "human rights", "rule of law" and "civil society", not only in the West, but in the targeted countries? This is powerful, perfidious propaganda. It immediately puts the targeted countries on the defensive, if they resist accepting these fifth column regime changers in their midst. The Western media, which is totally infested with minders from the CIA, et al., can crank up the propaganda foghorns behind the Great Western Firewall with frightening headlines: "CHINA IS AGAINST HUMAN RIGHTS", "RUSSIA OPPOSES CIVIL SOCIETY" and "VENEZUELA FLAUNTS THE RULE OF LAW".

The backhanded message in this propaganda is that all these countries targeted for imperial submission have no constitutions, functioning governments, democratic principles, cultures, civilizations and legal and social institutions. It is fundamentally very racist, subliminally suggesting that the world's Moral Majority, 85% dark skinned peoples are a bunch of hairy heathens, savages cannibalizing each other in wastelands across the planet. Only the "morally superior, righteous" West and its crusading NGOs can save them from their depravity and baseness.

Thus, all the countries on the West's regime change hit list are brilliantly demonized in the eyes of its brainwashed masses. In these targeted countries, local fifth column compradors use this disinformation to subvert their governments internally: Xi, Putin, Maduro, the Communist Party of China (CPC), the Russian and Venezuelan governments, etc., are against human rights, rule of law and civil society. How dare them!

Of course, all of this filthy corruption is codified into the laws of Western countries, making their multibillion dollar, panglobal regime change operations perfectly and insidiously "legal". Being "legal", this allows color revolutions another powerful tool: recruiting and working with neofascist and neocon private "foundations", "institutes" and "think tanks". No more worries about any 1975-esque Church Commissions. This was the US Senatorial commission that investigated and exposed many CIA psyops, black ops and false flags. No, the whole ball of wax can now be done right under the world's noses, "right and proper".

2. *Are the people of mainland China aware that Hong Kong's Umbrella Revolution is a: color revolution engineered by amongst others, George Soros?*

The short answer is "yes". Baba Beijing, my wry name for China's communist leadership, has been exposing Western regime change efforts, since liberation from Western/Japanese colonialism, in 1949. The Chinese media regularly reports on historical overthrow attempts in Tibet, Tiananmen Square and more recently, in Xinjiang. Baba Beijing also continuously covers Western regime change efforts going on around the world, such as Russia, the Ukraine, Latin America, the Middle East, Africa, etc. Searching "George Soros-color revolution-Hong Kong" on the Chinese internet pulls up hundreds of Chinese news articles, which are available for Baba Beijing's 1,370,000,000 citizens to peruse on this subject, as well as for the 50,000,000 overseas Chinese around the planet.

3. *We have heard recent rumblings about religious tensions in Western China between Muslims and Chinese authorities. It was said in western media that the government had forbidden Muslims to celebrate Ramadan, whilst in other sources this was refuted. Can you:*
   a) *Explain the nature of this area of China.*
   b) *To the best of your knowledge explain the facts.*
   c) *Do you see any tensions between Muslims in this area and the Chinese authorities being "bait" for a "color revolution" as has occurred in Syria between extremist Islamic groups and the general population and in Ukraine between Ukrainian speaking peoples and Russian speaking peoples that has resulted in civil wars in both countries?*

These propaganda reports behind the Great Western Firewall about forcing China's Muslims and Tibetan Buddhists to do this and not that, have to be taken with a huge dose of skepticism. Remember, every media outlet in the West, of any import, has CIA & Co. psyops minders on their editorial boards. Baba Beijing has been dealing with the ceaseless onslaught of Western regime change efforts in Tibet and Xinjiang, since liberation in 1949. Why would they want to force Buddhists and Muslims to contravene their religious precepts, only making these Western psyops efforts more successful? It would be playing into Empire's hands and Baba Beijing is not stupid.

Is it possible that Baba Beijing harasses and/or arrests known fifth column compradors, caught by human and signal intelligence? Sure. Do they sometimes go after the wrong person? Happens everywhere. Is it certain that fifth column compradors inside and outside China are ginning up scaremonger horror shows, to fill the Western mainstream media breech with hysterical propaganda? Absolutely. Is it conceivable that local officials sometimes get overzealous and do something stupid and inflammatory? Of course. This occurs all over the world, the West included. But a broad fiat by a big city, province or region? Simply ridiculous.

In our Beijing suburban neighborhood is a large Hui (Muslim) community and mosque, and it stays very busy. The faithful pray and fast at their leisure. Muslim businesses here, just like across much of the Islamic world (I worked in Africa and the Middle East for ten years), tend to stay open during Ramadan, with normal or reduced hours during the heat of the day, because people still work and life goes on. All those absurd, CIA-fabricated stories about Muslim businesses being forced to sell alcohol are laughable. Uighur businesses almost never offer alcohol. Hui establishments almost always do. Different cultures, different business plans, same Islam.

a) There is underlying tension between Xinjiang's Uighur Muslim people, whose native language belongs to the Turkic linguistic group, and Chinese Han, who are Mandarin speaking, Buddhist-Daoist-Confucian or atheist. This, just as there are historically and ongoing, violent tensions between Catholics, Protestants, Orthodox Christians, Jews, Muslims, Buddhists and Hindus around the world. So, to single out Xinjiang is just more Behind the Great Western Firewall foghorn propaganda. Religious strife is as human as civilization itself.

b) The problem is Western colonialism has been and continues to use this all too human divisiveness to divide and conquer. The list is exceptionally long, but a classic example is the multifaceted religious, cultural and nationalistic tinderbox that the British created in India, Pakistan and China, with Pakistan's partition and the division of Jammu-Kashmir-Tibet. Thus for China, the West is banally and lethally predictable in its efforts to destabilize and hopefully balkanize Xinjiang and Tibet, for rape and plunder.

c) Yes, all the West's investment in overthrowing the status quo in Xinjiang and Tibet, via spydom's psyops-black ops-false flags, NGOs, financing and training fifth column propagandists, compradors and terrorists, to return home and wreak havoc - keeps Baba Beijing very preoccupied and vigilant. Even if the West fails in its efforts to balkanize and rape China, all these machinations force Baba Beijing to invest billions to counteract it. China's Ministry of State Security and Russia's FSB (their equivalents of the CIA) must be working double time to stay on top. You can just imagine the fascinating human and signal intelligence they share together. So many ongoing threats and incoming subterfuge across the Eurasian continent and its high seas.

But, just as Western colonialism has been and continues to use the same, tired playbook, its targets are just as adept at resisting it. And now, for the first time, groups like the Bolivarian Alliance for the Peoples of Our America (ALBA), Community of Latin American and Caribbean States (CELAC), Nonaligned Movement (NAM), Brazil-Russia-India-China-South Africa (BRICS), Eurasian Economic Union (EAEU), Collective Security Treaty Organization (CSTO) and Shanghai Cooperation Organization (SCO) are integrating and harmonizing their efforts to defeat Western imperialism, more than ever before. Even the Organization for African Unity (OAU) is having some success stories. Not only that, but the anti-Western forces now have the one thing they've never had enough of in the past: billions upon billions of dollars to fight back. It's the battle royal of the 21st century: the World's 85% Moral Majority vs. the Conradian Heart of Darkness.

Jeff J. Brown's Interview with The Saker: Xi Jinping, Vladimir Putin, China and Russia, Modi, India and BRICS vs. Western Empire, Israel and World War III

No questions about the common goals and aspirations of Putin and Xi. From its racist, capitalist perspective, Western Empire should be very, very worried about the consequences.

Note: The Saker is a very popular website that specializes in news and events about Russia and the Ukraine. Jeff J. Brown is commissioned to write a monthly column on The Saker, entitled, the *Moscow-Beijing Express.*

The Saker: *Both Larchmonter445 and myself see the new relationship being built between China and Russia as one of symbiosis. Larchmonter445 speaks of a "double Helix" and I call it a "symbiosis". In my opinion, this symbiotic relationship between two empires/civilizations/superpowers is something unique in history and possibly one of the most important events in world history. Do you think that we are exaggerating the importance of what Putin and Xi have put in motion or not? If we are, how would you characterize and assess the type of relationship which is being built between Russia and China?*

Jeff J. Brown: While clearly coming from very different backgrounds and civilizations, Putin and Xi have much in common philosophically, because so many human values transcend cultures. The key is whether peoples' leaders choose to follow them, and clearly the West's haven't done so, for the last 500 years. I think it is clear that Xi and Putin are trying to change the sordid dynamic of Western colonialism and are working hand in hand to make the 21st century different from the past.

Putin and Xi obviously like and respect each other as humans and leaders, but both countries and their peoples also have much in common. Yes, Russia and China committed genocide, as they expanded across Siberia, and out of the Yellow and Yangtze River basins, respectively, to create their "natural" borders. But other than China colonizing Vietnam from about 100BC-900AD, neither country poured across the planet like Europe and then America and Israel, devouring, like locusts, everything in their colonial/settler paths.

Russia and China are brothers in arms, in the endless struggle against worldwide fascism, which is part and parcel of Western empire and its pillage capitalism. We can quibble over numbers, but there is no argument that China and Russia lost more lives, by several magnitudes, than any other country during World War II. Combined, their citizens — over 50,000,000 in all - gave their last full measure of devotion, to crush fascism. Now, China is working behind the scenes to help Russia fight the virulent fascist junta that the West has spawned in Ukraine, in order to try to overthrow the Russian government.

Also, both China and Russia have spiritual foundations that are different to the Catholic/Protestant/Jewish West, with China's Buddhist-Daoist-Confucian, 3-in-1 religion and Russia's Orthodox Church. Yes, Russia has dirty hands for colonizing China, along with Westerners, during the 19th-20th centuries, but both countries can empathize with each other for constantly being invaded: Mongols, Japanese and Europeans. Both have had huge impacts on world philosophy, science, technology, literature, the arts and music. Both countries have non-Latin languages, which are hard to learn for outsiders, making cultural connections with the rest of the world that much more difficult. Ironically, they often have to use an imperial European language to communicate with outsiders, even between themselves.

Appreciating all this commonality, it is an interesting speculation of history to wonder what would have happened if Mao and Khrushchev had not had their infamous, and ultimately, disastrous split in 1960 (I put more of the blame on Mao, to be honest). Just think of the possibilities for the world, if they had hung together against the West, especially now that we know Khrushchev was an early day Gough Whitlam, working tirelessly with John Kennedy behind the scenes for world peace, until America's deep state coup d'état on Dealey Plaza, three years later.

So in fact, the Putin-Xi-Russia-China alliance is not an anomaly. It was simply put on hold for 55 years.

The Saker: There has been amazingly little coverage in the West of the new Russian Chinese Strategic Partnership (RCSP) and when there has been coverage of it, it was mostly looking at the tree and missing the forest, that is to say that contracts between the two countries were mentioned, joint military maneuvers described, and even some commentaries were made about a "rapprochement" between the two countries. But the staggering implication of the two countries essentially joining each other at the hip in economic and military terms are never discussed in the West. How much coverage of this new symbiosis has there been in China? Are most Chinese people aware of the fact that Xi and Putin have basically made the two countries interdependent?

Jeff J. Brown: You can talk to any Chinese person on the street and they know the score. Russia good. America bad. Right now, Western Europe is getting a pass, for the most part, in the media. Like Putin & Co., I think Baba Beijing is hoping that Europe, especially Germany, will break the chains of its demonic slavery to all things Uncle Sam, and come over from the dark side. That is still very much open to debate, especially after the shameless war crimes against humanity unfolding in the Ukraine, and Macedonia, and Serbia, and Gladio, and NATO, and Greece, and NSA/MI6/BND – did I leave anything out?

Every time Putin and Xi talk on the phone, every meeting between their foreign ministers, Sergei Lavrov and Wang Yi, every Russian dignitary who comes to China for an official visit, everytime Baba Beijing sends someone to Russia for a tête-à-tête, every deal signed – it all gets reported in China on Page One. The May 9th, 70th Anniversary Great Victory Moscow parade, with Xi sitting on Putin's right side, as they watched the PLA proudly marching on Red Square below, was an 18-month culmination of Baba Beijing planting in the consciousness of the Chinese their commonality with the Russians, in victory over fascism. This new consciousness is going to be brought to dizzying heights in Beijing, on September 3rd, when Putin sits with Xi overlooking Tiananmen Square, as China celebrates its 70th anniversary and an official, new national holiday: "Victory in the War of Resistance against Japanese Aggression and World Fascism". By including Japan's name in the new holiday, Baba

Beijing is almost daring Western leaders not to attend the parade, thus bonding China's and Russia's unique role in World War II history. In effect, it is not Russia's celebration, nor just China's celebration. It is their and their peoples' collective victory. The importance of these two parades, their massive show of military force and solidarity, in the face of Western Empire, cannot be understated.

The Saker: There is little doubt that the US has done everything possible to alienate and antagonize Russia. As for Europe, it has convincingly shown Russia that it is a US-run colony with no opinion or policy of its own. So the Russian re-direction to the East, South and North is rather easy to explain. But what has motivated China to decide join Russia in such a symbiotic relationship? Did the USA not have much more to offer to China than Russia?

Jeff J. Brown: Both Russian and Chinese leadership know the classic book, Admiral Alfred Mahan's *The Influence of Sea Power upon History, 1660–1783* (1890). This colonial-empire concept was fleshed out by Halford Mackinder, in a paper he wrote in 1904, *The Geographical Pivot of History*. Its thesis is simple: control the high seas around Russia, China and the rest of Eurasia/Middle East, and you control the human and natural resources of Earth's biggest continent. Then, in post 1990 Russia and with China's meteoric economic rise, both sides saw the light (actually, until Putin was elected Prime Minister/President in 1999-2000, it was Kazakhstan's Nursultan Nazarbaev, who was reading *Sea Power*). At first independently, and then together, Russia and China informally wrote their own Eurasian manifesto: Western Empire can control the high seas around us, but they cannot control the landmass of our continent, unless we let them. And thus, organizations like China's Shanghai Cooperation Organization (SCO), Belts and Roads Initiative (B&R), and Russia's Collective Security Treaty Organization (CSTO) and Eurasian Economic Union (EEU= EAEU) have become part and parcel of Asia's lexicon and vision.

Foreigners laugh when I say this, but the Chinese simply don't like the West. And with America as the Empire's viper head, Uncle Sam comes in last place. The Chinese understand history much better than Westerners. They will never forget their century of humiliation, 1840-1949, when the UK and the US engaged in what is called, "the longest running and largest global criminal enterprise in world history" – enslaving the Chinese people with opium. They, along with the European colonial powers, then proceeded to cart off the nation's silver bullion and rob it of its agricultural, mineral, forest and human resources.

When the slave trade was abolished in the United States in 1865, it was the Americans who took this fabulously profitable business model to China, where US flagships kidnapped and enslaved an estimated one million Chinese coolies, who were sold in the New World, principally the United States, South Africa, Peru and Cuba. The Americans raked in this filthy lucre, until they were shamed into finally stopping it in 1874.

During China's Civil War, 1937-1949, the Americans plied the corrupt Chiang Kai-Shek with billions in cash and weapons (a chunk of which he stole), ostensibly defeat the fascist Japanese, who were occupying much of Northern China. But Chiang kept retreating against the Japanese to devote all of his energy into fighting Mao Zedong and the Red Army, whom he hated with a visceral passion. In spite of Presidents Roosevelt's and Truman's massive Lend Lease Program, to arm and fund Chiang to the hilt, he still got his ass whipped anyway. Then the US made sure that Chiang and his mafia KMT made it safely to Taiwan, to be the West's "real" China.

Since liberation in 1949 up till today, the US has relentlessly tried to destabilize and overthrow China's communist government, via Taiwan, Tibet, Xinjiang, Burma, Vietnam, Japan, Korea and on and on.

For the Chinese, what is there to like about the West, especially the USA?

The Saker: *You have recorded three very interesting radio shows about China and Russia (see* http://chinarising.puntopress.com/2015/05/10/mao-zedong-ow-or-wow-44-days-radio-sinoland-show-15-5-1-2/, http://chinarising.puntopress.com/2015/05/11/mao-zedong-ow-or-wow-44-days-radio-sinoland-show-15-5-1-2-2/ *and* http://chinarising.puntopress.com/2015/05/17/china-russia-india-family-style-44-days-radio-sinoland-show-15-5-1-2-2-2/). *Can you please summarize for us what you think the Chinese want from their relationship with Russia in the* *middle to long term? While the two countries will not fuse to become one, or even form a confederacy, do you think that China would be interested in joining the Eurasian Union or negotiate some kind of open borders agreement with Russia?*

Jeff J. Brown: I earlier mentioned the CSTO, EEU, SCO and B&R. The first two are Russian inspired, the latter two are Chinese. The first of each pair is security and strategy oriented. The latter pair are trade based. During his May trip to Moscow with Putin, Xi stopped and met with Nazarbaev in Kazakhstan and then with Belarus' President, Alexander Lukashenko. The Chinese press said they all talked about synthesizing these organizations into a holistic, Asian whole. Obviously, both sides want their influence, but I am confident they will sort it out. They have to. America's Sixth fleet is parked off China's and Russia's Eastern shores, the US is militarizing Japan, threatening them both, not to mention, banks of NATO missiles are all pointed their way from Europe.

For cross border relations, rail and transport bridges are open across the Sino-Russian border. China and Russia are proposing a high speed rail line between Jilin Province (in Manchuria) and Vladivostok. The largest engineering project in human history, the gas and oil pipeline system between Russia and China is being built. All of this is going to continue to intensify and diversify. While I don't think we will see a Maastricht Treaty, with the free movement of nationals moving from one country to another, I do foresee a day when Russia and China have a border like Canada and the US: no visa, register your passport, vehicle and go through customs, coming and going. I think Mongolia will eventually be included in the deal.

The Saker: Russia and China have engaged in unprecedented joint military exercises and Chinese officials have even been given access to Russian strategic command posts. Russian and Chinese admirals have given joint reports to Xi and Putin during a video conference organized by the Russian military. Russia is now facing a direct US/NATO threat in Europe while China is threatened by the USA from Japan, Taiwan, Korea and over the Spratlys. If it ever came to a real, shooting, war between the USA and Russia or between the USA and

China, do you expect that Russia and China would be willing to get involved and actively support their partners even against the USA?

Jeff J. Brown: Great question, Saker. If the US strikes either China or Russia first, it's probably World War III and humanity ceases to function as we know it. While there is no announced treaty alliance, we have no way of knowing what Russia and China have agreed to secretly. It is also possible that China and Russia have told NATO back channel to the effect, "You mess with one of us, you deal with us both". I've always wondered if that might be the case, given America's reluctance to push the pedal to the metal in the Ukraine and the South China Sea. Working together, China and Russia maybe wouldn't even need to fire a shot. Just use all their technology and tricks of the trade to neutralize NATO's satellites, radars, communications, computer systems, etc. Or either one of them could start selling off their mountains of US Treasury debt. In fact, both of them may have told Obama that if he pushes too far, they will start dumping US bonds. Napoléon Bonaparte famously said that whoever is the creditor calls the shots.

What if Russia feels the need to intervene militarily in the Donbass, or if the Americans can get the Japanese or Taiwanese to do something really stupid? Or of course, the tried a true method of manipulating history: a big, fat false flag in either region, to get the desired result? I guess we will find out the hard way. But think of it this way: the B&R/SCO-EEU/CSTO framework and all its tremendous synergies and potential, just dissolve away, if either China or Russia fall to Western Empire. If you were Putin or Xi, would you just stand there and let the 21st century and humanity go down the drain?

Then again, both getting involved probably means WWIII and we know how the history books will probably be written as a result, if there is anybody left to write them. What is so scary about all these ponderings is that while Putin and Xi are keeping their heads down and taking care of business around the Asian continent and across the planet, America is so wantonly reckless and out of control. Uncle Sam is like an overdosed meth freak on PCP. It makes me shudder.

The Saker: It is rather obvious that both China and Russia need a de-dollarization of the world economy, but that they don't want to trigger such a brutal collapse as to crash their own economy. This is especially true of China which is heavily invested in the US economy. Russia is trying to slowly and smoothly pull herself out of the dollar-centered markets. What is China doing? Do you believe that there are plans in China to "de-Walmartize" the Chinese economy or is it still way too early for that?

Jeff J. Brown: Let's face it, Saker, when the US dollar economy collapses, it could easily trigger WWIII. It is going to be that cataclysmic. And when it does happen, Israel knows they can start counting the days when the gates of Jerusalem change hands for the 45th time, in that city's heralded 5,000-year history. Israel is at least as out of control as the US, maybe even more so. Their 200-300 undeclared nukes would surely make a mess of Mother Earth and what they started would surely trigger a global nuclear holocaust, with all the depressing outcomes to go with it.

So I think Baba Beijing, as well as everybody else in the world, Russia included, are hoping that the Western financial house of smoke, mirrors and cards can keep going on for as long as possible. Why? Because like ants harvesting for the winter, BRICS, CELAC, NAM and all the other anti-Empire coalitions are working feverishly to organize, plan, implement, found and institute as many entities, agreements and systems as possible, to soften the eventual economic Armageddon. Great examples include the Sino-Russian CRIFT (anti-SWIFT), UCRG (anti-big three credit agencies), BRICS New Development Bank (NDB= anti-World Bank), Asian Infrastructure Investment Bank (AIIB= anti-Asian Development Bank), Banco del Sur, PetroCaribe and on and on. China is setting up the world's largest gold fund ($16.1 billion), with 60 countries already signed up, to develop gold mining and commerce along, where else – the Asian continent's Silk Roads, which Admiral Mahan's ghost can only dream about controlling.

About the Chinese economy de-Walmartizing itself: ironically, to get over the need to drive the economy based on exports and capital investment, Baba Beijing is doing everything in its power to increase internal consumption. Environmentally, with 1.3 billion citizens, that's kind of a frightening thought, if the Chinese try to imitate the US model of gluttonous, Hampshire hog overconsumption. But the key words in Xi's Chinese Dream are, "moderately prosperous, socialist society". I believe Xi, with all his upbringing about frugality and simplicity, finds American "shop till you drop" consumerism to be a modern day Sodom and Gomorrah. After 35 years of the Deng Era, with its crass, US style materialism, Xi is setting a new philosophical course for the Chinese nation: the very Buddhist mantra of "less is more". A jet ski, a Harley and a SUV in the three-car garage are not going to buy you inner peace and happiness, nor is the newest model BMW or Hermes handbag.

The Saker: What about India in all this? There apparently still is a lot of suspicion in India about the true motives of the Chinese, not only about "South Tibet" and border issues, but also about Chinese support for Pakistan and a general suspicion that China might use military force as it did in 1962 and 1967. What are, in your opinions, Chinese goals towards India? Does China still have expansionist plans towards India? Are Indian suspicions still warranted? Furthermore, Russia, China and India are members of the BRICS. It appears to me that for Russia to achieve a comprehensive and long term peace treaty between China and India would be a top strategic objective as tensions between China and India only benefit the US Empire. Likewise, it appears to me that for China it would be far more important to achieve a comprehensive and long term peace deal with India than to resolve petty border disputes and give support to Pakistan. Am I correct here, or am I missing something? Do you think that Russia and the other BRICS countries have the means to push both China and India away from their current "cool and cautious" relationship and into a real alliance? What kind of relationship with India would China ideally want?

Jeff J. Brown: India truly is the $64,000 dollar, er, yuan/ruble question, isn't it? We have to go back to postwar history to get a proper perspective. Comparing China and India since then, has been nothing but a study in contrast. India got its independence in 1947, two years before China's. It was (and still is) the world's largest "Western" democracy. China's liberation launched one of the greatest experiments in human history, in political, social and economic revolution. India was the Crown Jewel of the British Empire, with decent infrastructure, governing bodies, institutions and "civil society", at least among the country's educated elite, who helped run India during the UK's 300 year, colonial rule.

Mao inherited a devastated, 19th century hellhole, with drug addiction and almost no infrastructure, outside what the colonialists built to ship in the opium and haul off all the loot. The British Raj made sure he would leave a legacy of tension and religious strife, by partitioning off Pakistan and messing up the borders between India, China and Pakistan. The US made sure that the communists had their anti-China, by helping Chiang Kai-Shek and his fascist KMT escape to establish Taiwan. Both China and India had vast land masses and huge populations to drive their economies.

Before Russia and China ended their split in 1989, Deng Xiaoping famously said that if the 21st century was to be Asia's, then China and India had to do it together, to make it happen. But it hasn't turned out that way, at least until now, has it? India had what the French call, a "champagne and caviar" revolution, where the local Indian colonial elite took over where the British left off. Departing Lord Mountbatten appointed Jawaharlal Nehru as prime minister, King George VI's royal pick, Mr. Indian Establishment. The colonial hierarchy and all its institutions largely stayed, only to be managed by the Indian elite. This sclerotic, corrupt system was kept in place.

Contrast that to China's democratic dictatorship of the people, where Mao and the communists cleaned up their political, social and economic house. Out with the colonial compradors and running dog capitalists, in with taking China from the 19th to the 20th century in one generation, standing tall and proud, without any help from the West. And they did it, with massive success across the country. The Mao Era transformed China and dramatically improved the lives of the vast majority of the people, turning it into a modern, developing economy and agricultural and industrial powerhouse. This, while "Western democratic" India floundered economically and politically, going through prime ministers like poop through a goose.

It was a bitter pill for Indians to swallow. And that was even before the Deng Era, with its double digit growth and another economic and social revolution, which world history had never seen before, and probably never will again. So, it is easy to see why Indians are a little bit techy about comparing themselves to the Chinese, and why they have a bit of a chip on their shoulders. It's only human nature.

Recently, more frustrations set in, with the Xi-Putin-China-Russia Express flying at breakneck speed. Wasn't Russia India's longtime friend? What's going on? Again, the Indians felt slighted by the Chinese. However, it often boils down to leadership and India seems to have finally gotten a prime minister worth his salt, someone who can belly up to the geopolitical bar and state India's case, Mr. Narendra Modi. With the Indian Grenadier regiment marching alongside China's PLA in Moscow on May 9th, reciprocal Xi-Modi state visits, Putin's state visit to Delhi and Modi's scheduled two visits to Russia later this year, it looks like Deng's vision may finally be realized. Western Empire is still a dangerous giant straddling the world. I am sure that Deng is smiling in his grave, knowing that his China-India dream now includes China's long lost socialist brother-in-revolution, Russia.

But it will not be all that easy. The British Raj intentionally left that terrible border legacy between China and India, and with Pakistan as well. China and India had a border war in 1962, which the Chinese won. Ouch. More Indian egos bruised. But India got even, taking back Sikkim in 1967. The fact that much of it is religiously fueled, makes it that much more intractable. Hindus believe that the map of India is in the shape of Bharat Mata, the Mother Goddess of India, and any land conceded to China or Pakistan is tantamount to removing part of her head. Nor are we talking about a few islands in the Amur River and some slivers of land between Russian, Mongolia, North Korea and China, all of which have signed formal treaties in the last 25 years, to settle their boundary disputes. Modi and Xi have 138,000 km^2 on the table, with Tibetan Buddhists, Pakistani Muslims and Indian Hindus glaring menacingly over their shoulders. It's a nightmare. The world's highest highway, running between China and Pakistan over the Khunjerab Pass, then down to the Port of Gwadar, which the Chinese are managing? Baba Beijing pitched it to India first and was given the cold shoulder, largely due to public pressure on the government not to "give in" to the Chinese on the border dispute.

Leaving out Pakistan for the moment, the Indians have much more to lose over this than the Chinese. While it would be hard for China to give all its disputed land back to India, I think Baba Beijing could go to the Chinese people and explain why they gave back, not all, but more than half. I believe this is what Modi meant, when he gave his speech in Beijing, asking the Chinese to please consider India's "special situation" (about the border dispute). He asked publically, like a gentleman, rebuffing India's very vocal and volatile nationalists.

Huge steps were taken during Modi's visit. There has been no real diplomatic or military contact between China and India, since the 1962 and 1967 wars, to address the border issue, just pot shots over each other's heads and the occasional skirmish. Now there are red phones installed in Beijing and Delhi. Generals along the border will now regularly meet to discuss any sore spots. And most importantly, there will be high level, diplomatic discussions every six months, to specifically settle the border terms. The Raj was a demonic genius and it's been a long, destructive half century.

The Indian-Chinese border dispute is the biggest weak link in forging an alliance between Russia, China and India. Russia, with its historical warm relations with India, has signaled a willingness to play the intermediary. Let's hope these three countries prove the Washington-London-Paris-Tokyo consensus wrong. A locked-arm, trident alliance between China, Russia and India might even give Western Empire pause. Throw in Iran and maybe Uncle Sam might even want to sit down to talk.

The Saker: There are regular rumors and speculations about a new joint reserve currency to replace the dollar. Some speak of a Ruble-Yuan currency, others of a "BRICS" currency, possibly backed by gold. These rumors are strengthened by the fact that both Russia and China have been and, apparently, still are buying all the gold they can. Is there support in China for such a "gold-backed BRICS currency basket"?

Jeff J. Brown: China and Russia are the two largest gold miners in the world. They are both buying gold at a prodigious rate. It is no secret that China wants to have as much gold as the US's supposed 8,500MT. China's gold reserves are a state secret, but estimates are Baba Beijing has somewhere around 3,500MT, maybe a little more. China will be required to officially declare its gold reserves, in order to have the renminbi considered as a currency in the IMF's special drawing rights (SDR) basket. I think they will want to be able to say they have more gold reserves than #2 Germany, which officially has 3,400MT (if only the Bundesbank could get it out of American vaults, which seem to be having a hard time coughing it up).

There is a talk of the "Brisco", a BRICS currency. The new BRICS NDB will help make that vision become a reality. That would pull in Russia and China together for trade and financing, along with India, Brazil and South Africa. Russia has apparently invited Greece to join BRICS too, and would have not done so, without consulting the other members first.

Yuan-ruble trade will increase exponentially, when the gas and oil pipelines start flowing in 2018, with CRIFT and UCRG humming at full speed. But I don't think Russia and China are envisioning a "Ruyuan" binational currency. There is just not enough critical mass there. The Brisco seems much more fungible and international.

The Saker: *Lastly, what kind of future do you see for China in the next couple of decades? Where is this country headed and what kind of role do you think it sees for itself in the future world?*

Jeff J. Brown: For hundreds of years, China had the world's largest economy. Finally, in 1872, in the depths of opium addiction, coolie slavery trade and extractive Western colonialism, it fell from its longstanding pinnacle, against the rapidly expanding settler/colonial American Empire. So, China is accustomed to greatness. Now being declared the world's biggest Purchasing Power Parity (PPP) economy just feels natural around here, and that century of humiliation was simply a nadir not to be repeated.

China had the world's greatest naval fleet 200-300 years before Europe, possessed gunpowder and invented firearms. They sailed all up and down the Asian, African and Middle Eastern coasts and into the Indonesian archipelago, long before Columbus. Unlike the West, it only wanted one thing: win-win trade and cultural exchanges. Other than Vietnam, China has never had imperial ambitions, nor a hegemonic drive to control the world's resources, while enslaving the natives who own them. It has always been, "Let's do business". Xi's "win-win" diplomacy is not Potemkin fluff. Baba Beijing means what it says. Xi and Li Keqiang (China's Premier) are crisscrossing the globe, signing billions upon billions of bilateral and regional trade, energy, aerospace, telecommunications, infrastructure, cultural, educational and scientific deals, all at lightning speed. But historically, this is what the Chinese have always been doing with the outside world, for the last 3,000 years: Maritime Belts and Silk Roads.

Saker, whether the West likes it or not, Napoléon's oriental sleeping lion is back in historical form. The West has two choices: come to the negotiating table with BRICS or take our Pale Blue Dot down in a fog of nuclear oblivion. Empire is so evil and corrupt, I'm leaning towards the latter scenario, to be honest. But I am also an eternal optimist. Here is to hoping that some superhero, American Vasili Arkhipov or Stanislav Petrov (they both defused potential nuclear war with the US, back in the day) can somehow short circuit the Joint Chiefs of Staff/CIA/Wall Street deep state, which has been ruling the United States since WWII, and bring humanity back from the brink.

Either way world, welcome to the Xi Era – and the Putin Era – and with fingers crossed – the Modi Era too. Greetings from the belly of the New Century Beast, China.

ACKNOWLEDGEMENTS

I would first like to thank Pepe Escobar, who has been an inspiration and encouragement for me during my nascent writing and journalism career. His endorsement of *China Rising* is very special to me.

Next, a big thanks to my editor, John Chan, for taking a pile of inspired, but terribly disparate, disjointed articles, columns, blogs and letters, to help me turn it all into the book you are reading. Getting back John's first edit was a wakeup call of just how much more work needed to be invested before *China Rising* could be published. It would not be in your hands without his critical eye and frank opinions.

Cherie Chow Pui Yee gets a hearty thank you for getting *China Rising* in acceptable format for publishing in ebook form. With about 200 audiovisual images, it took a lot of time and patience. Because of her, it looks great on your screen.

Thanks to my wife, Florence B. Langlois, who keeps putting up with my thousands of hours and years and years of research and writing. It gets in the way sometimes.

I am proud that my daughter, Chara Vega Langlois Brown, designed the original book cover. It did not make it on the front cover, but is included in one of the funnier chapters of the book, the Mao & Jiang used car seller montage. Bravo.

As expressed in this book's dedication, hats off to the peoples of China. What an amazing civilization, history and story to tell, ongoing. I feel honored and lucky to be a part of it and their local neighbor for thirteen years.

Finally, a hearty "cheers" to all my comrades at The Greanville Post and Punto Press. Our work together over the last year has been most rewarding and intellectually satisfying. May we continue to fight the good fight against Western imperialism and capitalism, far into the future.

ABOUT THE AUTHOR

Jeff J. Brown is the author of _44 Days_ (2013) and _Doctor WriteRead's Treasure Trove to Great English_ (2015). Punto Press released China Rising, Capitalist Roads, Socialist Destinations – The Truth behind Asia's Enigmatic Colossus (2016). For Badak Merah, Jeff authored China Is Communist, Dammit! – Dawn of the Red Dynasty (2016). He is also currently penning an historical fiction, _Red Letters – The Diaries of Xi Jinping_, to be published in late 2016. Jeff is a contributing editor with the Greanville Post, where he keeps a monthly column, _Dispatch from Beijing_. He also writes a monthly column for The Saker, called the _Moscow-Beijing Express_. Jeff interviews and podcasts on his own program, _China Rising Radio Sinoland_, which is also available on YouTube, Stitcher Radio and iTunes.

In China, he has been a speaker at TEDx, the Bookworm and Capital M Literary Festivals, the Hutong, as well as being featured in an 18-part series of interviews on Radio Beijing AM774, with former BBC journalist, Bruce Connolly. He has guest lectured at international schools in Beijing and Tianjin.

Jeff grew up in the heartland of the United States, Oklahoma, much of it on a family farm, and graduated from Oklahoma State University. He went to Brazil while in graduate school at Purdue University, to seek his fortune, which whet his appetite for traveling the globe. This helped inspire him to be a Peace Corps Volunteer in Tunisia in 1980 and he lived and worked in Africa, the Middle East, China and Europe for the next 21 years. All the while, he mastered Portuguese, Arabic, French and Mandarin, while traveling to over 85 countries. He then returned to America for nine years, whereupon he moved back to China in 2010. He lives in China with his wife, where he teaches passionately in an international school. Jeff is a dual national French-American.

China Rising Radio Sinoland and Jeff J Brown's social media outlets:

Facebook: https://www.facebook.com/44DaysPublishing
Flickr: http://www.flickr.com/photos/113187076@N05/
Google+: https://plus.google.com/110361195277784155542
Linkedin: https://cn.linkedin.com/in/jeff-j-brown-0517477
Pinterest: https://www.pinterest.com/jeffjb/
Sinaweibo (for Jeff's ongoing photos and comments on daily life in China, in both English and Chinese): http://weibo.com/u/5859194018
Stumbleupon: http://www.stumbleupon.com/stumbler/jjbzaibeijing
Tumblr: http://jjbzaibeijing.tumblr.com/
Twitter: https://twitter.com/44_Days
Wechat group: search China Rising Radio Sinoland

As well, email: jeff@brownlanglois.com and Wechat/Whatsapp: +8618618144837

THE END

Made in the USA
San Bernardino, CA
09 August 2017